9

Hiro Mashima

Translated and adapted by William Flanagan
Lettered by North Market Street Graphics

Ballantine Books · New York

Fairy Tail volume 9 is a work of fiction. Names, characters, places, and incidents are the products of the author's imagination or are used fictitiously. Any resemblance to actual events, locales, or persons, living or dead, is entirely coincidental.

A Del Rey Manga/Kodansha Trade Paperback Original

Published in the United States by Del Rey, an imprint of The Random House Publishing Group, a division of Random House, Inc., New York.

DEL REY is a registered trademark and the Del Rey colophon is a trademark of Random House, Inc.

Publication rights arranged through Kodansha Ltd.

First published in Japan in 2008 by Kodansha Ltd., Tokyo

ISBN 978-0-345-51233-8

Printed in the United States of America

www.delreymanga.com

9 8 7 6 5 4 3

Translator/Adapter—William Flanagan
Lettering—North Market Street Graphics

Contents

Photo of the Mashima Group and
Yoshikawa Group combined.

I've been hanging out with Miki
Yoshikawa-sensei (I usually follow
her name with "-chan" but...) for
more than five years. She has been
a good friend at times, and at other
times a good rival. Although she
started in manga after me, she's a
well-respected member of my circle
of friends. Since we're both so
busy, we are only able to hang out
together once or twice a year, but
during the times we can get both
of our groups together, it's really
fun! On the day of this picture, we
were playing video games from the
morning on....What a great group
of adults, huh? Ah ha ha ha!! They
were really fun people!

—Hiro Mashima

Honorifics Explained

Throughout the Del Rey Manga books, you will find Japanese honorifics left intact in the translations. For those not familiar with how the Japanese use honorifics and, more important, how they differ from American honorifics, we present this brief overview.

Politeness has always been a critical facet of Japanese culture. Ever since the feudal era, when Japan was a highly stratified society, use of honorifics—which can be defined as polite speech that indicates relationship or status—has played an essential role in the Japanese language. When addressing someone in Japanese, an honorific usually takes the form of a suffix attached to one's name (example: "Asuna-san"), is used as a title at the end of one's name, or appears in place of the name itself (example: "Negi-sensei," or simply "Sensei").

Honorifics can be expressions of respect or endearment. In the context of manga and anime, honorifics give insight into the nature of the relationship between characters. Many English translations leave out these important honorifics and therefore distort the feel of the original Japanese. Because Japanese honorifics contain nuances that English honorifics lack, it is our policy at Del Rey not to translate them. Here, instead, is a guide to some of the honorifics you may encounter in Del Rey Manga.

-san: This is the most common honorific and is equivalent to Mr., Miss, Ms., or Mrs. It is the all-purpose honorific and can be used in any situation where politeness is required.

-sama: This is one level higher than "-san" and is used to confer great respect.

-dono: This comes from the word "tono," which means "lord." It is an even higher level than "-sama" and confers utmost respect.

-kun: This suffix is used at the end of boys' names to express familiarity or endearment. It is also sometimes used by men among friends, or when addressing someone younger or of a lower station.

-chan: This is used to express endearment, mostly toward girls. It is also used for little boys, pets, and even between lovers. It gives a sense of childish cuteness.

Bozu: This is an informal way to refer to a boy, similar to the English terms "kid" and "squirt."

Sempai/
Senpai: This title suggests that the addressee is one's senior in a group or organization. It is most often used in a school setting, where underclassmen refer to their upperclassmen as "sempai." It can also be used in the workplace, such as when a newer employee addresses an employee who has seniority in the company.

Kohai: This is the opposite of "sempai" and is used toward under-classmen in school or newcomers in the workplace. It connotes that the addressee is of a lower station.

Sensei: Literally meaning "one who has come before," this title is used for teachers, doctors, or masters of any profession or art.

-[blank]: This is usually forgotten in these lists, but it is perhaps the most significant difference between Japanese and English. The lack of honorific means that the speaker has permission to address the person in a very intimate way. Usually, only family, spouses, or very close friends have this kind of permission. Known as *yobisute*, it can be gratifying when someone who has earned the intimacy starts to call one by one's name without an honorific. But when that intimacy hasn't been earned, it can be very insulting.

FAIRY TAIL

9

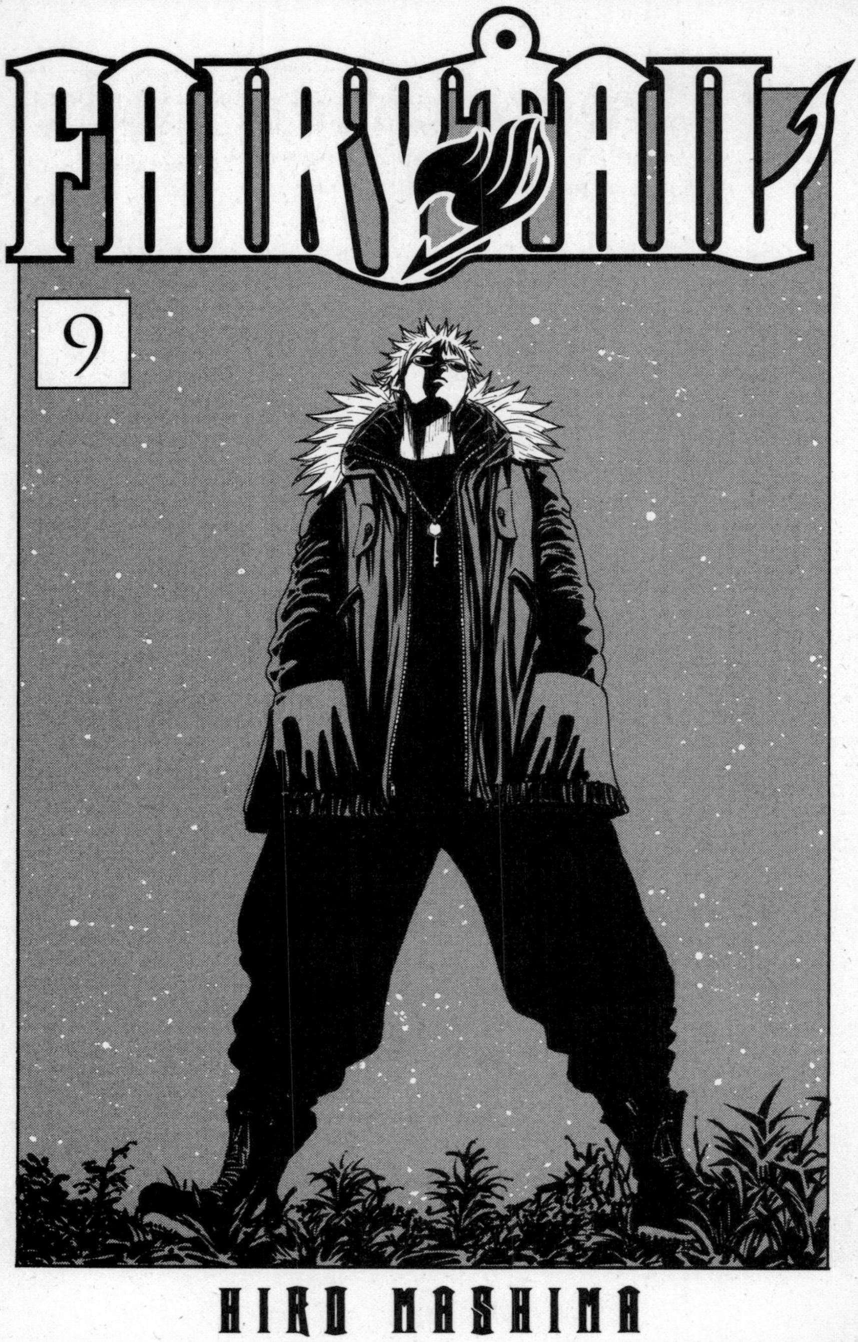

HIRO MASHIMA

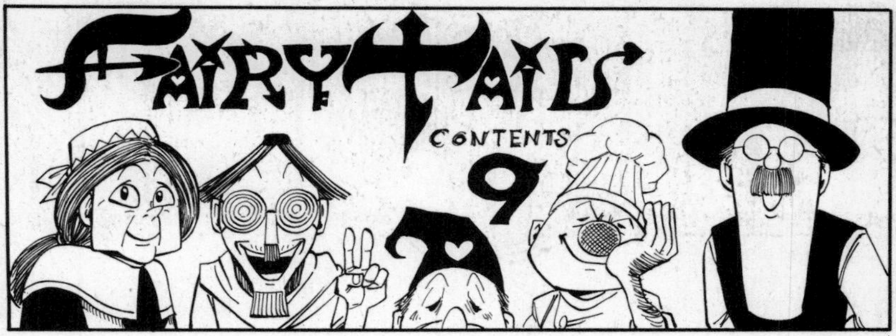
FAIRY TAIL
CONTENTS
9

FAIRY TAIL

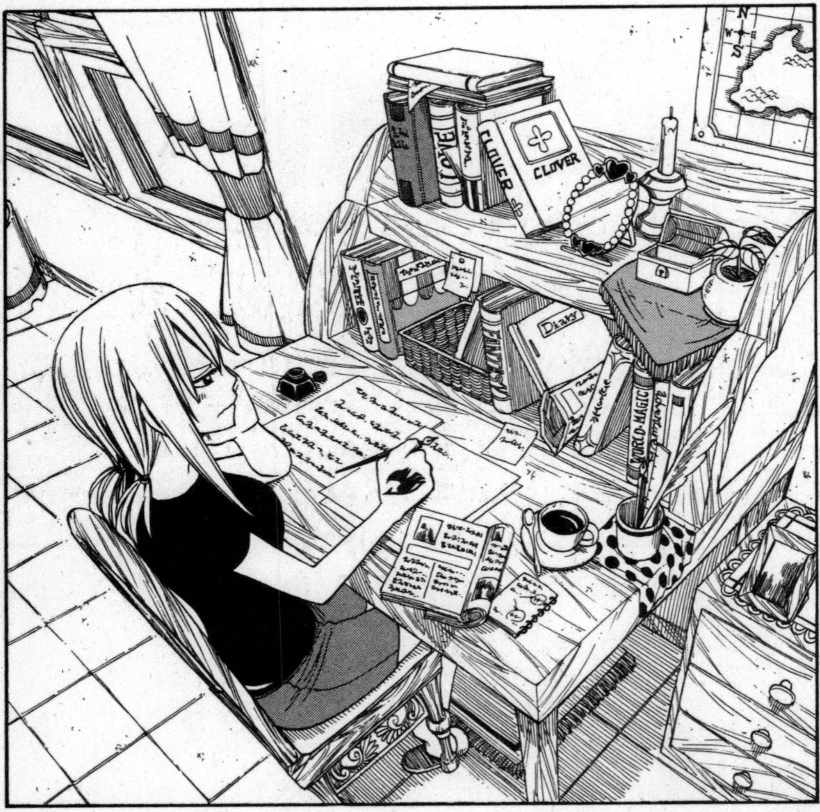
CLOVER
CLOVER
Diary
WORLD-MAGIC

Chapter 66: Like-Minded

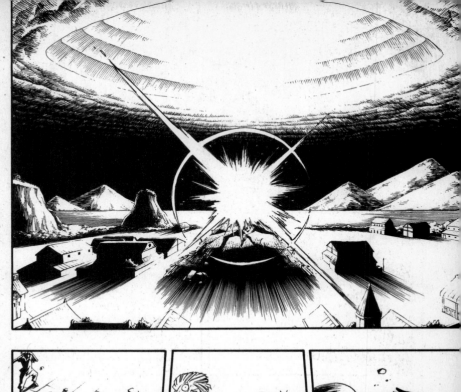

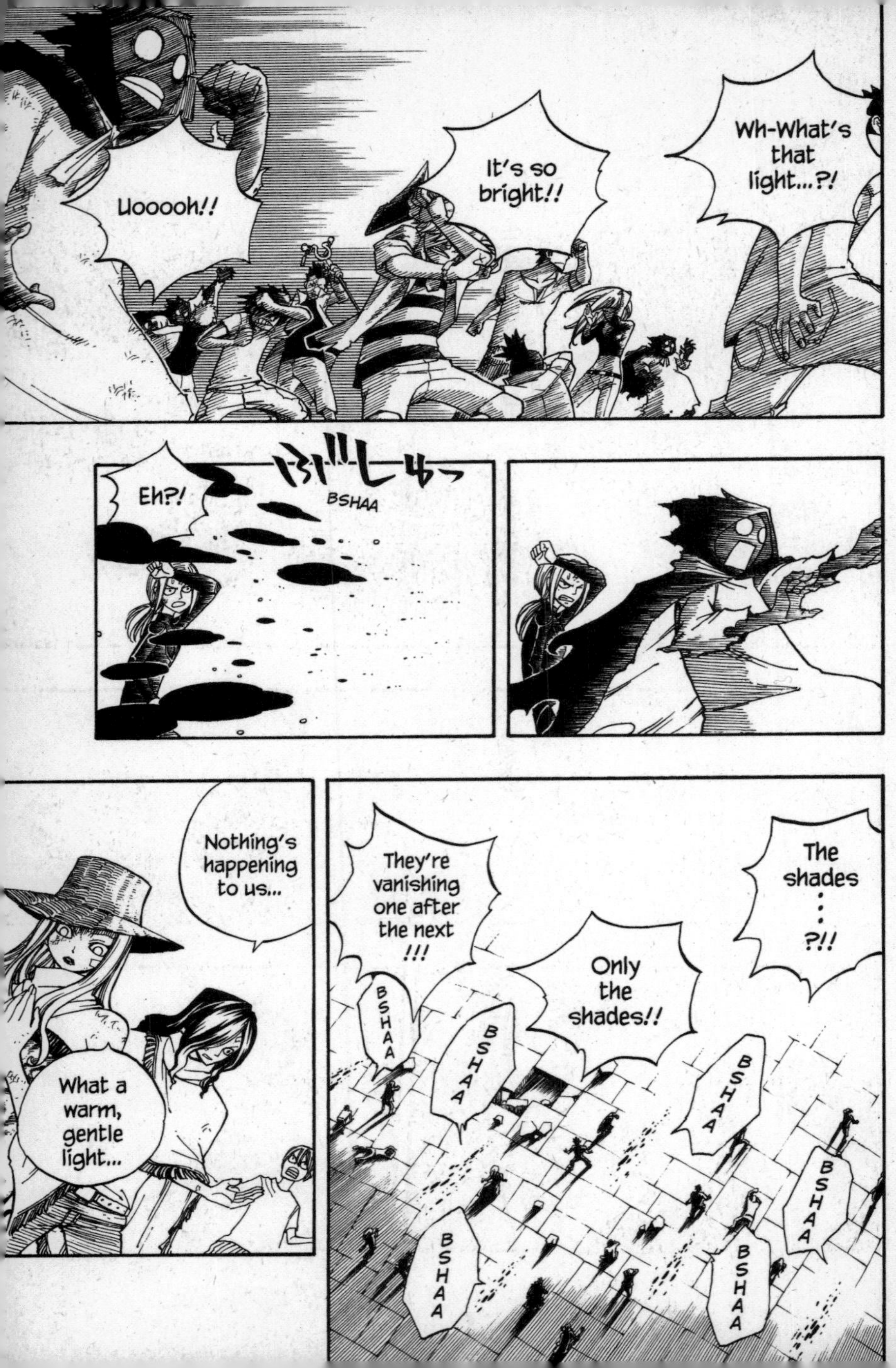
Wh-What's that light...?!
It's so bright!!
Uooooh!!
Eh?!
BSHAA
The shades...?!!
They're vanishing one after the next!!!
Only the shades!!
BSHAA
BSHAA
BSHAA
BSHAA
BSHAA
BSHAA
BSHAA
Nothing's happening to us...
What a warm, gentle light...

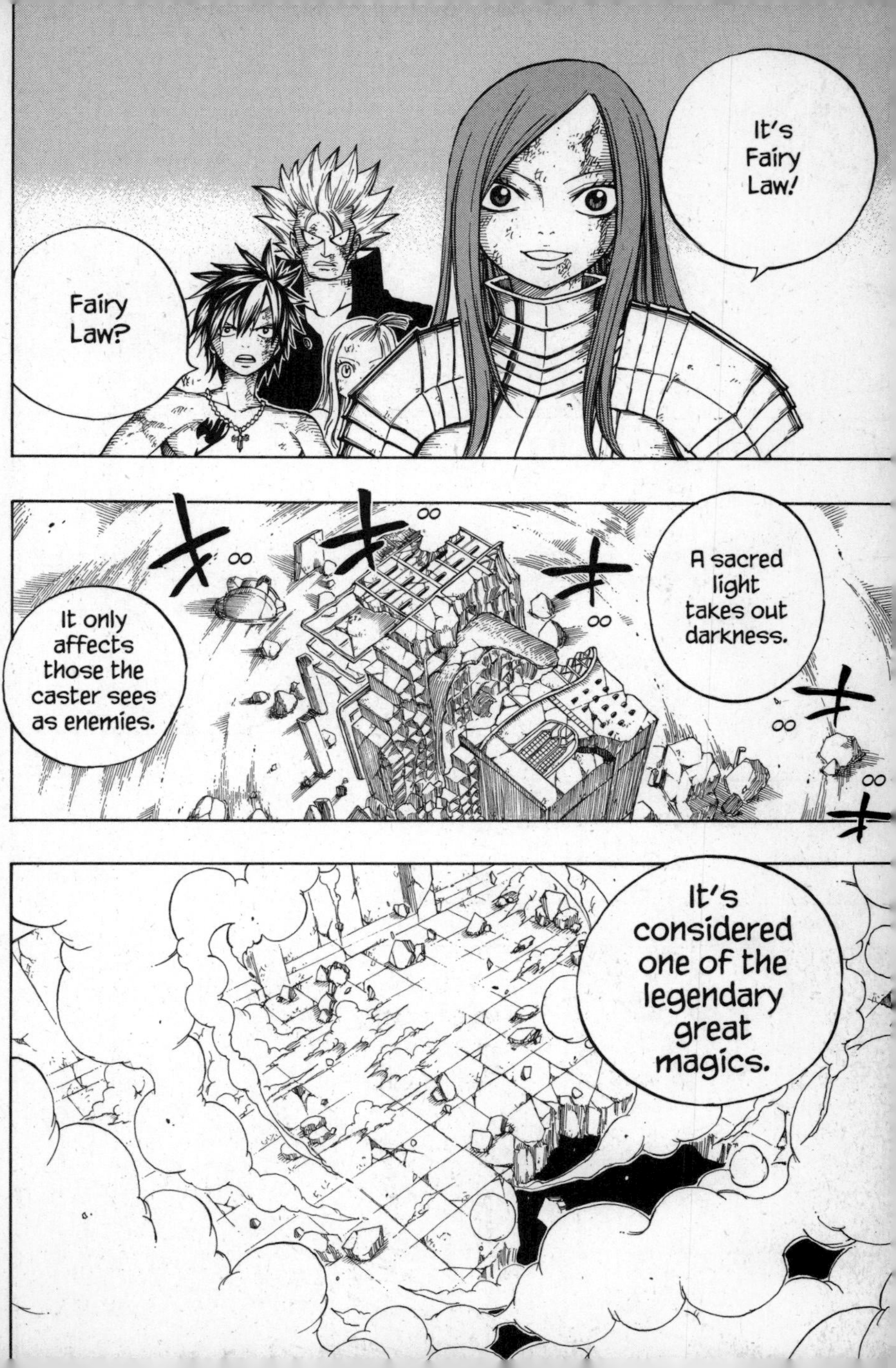
It's Fairy Law!
Fairy Law?
A sacred light takes out darkness.
It only affects those the caster sees as enemies.
It's considered one of the legendary great magics.

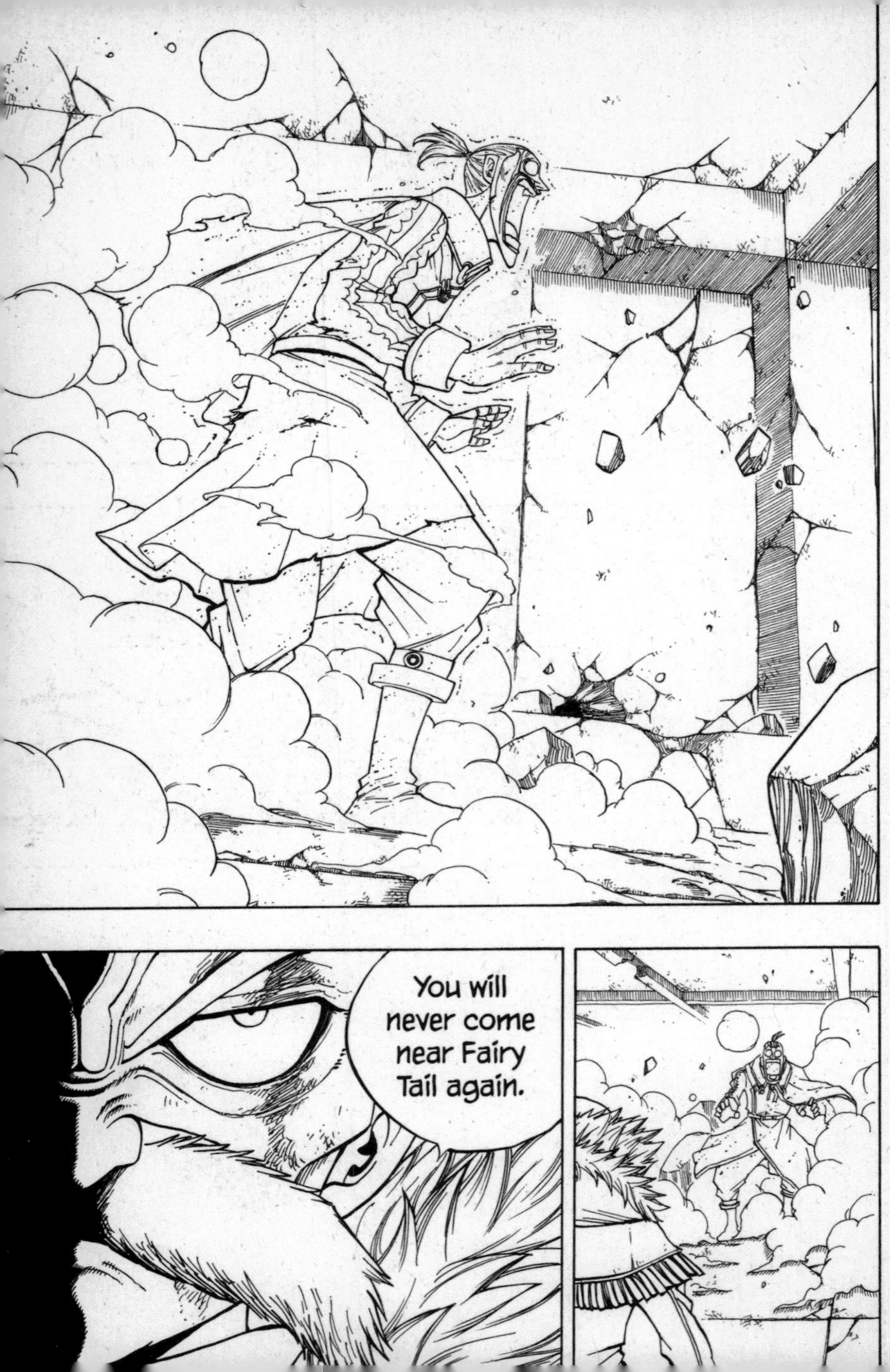
You will never come near Fairy Tail again.

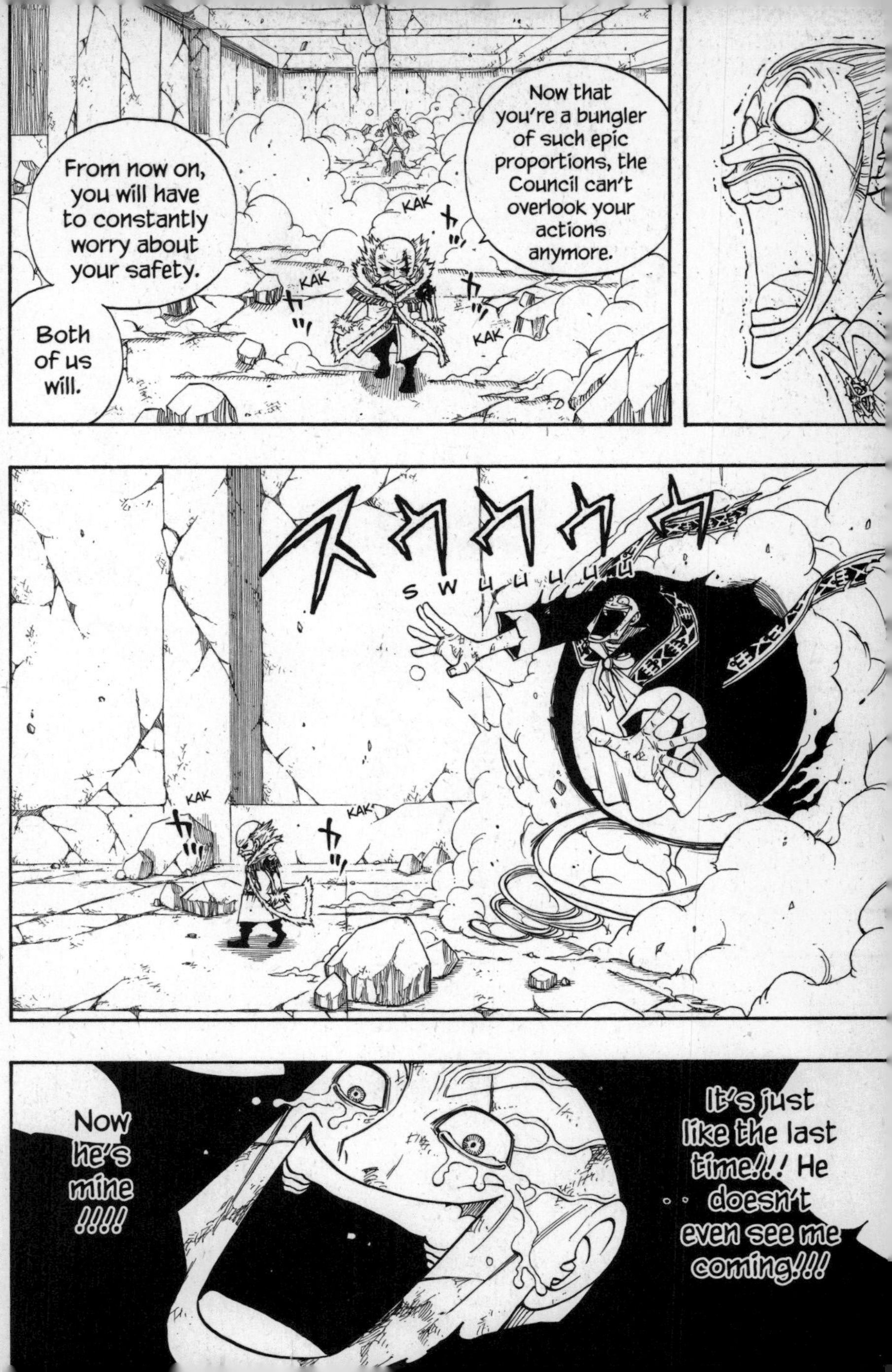
Now that you're a bungler of such epic proportions, the Council can't overlook your actions anymore.
KAK
KAK
KAK
From now on, you will have to constantly worry about your safety.
Both of us will.
SWUUUUUU
KAK
KAK
It's just like the last time!!! He doesn't even see me coming!!!
Now he's mine !!!!

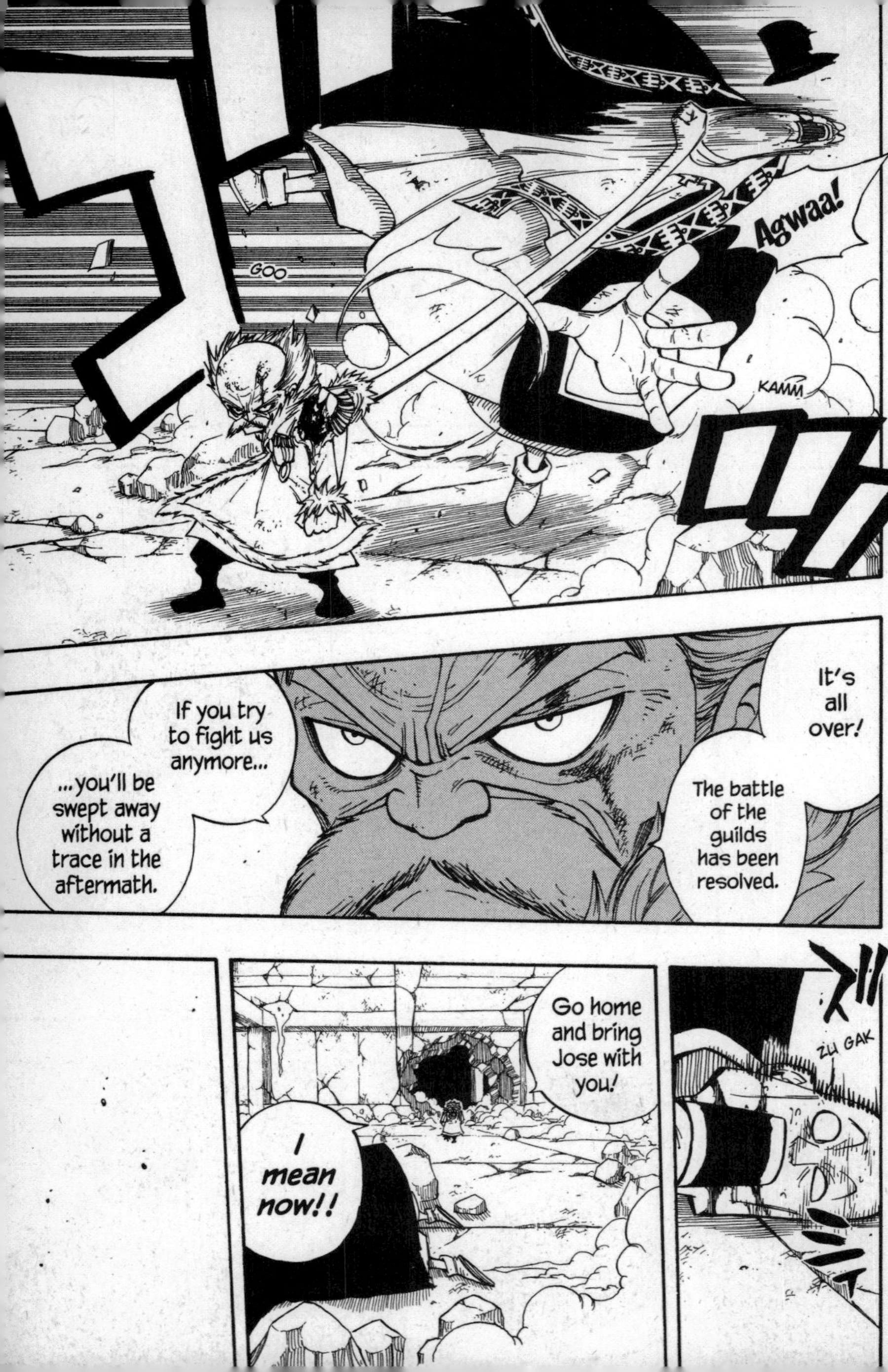
Agwaa!
GOO
KAMM
It's all over!
The battle of the guilds has been resolved.
If you try to fight us anymore...
...you'll be swept away without a trace in the aftermath.
ZU GAK
Go home and bring Jose with you!
I mean now!!

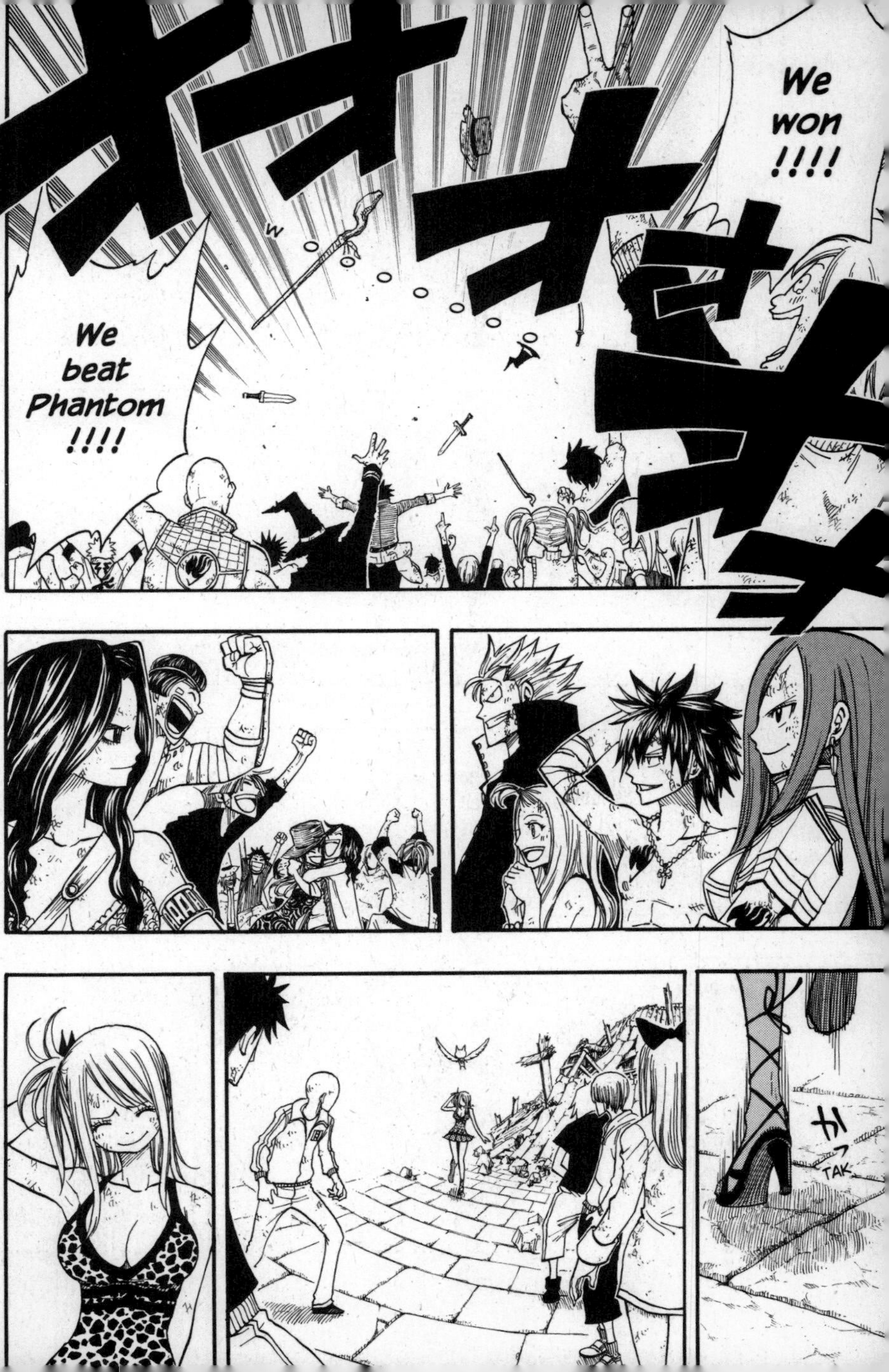
We won !!!!
We beat Phantom !!!!
TAK

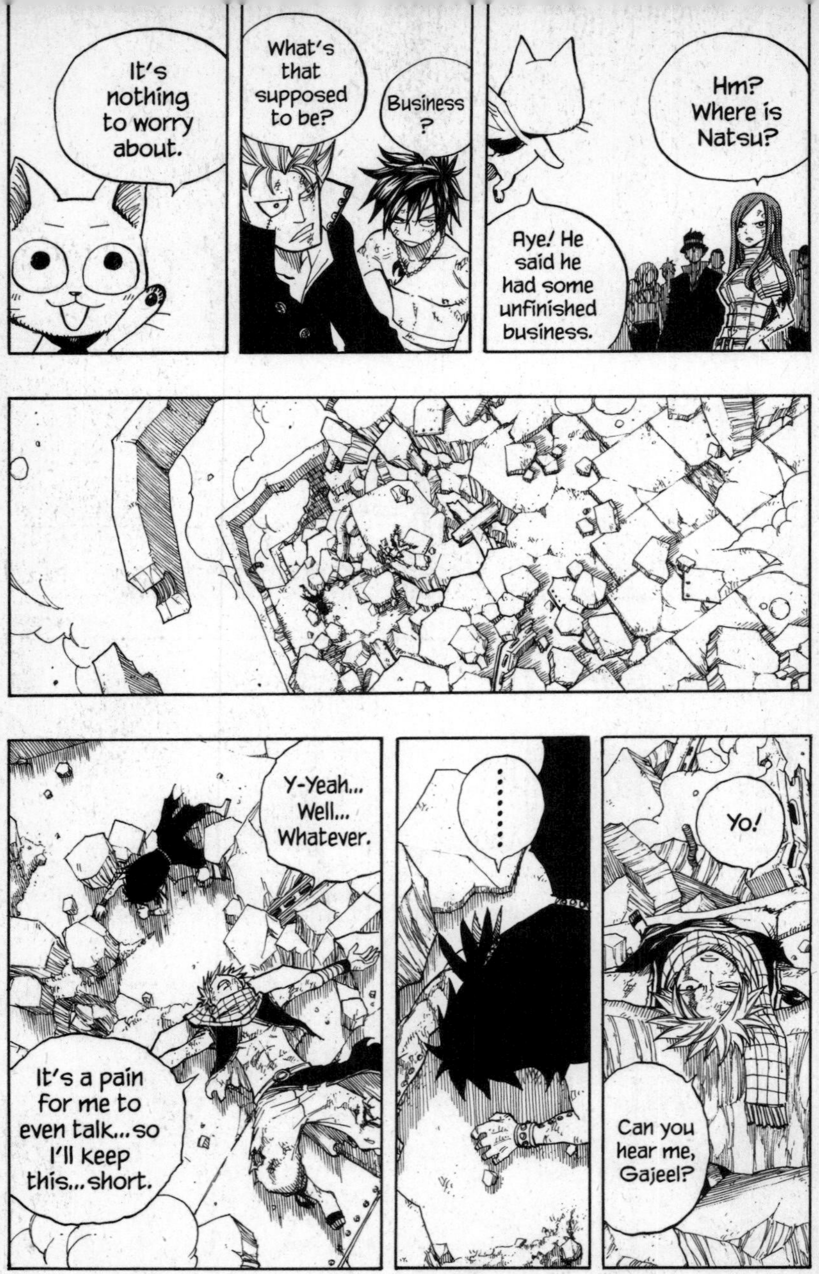
Hm? Where is Natsu?
Aye! He said he had some unfinished business.
Business?
What's that supposed to be?
It's nothing to worry about.
Yo!
Can you hear me, Gajeel?
......
Y-Yeah... Well... Whatever.
It's a pain for me to even talk...so I'll keep this...short.

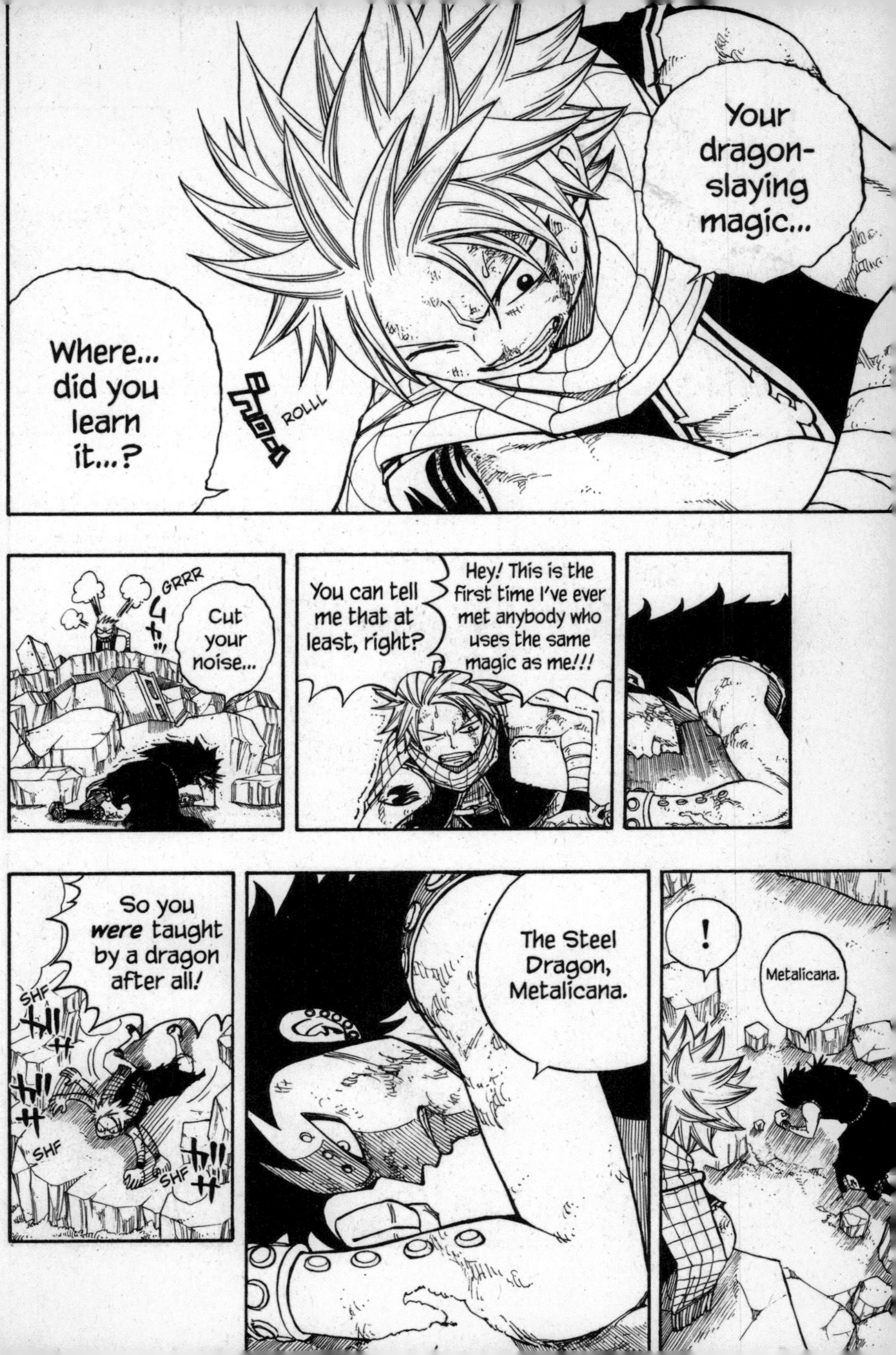
Your dragon-slaying magic...
Where... did you learn it...?
ROLLL
Hey! This is the first time I've ever met anybody who uses the same magic as me!!!
You can tell me that at least, right?
GRRR
Cut your noise...
!
Metalicana.
The Steel Dragon, Metalicana.
So you *were* taught by a dragon after all!
SHF
SHF
SHF

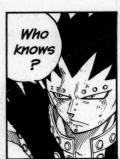

You too?
What happened to the dragon?
Who knows?
I • asked • you • what • happened ?!!!
And I told you that I don't know, you trash!!!
GONK
Oww...
Ouch...
Just talking to you makes me feel like my brains have burned down to ash!!
What did you say?!!
It disappeared on me!!
?!!

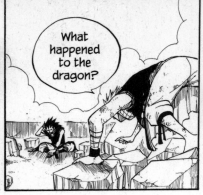

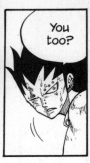

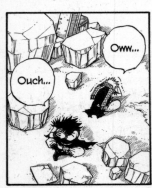

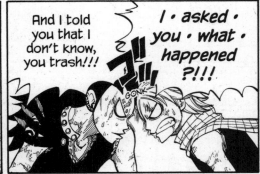

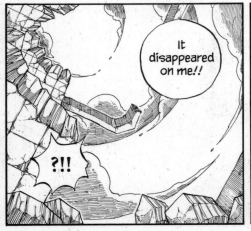

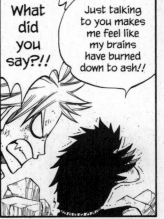

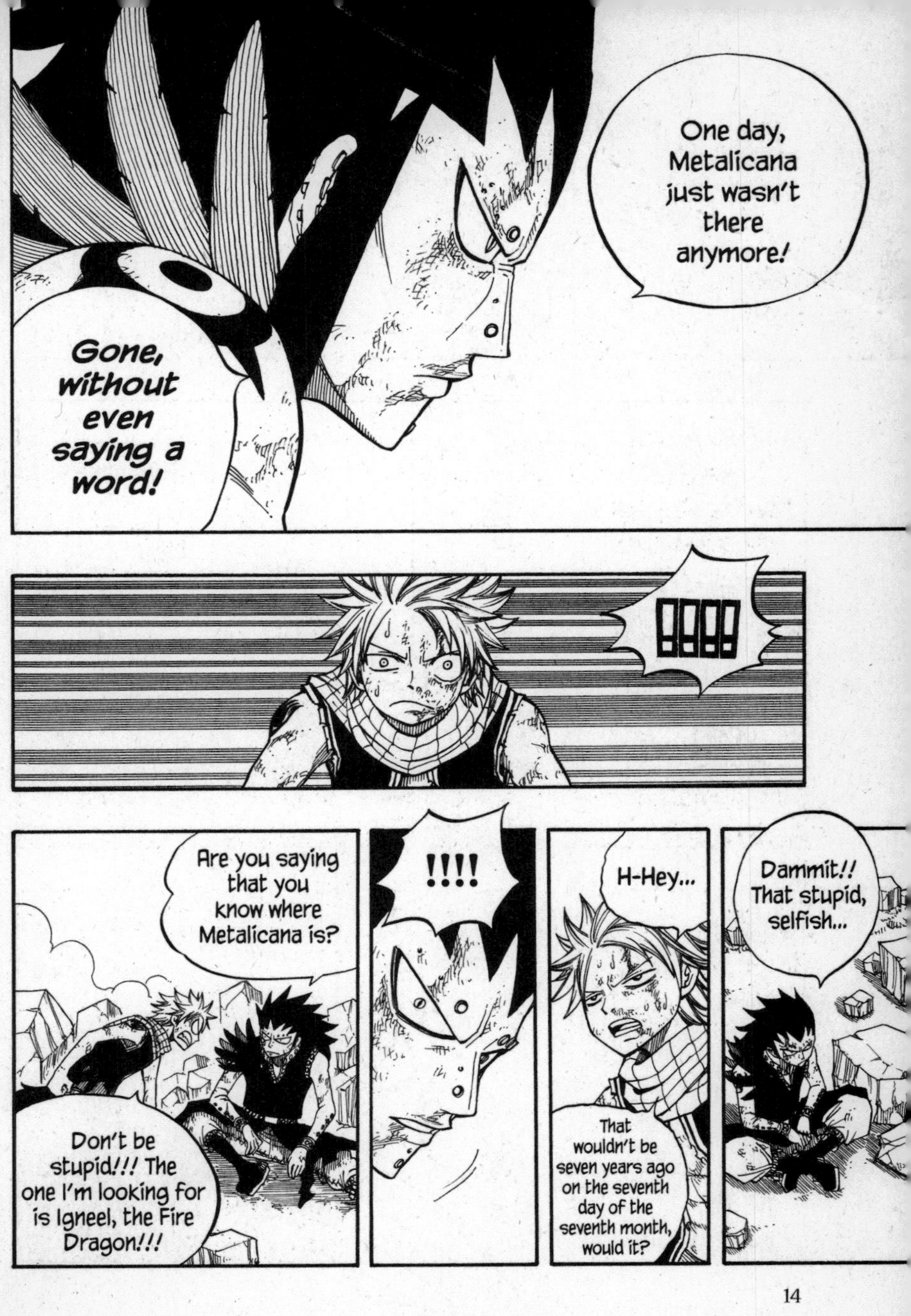
One day, Metalicana just wasn't there anymore!
Gone, without even saying a word!
!!!!
Dammit!! That stupid, selfish...
H-Hey...
That wouldn't be seven years ago on the seventh day of the seventh month, would it?
!!!!
Are you saying that you know where Metalicana is?
Don't be stupid!!! The one I'm looking for is Igneel, the Fire Dragon!!!

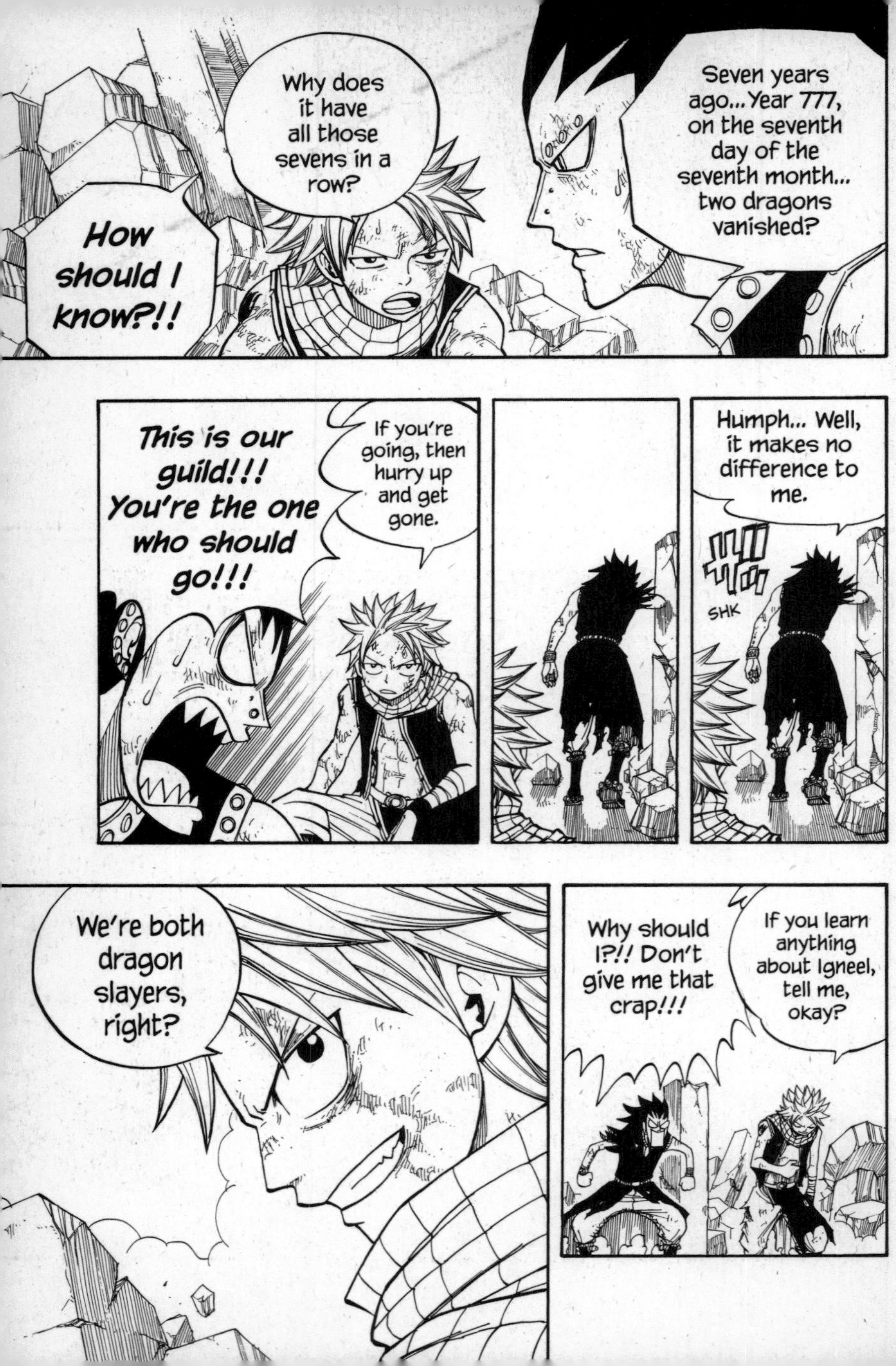
Seven years ago...Year 777, on the seventh day of the seventh month... two dragons vanished?
Why does it have all those sevens in a row?
How should I know?!!
Humph... Well, it makes no difference to me.
SHK
If you're going, then hurry up and get gone.
This is our guild!!! You're the one who should go!!!
If you learn anything about Igneel, tell me, okay?
Why should I?!! Don't give me that crap!!!
We're both dragon slayers, right?

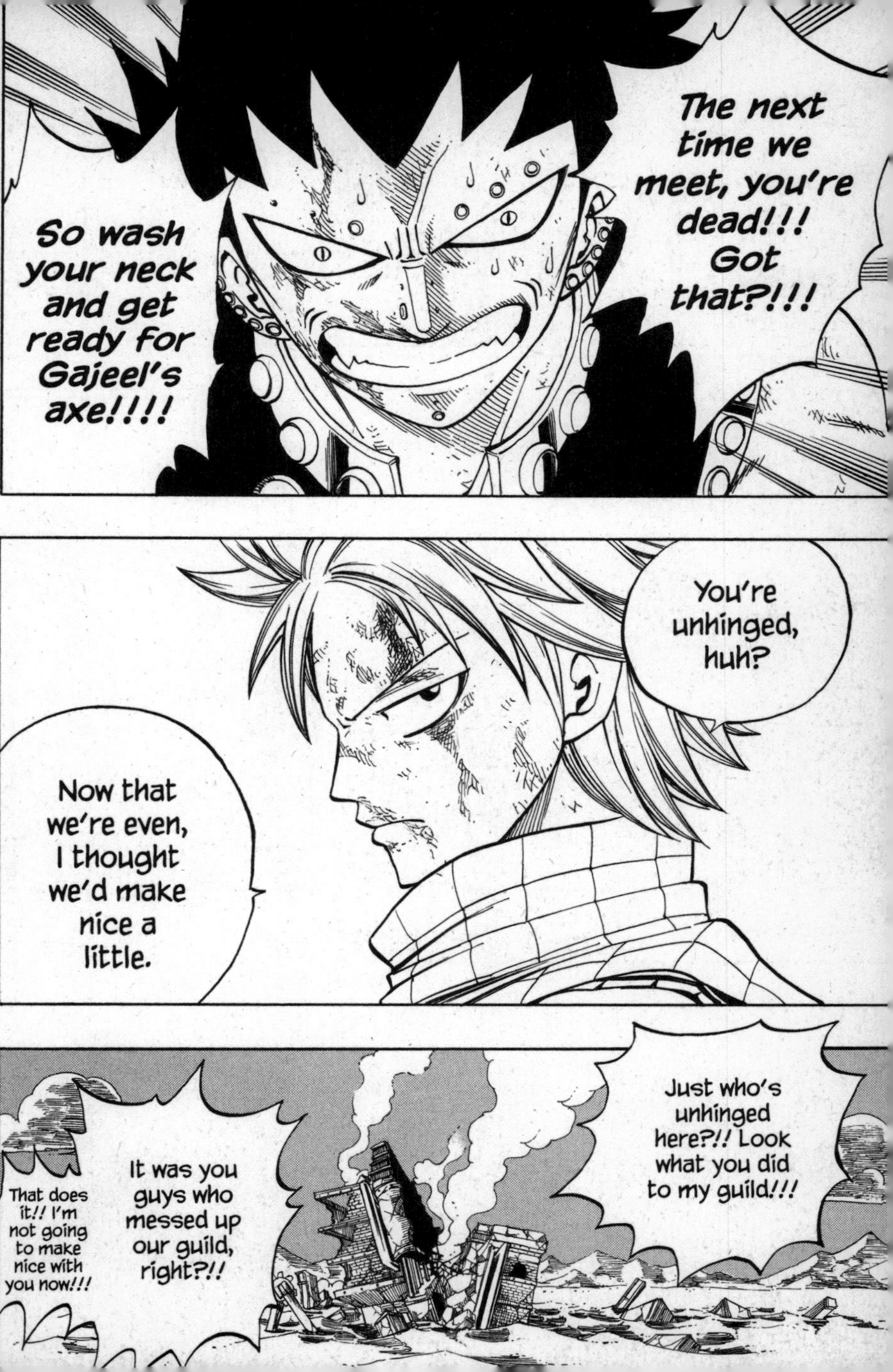
The next time we meet, you're dead!!! Got that?!!!
So wash your neck and get ready for Gajeel's axe!!!!
You're unhinged, huh?
Now that we're even, I thought we'd make nice a little.
Just who's unhinged here?!! Look what you did to my guild!!!
It was you guys who messed up our guild, right?!!
That does it!! I'm not going to make nice with you now!!!

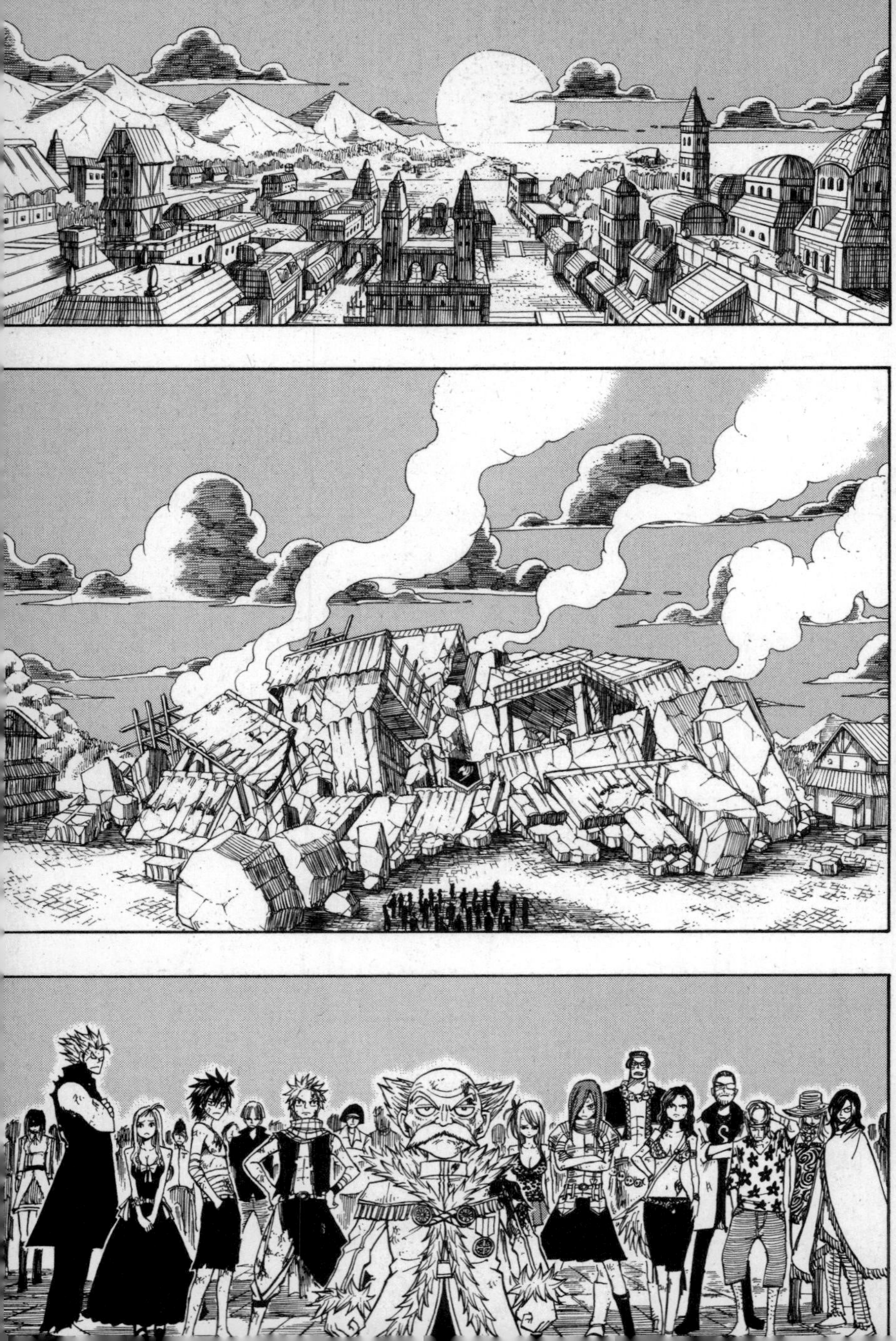

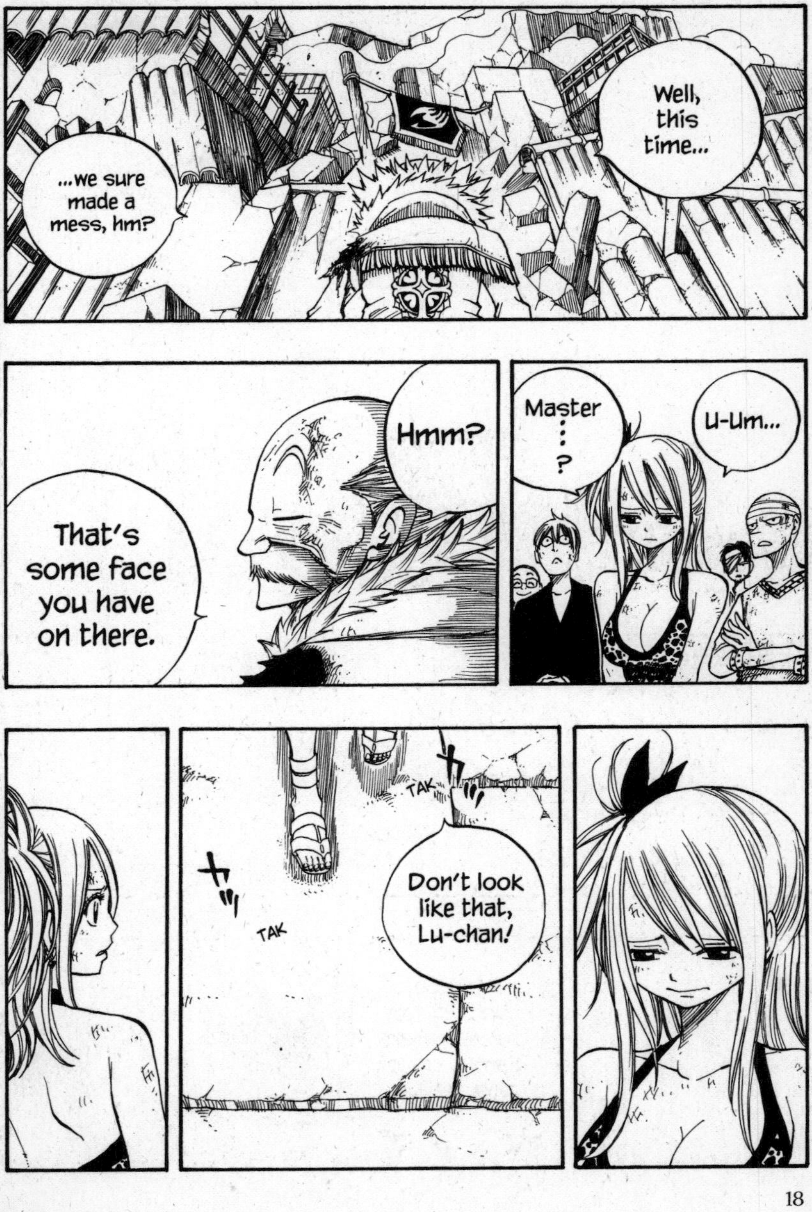
Well, this time...
...we sure made a mess, hm?
U-Um...
Master...?
Hmm?
That's some face you have on there.
TAK
Don't look like that, Lu-chan!
TAK

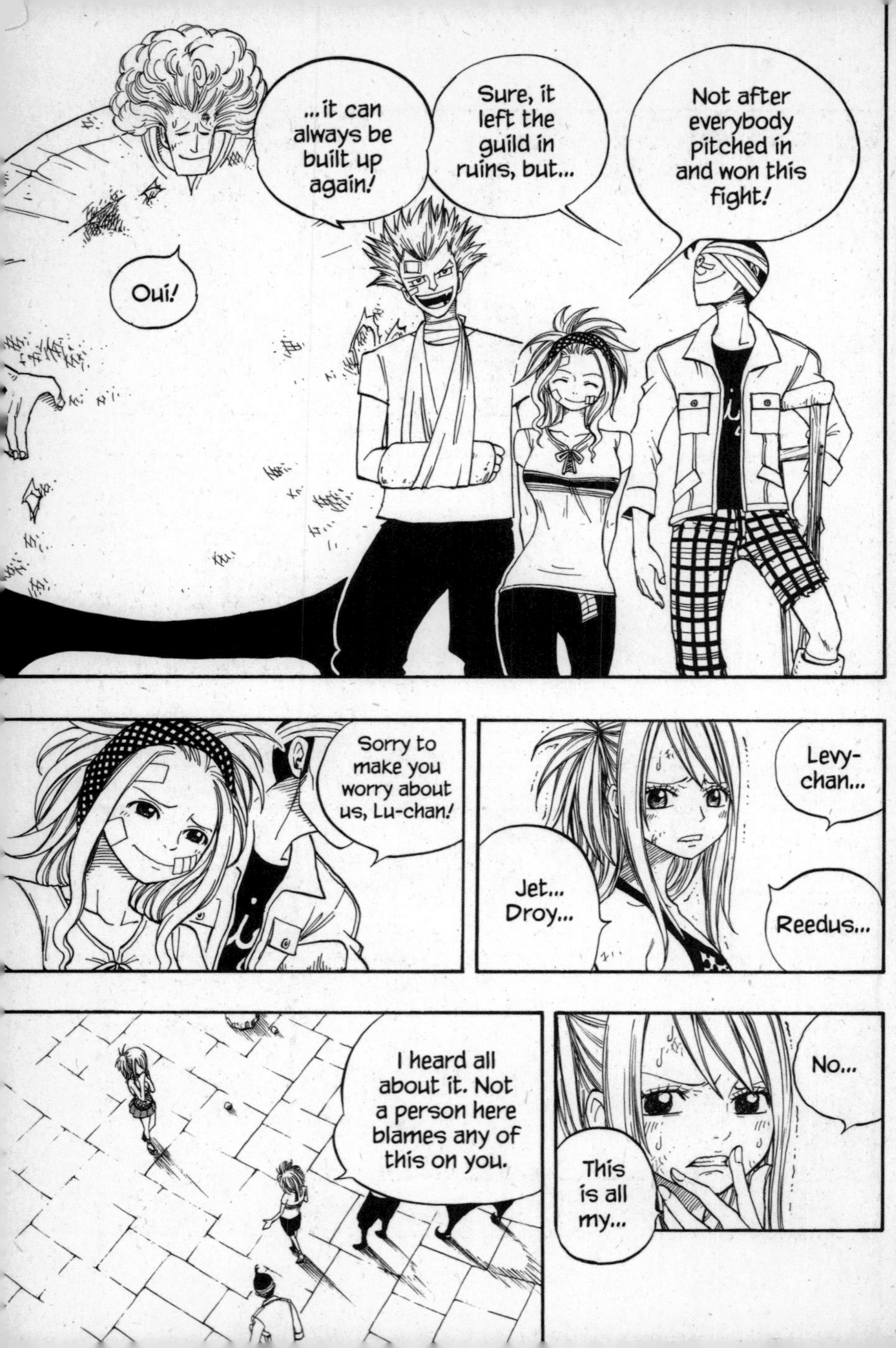
Not after everybody pitched in and won this fight!
Sure, it left the guild in ruins, but...
...it can always be built up again!
Oui!
Levy-chan...
Jet... Droy...
Reedus...
Sorry to make you worry about us, Lu-chan!
No...
This is all my...
I heard all about it. Not a person here blames any of this on you.

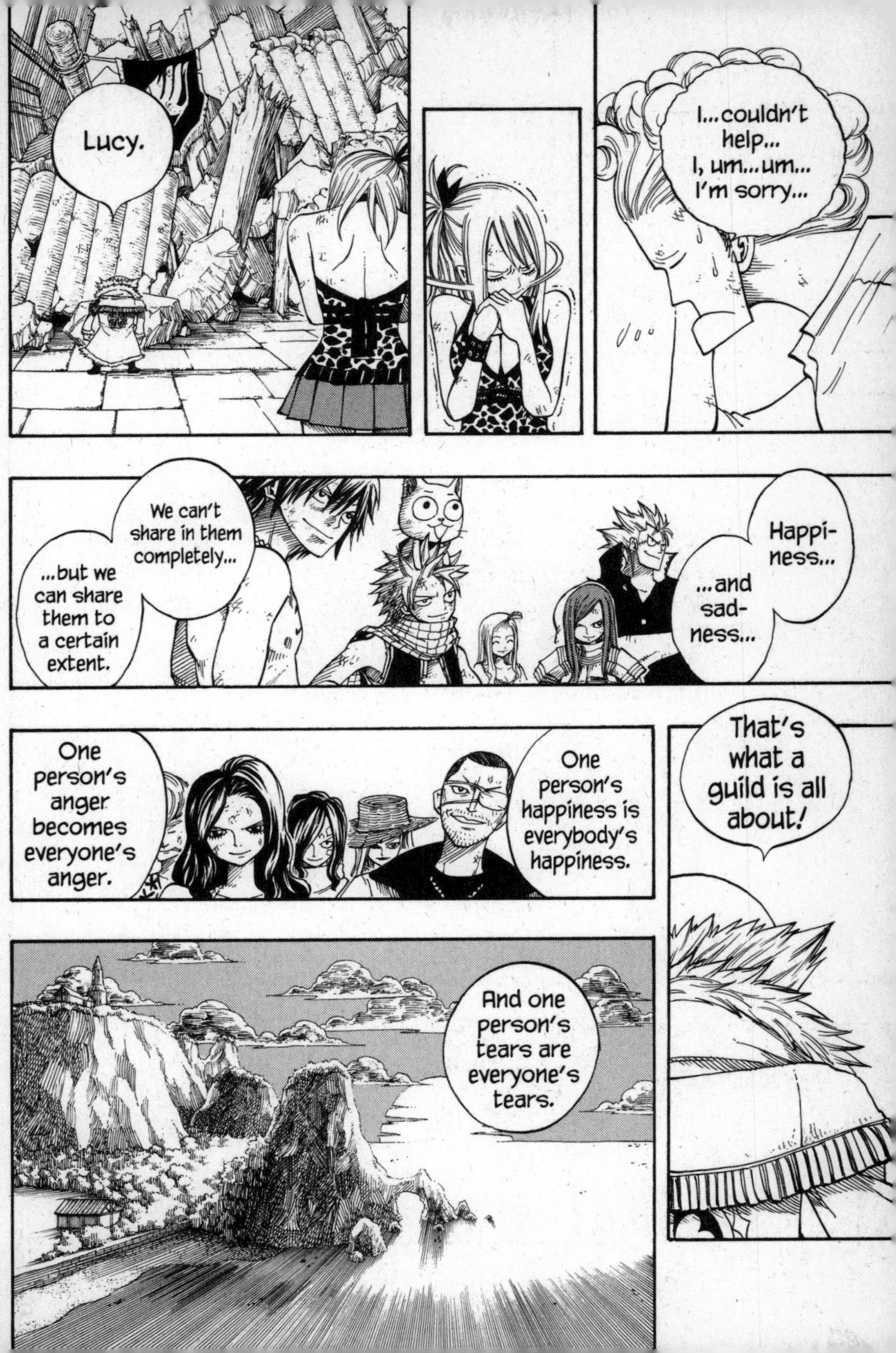
I...couldn't help... I, um...um... I'm sorry...
Lucy.
Happiness...
...and sadness...
We can't share in them completely...
...but we can share them to a certain extent.
That's what a guild is all about!
One person's happiness is everybody's happiness.
One person's anger becomes everyone's anger.
And one person's tears are everyone's tears.

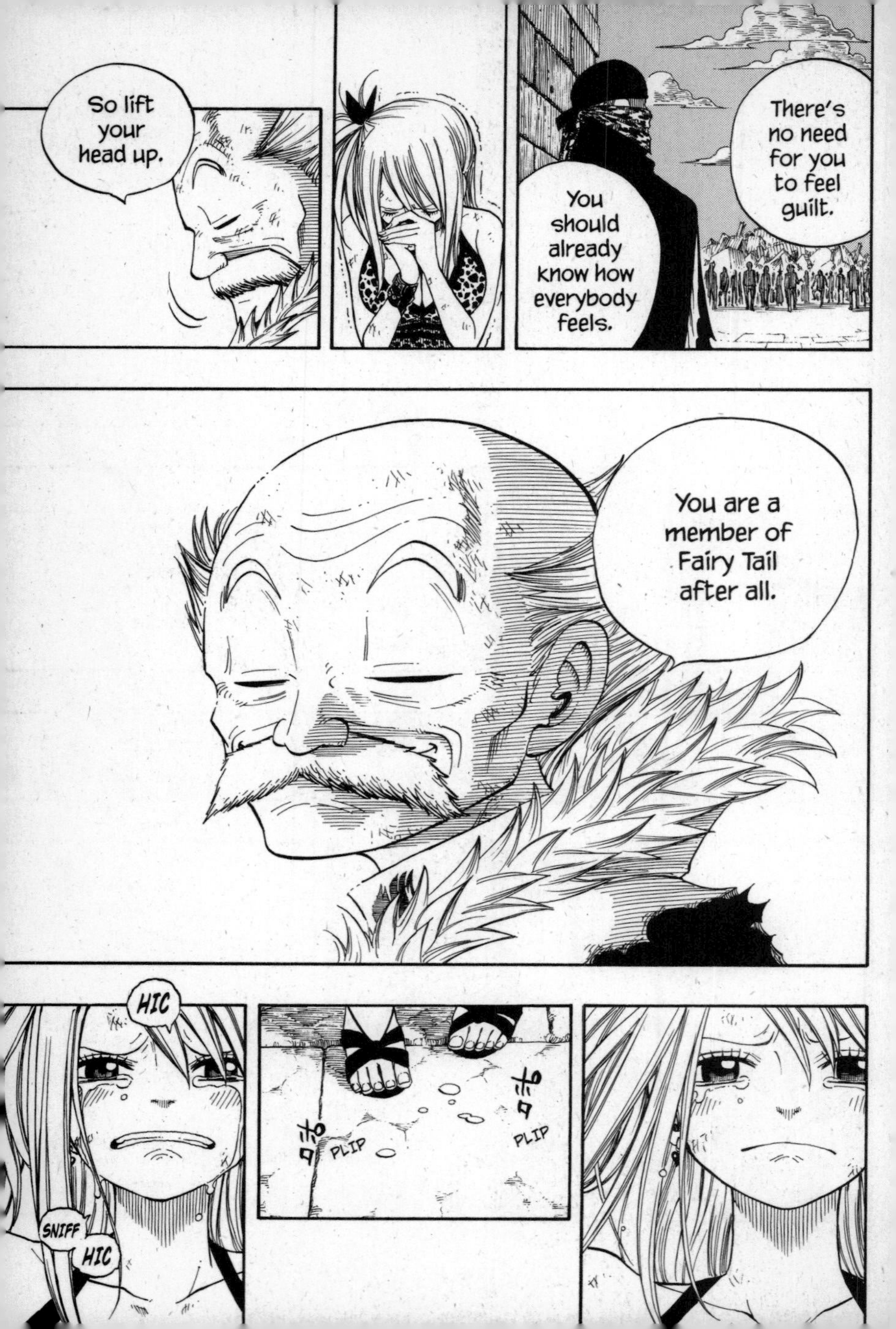
There's no need for you to feel guilt.
You should already know how everybody feels.
So lift your head up.
You are a member of Fairy Tail after all.
ポロ
PLIP
ポロ
PLIP
HIC
SNIFF
HIC

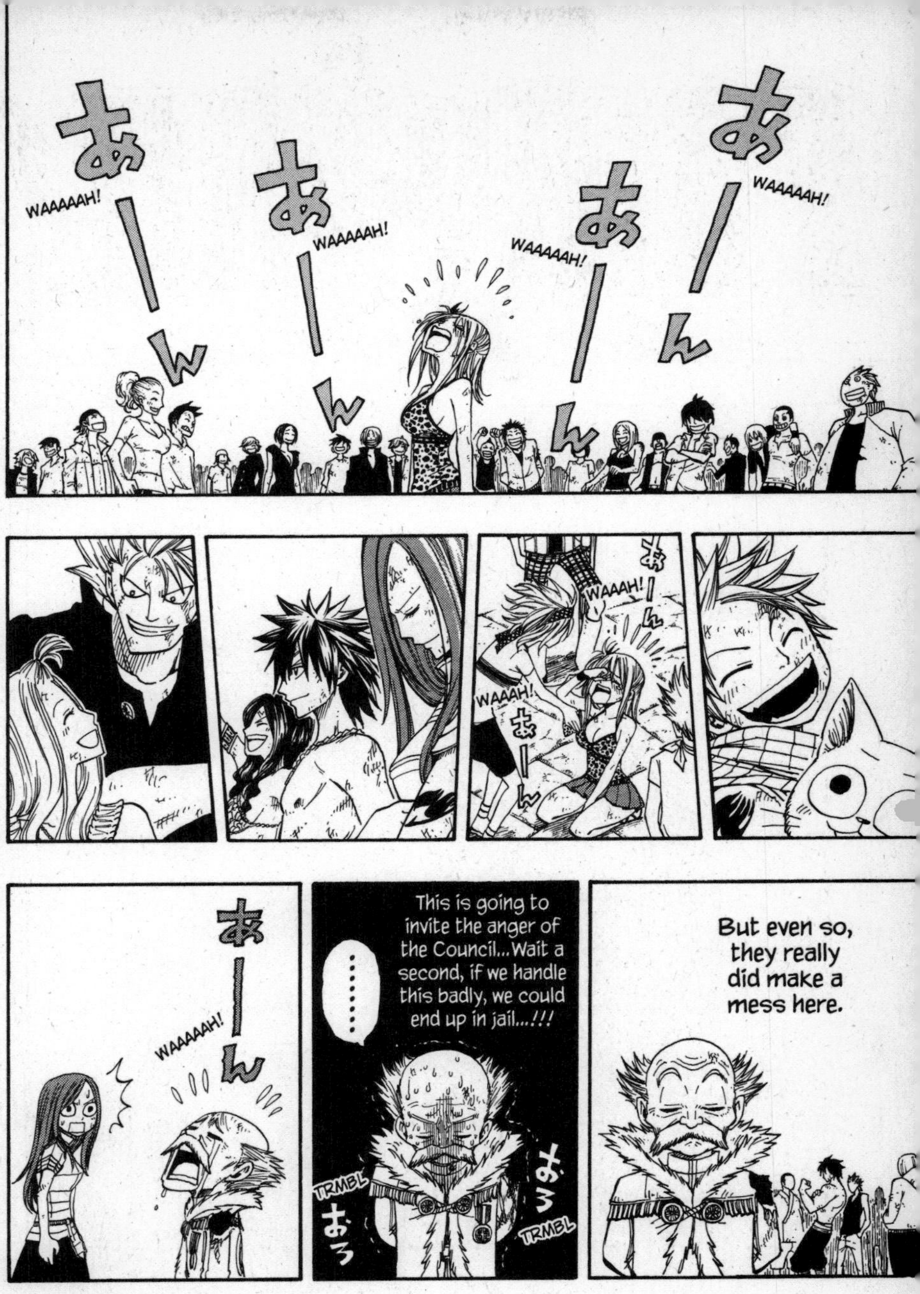
あーん
WAAAAAH!
あーん
WAAAAAH!
あーん
WAAAAAH!
あーん
WAAAAAH!
WAAAH!
WAAAH!
But even so, they really did make a mess here.
This is going to invite the anger of the Council...Wait a second, if we handle this badly, we could end up in jail...!!!
......
TRMBL
おろ
TRMBL
おろ
あーん
WAAAAAH!

FAIRY TAIL

Chapter 67: My Decision

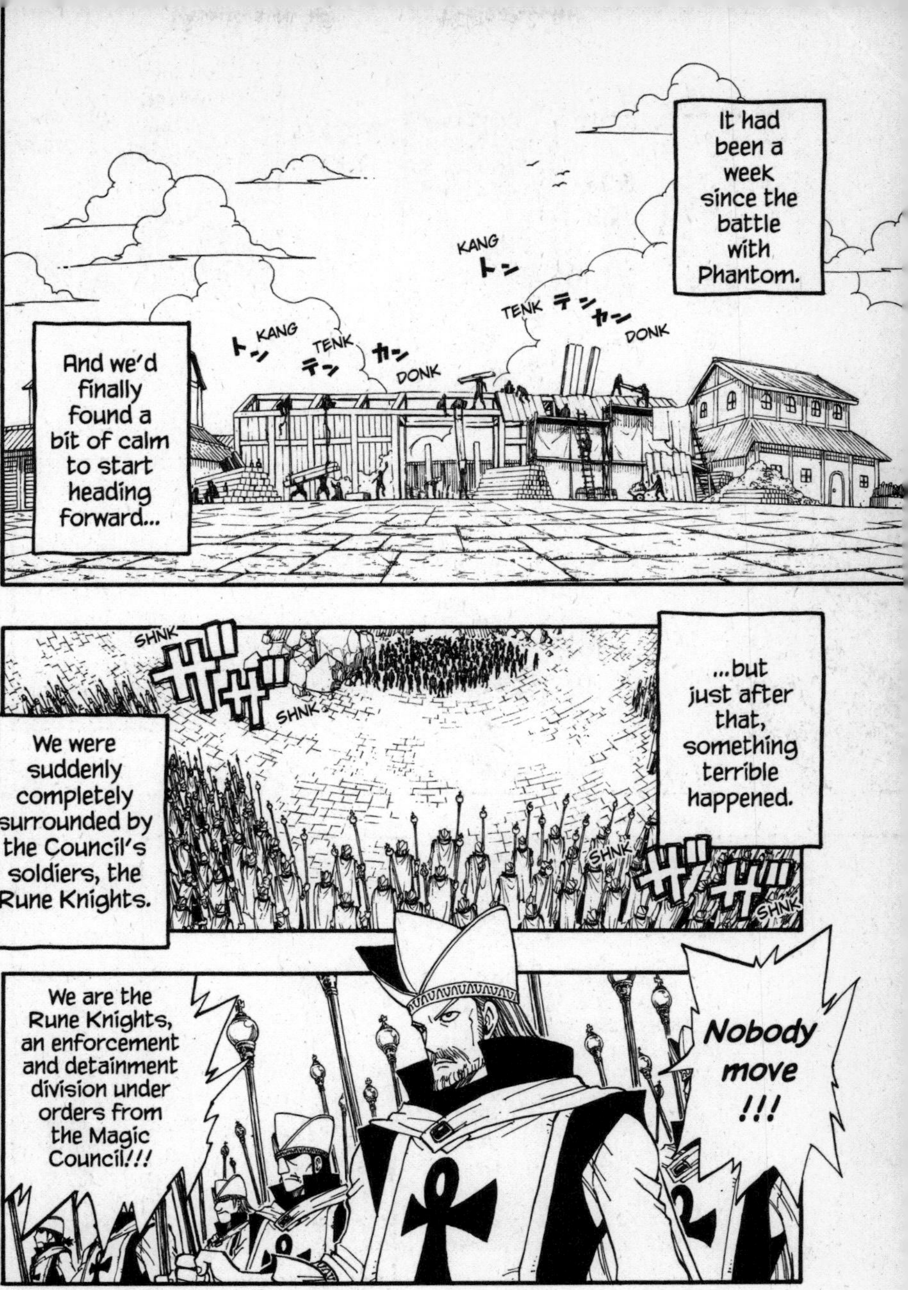
It had been a week since the battle with Phantom.
KANG
TENK
DONK
And we'd finally found a bit of calm to start heading forward...
KANG
TENK
DONK
...but just after that, something terrible happened.
SHNK
SHNK
We were suddenly completely surrounded by the Council's soldiers, the Rune Knights.
SHNK
SHNK
Nobody move!!!
We are the Rune Knights, an enforcement and detainment division under orders from the Magic Council!!!

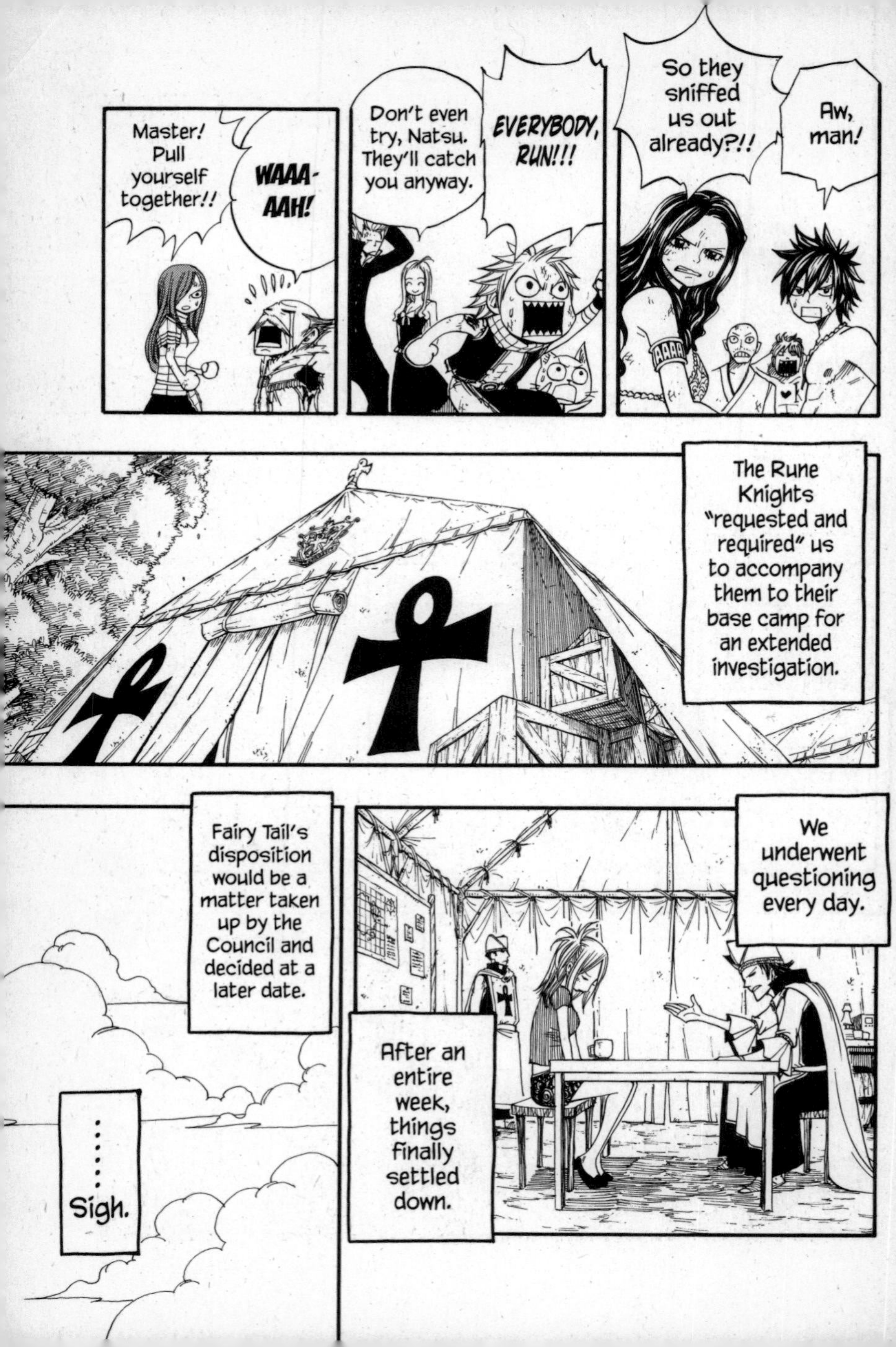
So they sniffed us out already?!!
Aw, man!
EVERYBODY, RUN!!!
Don't even try, Natsu. They'll catch you anyway.
WAAAAAH!
Master! Pull yourself together!!
The Rune Knights "requested and required" us to accompany them to their base camp for an extended investigation.
We underwent questioning every day.
After an entire week, things finally settled down.
Fairy Tail's disposition would be a matter taken up by the Council and decided at a later date.
...... Sigh.

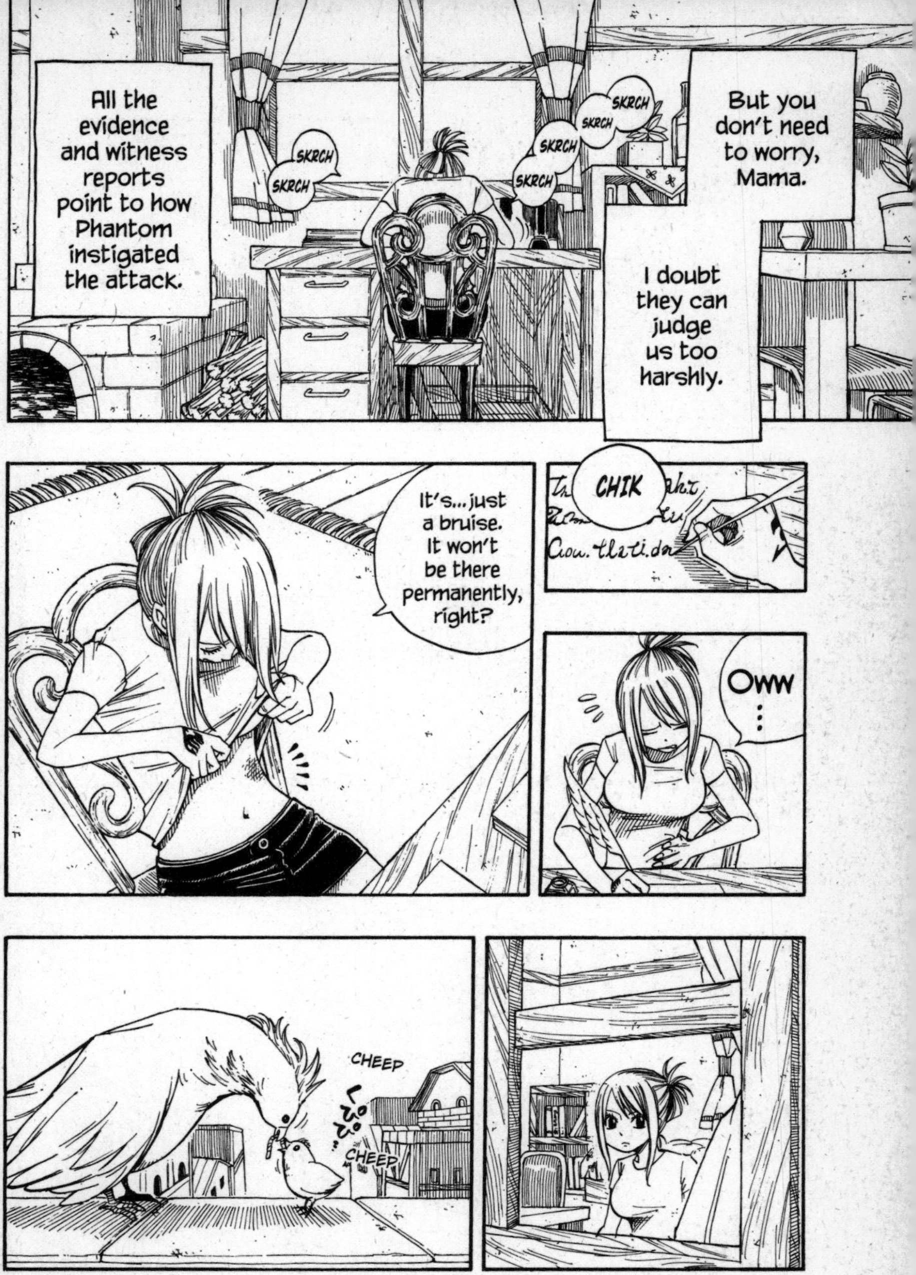
But you don't need to worry, Mama.
SKRCH
SKRCH
SKRCH
SKRCH
SKRCH
SKRCH
All the evidence and witness reports point to how Phantom instigated the attack.
I doubt they can judge us too harshly.
CHIK
Oww...
It's...just a bruise. It won't be there permanently, right?
CHEEP
CHEEP

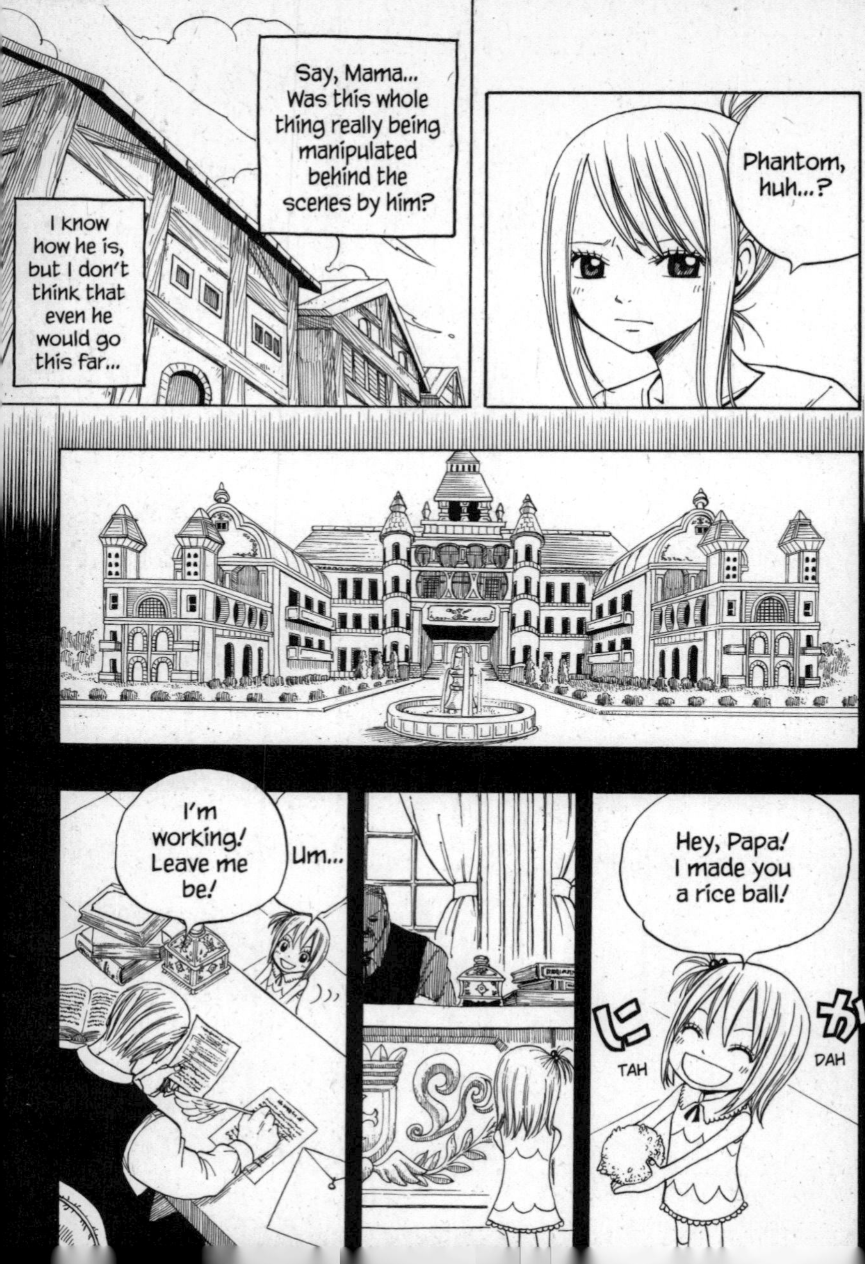
Phantom, huh...?
Say, Mama... Was this whole thing really being manipulated behind the scenes by him?
I know how he is, but I don't think that even he would go this far...
Hey, Papa! I made you a rice ball!
に TAH
か DAH
Um...
I'm working! Leave me be!

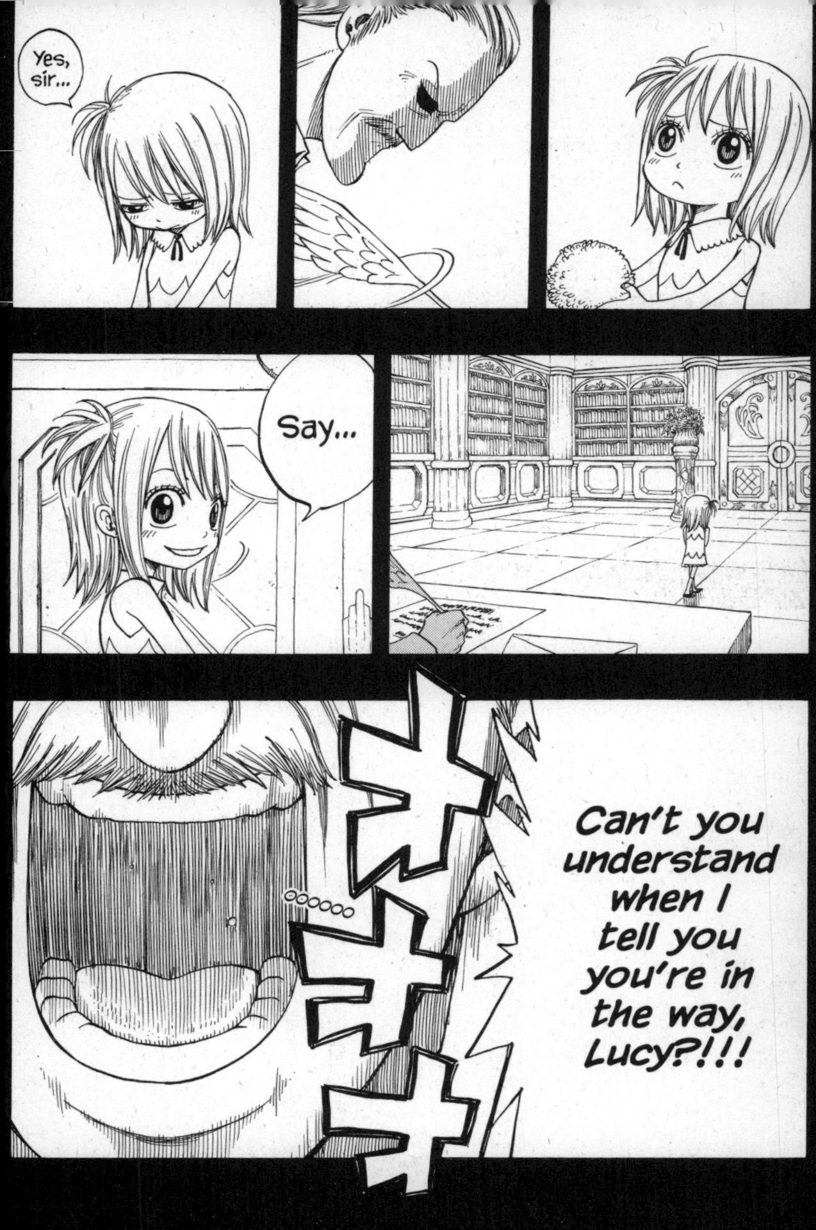
Yes, sir...
Say...
Can't you understand when I tell you you're in the way, Lucy?!!!
oooooo

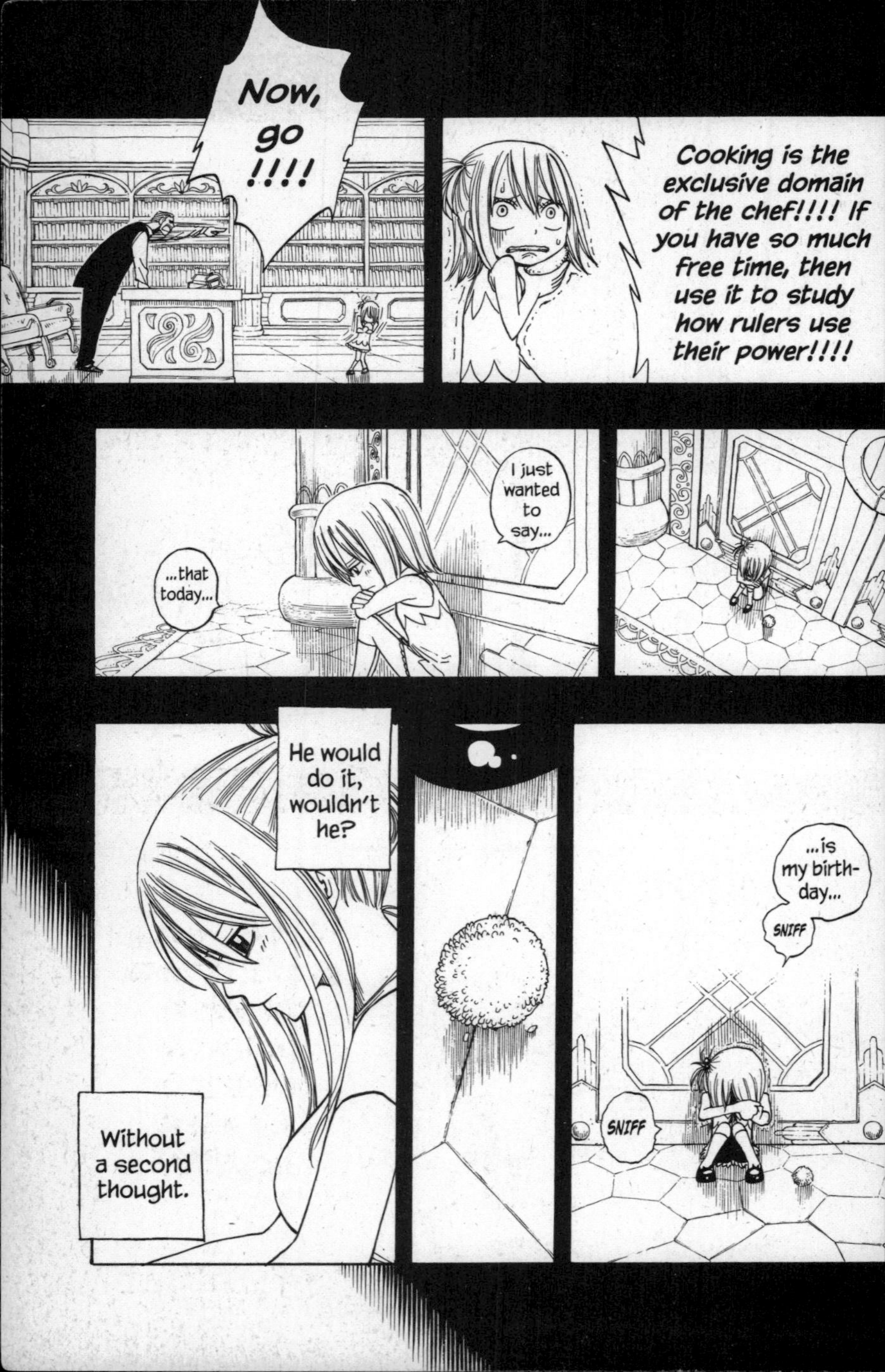

Cooking is the exclusive domain of the chef!!!! If you have so much free time, then use it to study how rulers use their power!!!!
Now, go !!!!
I just wanted to say...
...that today...
...is my birth-day...
SNIFF
SNIFF
He would do it, wouldn't he?
Without a second thought.

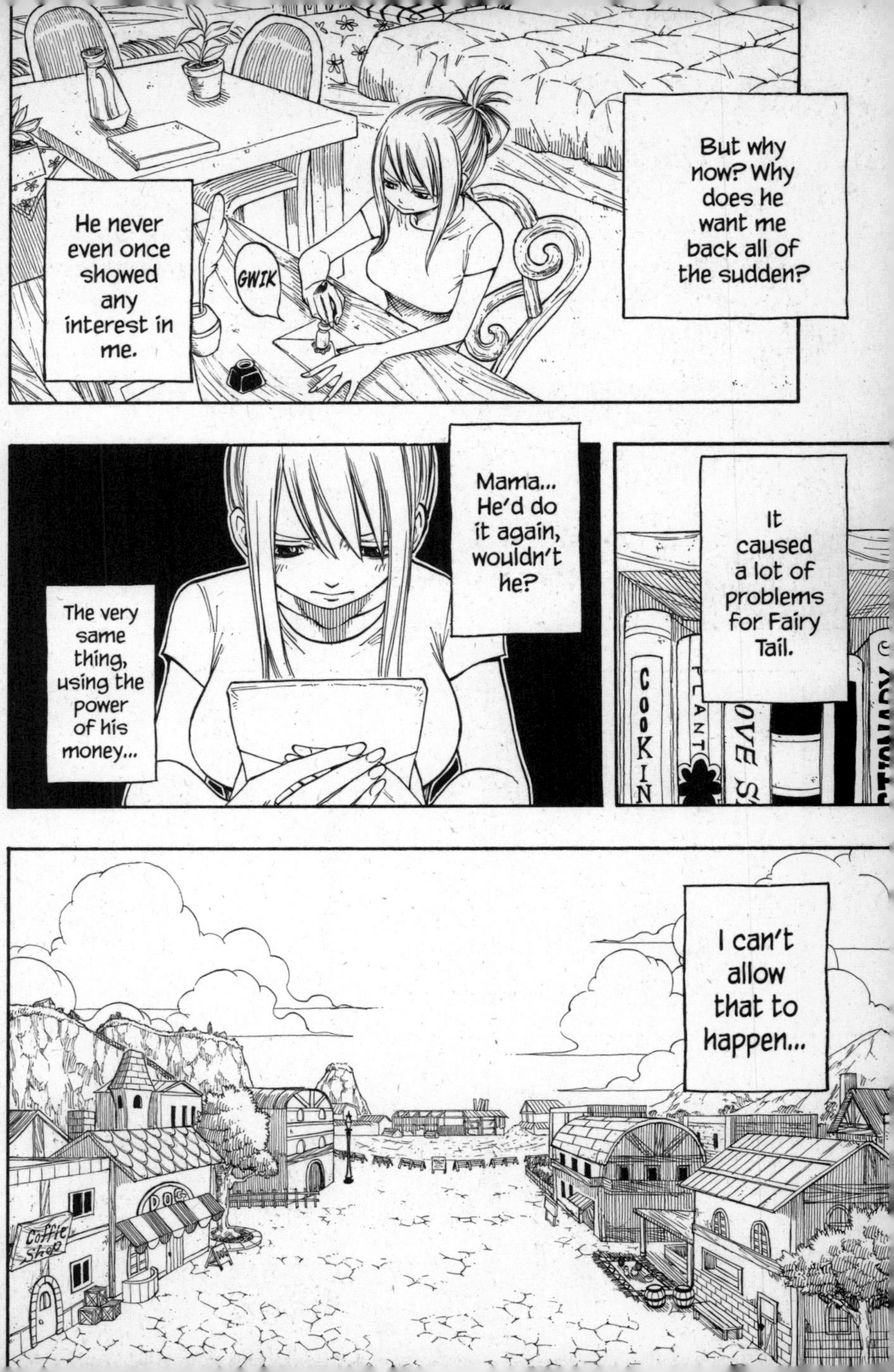
But why now? Why does he want me back all of the sudden?
He never even once showed any interest in me.
GWIK
It caused a lot of problems for Fairy Tail.
COOKIN
PLANT
Mama... He'd do it again, wouldn't he?
The very same thing, using the power of his money...
I can't allow that to happen...
DOG
Coffie Shop

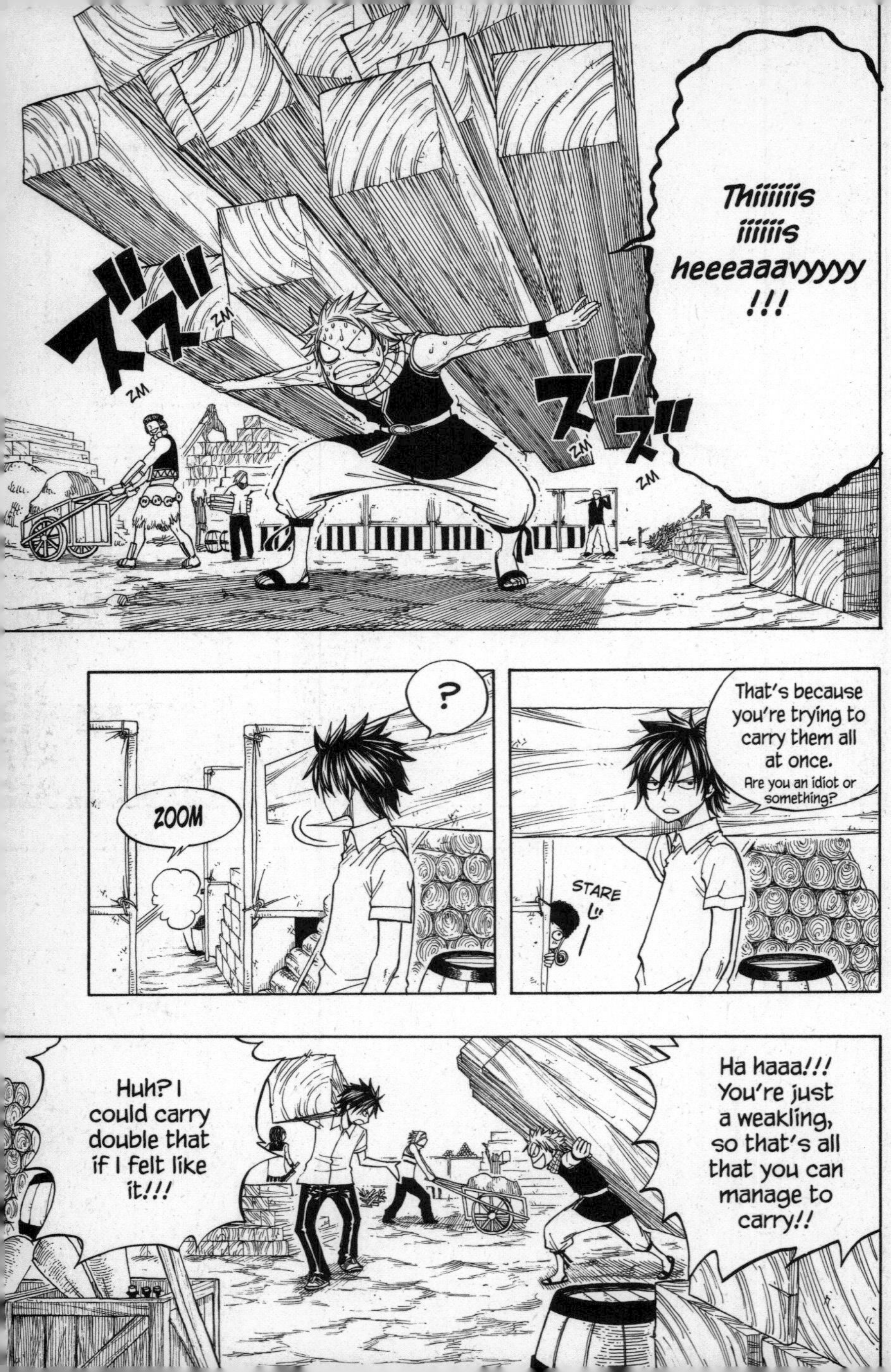
Thiiiiiis iiiiiis heeeaaavyyyy!!!
ZM
ZM
ZM
ZM
That's because you're trying to carry them all at once.
Are you an idiot or something?
STARE
?
ZOOM
Ha haaa!!! You're just a weakling, so that's all that you can manage to carry!!
Huh? I could carry double that if I felt like it!!!

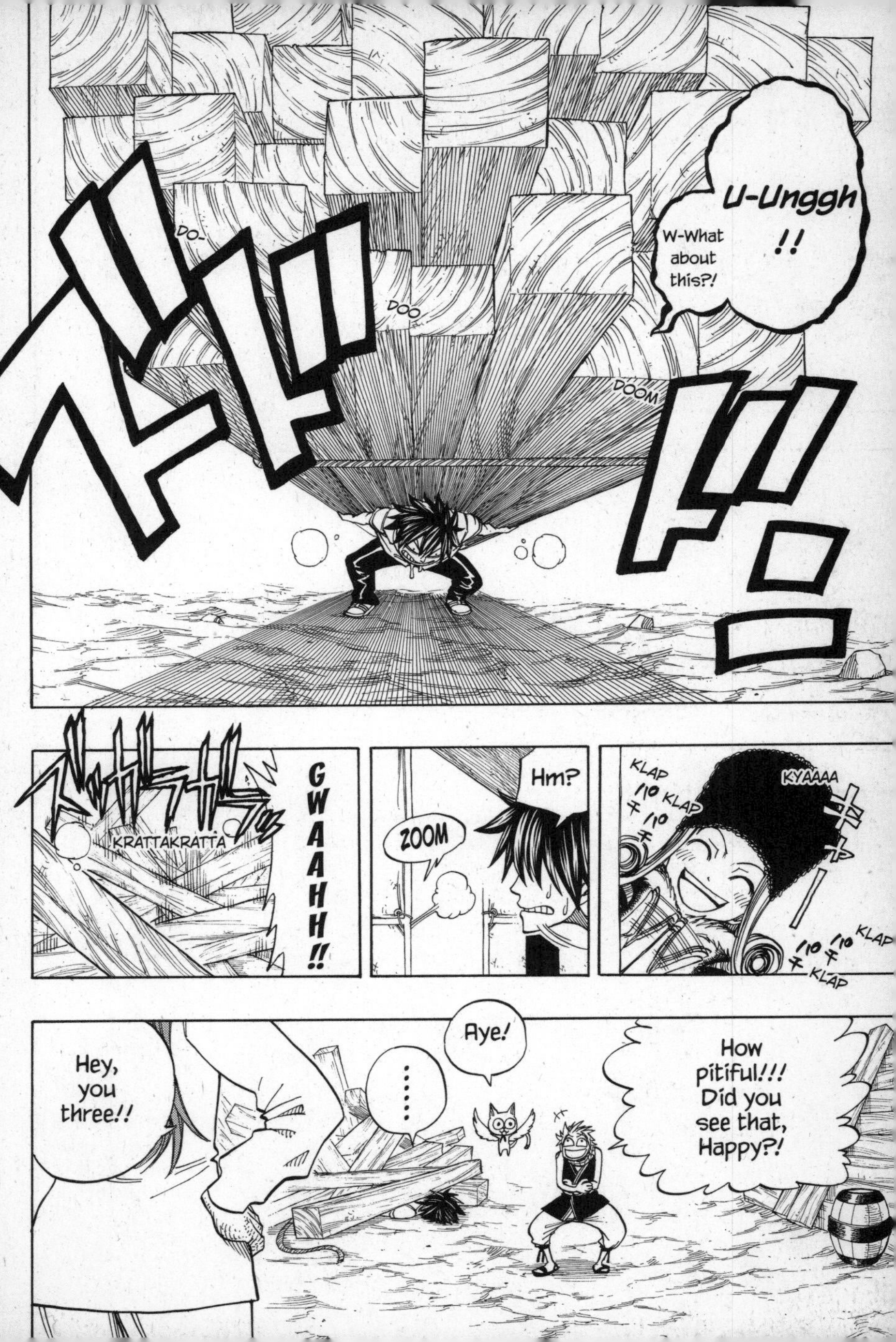
U-Unggh!!
W-What about this?!
DO-
DOO
DOOM
KYAAAA
KLAP KLAP
KLAP KLAP
Hm?
ZOOM
GWAAAHH!!
KRATTAKRATTA
How pitiful!!! Did you see that, Happy?!
Aye!
......
Hey, you three!!

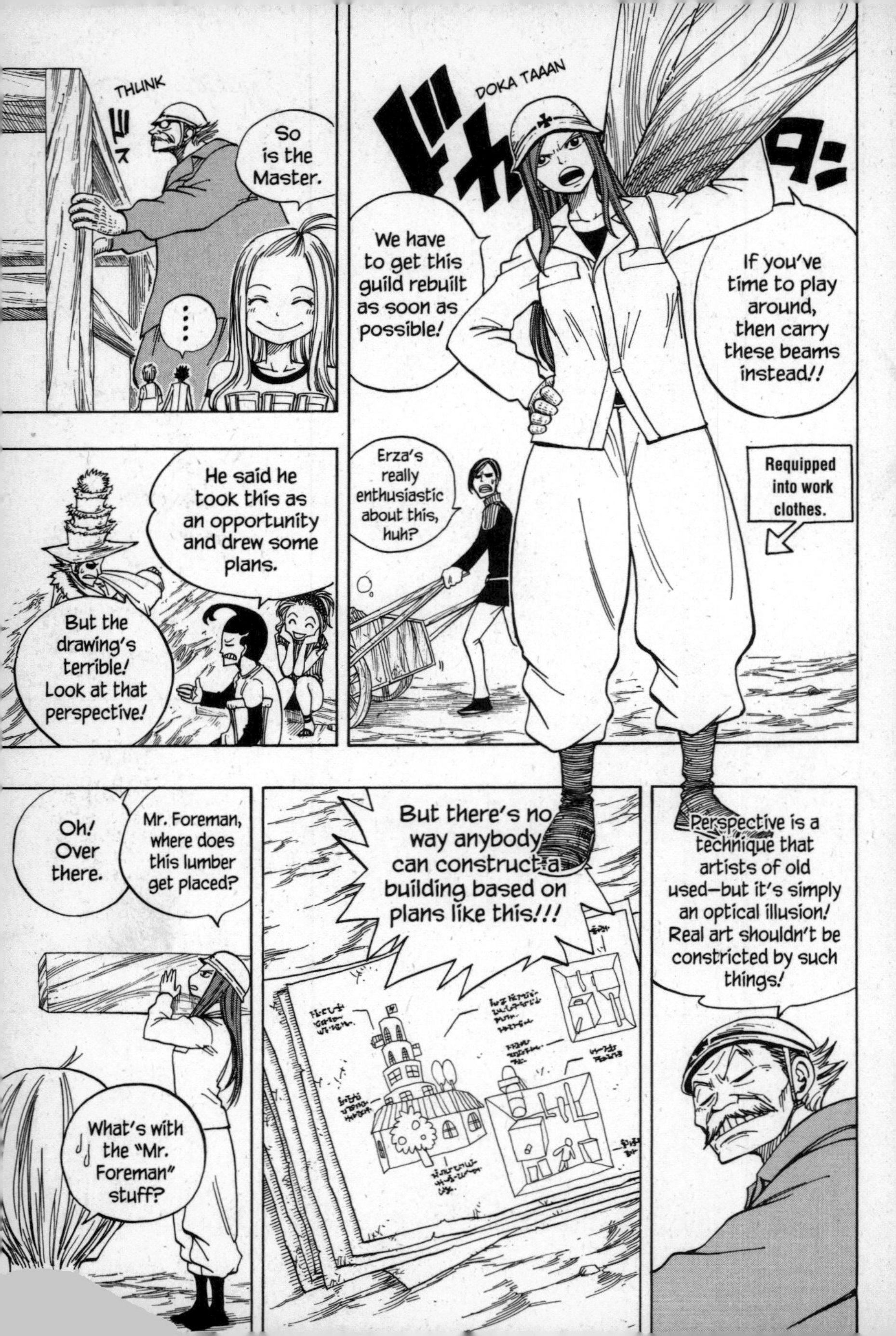
DOKA TAAAN
If you've time to play around, then carry these beams instead!!
We have to get this guild rebuilt as soon as possible!
Erza's really enthusiastic about this, huh?
Requipped into work clothes.
THUNK
So is the Master.
....
He said he took this as an opportunity and drew some plans.
But the drawing's terrible! Look at that perspective!
Perspective is a technique that artists of old used—but it's simply an optical illusion! Real art shouldn't be constricted by such things!
But there's no way anybody can construct a building based on plans like this!!!
Mr. Foreman, where does this lumber get placed?
Oh! Over there.
What's with the "Mr. Foreman" stuff?

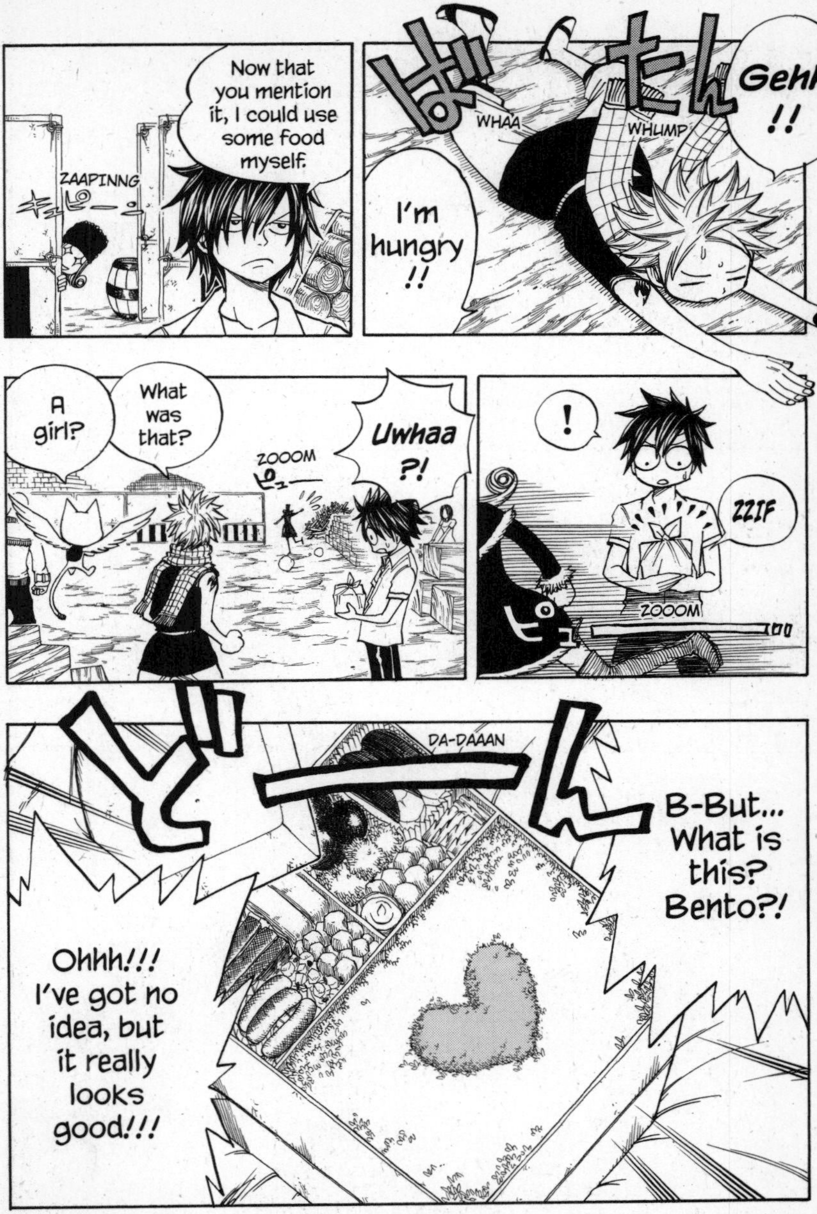

ばたん
Gehh!!
WHAA
WHUMP
I'm hungry!!
Now that you mention it, I could use some food myself.
ZAAPINNG
!
ZZIF
ZOOOM
Uwhaa?!
What was that?
A girl?
ZOOOM
DA-DAAAN
どーん
B-But... What is this? Bento?!
Ohhh!!! I've got no idea, but it really looks good!!!

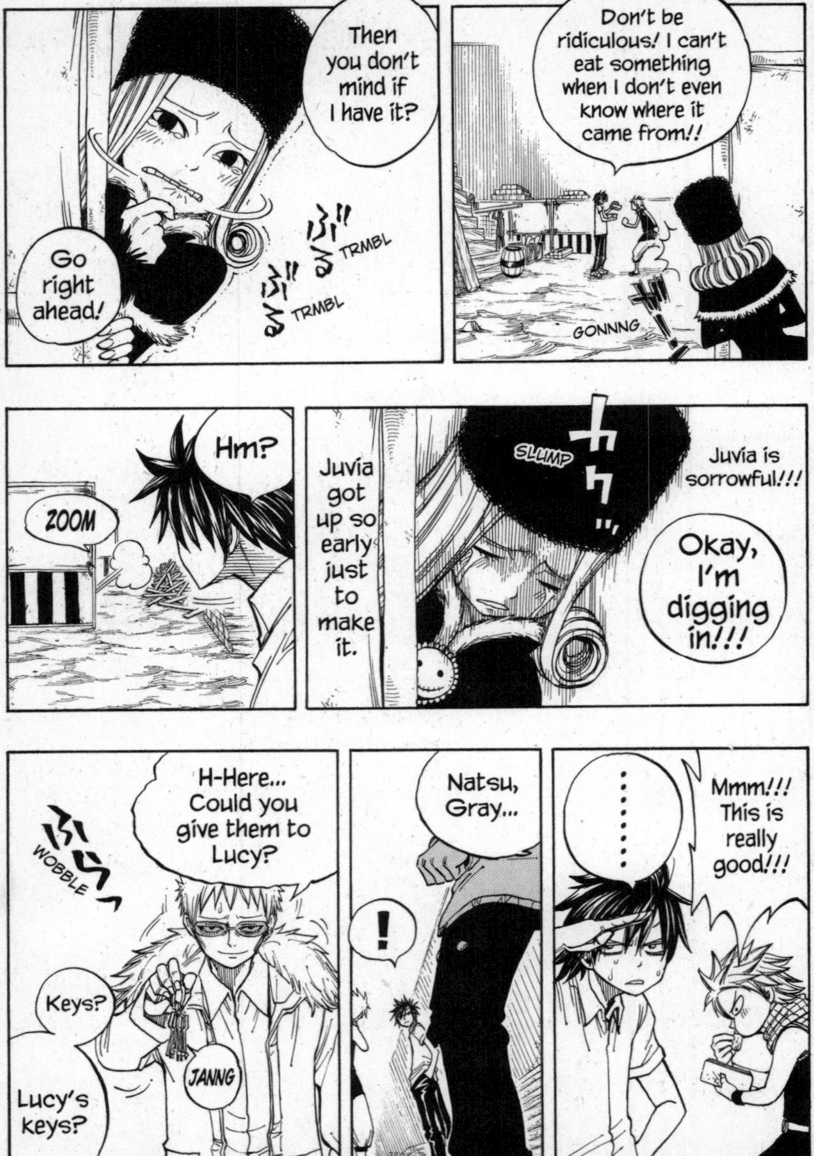
Don't be ridiculous! I can't eat something when I don't even know where it came from!!
GONNNG
Then you don't mind if I have it?
TRMBL
TRMBL
Go right ahead!
Juvia is sorrowful!!!
SLUMP
Juvia got up so early just to make it.
Okay, I'm digging in!!!
Hm?
ZOOM
Mmm!!! This is really good!!!
......
Natsu, Gray...
!
H-Here... Could you give them to Lucy?
WOBBLE
Keys?
JANNG
Lucy's keys?

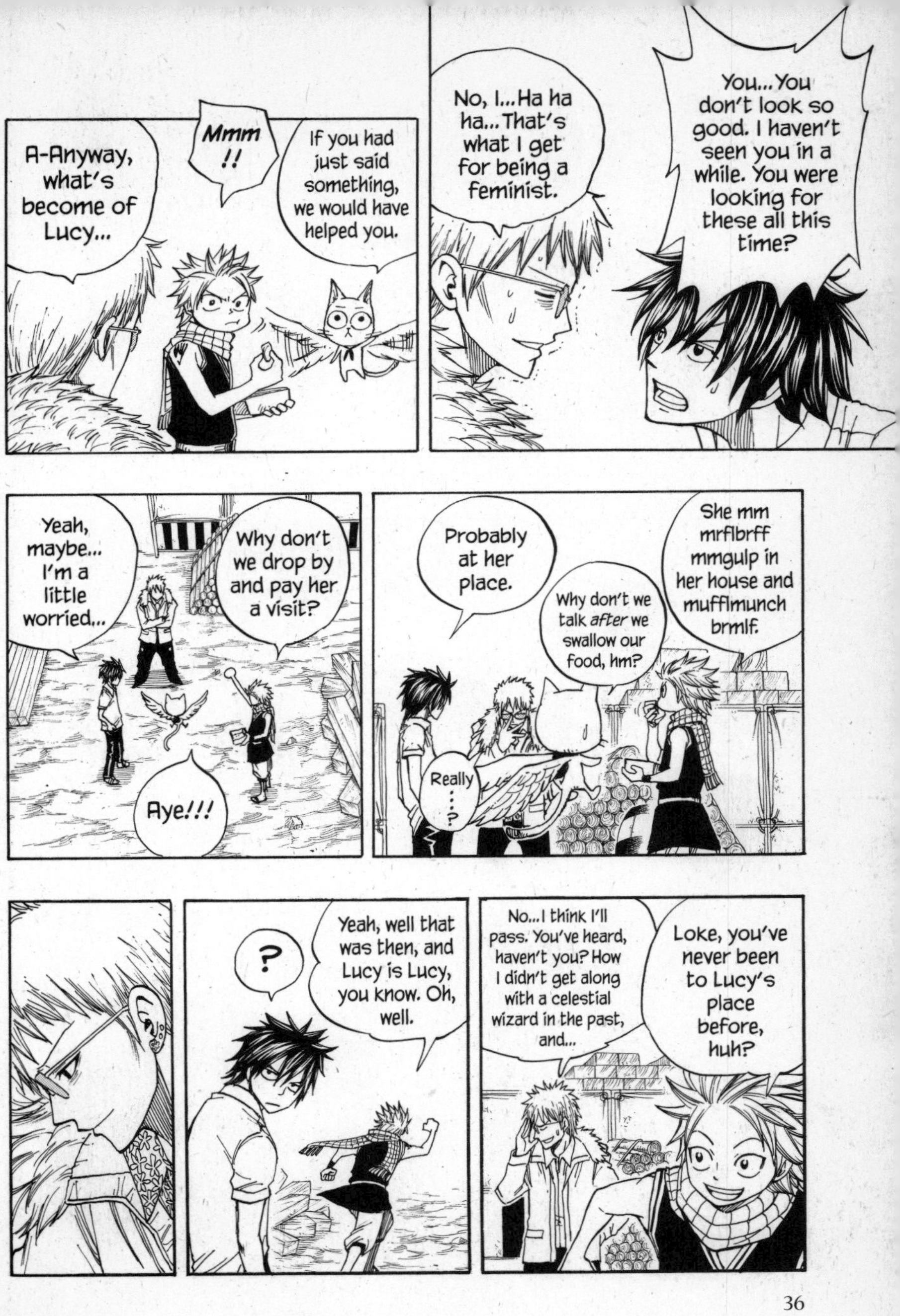
You...You don't look so good. I haven't seen you in a while. You were looking for these all this time?
No, I...Ha ha ha...That's what I get for being a feminist.
If you had just said something, we would have helped you.
Mmm !!
A-Anyway, what's become of Lucy...
She mm mrflbrff mmgulp in her house and mufflmunch brmlf.
Why don't we talk *after* we swallow our food, hm?
Probably at her place.
Really...?
Why don't we drop by and pay her a visit?
Yeah, maybe... I'm a little worried...
Aye!!!
Loke, you've never been to Lucy's place before, huh?
No...I think I'll pass. You've heard, haven't you? How I didn't get along with a celestial wizard in the past, and...
Yeah, well that was then, and Lucy is Lucy, you know. Oh, well.
?

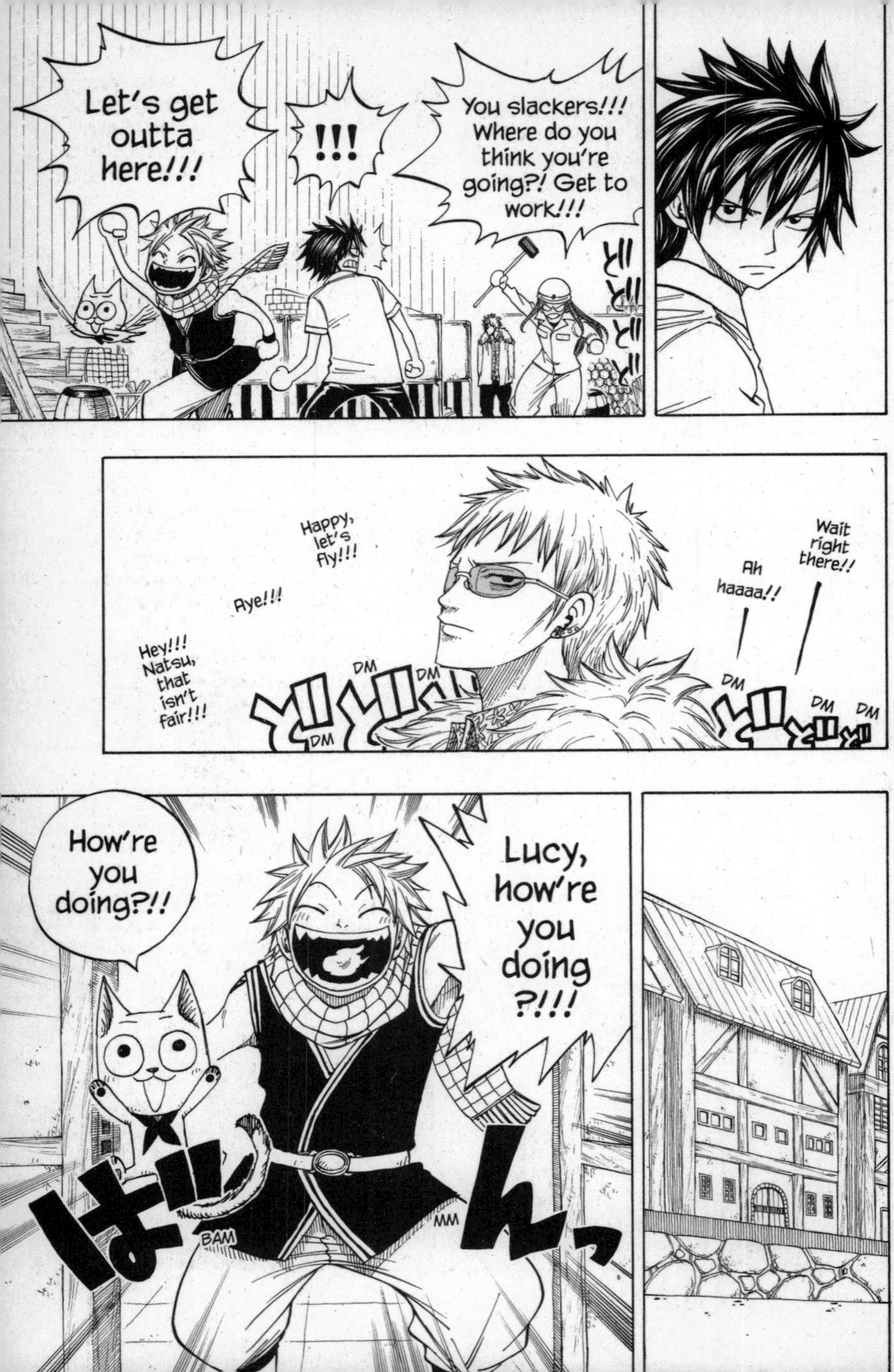
You slackers!!! Where do you think you're going?! Get to work!!!
!!!
Let's get outta here!!!
Wait right there!!
Ah haaaa!!
DM DM DM
Happy, let's fly!!!
Aye!!!
DM DM DM
Hey!!! Natsu, that isn't fair!!!
Lucy, how're you doing?!!!
MM
How're you doing?!!
BAM

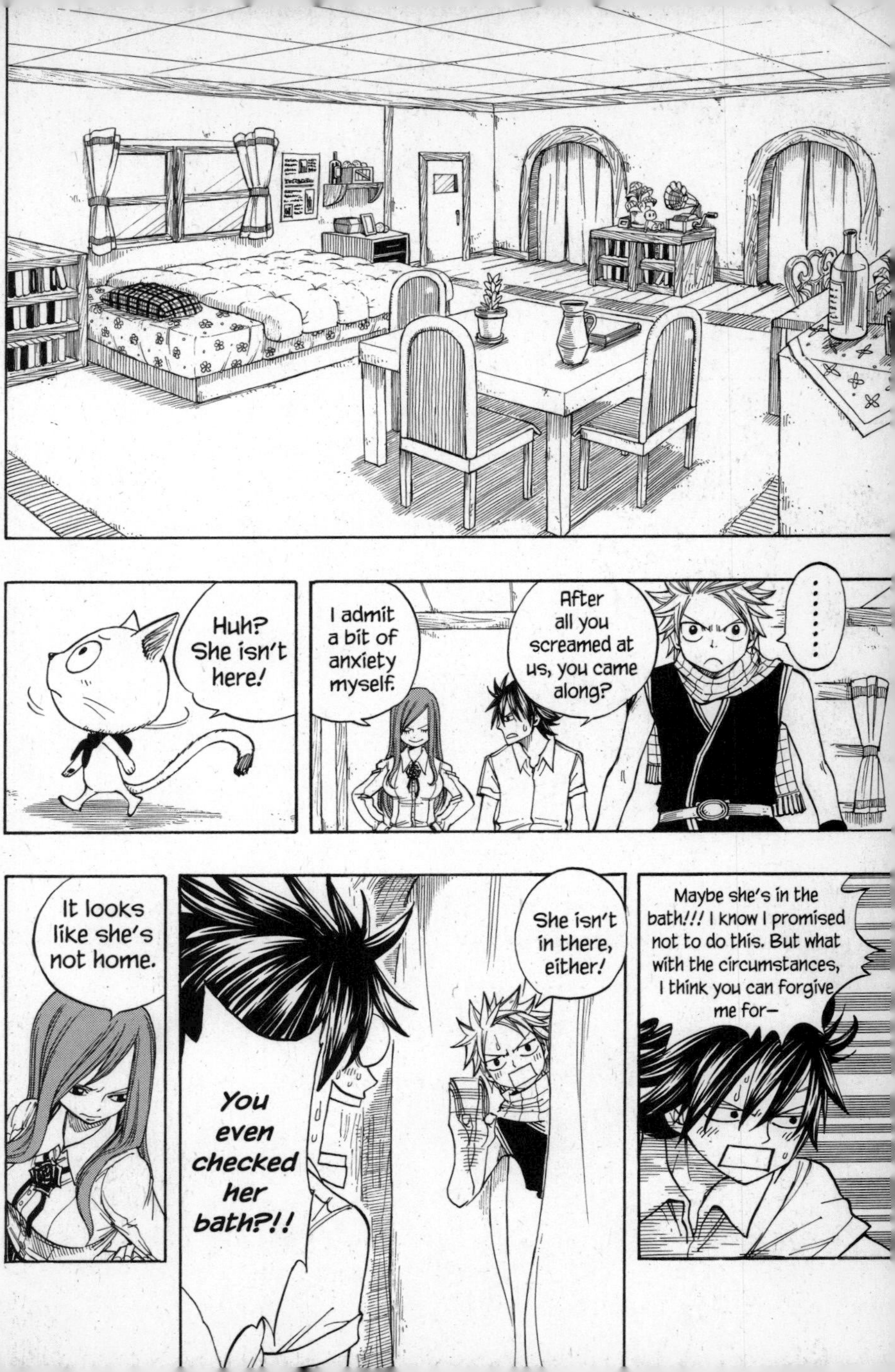
......
After all you screamed at us, you came along?
I admit a bit of anxiety myself.
Huh? She isn't here!
Maybe she's in the bath!!! I know I promised not to do this. But what with the circumstances, I think you can forgive me for—
She isn't in there, either!
You even checked her bath?!!
It looks like she's not home.

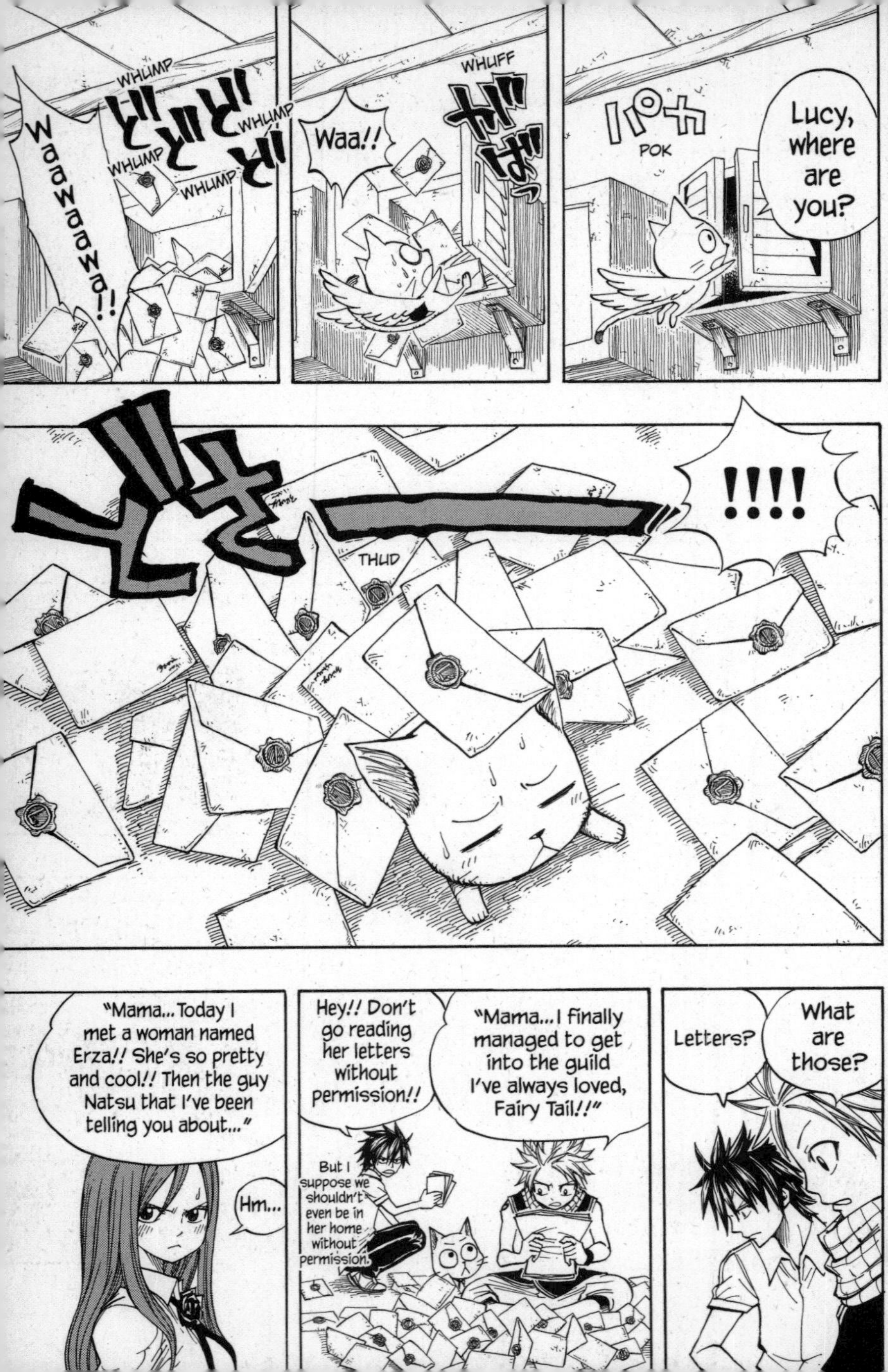
Lucy, where are you?
POK
WHUFF
Waa!!
WHUMP
WHUMP
WHUMP
WHUMP
Waawaawawa!!
!!!!
THUD
What are those?
Letters?
"Mama...I finally managed to get into the guild I've always loved, Fairy Tail!!"
Hey!! Don't go reading her letters without permission!!
But I suppose we shouldn't even be in her home without permission.
"Mama...Today I met a woman named Erza!! She's so pretty and cool!! Then the guy Natsu that I've been telling you about..."
Hm...

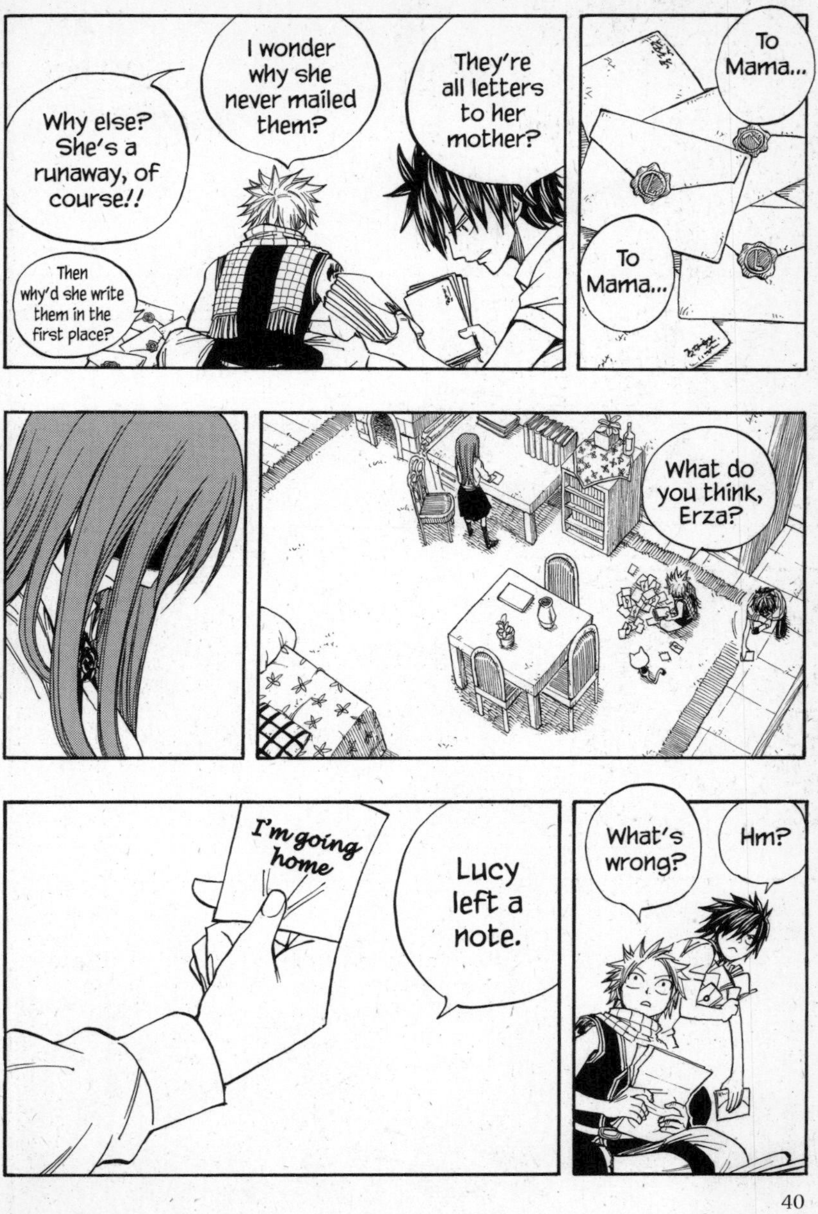
To Mama...
To Mama...
They're all letters to her mother?
I wonder why she never mailed them?
Why else? She's a runaway, of course!!
Then why'd she write them in the first place?
What do you think, Erza?
Hm?
What's wrong?
Lucy left a note.
I'm going home

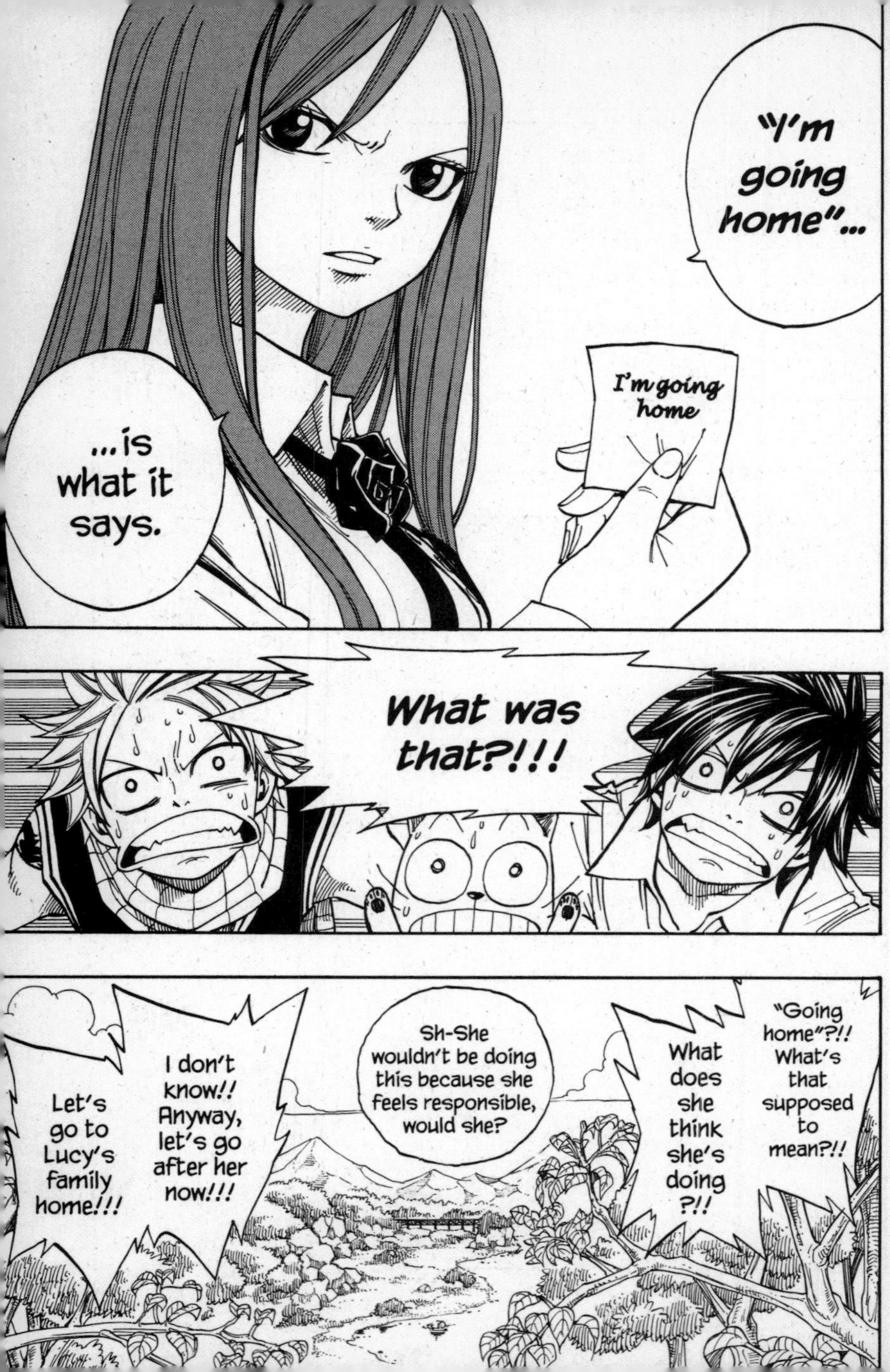
"I'm going home"...
I'm going home
...is what it says.
What was that?!!!
"Going home"?!! What's that supposed to mean?!!
What does she think she's doing?!!
Sh-She wouldn't be doing this because she feels responsible, would she?
I don't know!! Anyway, let's go after her now!!!
Let's go to Lucy's family home!!!

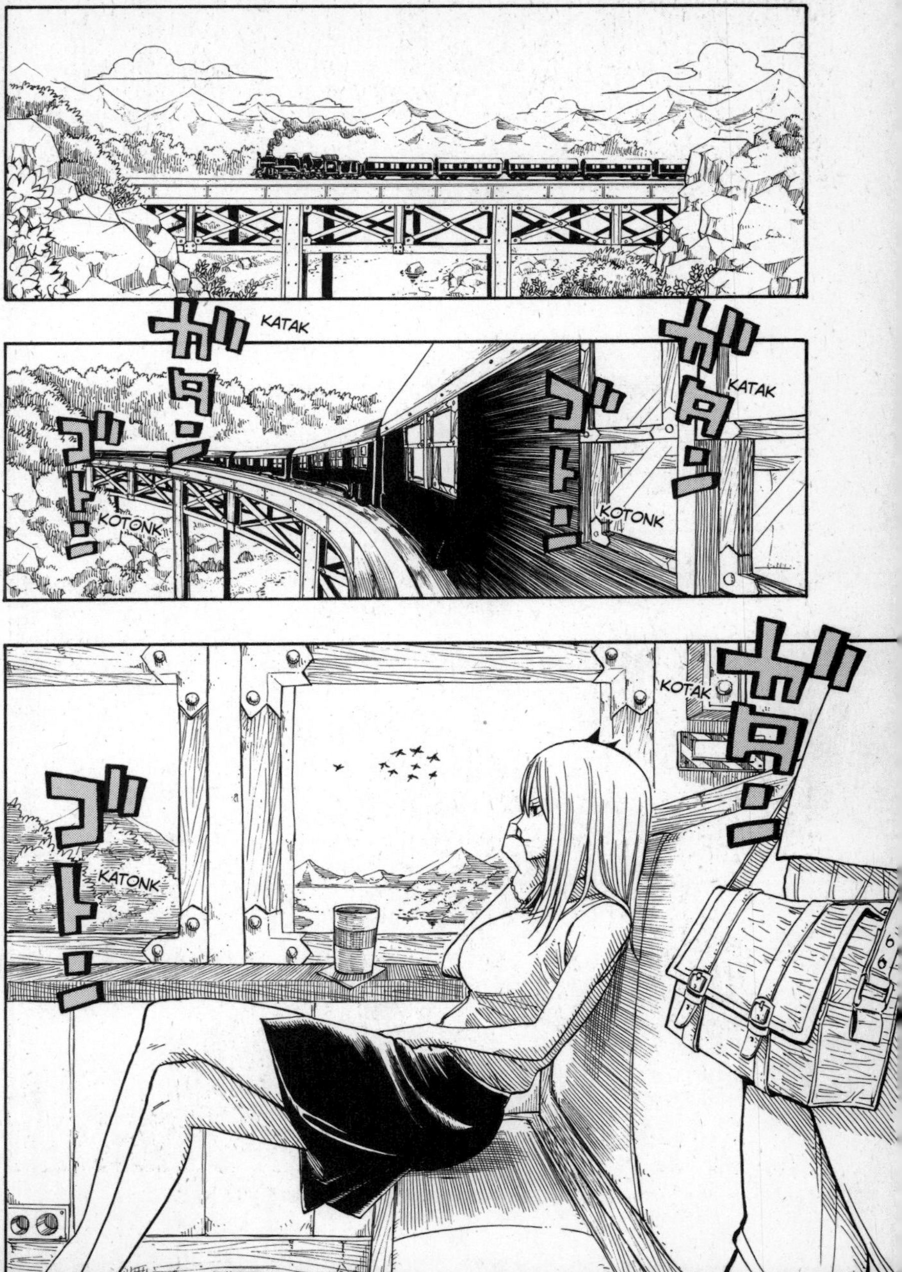
ガタン
KATAK
ゴトン
KOTONK
ガタン
KATAK
ゴトン
KOTONK
ガタン
KOTAK
ゴトン
KATONK

FAIRY TAIL

Chapter 68: Goodbye

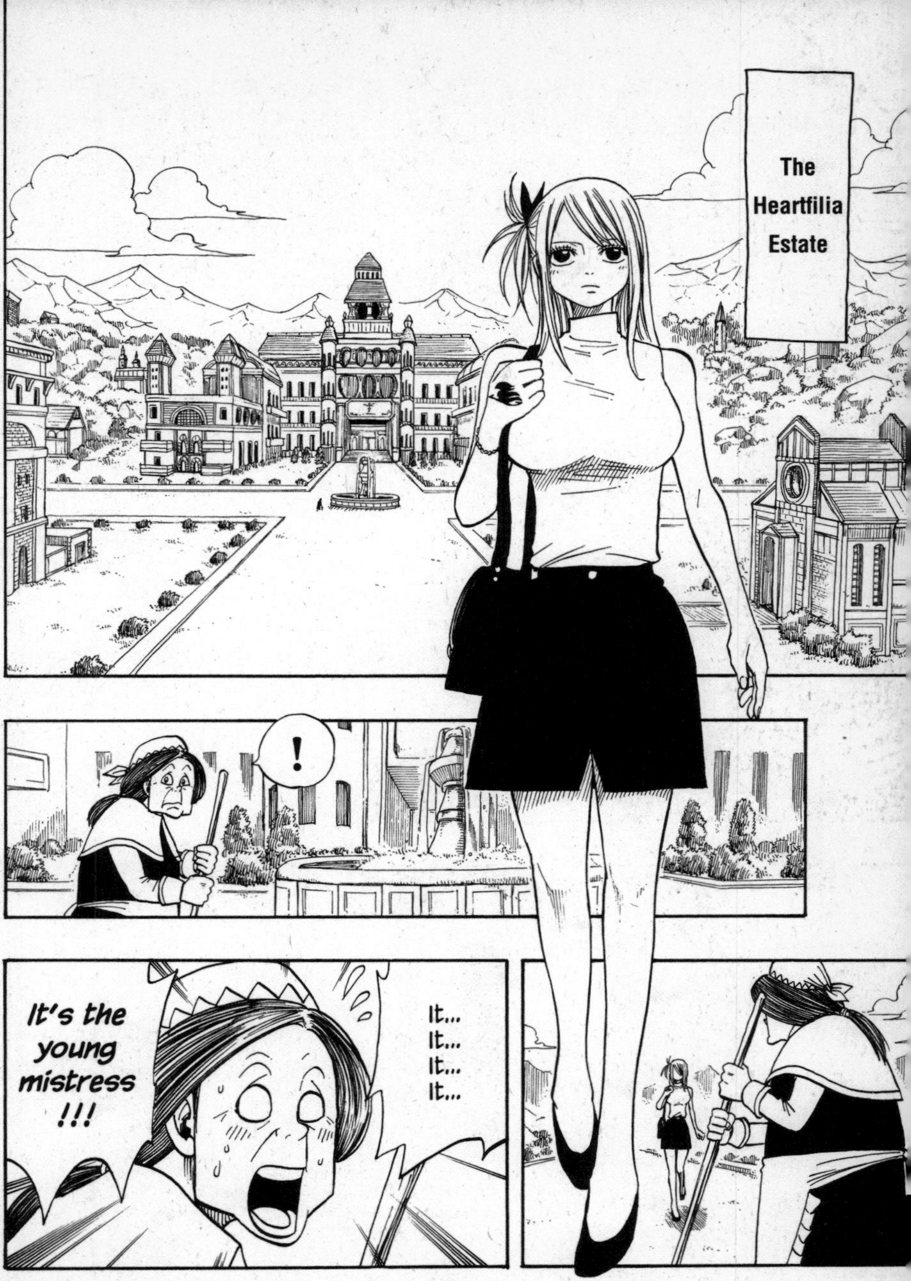
The Heartfilia Estate
!
It... It... It... It...
It's the young mistress!!!

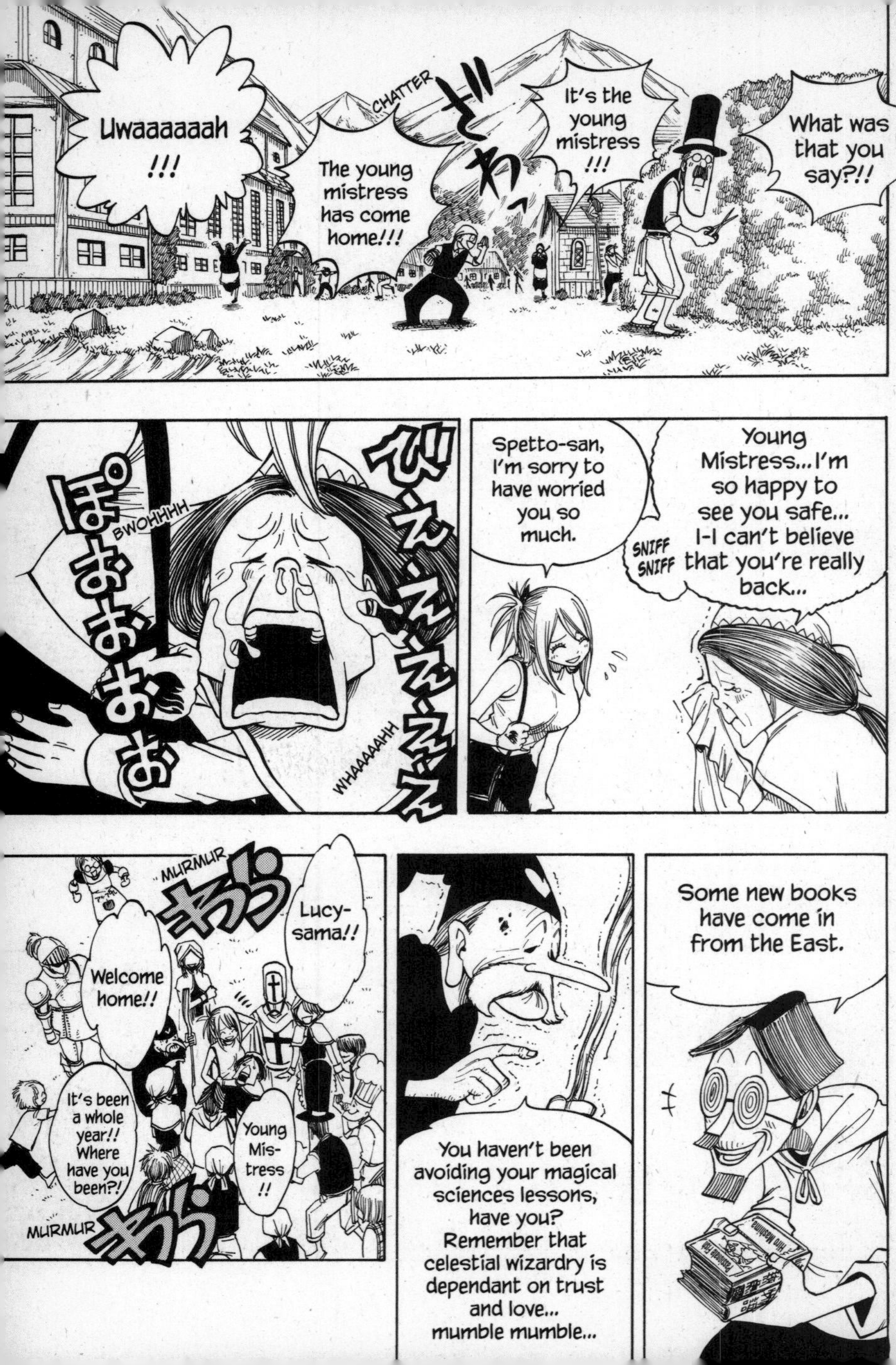
What was that you say?!!
It's the young mistress!!!
CHATTER
The young mistress has come home!!!
Uwaaaaaah!!!
Young Mistress...I'm so happy to see you safe... I-I can't believe that you're really back...
SNIFF SNIFF
Spetto-san, I'm sorry to have worried you so much.
WHAAAAAHH
BWOHHHH
Some new books have come in from the East.
You haven't been avoiding your magical sciences lessons, have you? Remember that celestial wizardry is dependant on trust and love... mumble mumble...
Lucy-sama!!
MURMUR
Welcome home!!
Young Mis-tress!!
It's been a whole year!! Where have you been?!
MURMUR

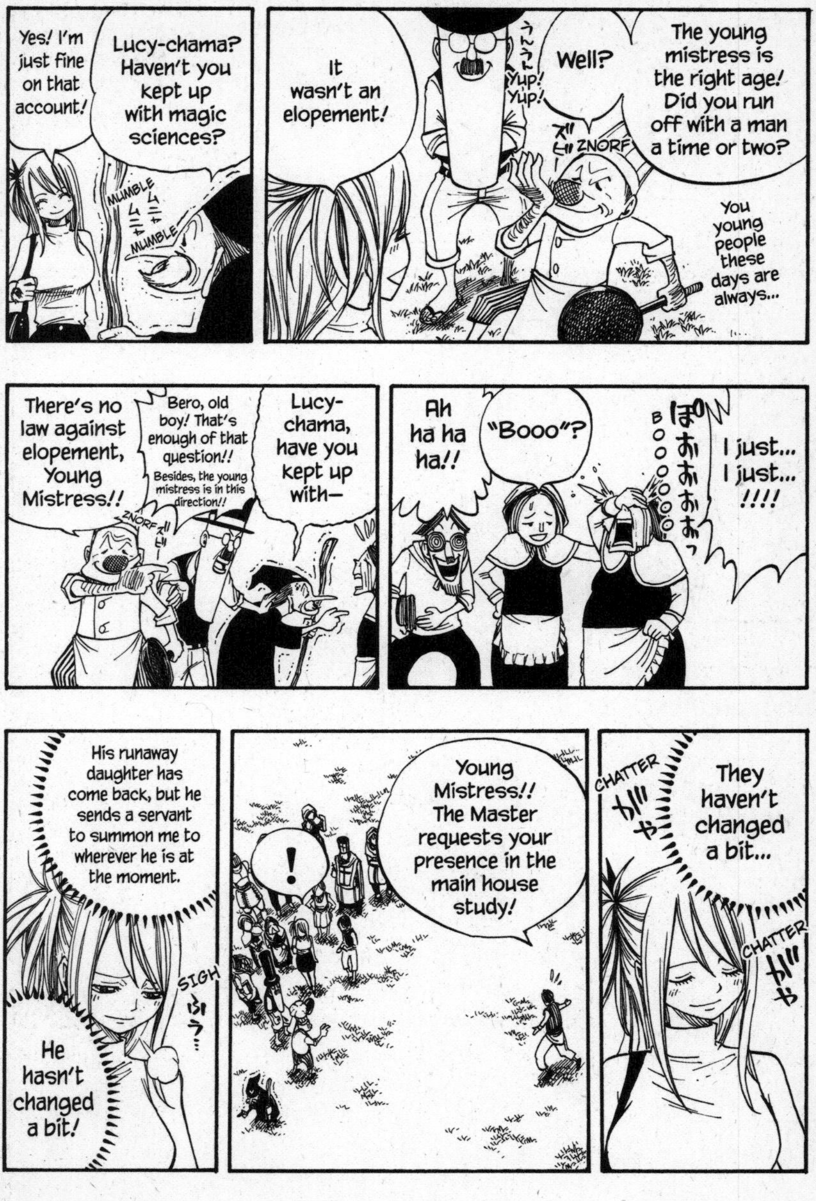
The young mistress is the right age! Did you run off with a man a time or two?
Well?
ZNORF
Yup! Yup!
It wasn't an elopement!
You young people these days are always...
Lucy-chama? Haven't you kept up with magic sciences?
Yes! I'm just fine on that account!
MUMBLE
MUMBLE
I just... I just... !!!!
BOOOOOOO
"Booo"?
Ah ha ha!!
Lucy-chama, have you kept up with—
Bero, old boy! That's enough of that question!! Besides, the young mistress is in this direction!!
There's no law against elopement, Young Mistress!!
ZNORF
They haven't changed a bit...
CHATTER
CHATTER
Young Mistress!! The Master requests your presence in the main house study!
!
His runaway daughter has come back, but he sends a servant to summon me to wherever he is at the moment.
SIGH
He hasn't changed a bit!

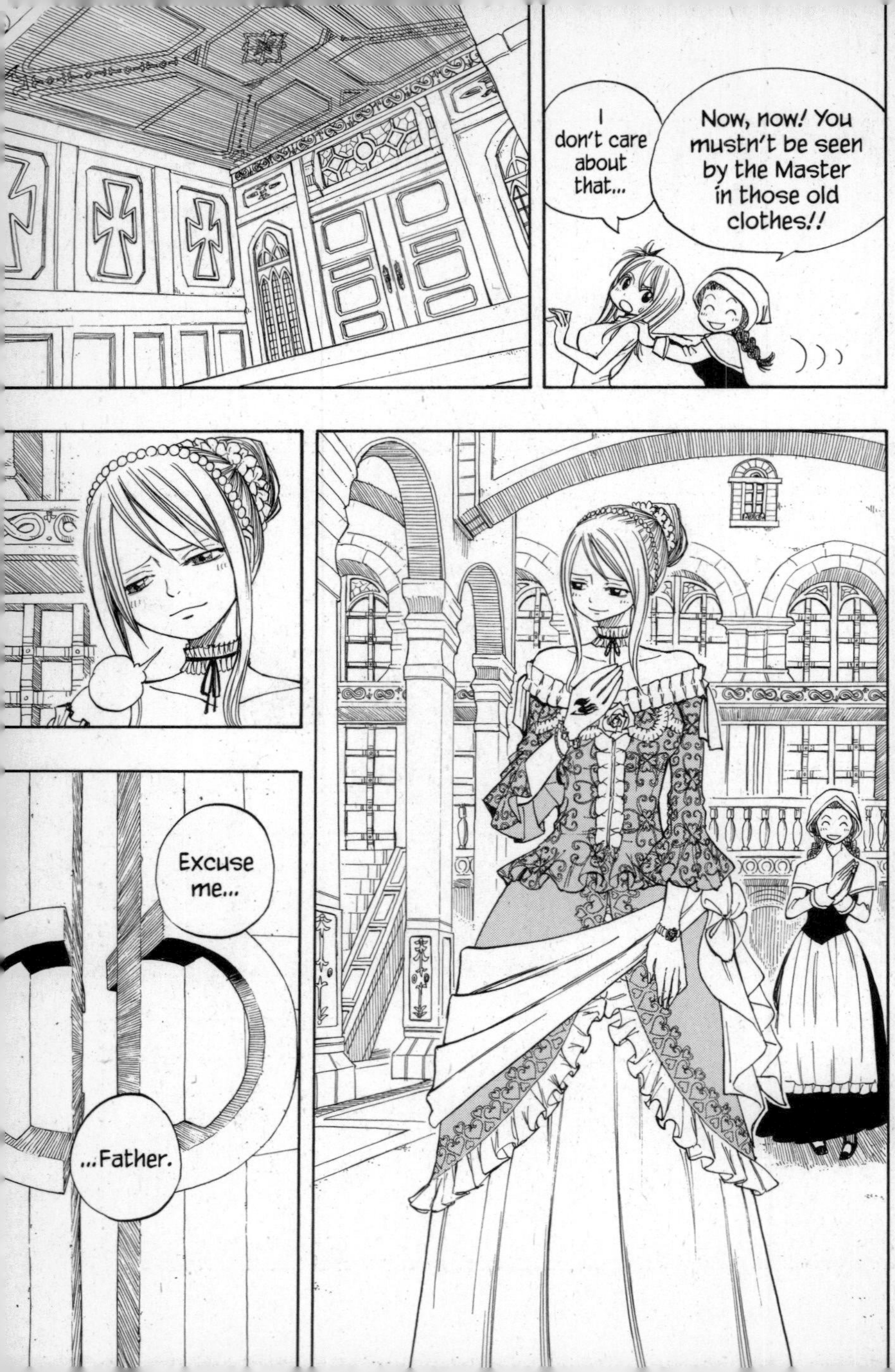
Now, now! You mustn't be seen by the Master in those old clothes!!
I don't care about that...
Excuse me...
...Father.

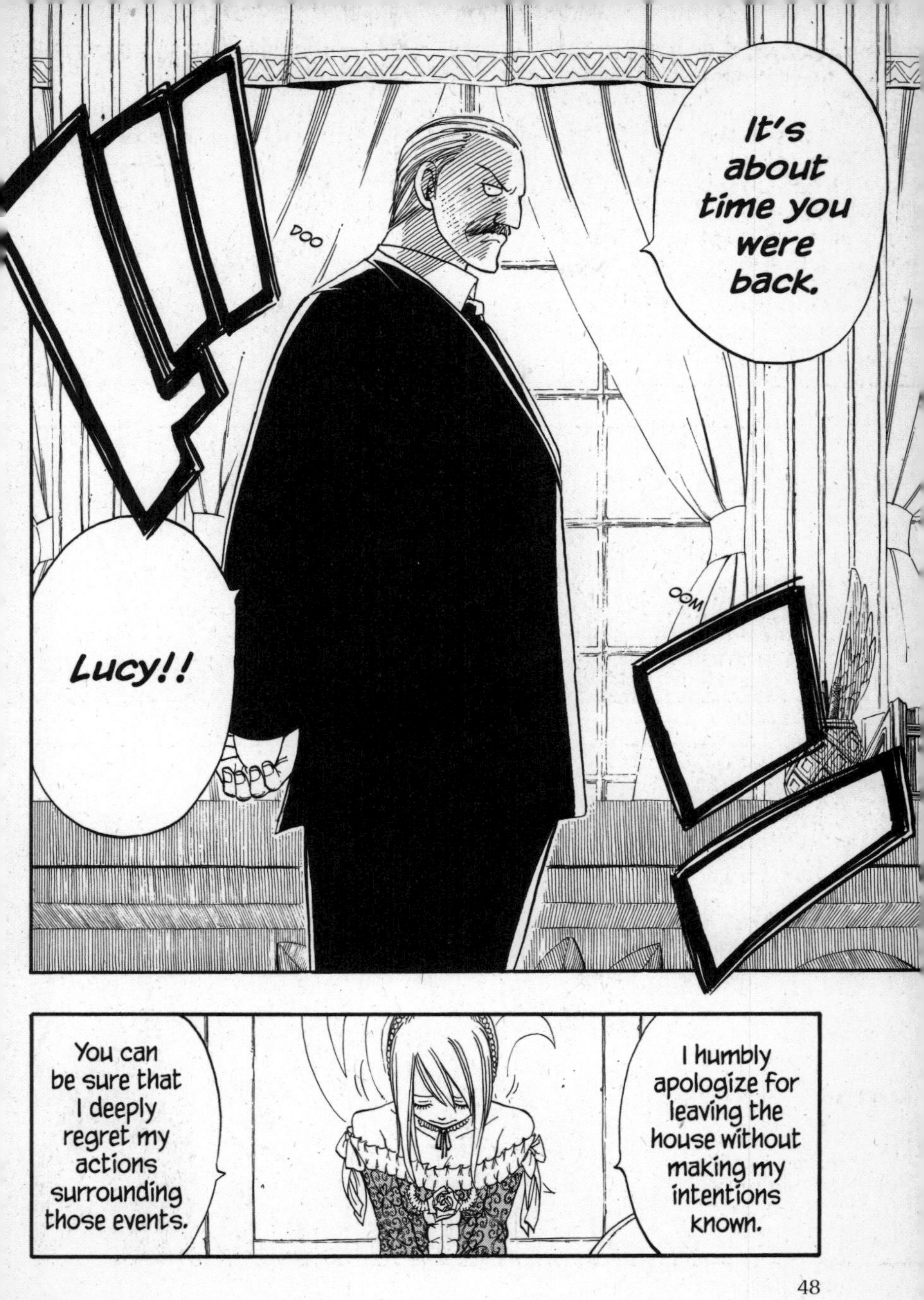
It's about time you were back.
DOO
OOM
Lucy!!
I humbly apologize for leaving the house without making my intentions known.
You can be sure that I deeply regret my actions surrounding those events.

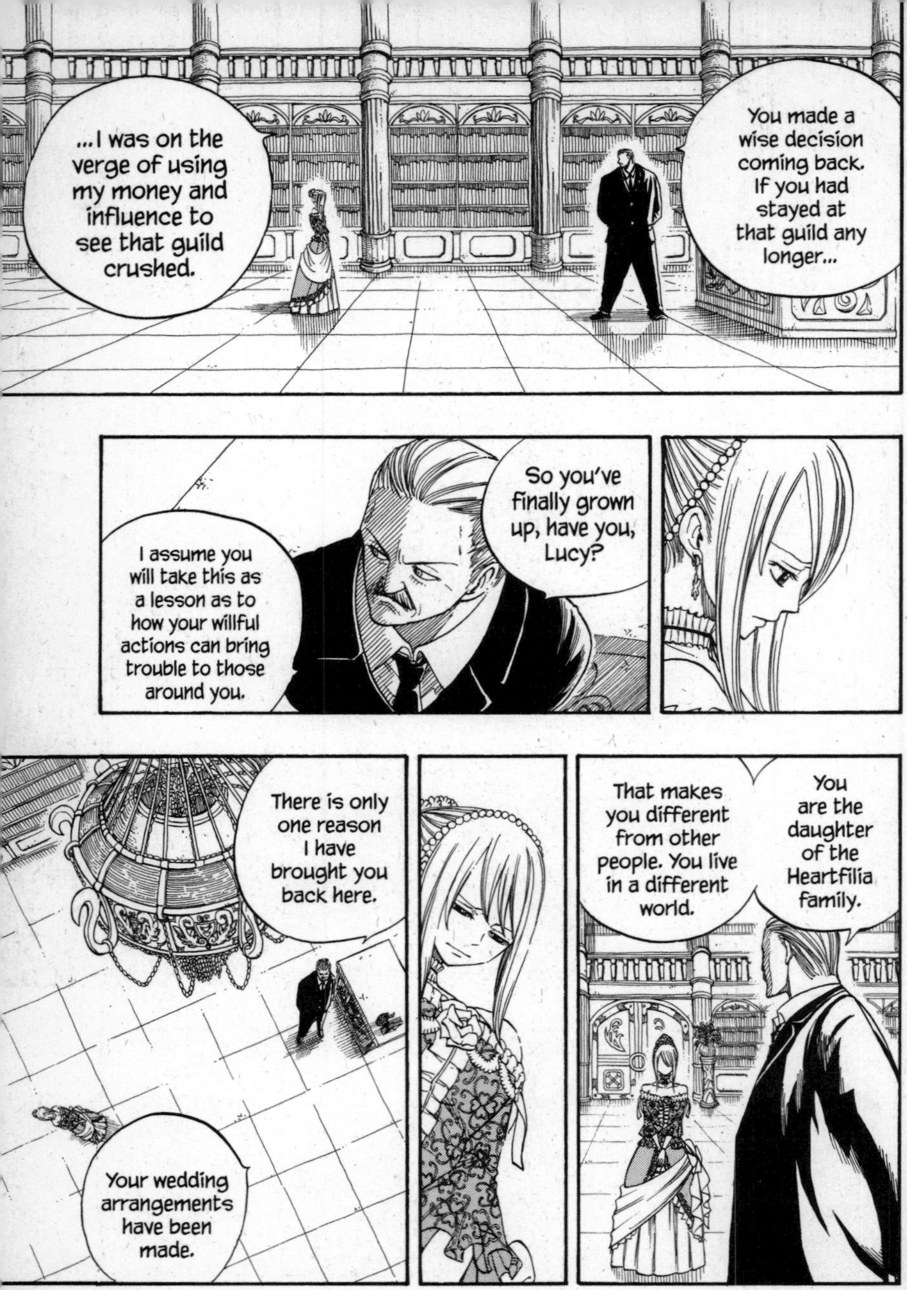
You made a wise decision coming back. If you had stayed at that guild any longer...
...I was on the verge of using my money and influence to see that guild crushed.
So you've finally grown up, have you, Lucy?
I assume you will take this as a lesson as to how your willful actions can bring trouble to those around you.
You are the daughter of the Heartfilia family.
That makes you different from other people. You live in a different world.
There is only one reason I have brought you back here.
Your wedding arrangements have been made.

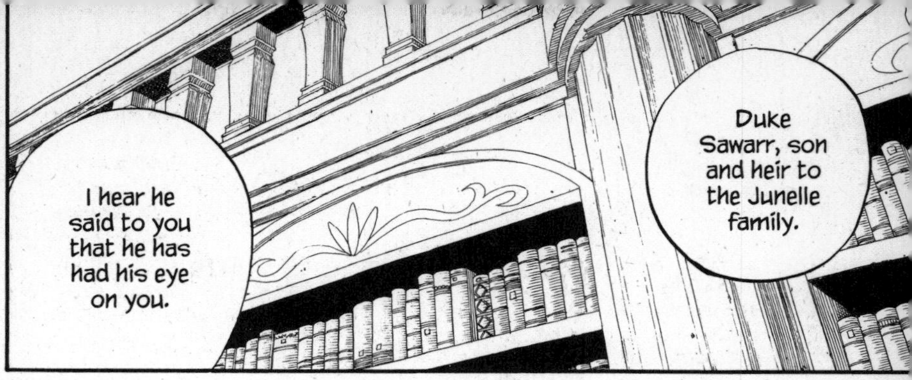
Duke Sawarr, son and heir to the Junelle family.
I hear he said to you that he has had his eye on you.

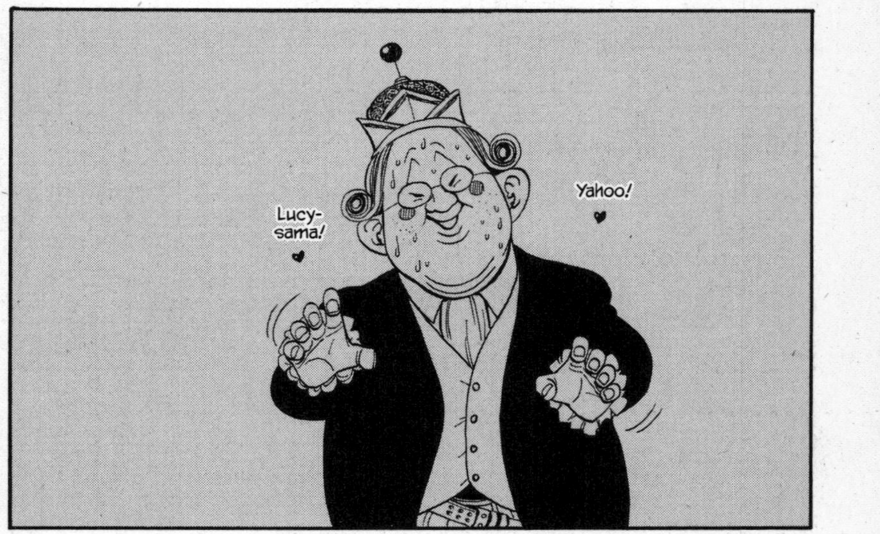
Yahoo!
Lucy-sama!

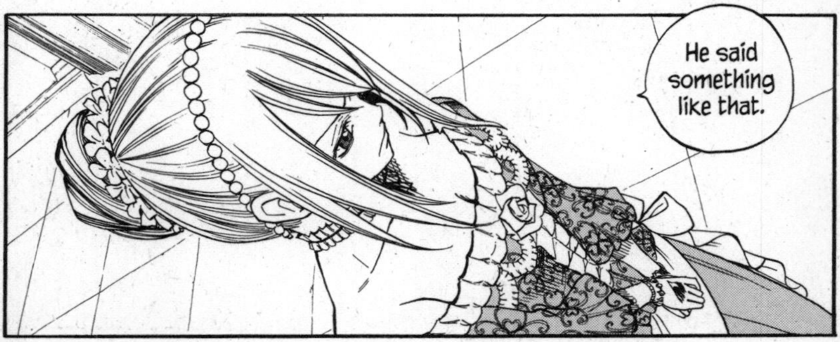
He said something like that.

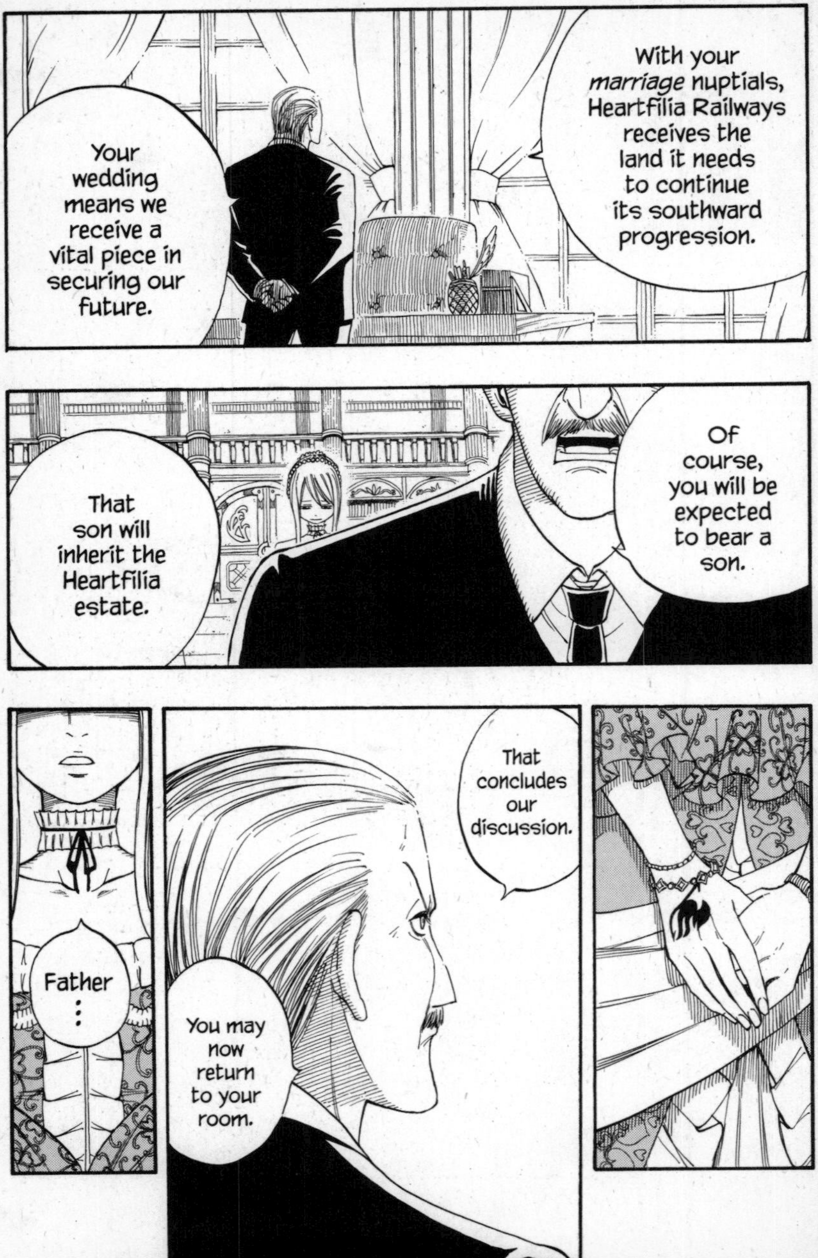
With your *marriage* nuptials, Heartfilia Railways receives the land it needs to continue its southward progression.
Your wedding means we receive a vital piece in securing our future.
Of course, you will be expected to bear a son.
That son will inherit the Heartfilia estate.
That concludes our discussion.
You may now return to your room.
Father ...

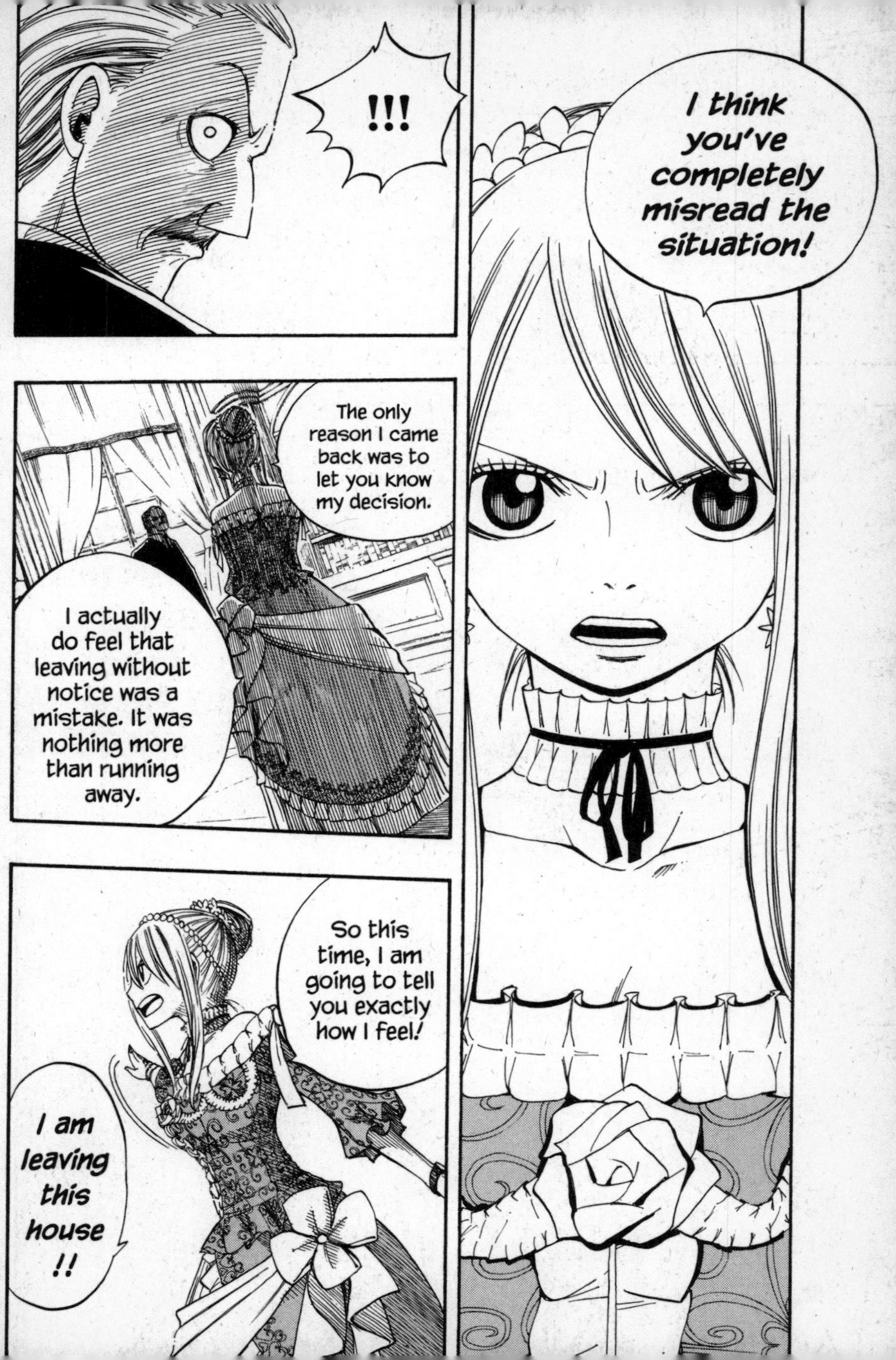
I think you've completely misread the situation!
!!!
The only reason I came back was to let you know my decision.
I actually do feel that leaving without notice was a mistake. It was nothing more than running away.
So this time, I am going to tell you exactly how I feel!
I am leaving this house !!

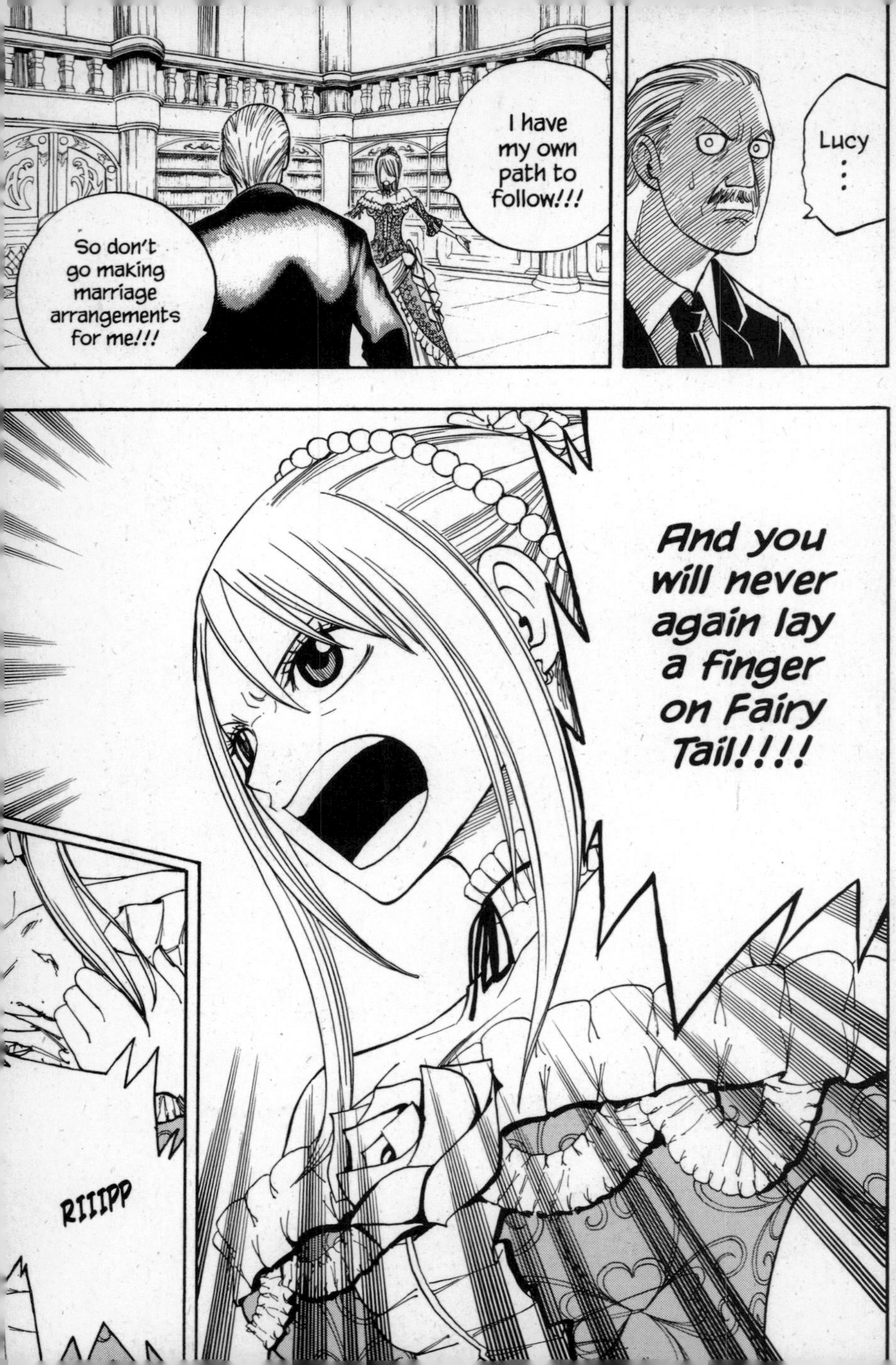
Lucy
...
I have my own path to follow!!!
So don't go making marriage arrangements for me!!!
And you will never again lay a finger on Fairy Tail!!!!
RIIIPP

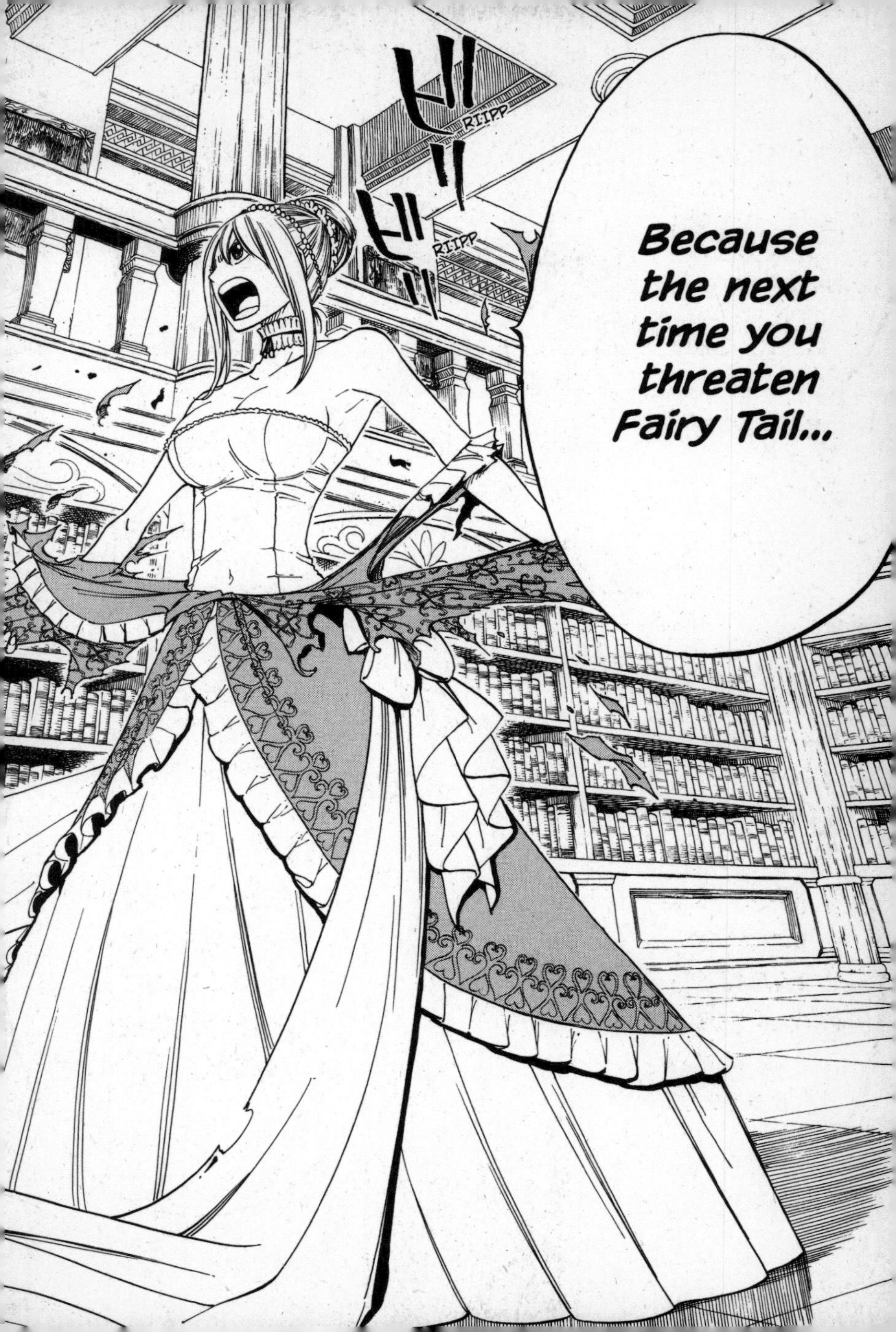

ビリ
RIIPP
ビリ
RIIPP
Because the next time you threaten Fairy Tail...

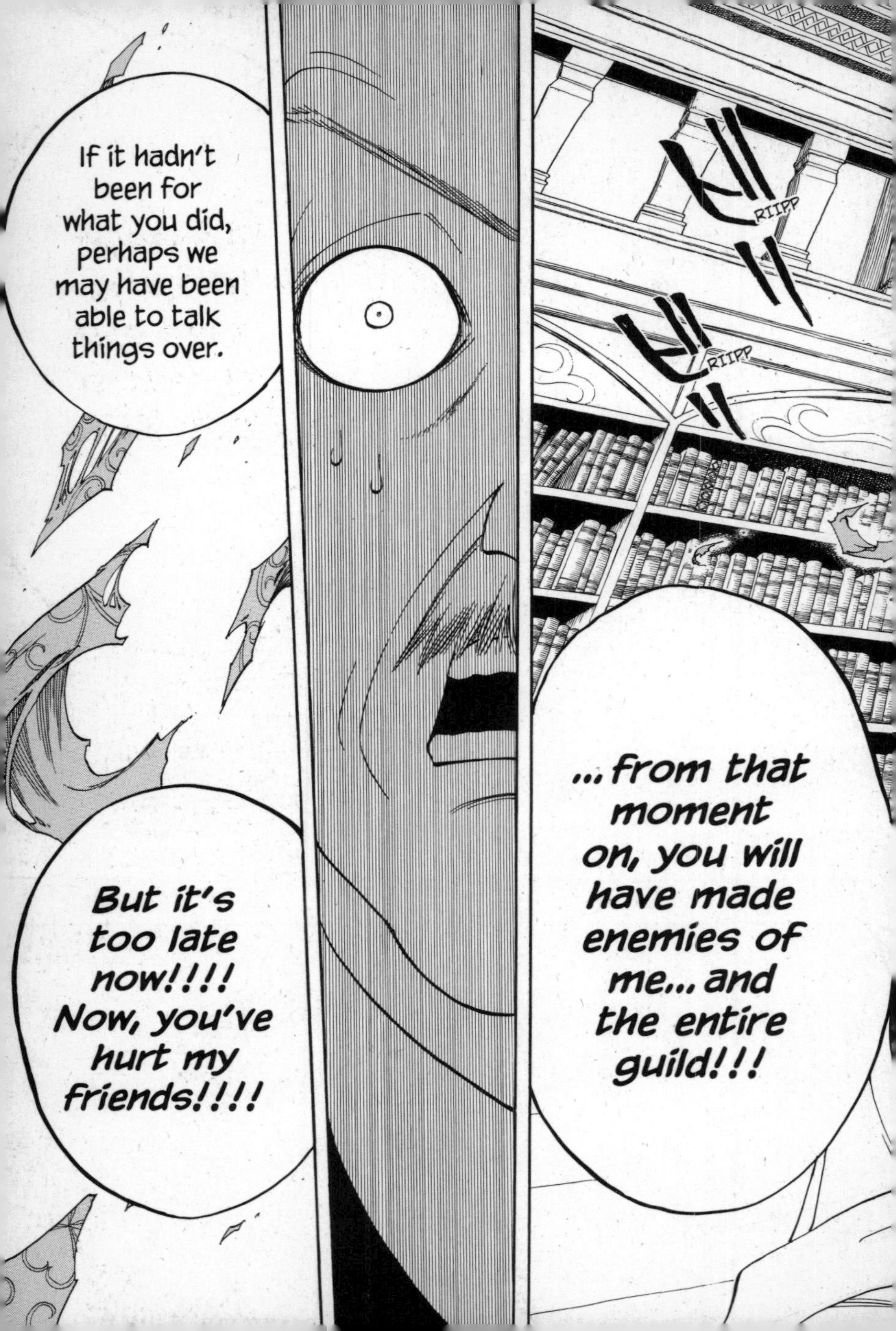
RIIPP
RIIPP
...from that moment on, you will have made enemies of me... and the entire guild!!!
If it hadn't been for what you did, perhaps we may have been able to talk things over.
But it's too late now!!!! Now, you've hurt my friends!!!!

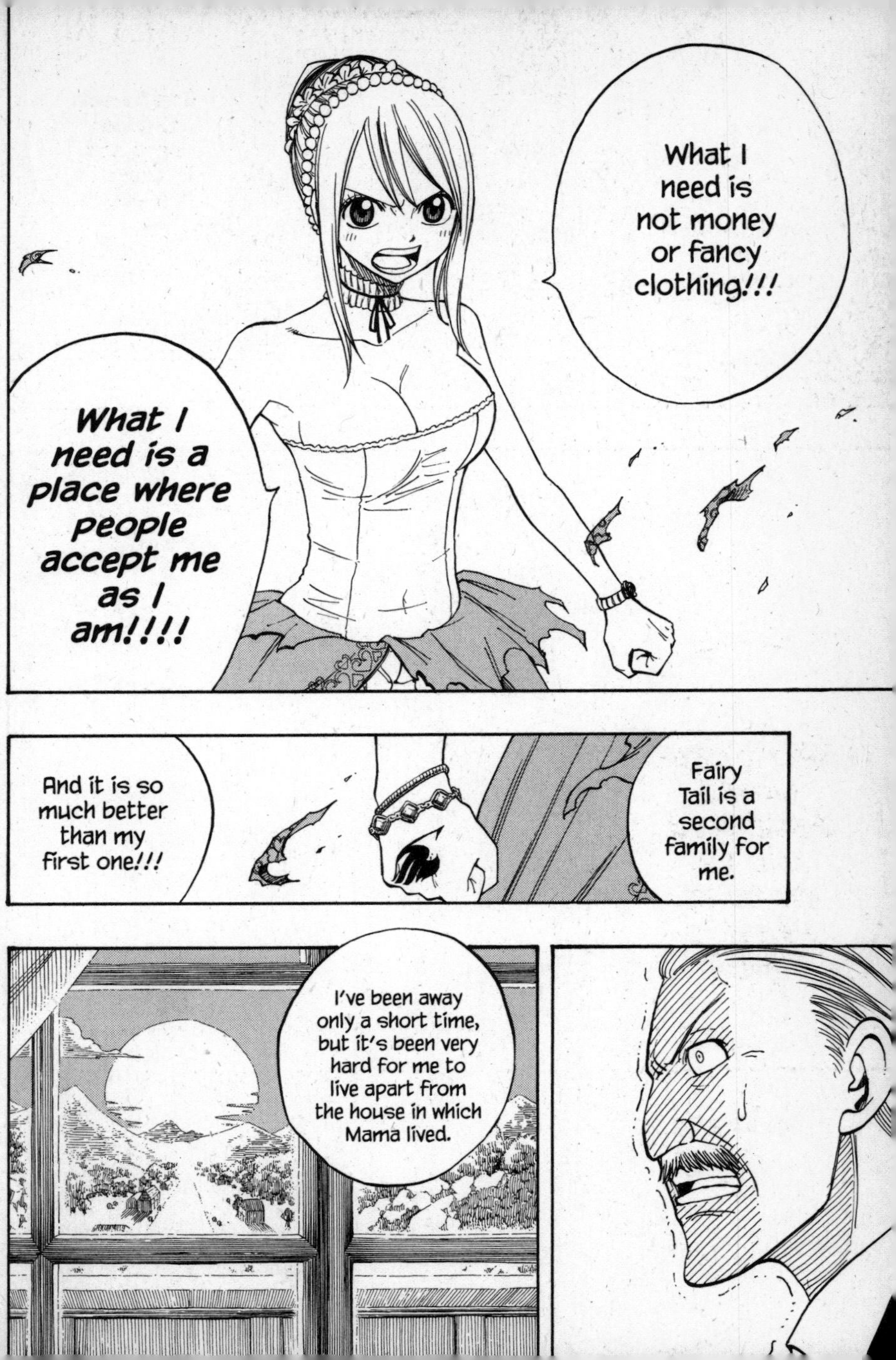
What I need is not money or fancy clothing!!!
What I need is a place where people accept me as I am!!!!
Fairy Tail is a second family for me.
And it is so much better than my first one!!!
I've been away only a short time, but it's been very hard for me to live apart from the house in which Mama lived.

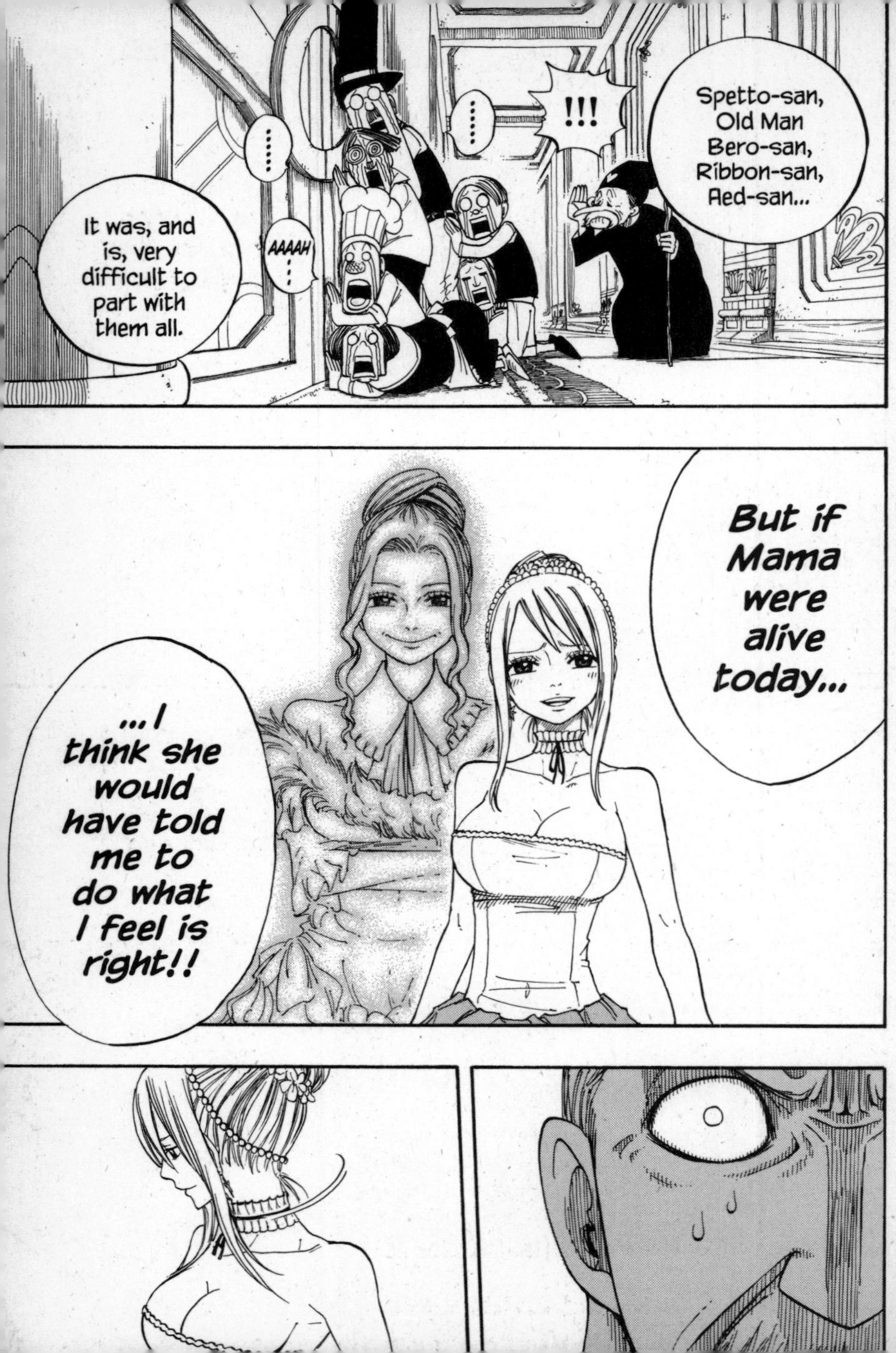
Spetto-san, Old Man Bero-san, Ribbon-san, Aed-san...
!!!
......
......
AAAAH...
It was, and is, very difficult to part with them all.
But if Mama were alive today...
...I think she would have told me to do what I feel is right!!

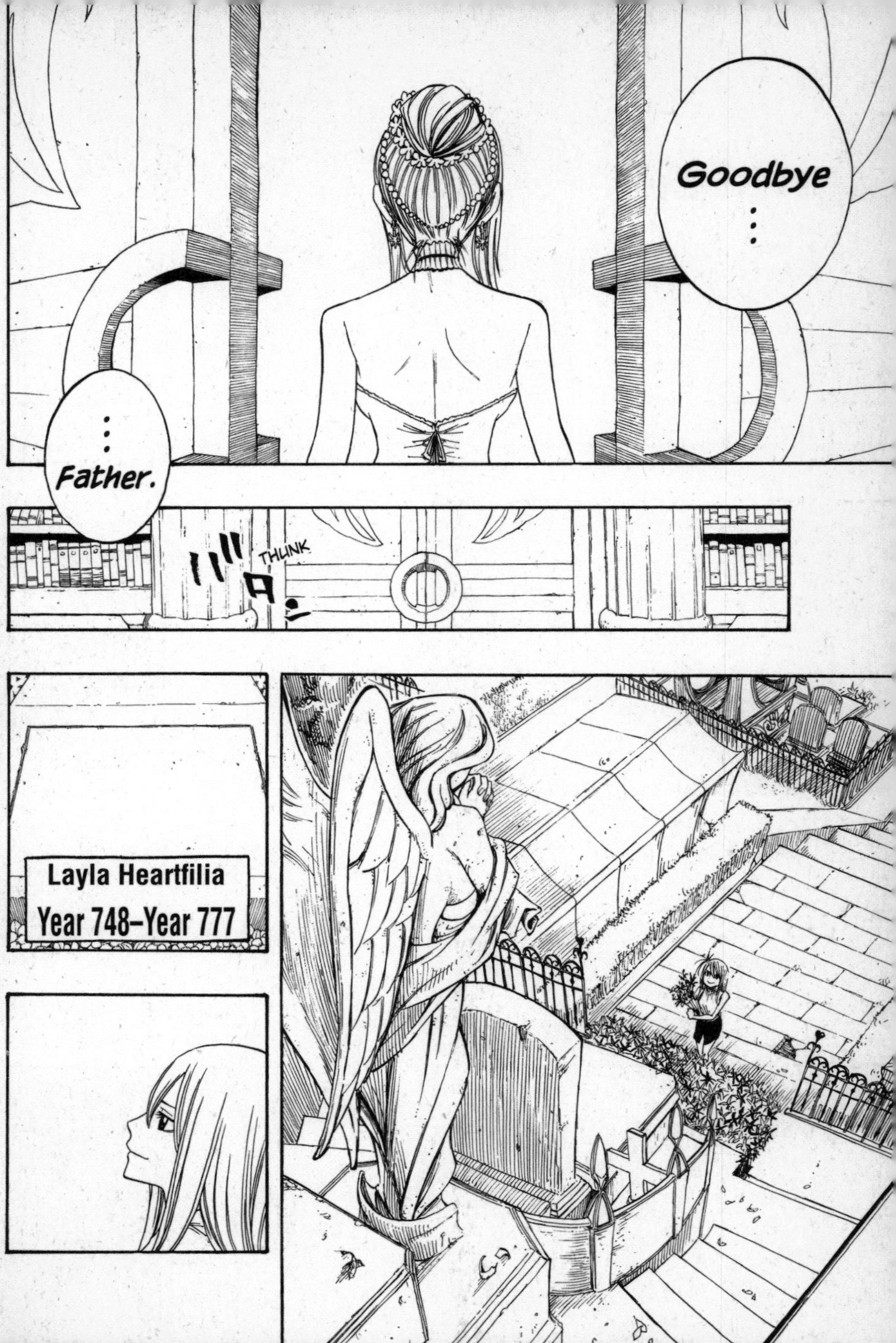
Goodbye
...
...
Father.
バタン
THUNK
Layla Heartfilia
Year 748–Year 777

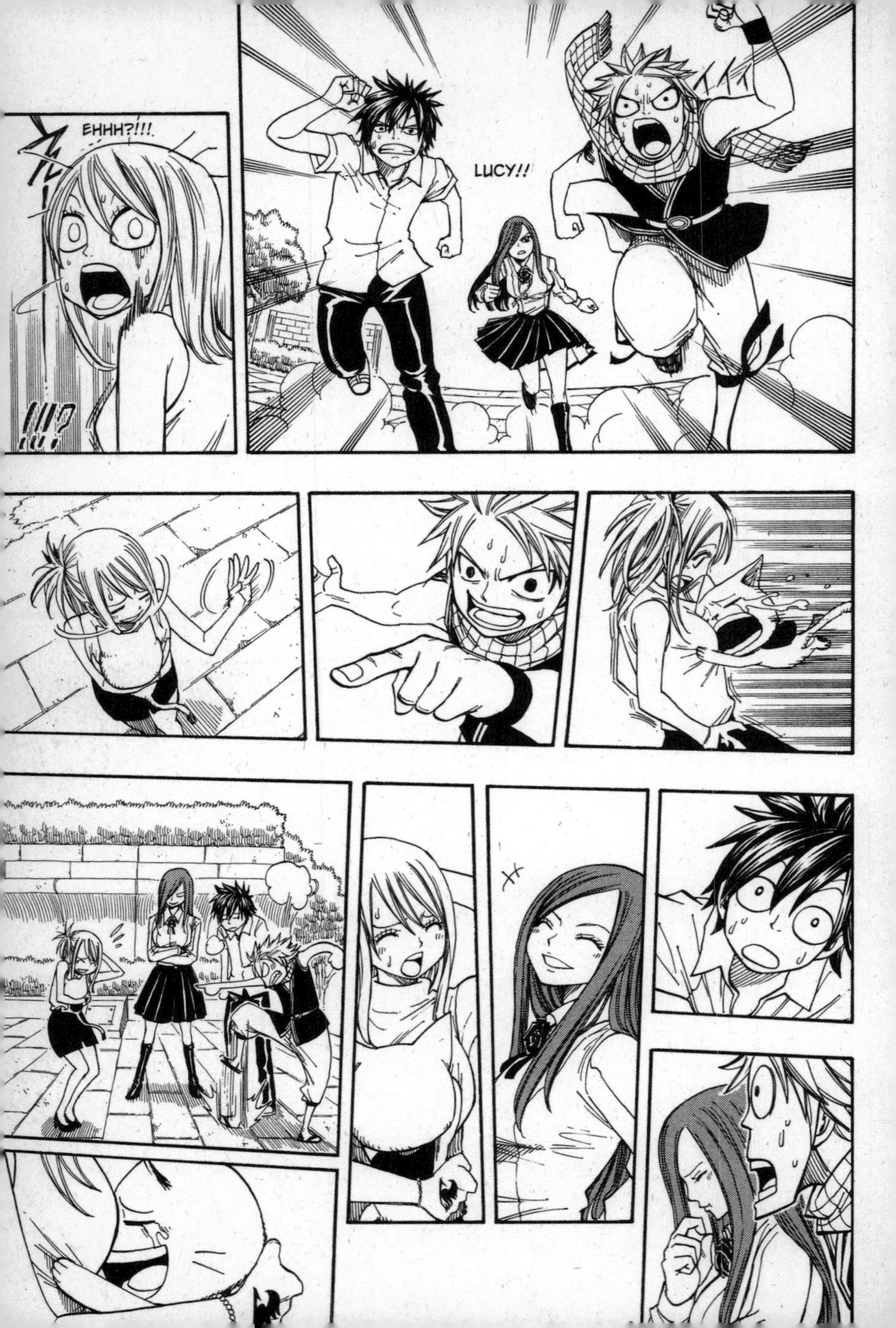
LUCY!!
EHHH?!!!.
!!!?

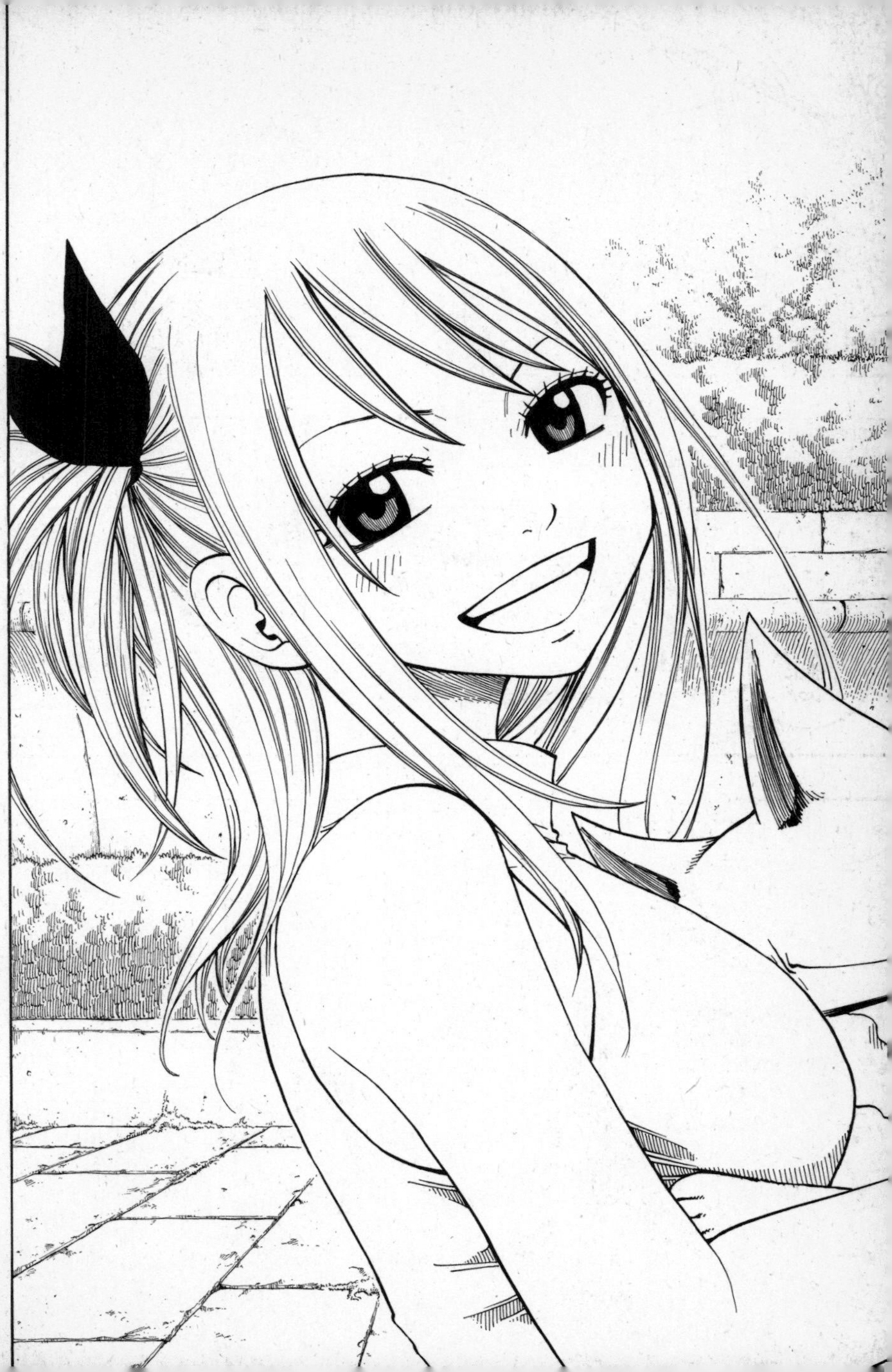

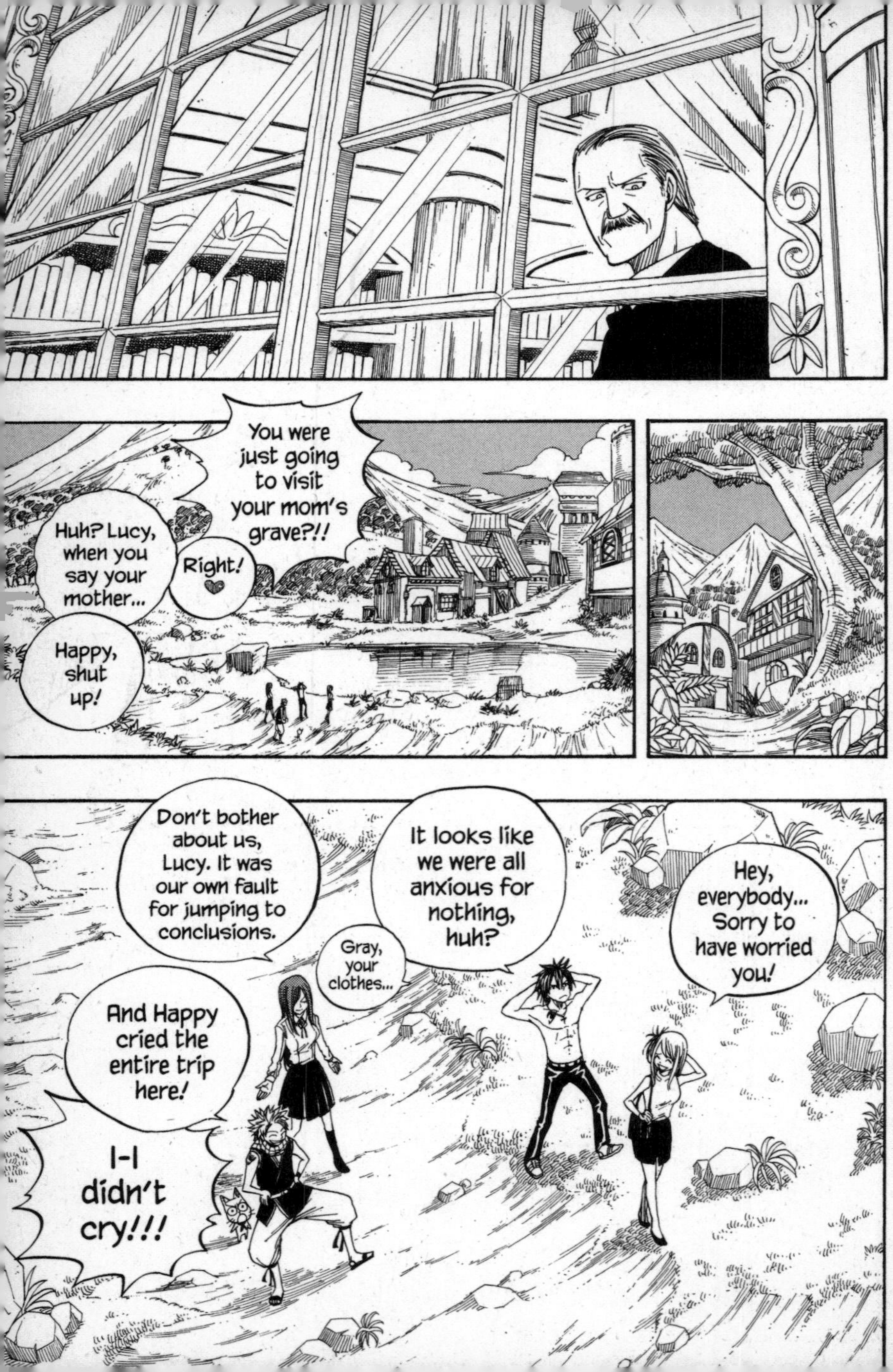
You were just going to visit your mom's grave?!!
Right! ♥
Huh? Lucy, when you say your mother...
Happy, shut up!
Hey, everybody... Sorry to have worried you!
It looks like we were all anxious for nothing, huh?
Don't bother about us, Lucy. It was our own fault for jumping to conclusions.
Gray, your clothes...
And Happy cried the entire trip here!
I-I didn't cry!!!

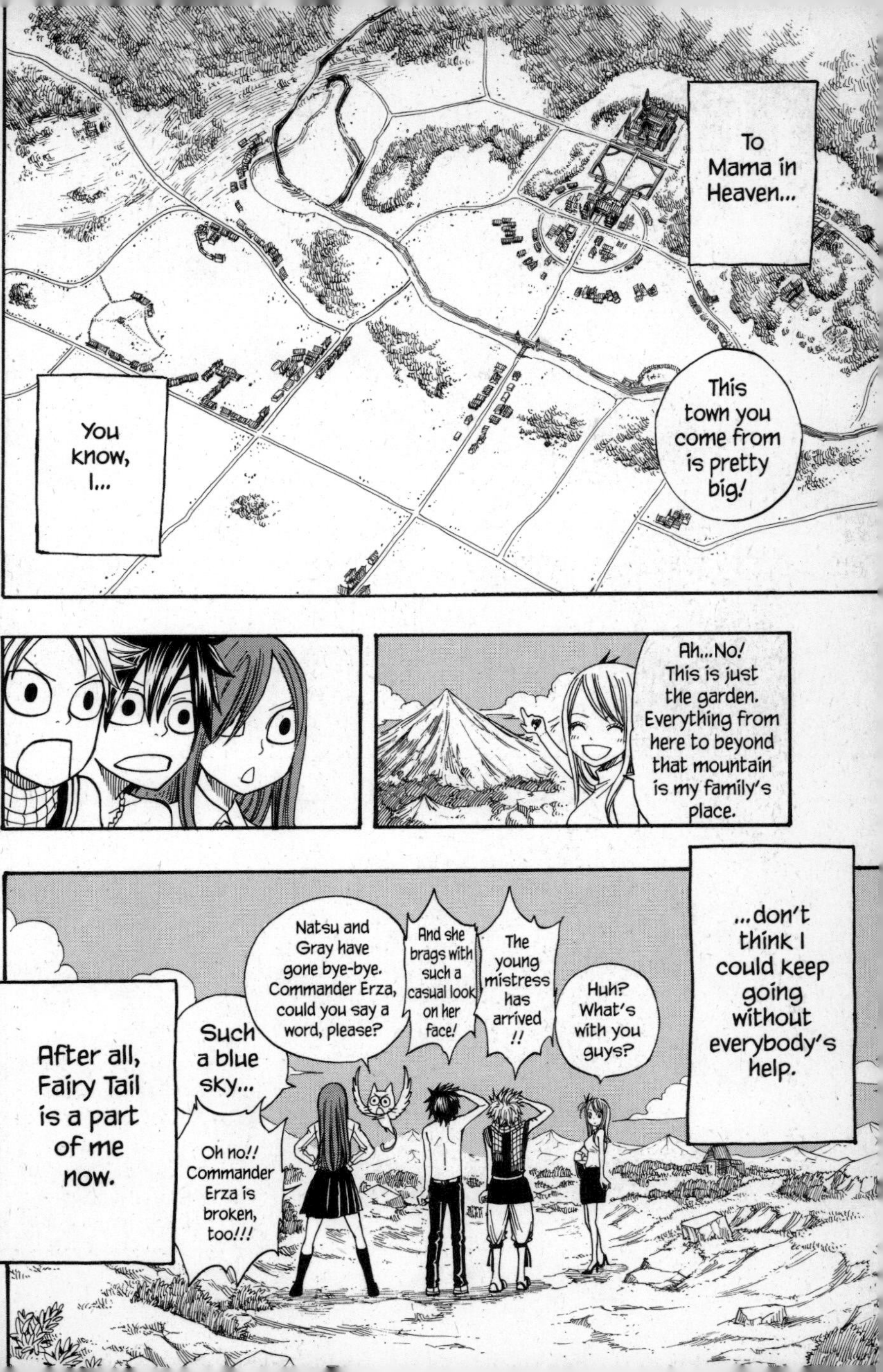
To Mama in Heaven...
This town you come from is pretty big!
You know, I...
Ah...No! This is just the garden. Everything from here to beyond that mountain is my family's place.
...don't think I could keep going without everybody's help.
Huh? What's with you guys?
The young mistress has arrived !!
And she brags with such a casual look on her face!
Natsu and Gray have gone bye-bye. Commander Erza, could you say a word, please?
Such a blue sky...
Oh no!! Commander Erza is broken, too!!!
After all, Fairy Tail is a part of me now.

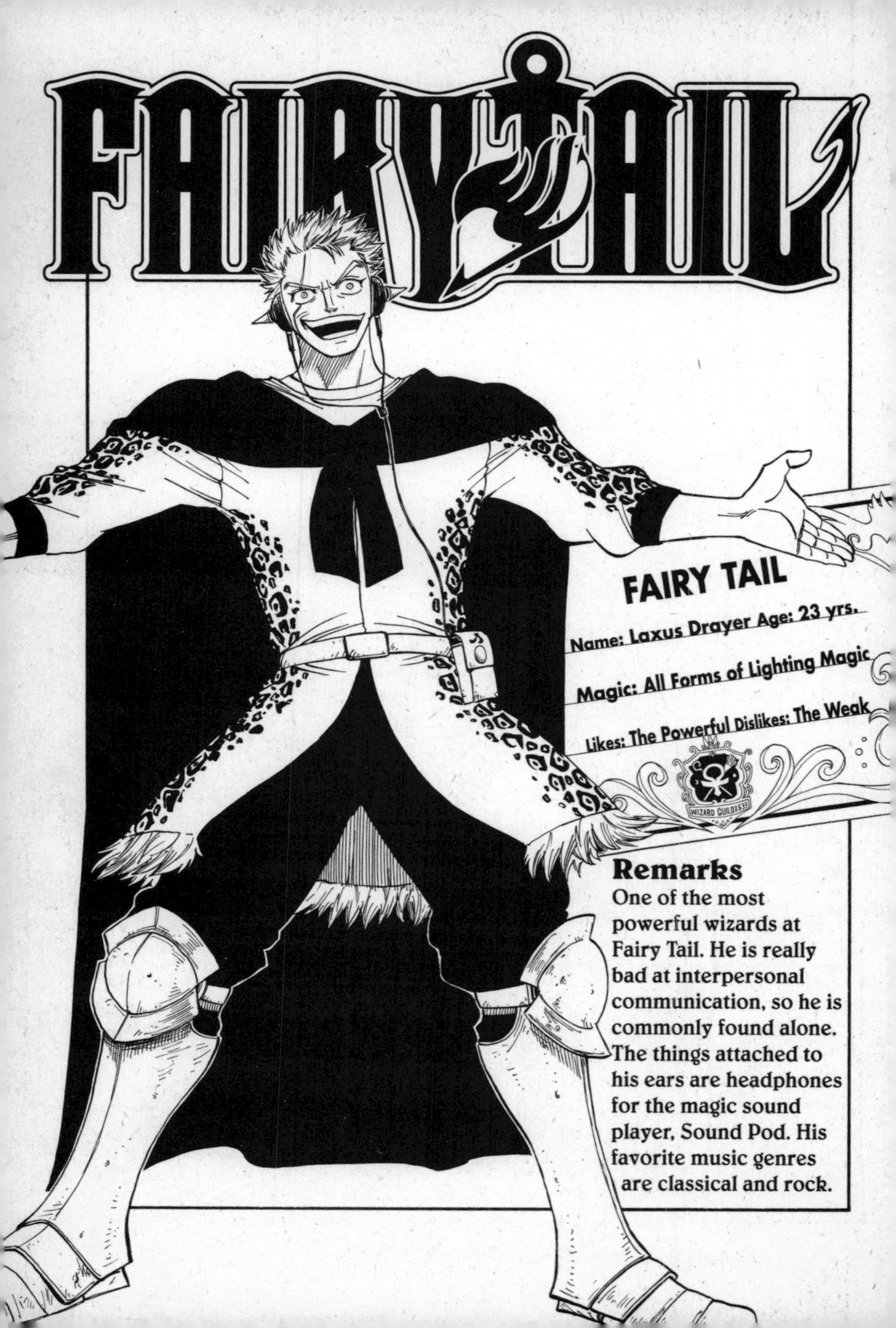
FAIRY TAIL
FAIRY TAIL
Name: Laxus Drayer Age: 23 yrs.
Magic: All Forms of Lighting Magic
Likes: The Powerful Dislikes: The Weak
WIZARD GUILDX633
Remarks
One of the most powerful wizards at Fairy Tail. He is really bad at interpersonal communication, so he is commonly found alone. The things attached to his ears are headphones for the magic sound player, Sound Pod. His favorite music genres are classical and rock.

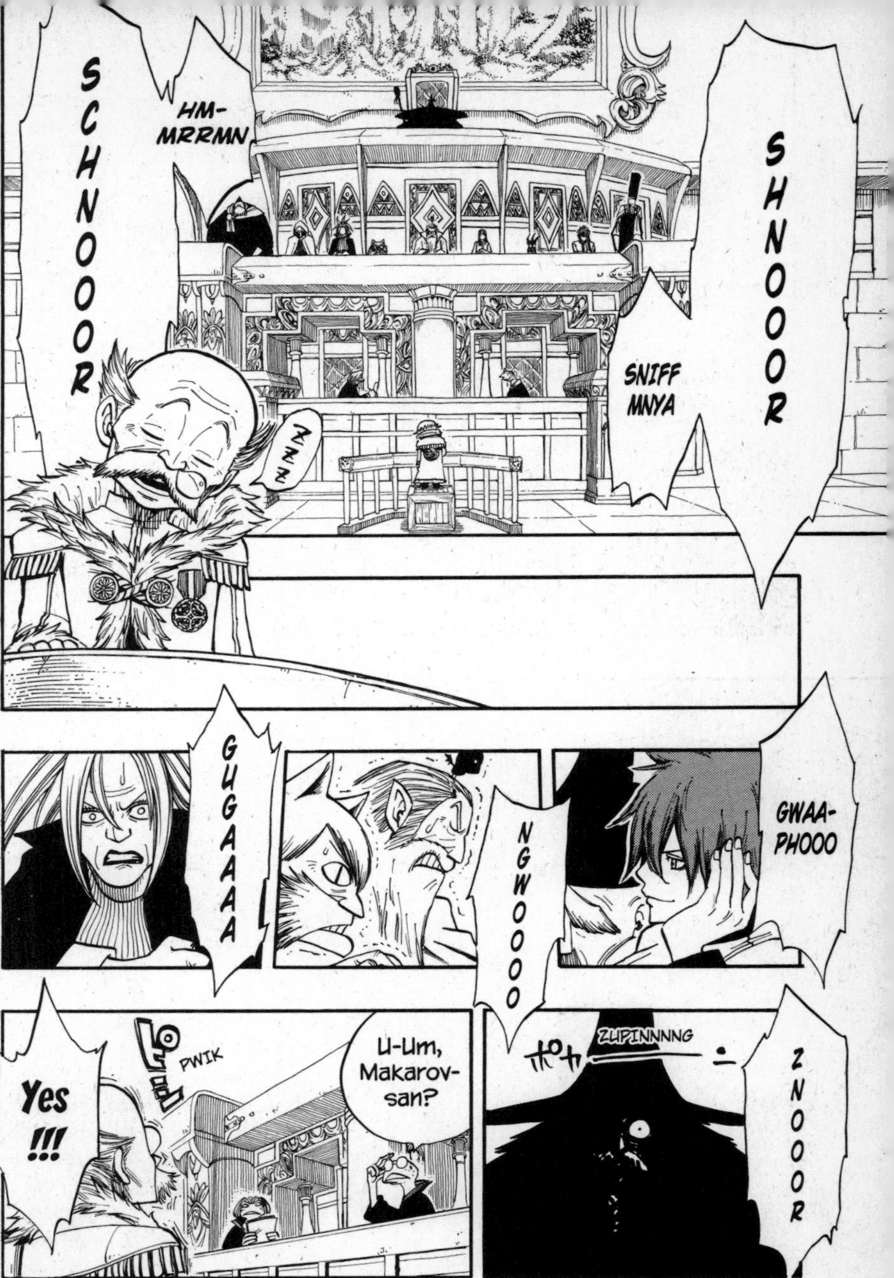
SHNOOOOR
HM-MRRMN
SCHNOOOOR
SNIFF MNYA
ZZZ
GWAA-PHOOO
NGWOOOOO
GUGAAAA
ZNOOOOR
ZUPINNNNG
U-um, Makarov-san?
PWIK
Yes!!!

Chapter 69: Next Generation

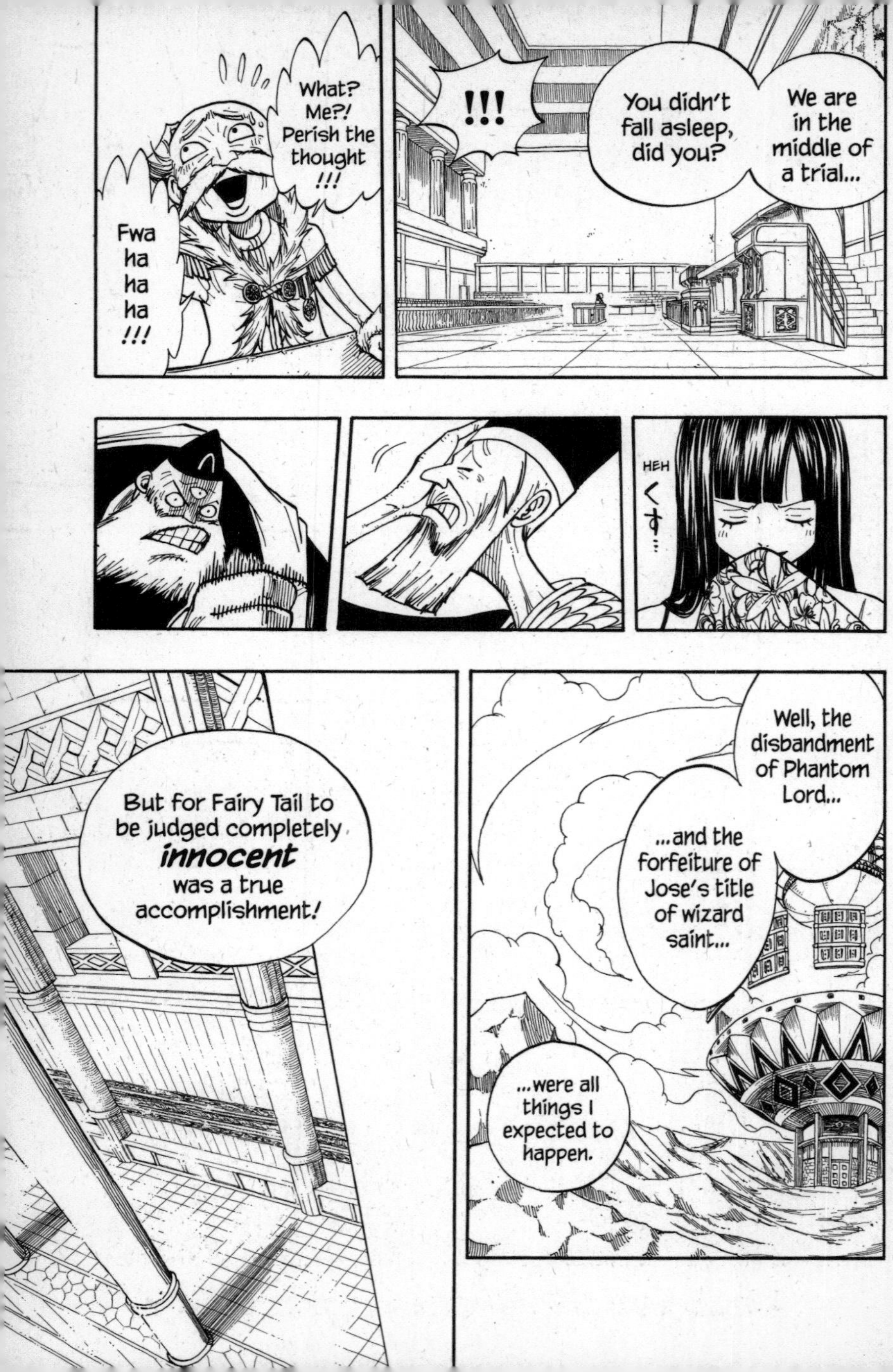
We are in the middle of a trial...
You didn't fall asleep, did you?
!!!
What? Me?! Perish the thought !!!
Fwa ha ha ha !!!
HEH
くす…
Well, the disbandment of Phantom Lord...
...and the forfeiture of Jose's title of wizard saint...
...were all things I expected to happen.
But for Fairy Tail to be judged completely *innocent* was a true accomplishment!

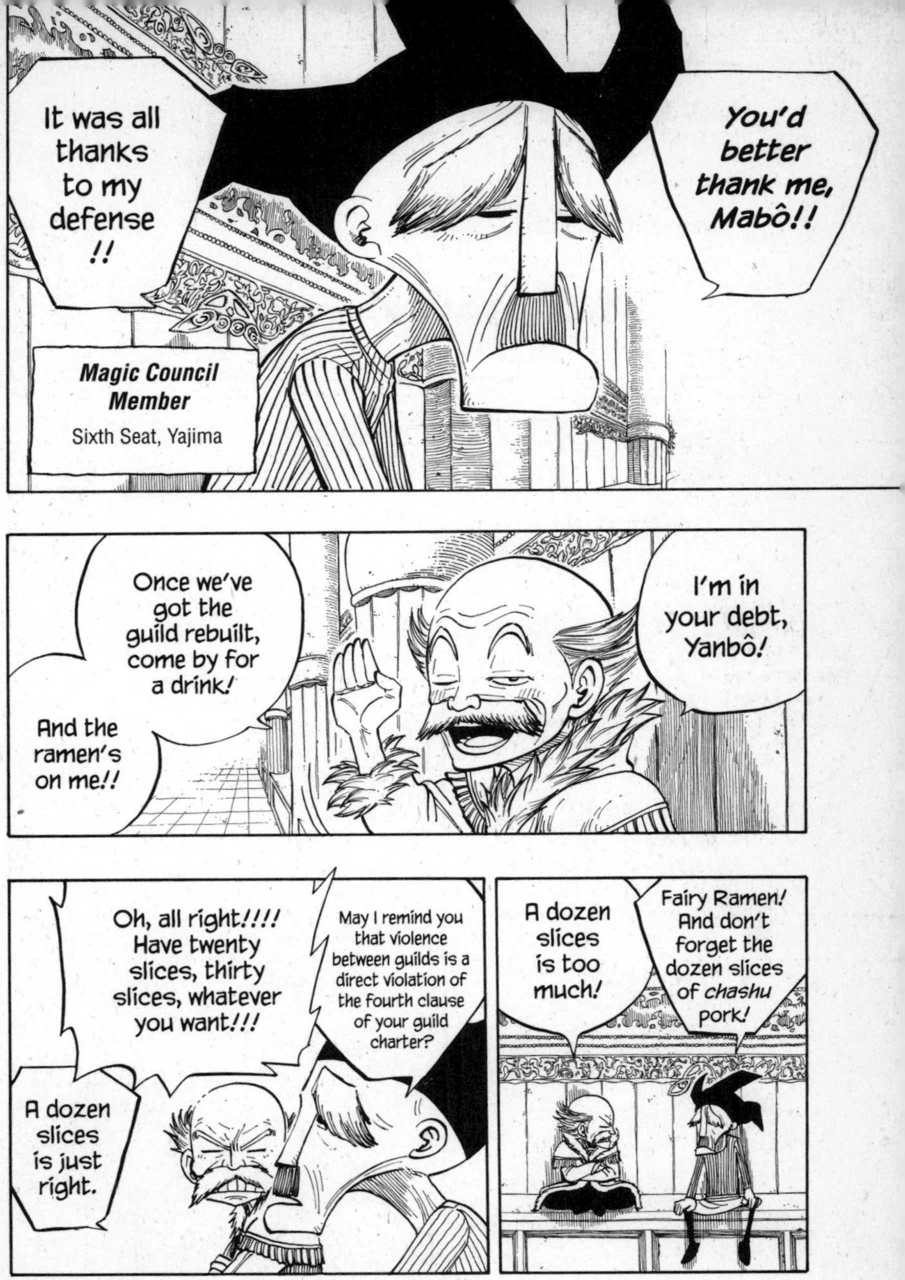
You'd better thank me, Mabô!!
It was all thanks to my defense!!
Magic Council Member
Sixth Seat, Yajima
I'm in your debt, Yanbô!
Once we've got the guild rebuilt, come by for a drink!
And the ramen's on me!!
Fairy Ramen! And don't forget the dozen slices of *chashu* pork!
A dozen slices is too much!
May I remind you that violence between guilds is a direct violation of the fourth clause of your guild charter?
Oh, all right!!!! Have twenty slices, thirty slices, whatever you want!!!
A dozen slices is just right.

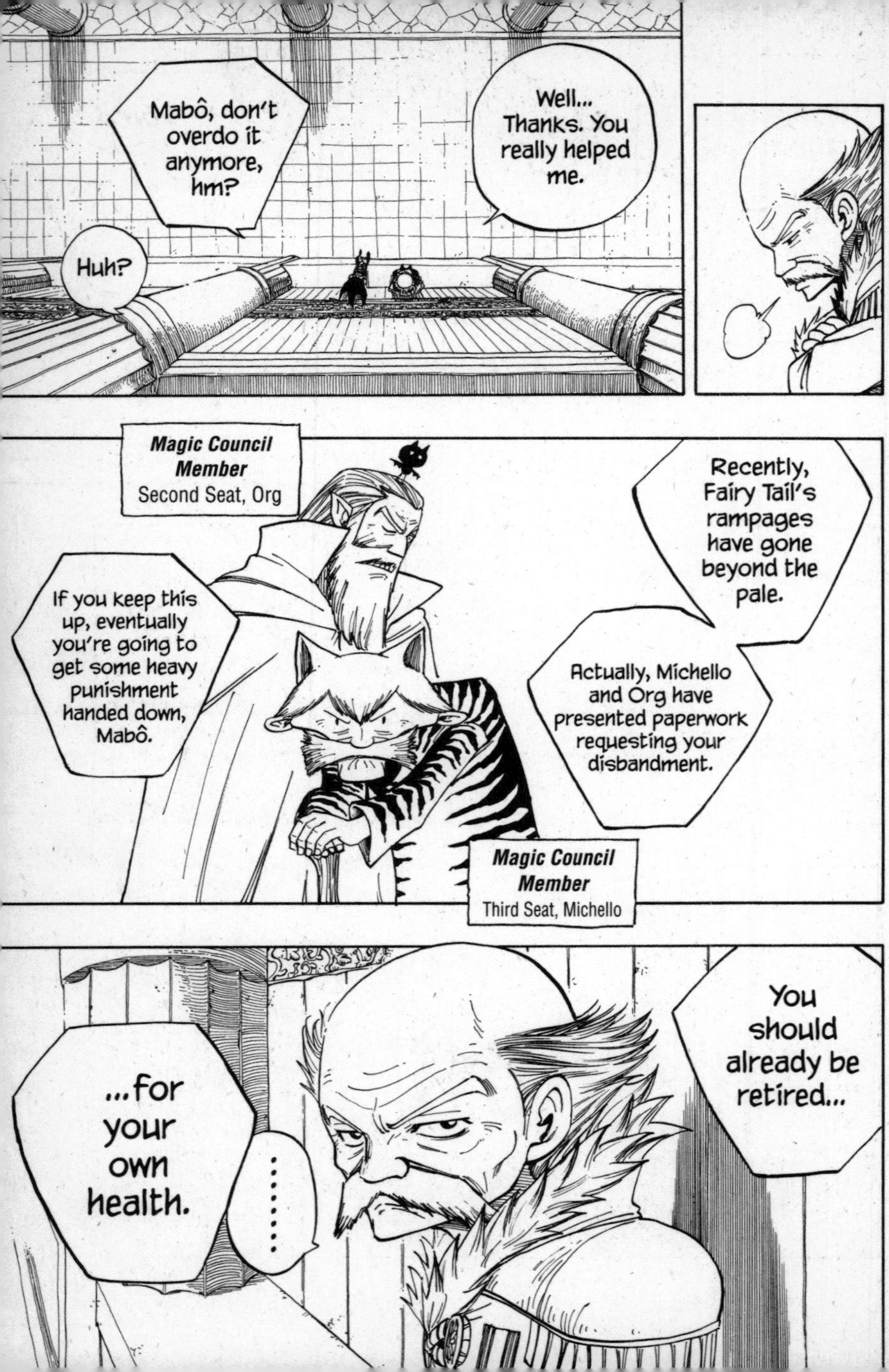
Well... Thanks. You really helped me.
Mabô, don't overdo it anymore, hm?
Huh?
Recently, Fairy Tail's rampages have gone beyond the pale.
Magic Council Member
Second Seat, Org
Actually, Michello and Org have presented paperwork requesting your disbandment.
If you keep this up, eventually you're going to get some heavy punishment handed down, Mabô.
Magic Council Member
Third Seat, Michello
You should already be retired...
......
...for your own health.

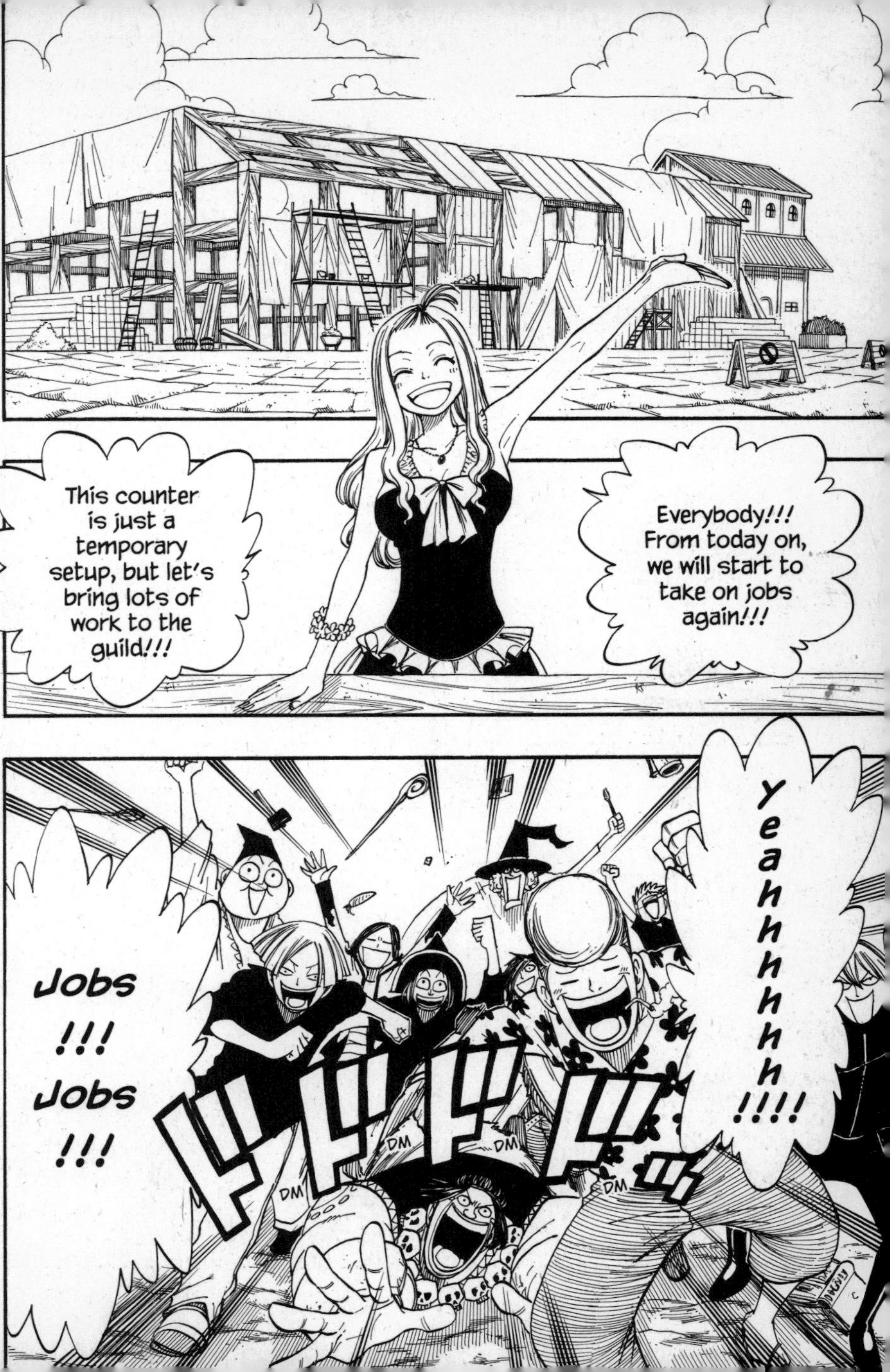
Everybody!!! From today on, we will start to take on jobs again!!!
This counter is just a temporary setup, but let's bring lots of work to the guild!!!
Yeahhhhhhh!!!!
DM DM DM DM
Jobs!!! Jobs!!!

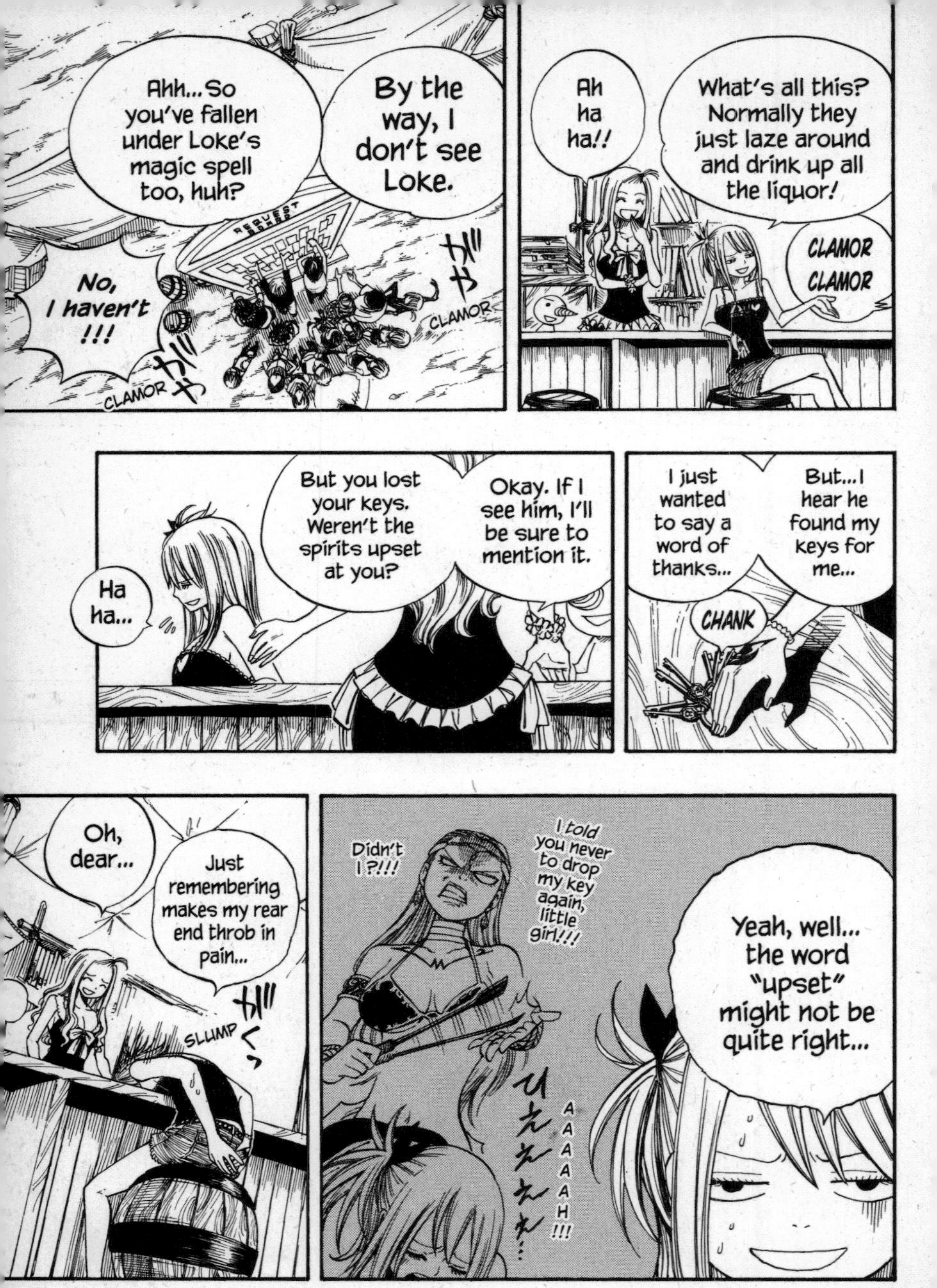
What's all this? Normally they just laze around and drink up all the liquor!
Ah ha ha!!
CLAMOR CLAMOR
By the way, I don't see Loke.
Ahh...So you've fallen under Loke's magic spell too, huh?
No, I haven't!!!
CLAMOR
CLAMOR
But...I hear he found my keys for me...
I just wanted to say a word of thanks...
CHANK
Okay. If I see him, I'll be sure to mention it.
But you lost your keys. Weren't the spirits upset at you?
Ha ha...
Yeah, well... the word "upset" might not be quite right...
I told you never to drop my key again, little girl!!!
Didn't I?!!!
AAAAAAH!!!
Oh, dear...
Just remembering makes my rear end throb in pain...
SLUMP

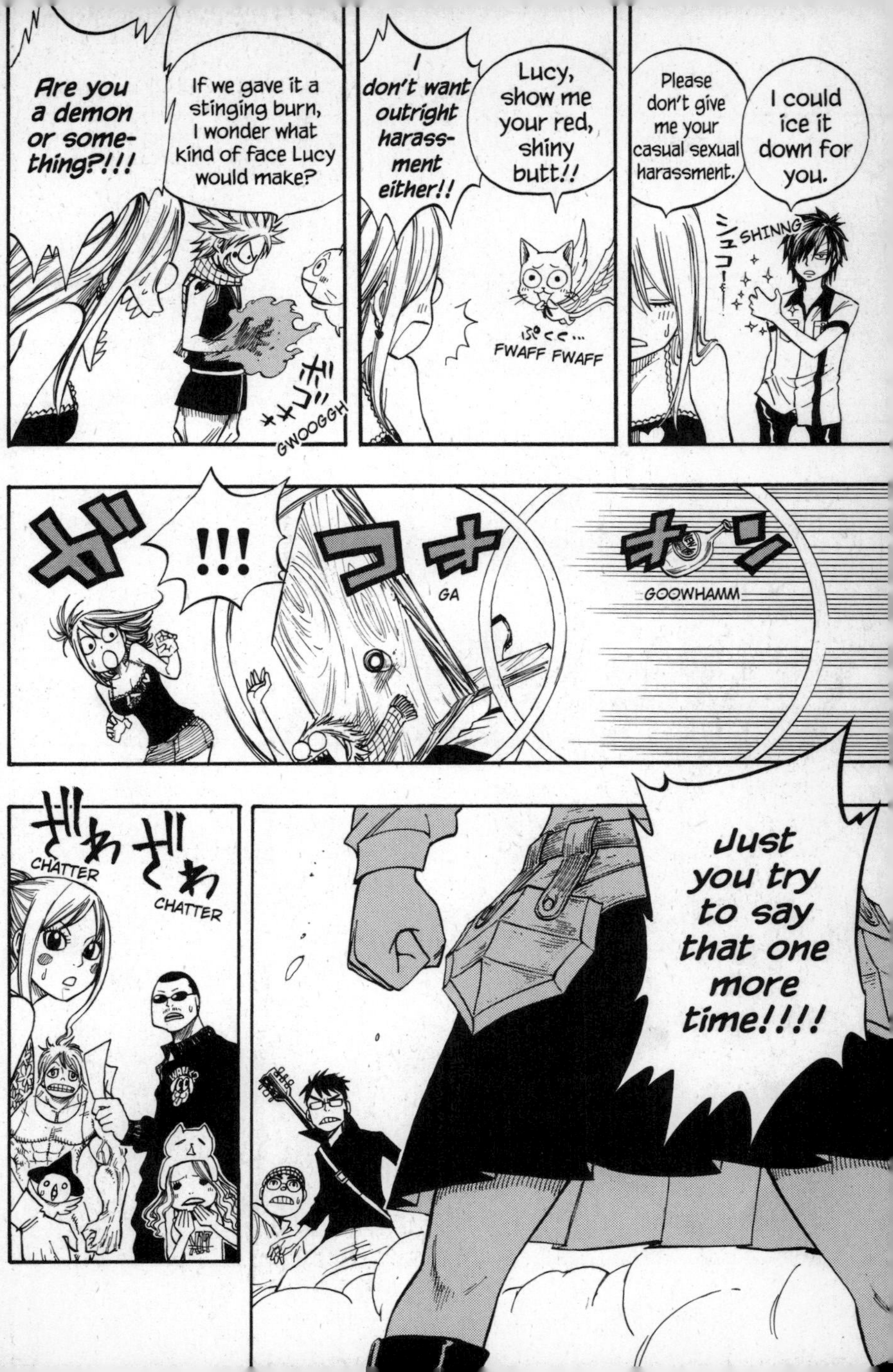
I could ice it down for you.
Please don't give me your casual sexual harassment.
SHINNG
Lucy, show me your red, shiny butt!!
I don't want outright harassment either!!
ぷくく...
FWAFF FWAFF
If we gave it a stinging burn, I wonder what kind of face Lucy would make?
Are you a demon or something?!!!
GWOOGGH
!!!
GA
GOOWHAMM
Just you try to say that one more time!!!!
CHATTER
CHATTER

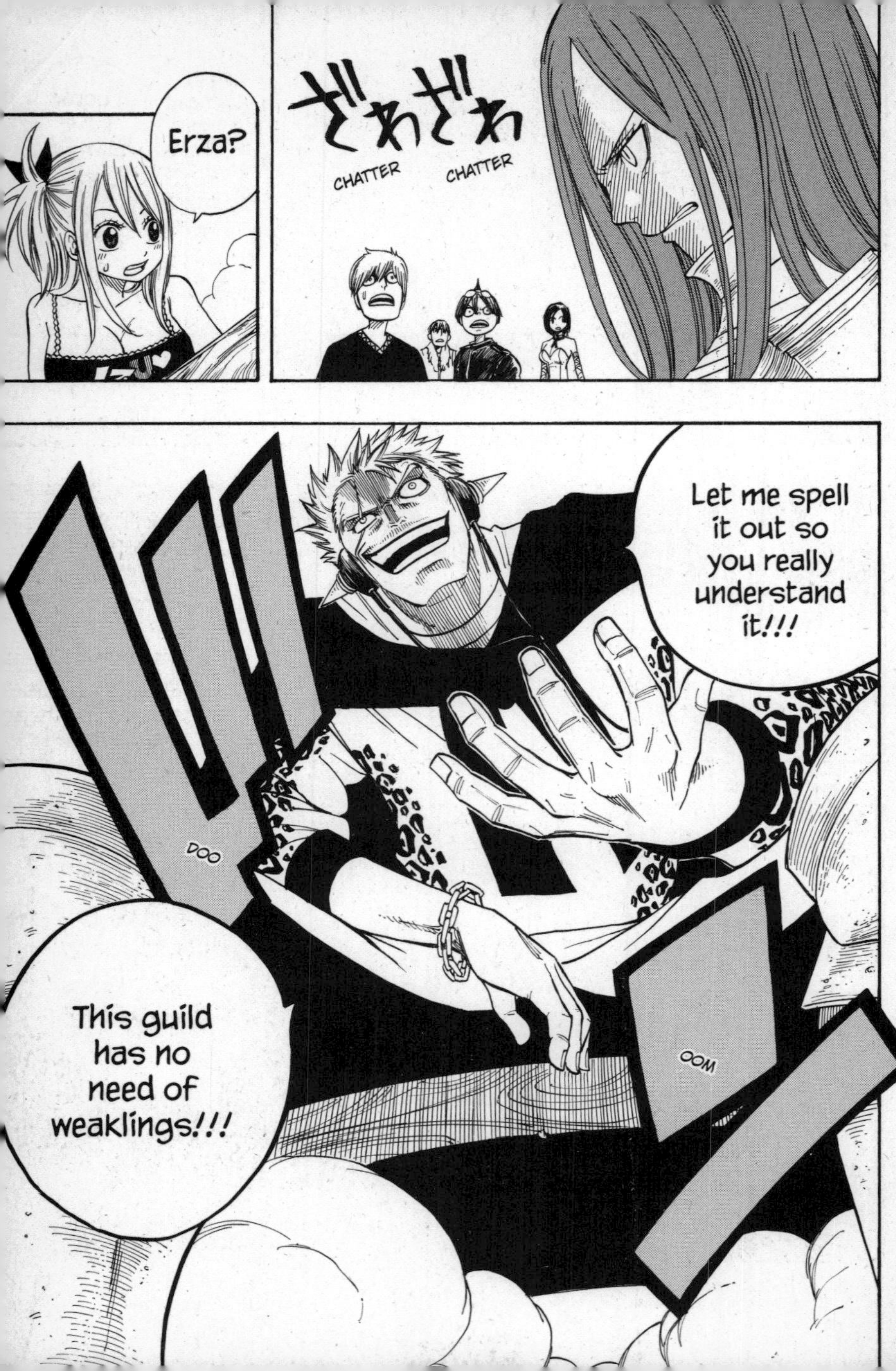
ざわざわ
CHATTER CHATTER
Erza?
Let me spell it out so you really understand it!!!
DOO
OOM
This guild has no need of weaklings!!!

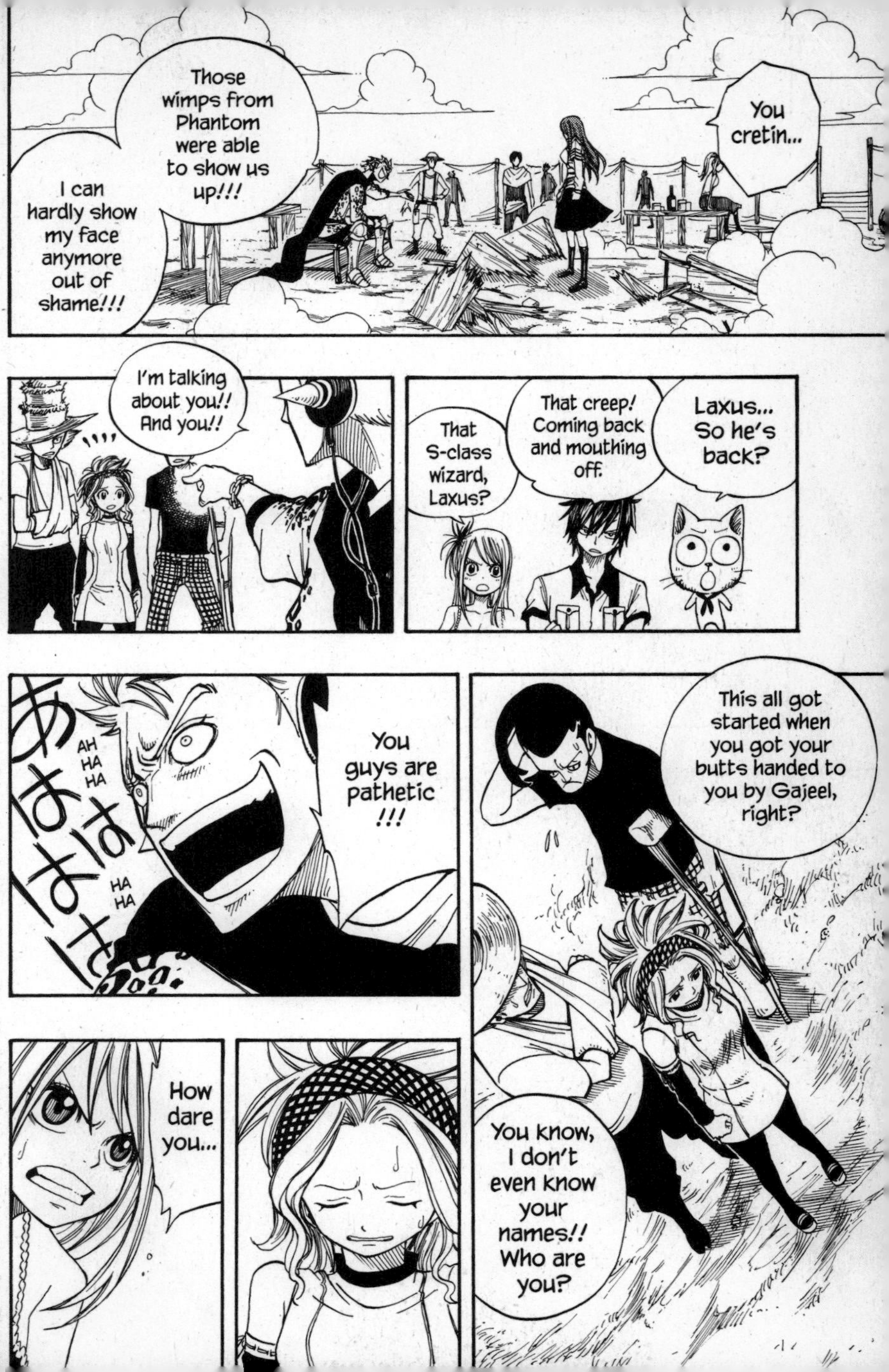
You cretin...
Those wimps from Phantom were able to show us up!!!
I can hardly show my face anymore out of shame!!!
Laxus... So he's back?
That creep! Coming back and mouthing off.
That S-class wizard, Laxus?
I'm talking about you!! And you!!
This all got started when you got your butts handed to you by Gajeel, right?
You know, I don't even know your names!! Who are you?
You guys are pathetic!!!
あははは
AH HA HA
HA HA
How dare you...

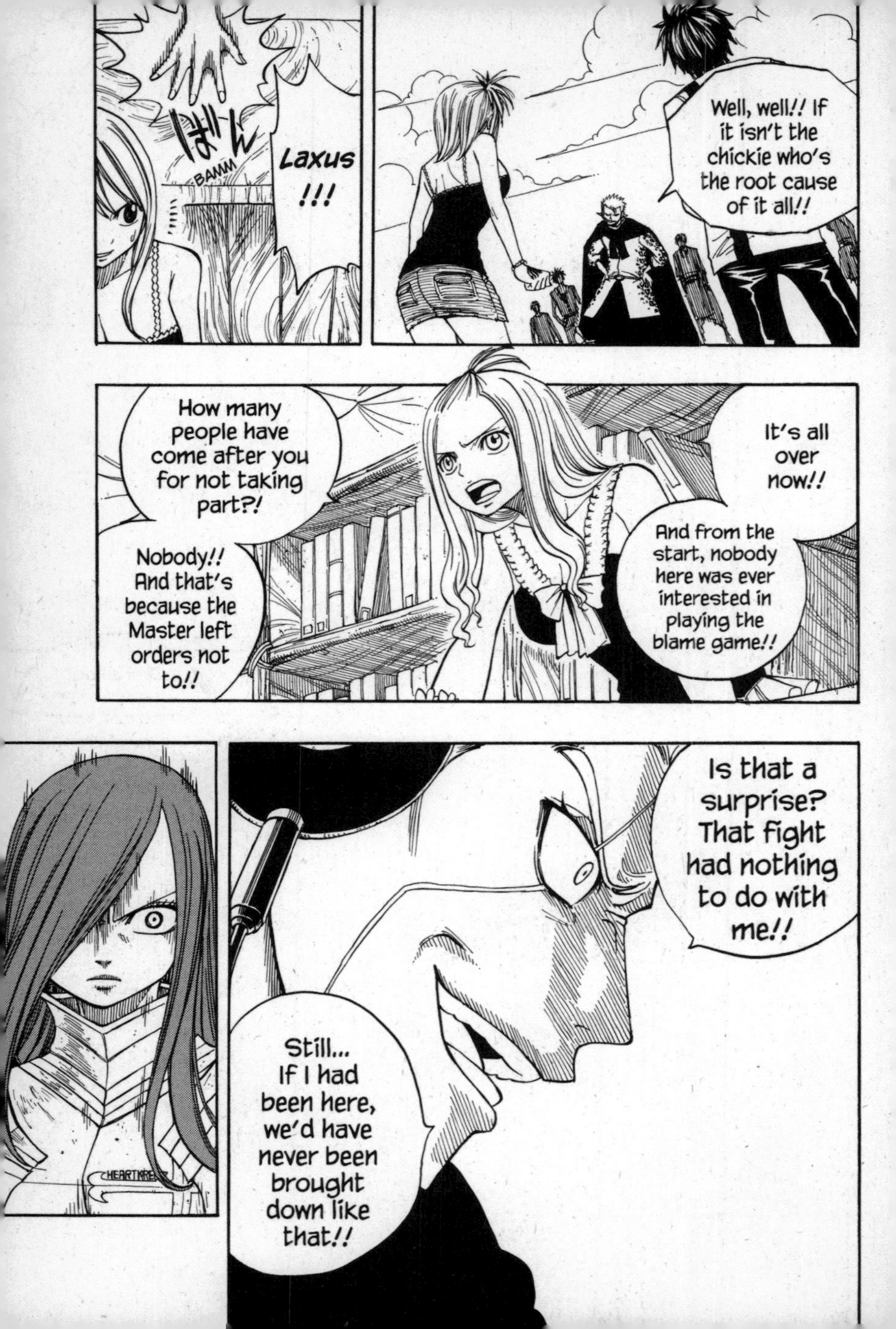
Well, well!! If it isn't the chickie who's the root cause of it all!!
BAMM
Laxus !!!
It's all over now!!
And from the start, nobody here was ever interested in playing the blame game!!
How many people have come after you for not taking part?!
Nobody!! And that's because the Master left orders not to!!
Is that a surprise? That fight had nothing to do with me!!
Still... If I had been here, we'd have never been brought down like that!!

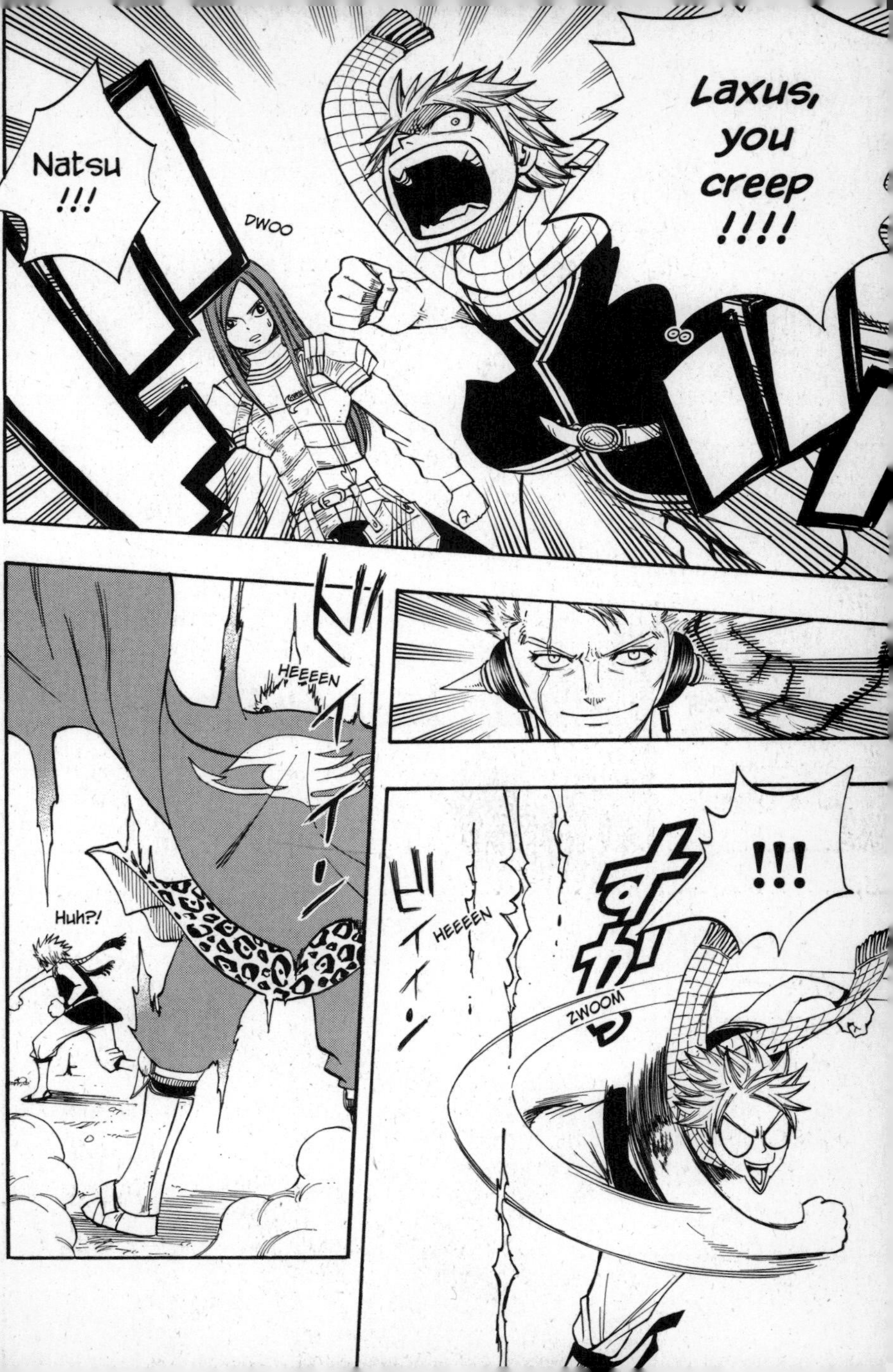
Laxus, you creep!!!!
Natsu!!!
DWOO
!!!
ZWOOM
HEEEEN
HEEEEN
Huh?!

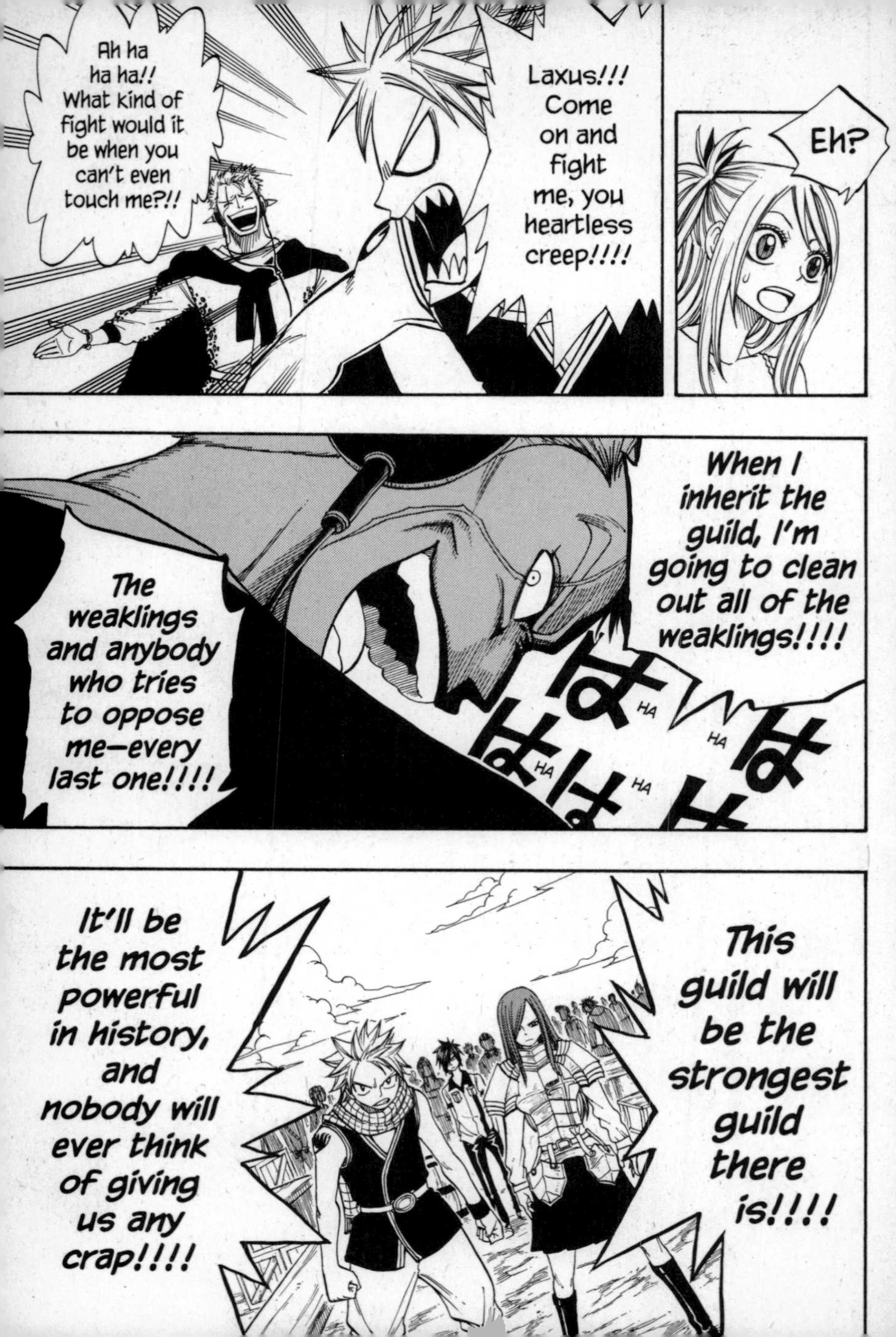

Eh?
Laxus!!! Come on and fight me, you heartless creep!!!!
Ah ha ha ha!! What kind of fight would it be when you can't even touch me?!!
When I inherit the guild, I'm going to clean out all of the weaklings!!!!
は HA は HA は HA は HA
The weaklings and anybody who tries to oppose me—every last one!!!!
This guild will be the strongest guild there is!!!!
It'll be the most powerful in history, and nobody will ever think of giving us any crap!!!!

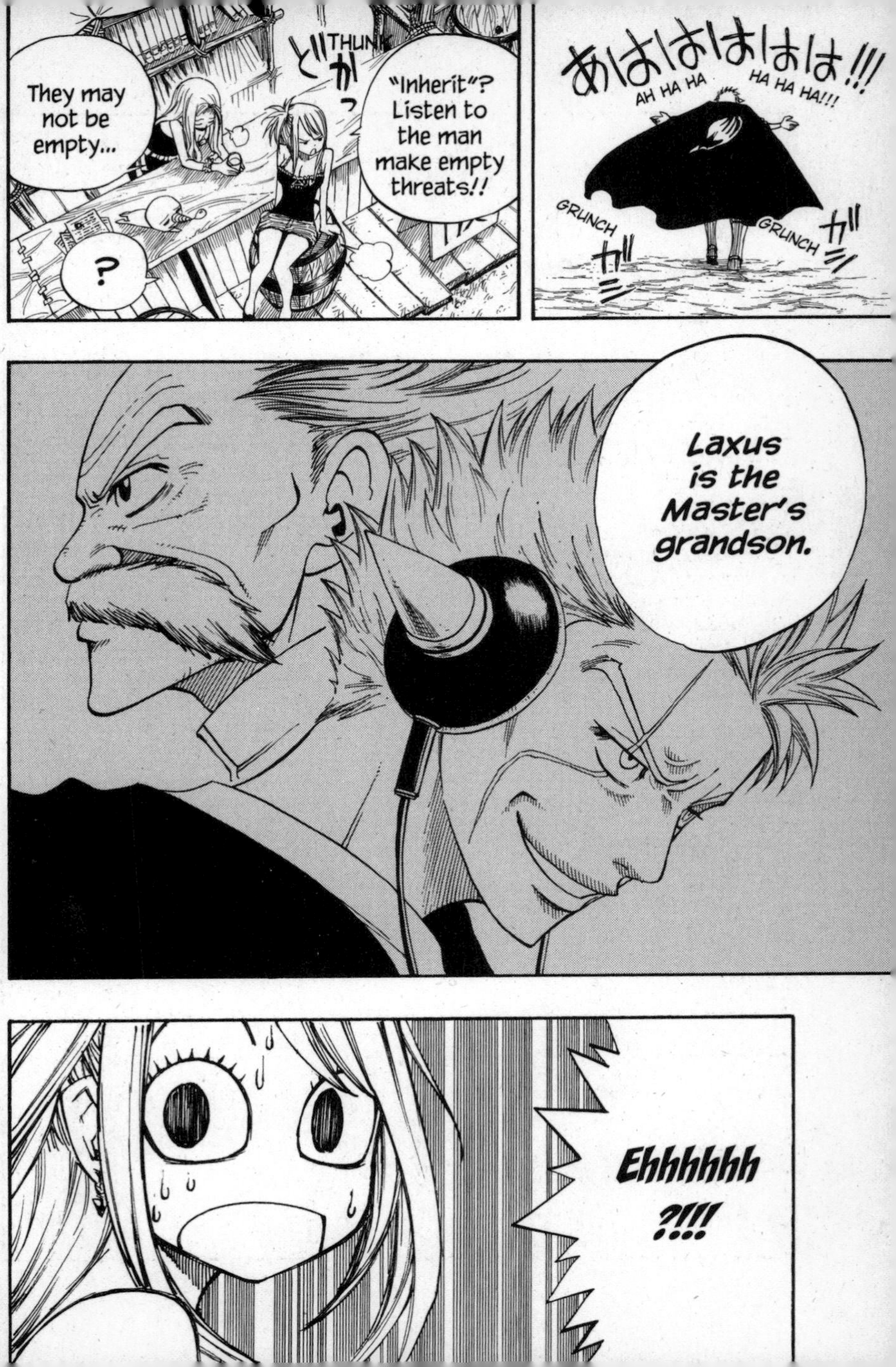
あははははは!!!
AH HA HA
HA HA HA!!!
GRUNCH
ガ
GRUNCH
ガ
THUNK
"Inherit"? Listen to the man make empty threats!!
They may not be empty...
?
Laxus is the Master's grandson.
Ehhhhhh ?!!!

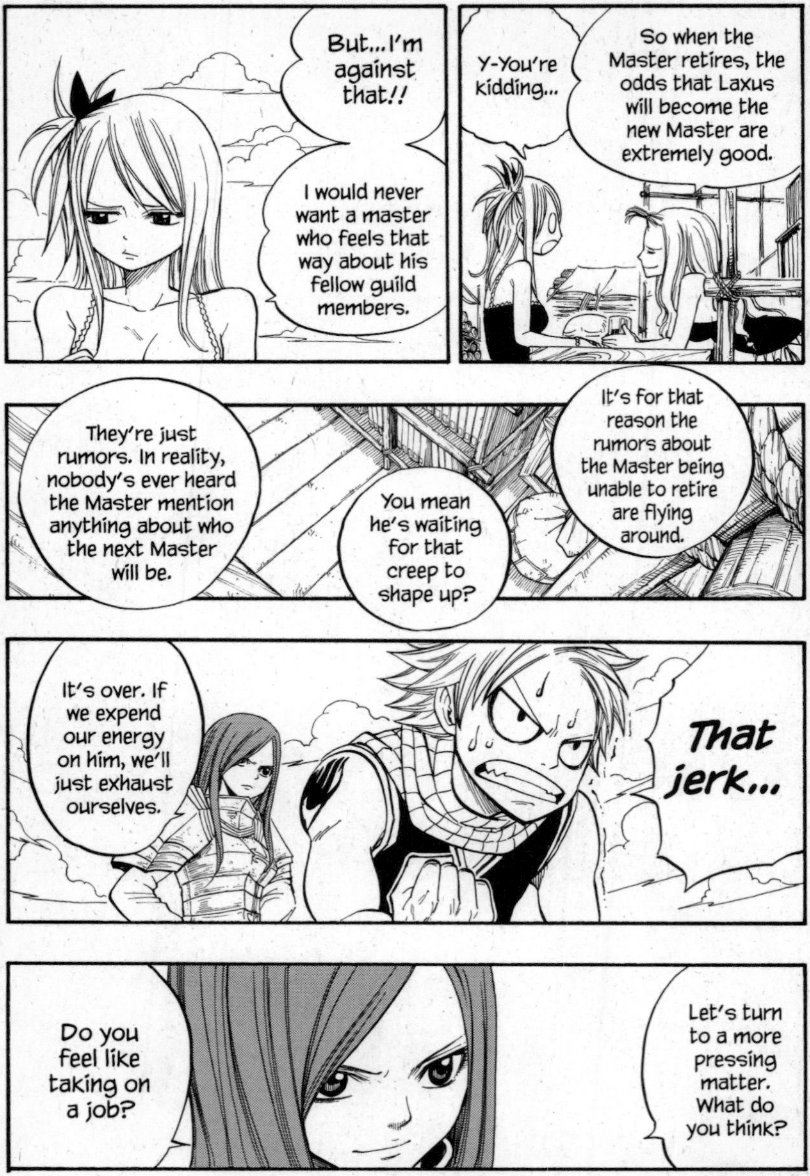
So when the Master retires, the odds that Laxus will become the new Master are extremely good.
Y-You're kidding...
But...I'm against that!!
I would never want a master who feels that way about his fellow guild members.
It's for that reason the rumors about the Master being unable to retire are flying around.
You mean he's waiting for that creep to shape up?
They're just rumors. In reality, nobody's ever heard the Master mention anything about who the next Master will be.
That jerk...
It's over. If we expend our energy on him, we'll just exhaust ourselves.
Let's turn to a more pressing matter. What do you think?
Do you feel like taking on a job?

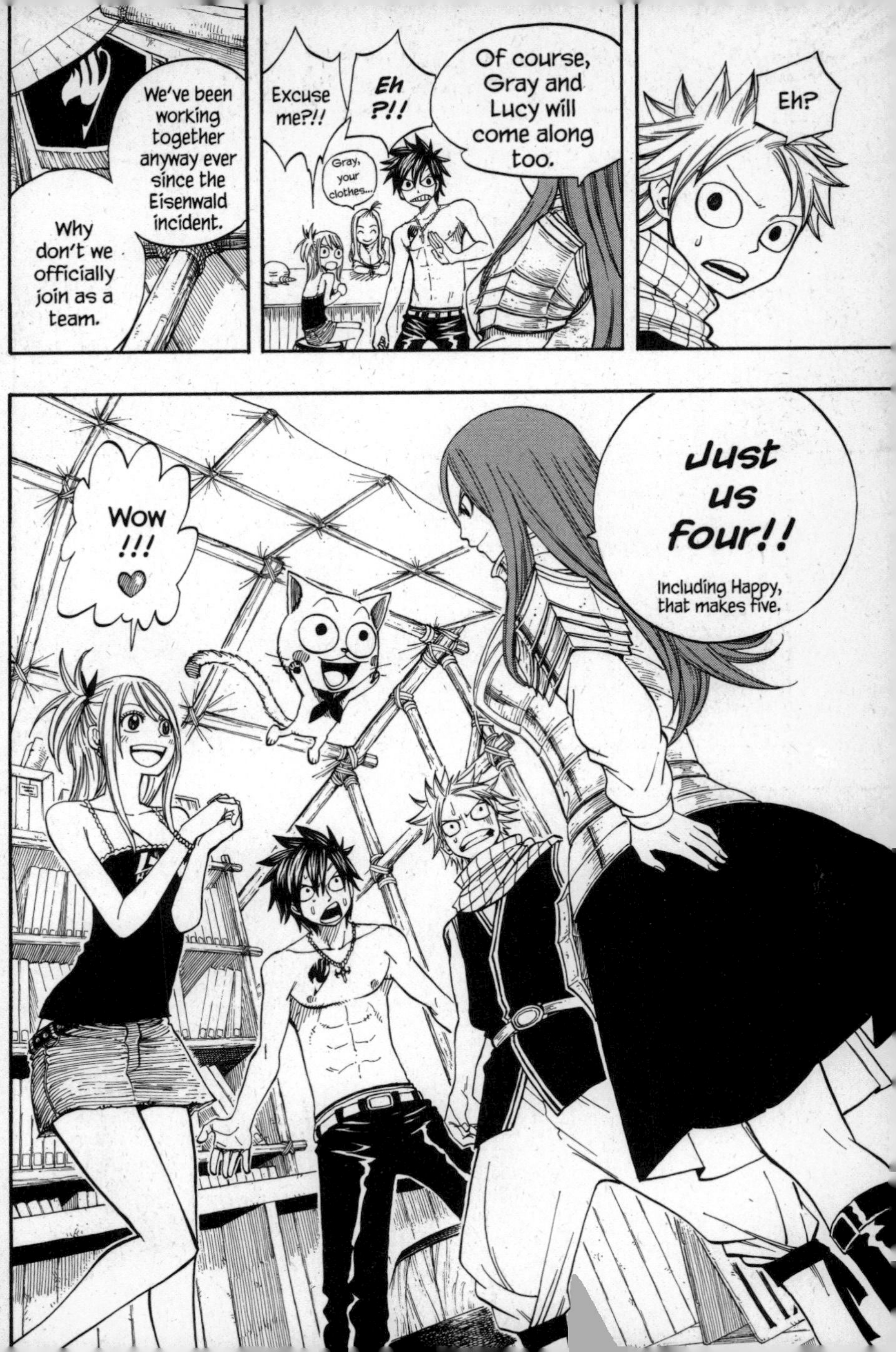
Eh?
Of course, Gray and Lucy will come along too.
Eh ?!!
Excuse me?!!
Gray, your clothes...
We've been working together anyway ever since the Eisenwald incident.
Why don't we officially join as a team.
Just us four!!
Including Happy, that makes five.
Wow !!! ♥

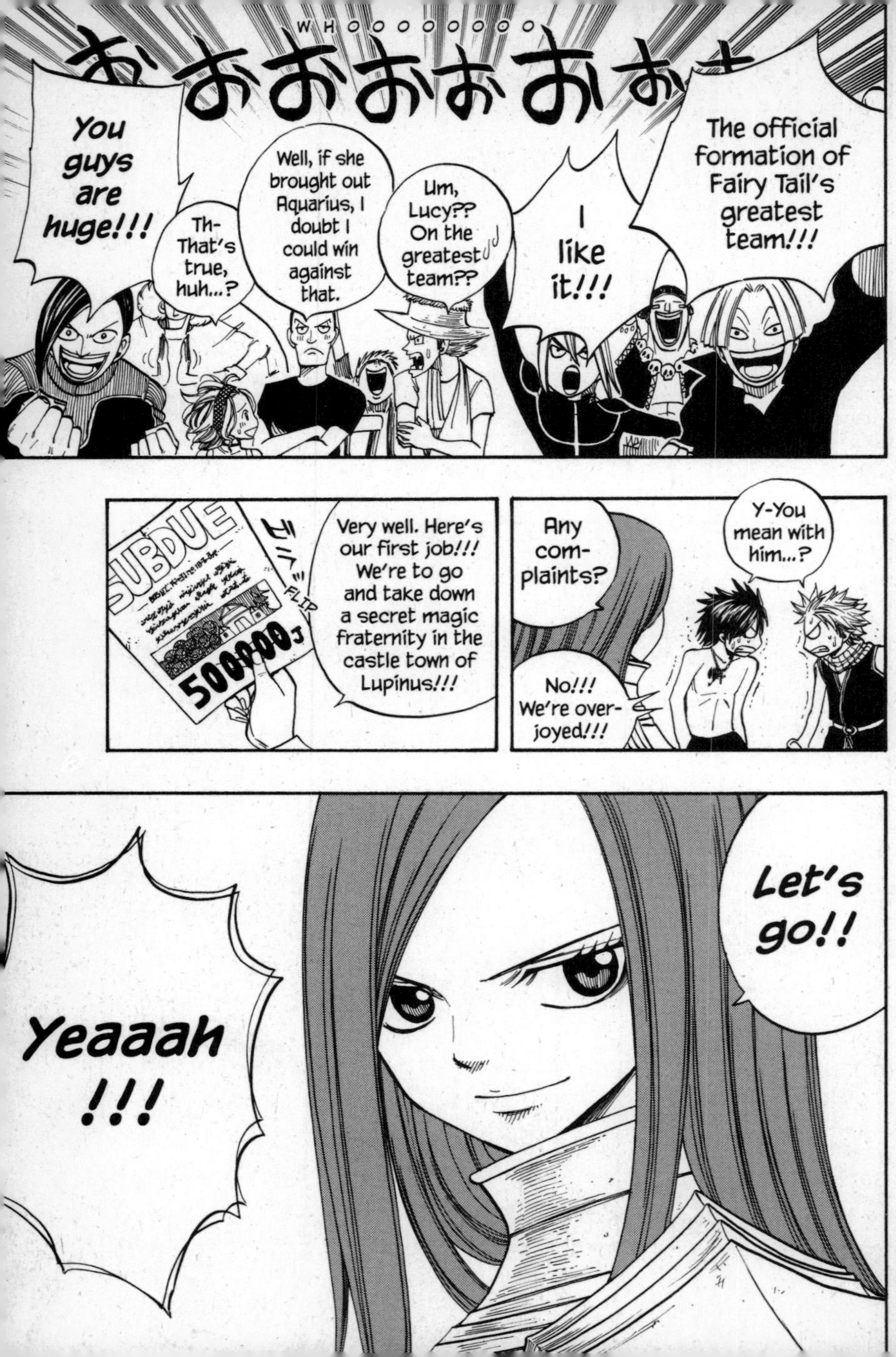
WHOOOOOOOOO
The official formation of Fairy Tail's greatest team!!!
I like it!!!
Um, Lucy?? On the greatest team??
Well, if she brought out Aquarius, I doubt I could win against that.
Th- That's true, huh...?
You guys are huge!!!
Y-You mean with him...?
Any com- plaints?
No!!! We're over- joyed!!!
Very well. Here's our first job!!! We're to go and take down a secret magic fraternity in the castle town of Lupinus!!!
FLIP
SUBDUE
500000J
Let's go!!
Yeaaaah!!!

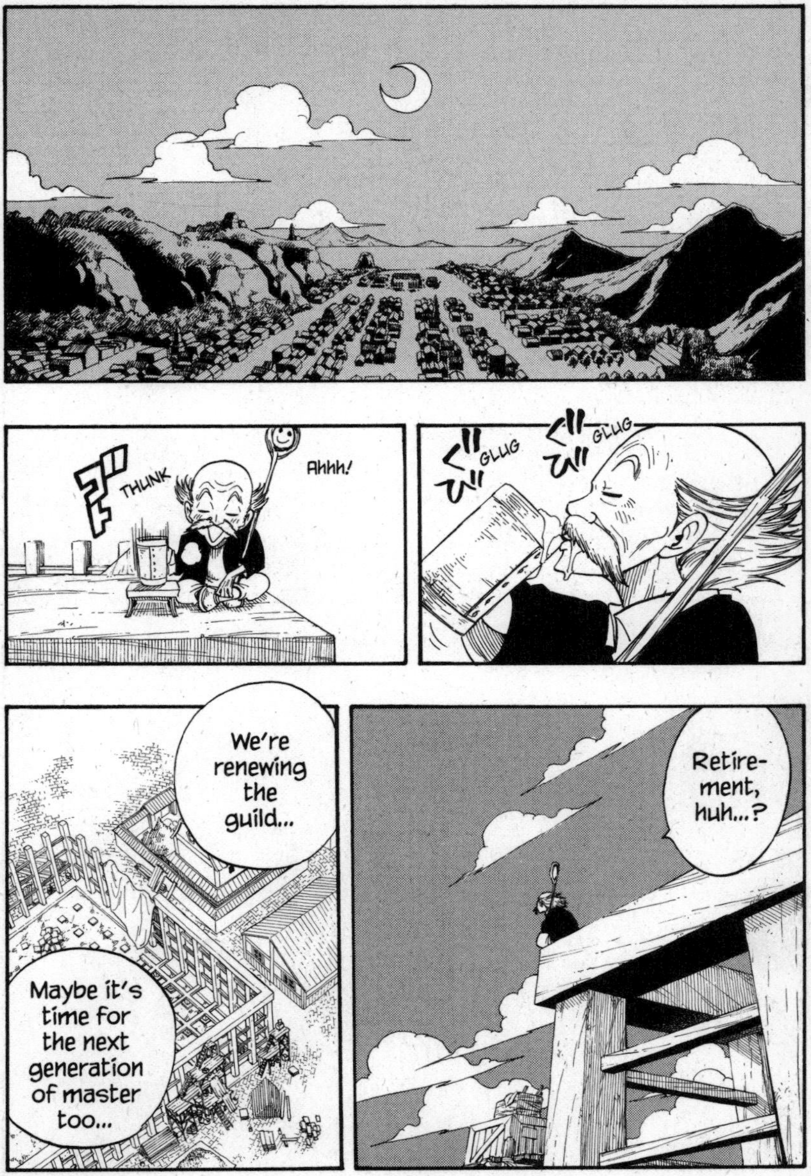
GLUG
GLUG
THUNK
Ahhh!
Retire-ment, huh...?
We're renewing the guild...
Maybe it's time for the next generation of master too...

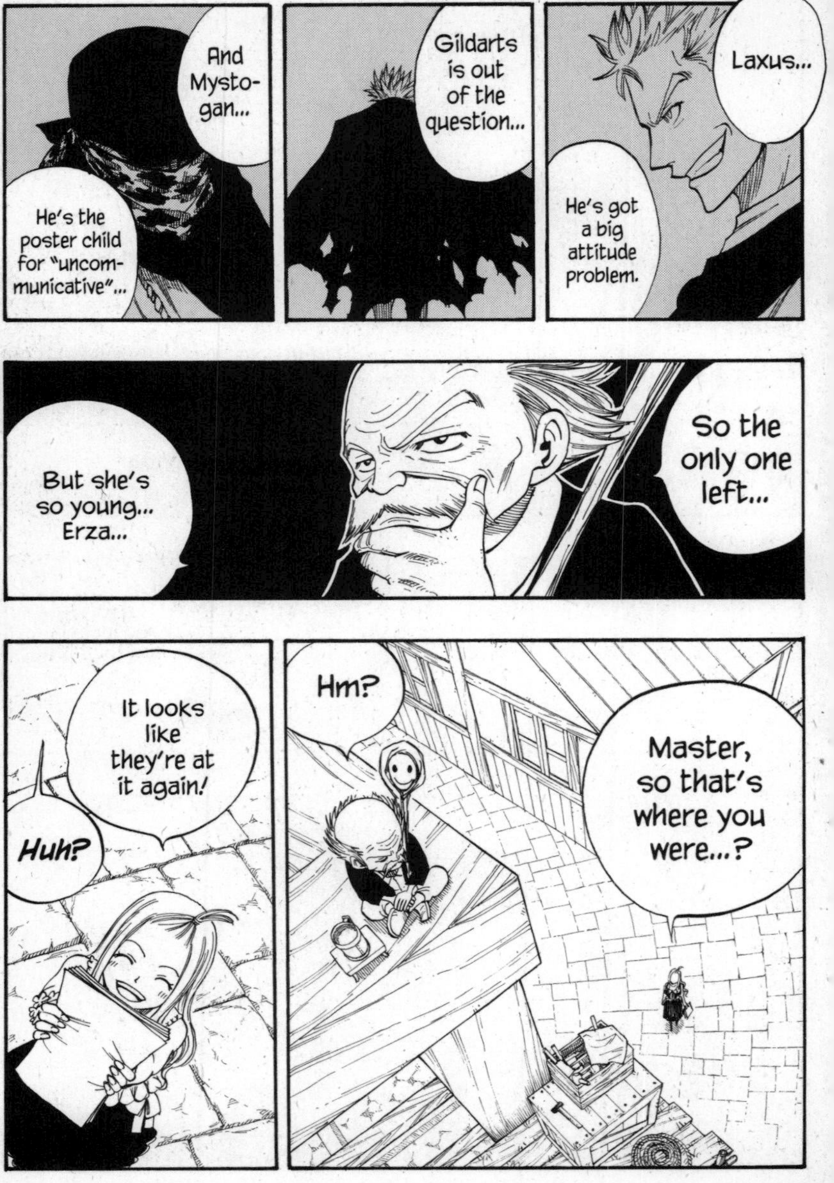
Laxus...
He's got a big attitude problem.
Gildarts is out of the question...
And Mysto-gan...
He's the poster child for "uncom-municative"...
So the only one left...
But she's so young... Erza...
Master, so that's where you were...?
Hm?
It looks like they're at it again!
Huh?

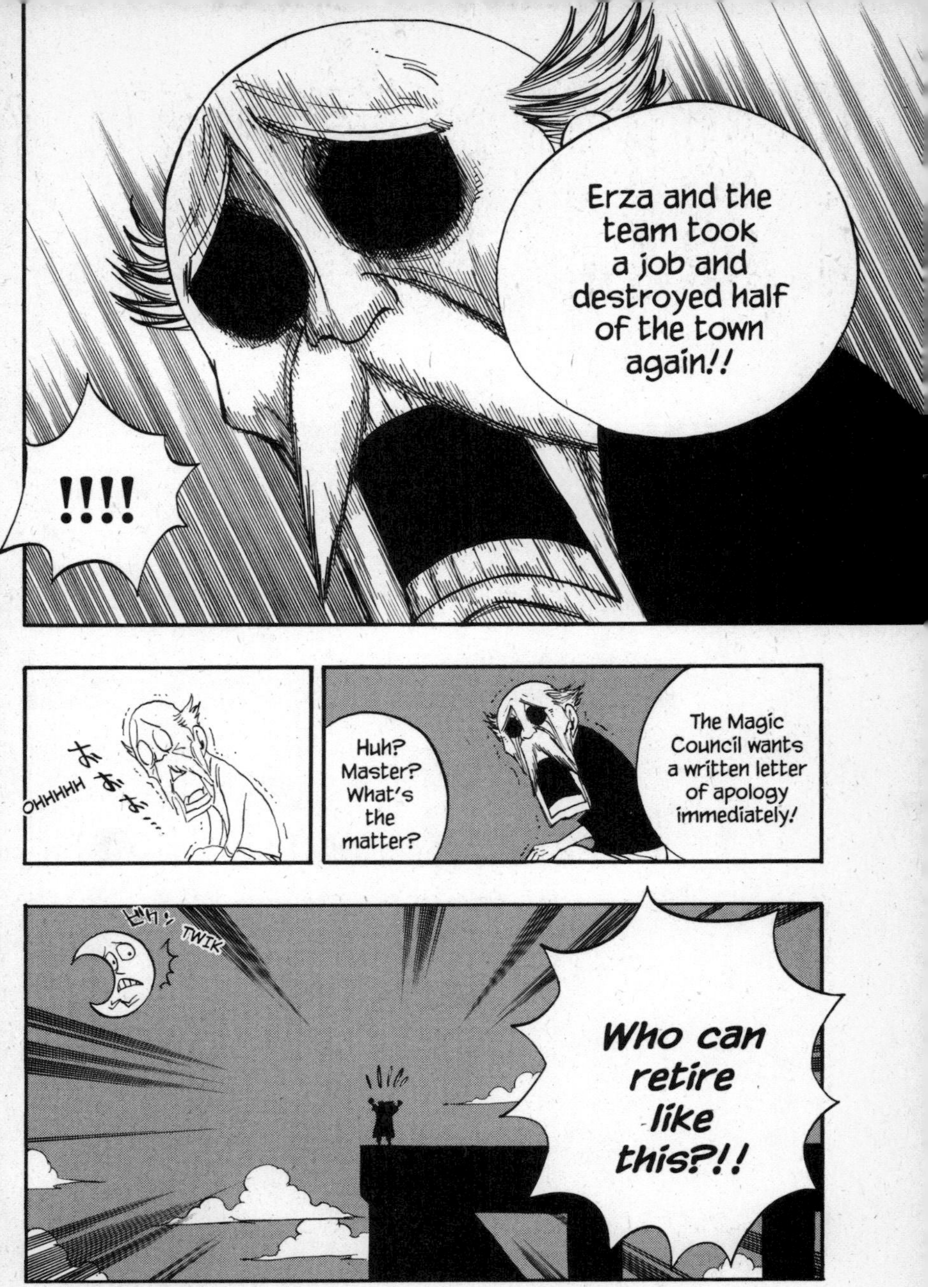
Erza and the team took a job and destroyed half of the town again!!
!!!!
The Magic Council wants a written letter of apology immediately!
Huh? Master? What's the matter?
おおお…
OHHHHH
Who can retire like this?!!
ビクッ
TWIK

FAIRY TAIL

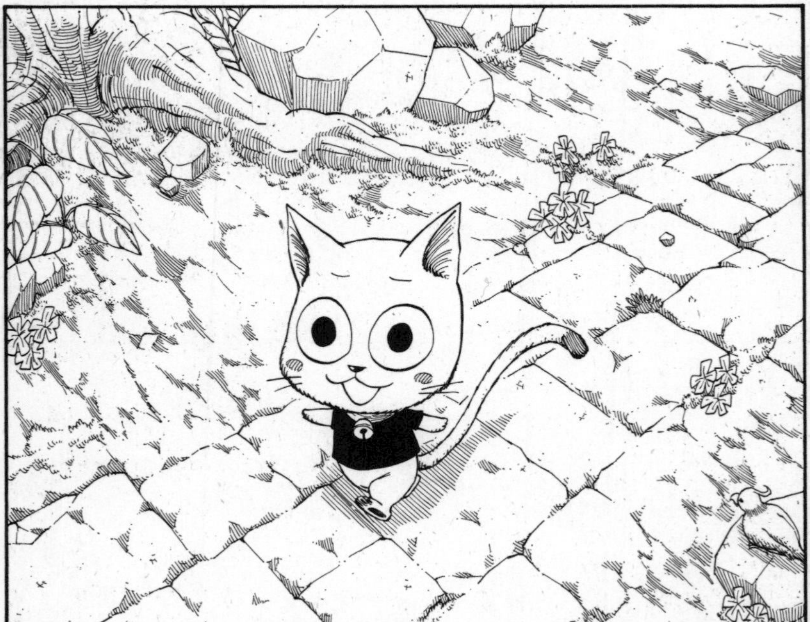

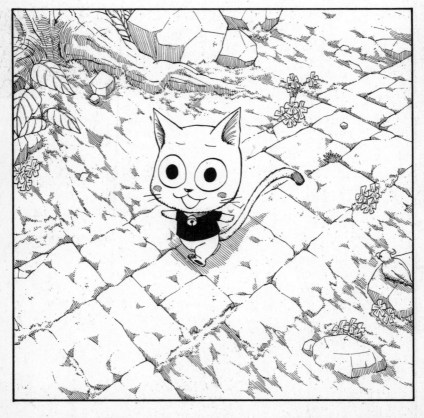

Chapter 70: Frederick & Yanderica

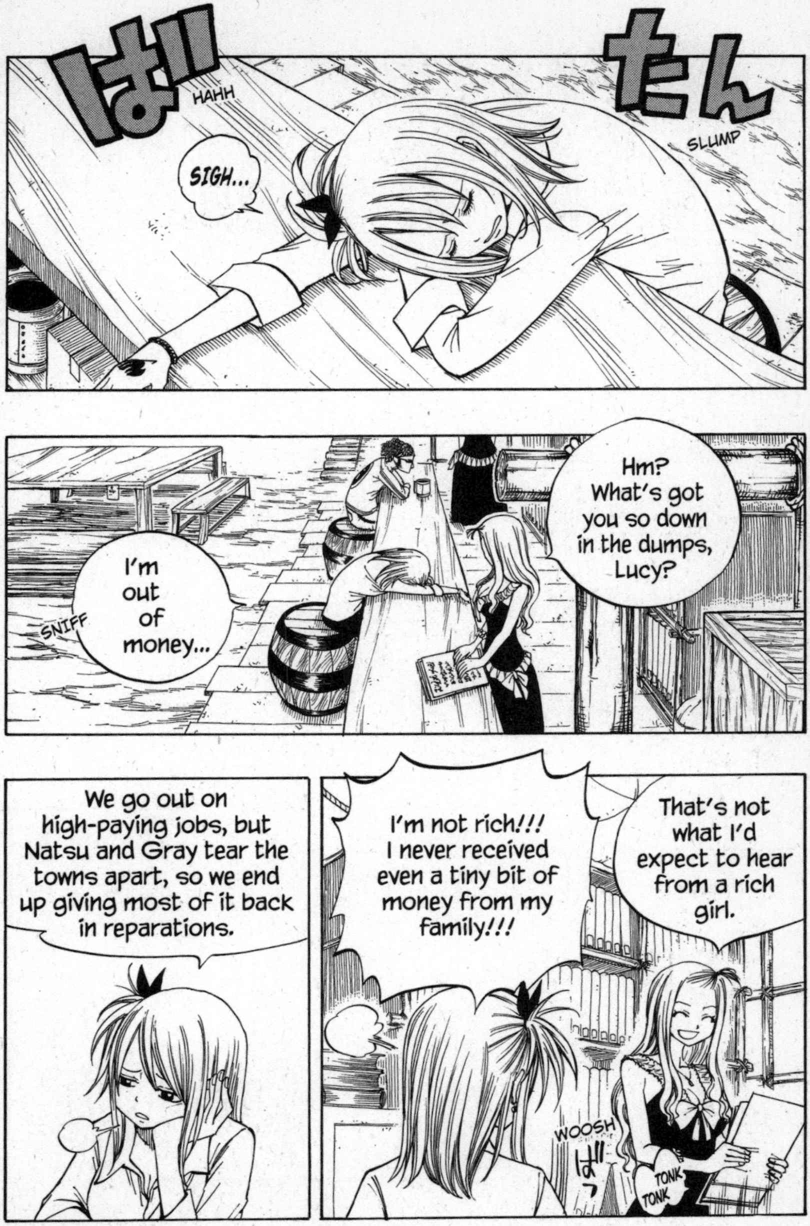

たん
SLUMP
SIGH...
ば
HAHH
Hm? What's got you so down in the dumps, Lucy?
I'm out of money...
SNIFF
That's not what I'd expect to hear from a rich girl.
I'm not rich!!! I never received even a tiny bit of money from my family!!!
WOOSH
ばっ
TONK TONK
We go out on high-paying jobs, but Natsu and Gray tear the towns apart, so we end up giving most of it back in reparations.

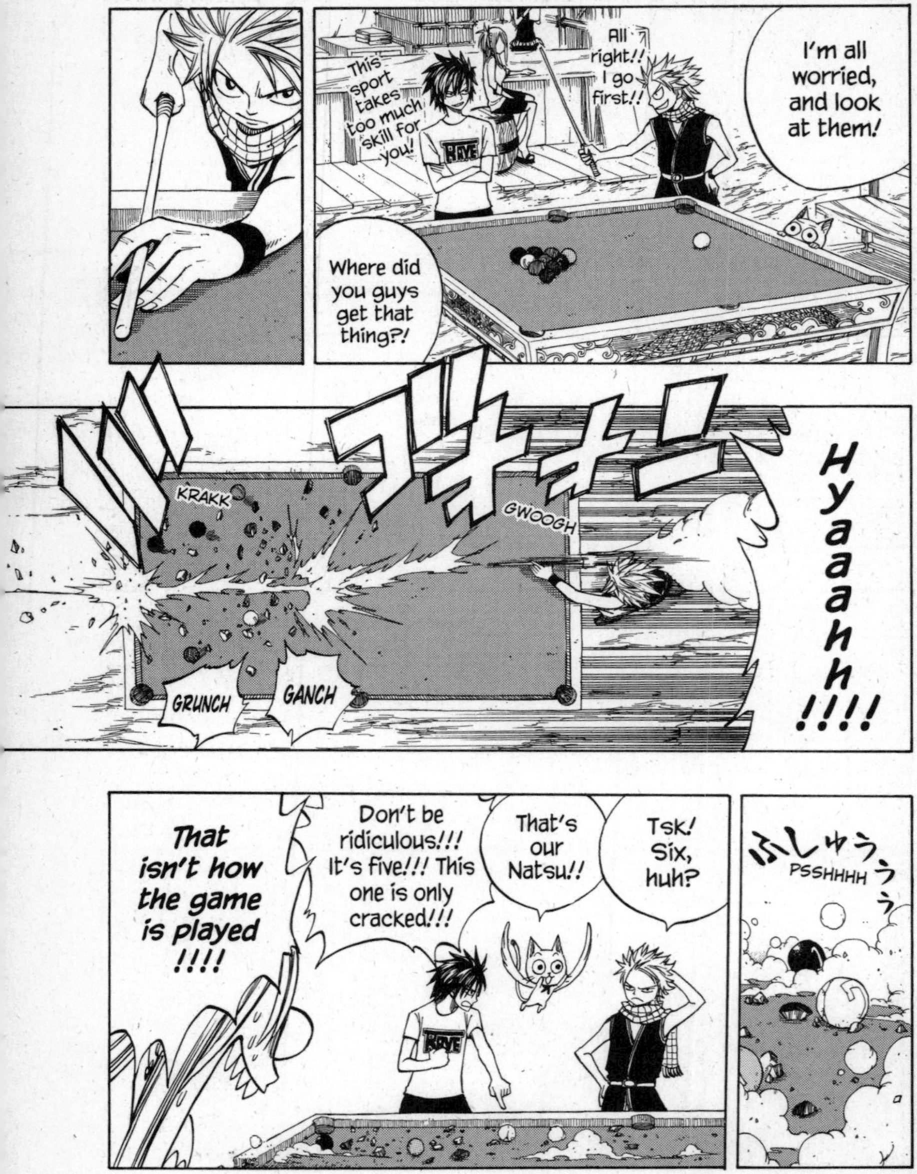
I'm all worried, and look at them!
All right!! I go first!!
This sport takes too much skill for you!
Where did you guys get that thing?!
Hyaaahh!!!!
GWOOGH
KRAKK
GANCH
GRUNCH
ふしゅううう
PSSHHHH
Tsk! Six, huh?
That's our Natsu!!
Don't be ridiculous!!! It's five!!! This one is only cracked!!!
That isn't how the game is played!!!!

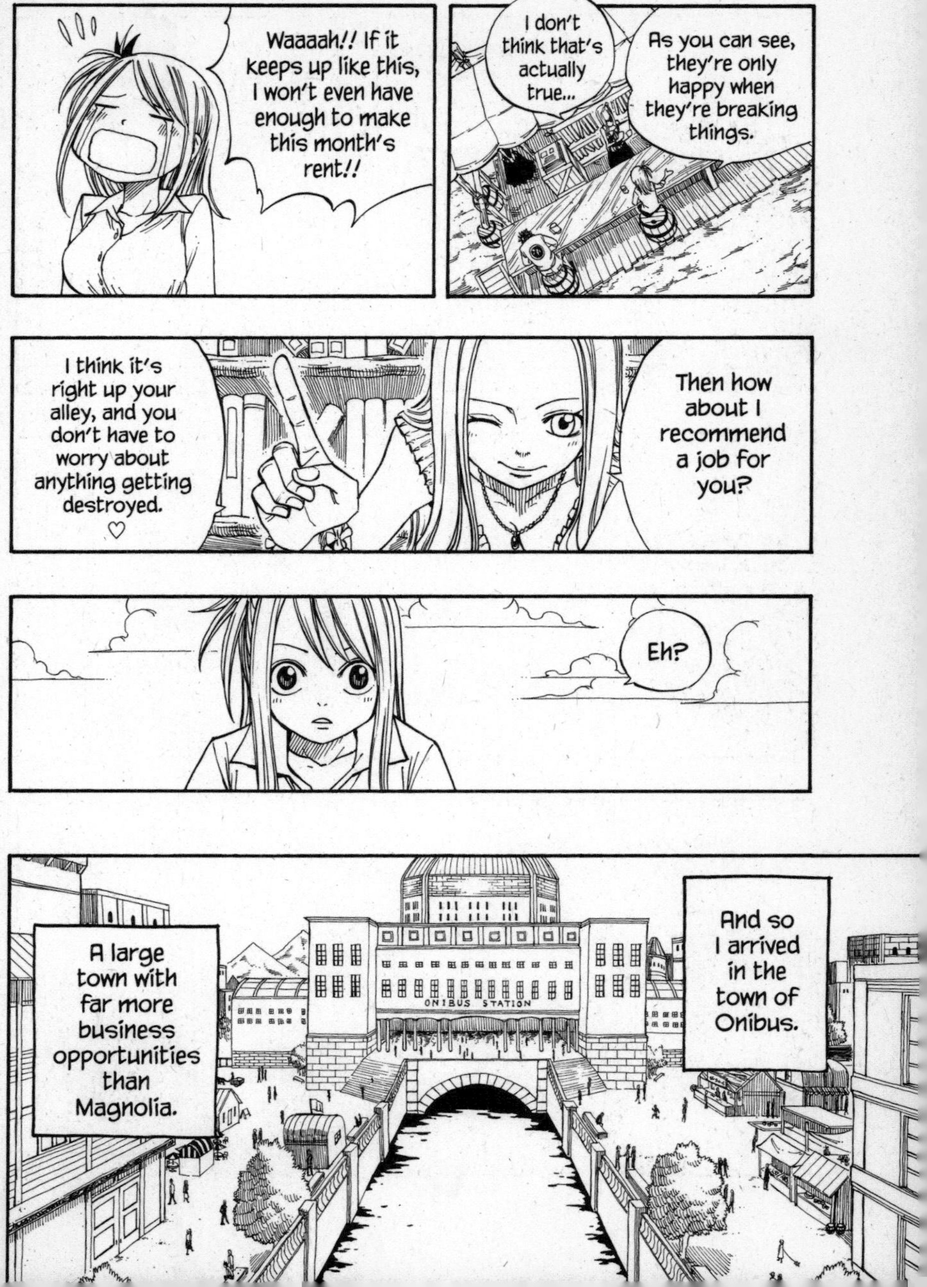
As you can see, they're only happy when they're breaking things.
I don't think that's actually true...
Waaaah!! If it keeps up like this, I won't even have enough to make this month's rent!!
Then how about I recommend a job for you?
I think it's right up your alley, and you don't have to worry about anything getting destroyed. ♡
Eh?
And so I arrived in the town of Onibus.
ONIBUS STATION
A large town with far more business opportunities than Magnolia.

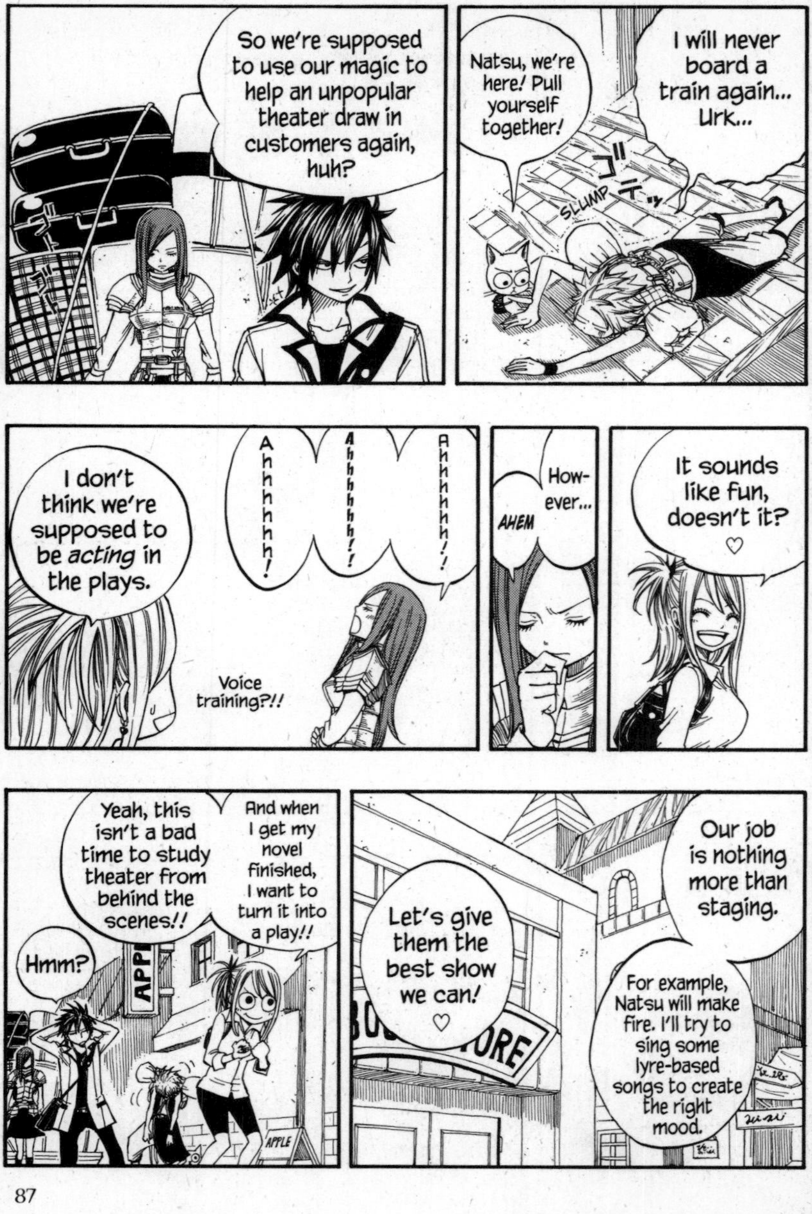
I will never board a train again... Urk...
Natsu, we're here! Pull yourself together!
SLUMP
So we're supposed to use our magic to help an unpopular theater draw in customers again, huh?
It sounds like fun, doesn't it? ♡
However...
AHEM
Ahhhhhhh!!
Ahhhhhhhh!!
Ahhhhhhh!
I don't think we're supposed to be *acting* in the plays.
Voice training?!!
Our job is nothing more than staging.
For example, Natsu will make fire. I'll try to sing some lyre-based songs to create the right mood.
Let's give them the best show we can! ♡
And when I get my novel finished, I want to turn it into a play!!
Yeah, this isn't a bad time to study theater from behind the scenes!!
Hmm?
APPLE

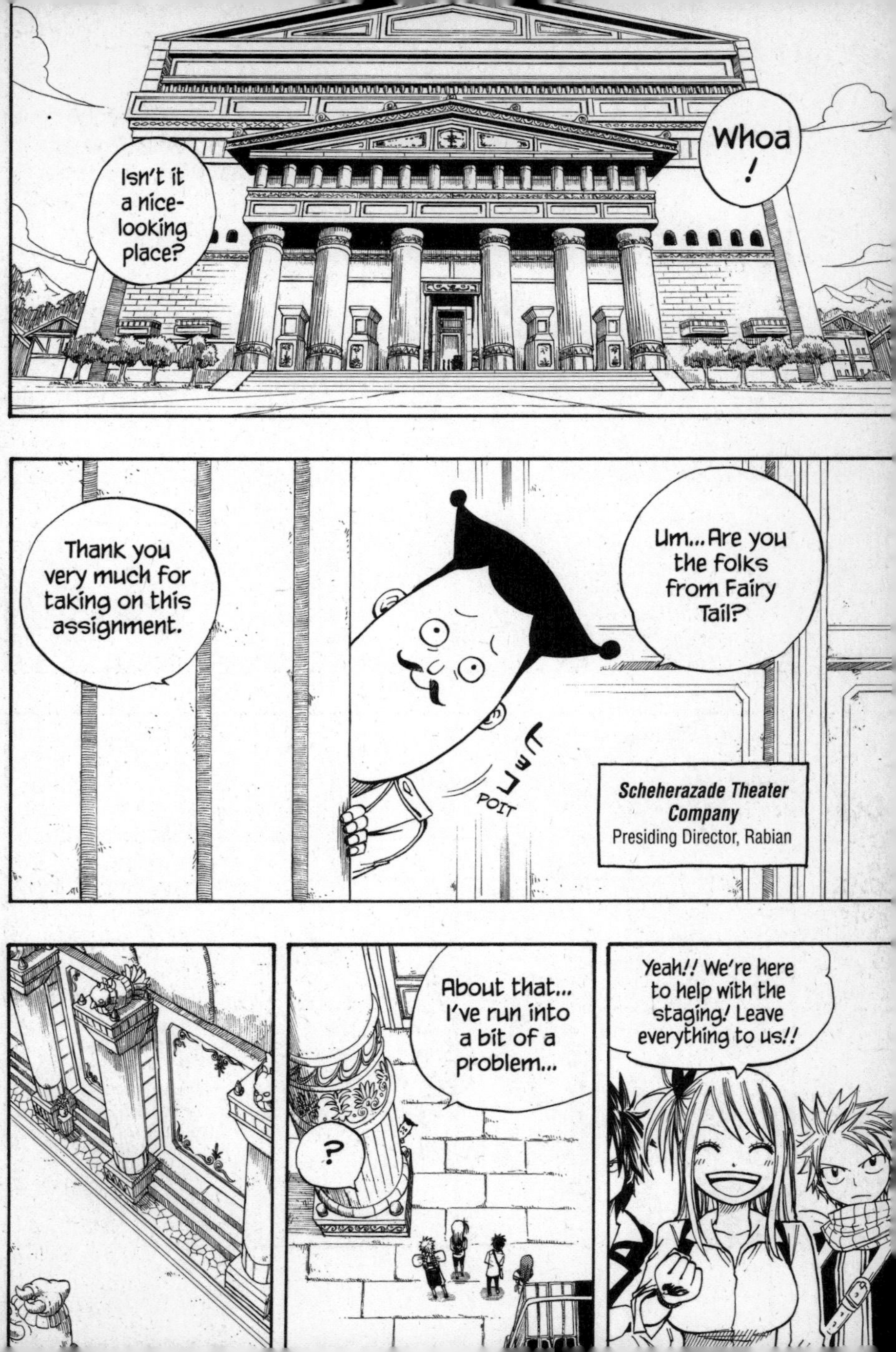
Whoa!
Isn't it a nice-looking place?
Um...Are you the folks from Fairy Tail?
POIT
Scheherazade Theater Company
Presiding Director, Rabian
Thank you very much for taking on this assignment.
Yeah!! We're here to help with the staging! Leave everything to us!!
About that... I've run into a bit of a problem...
?

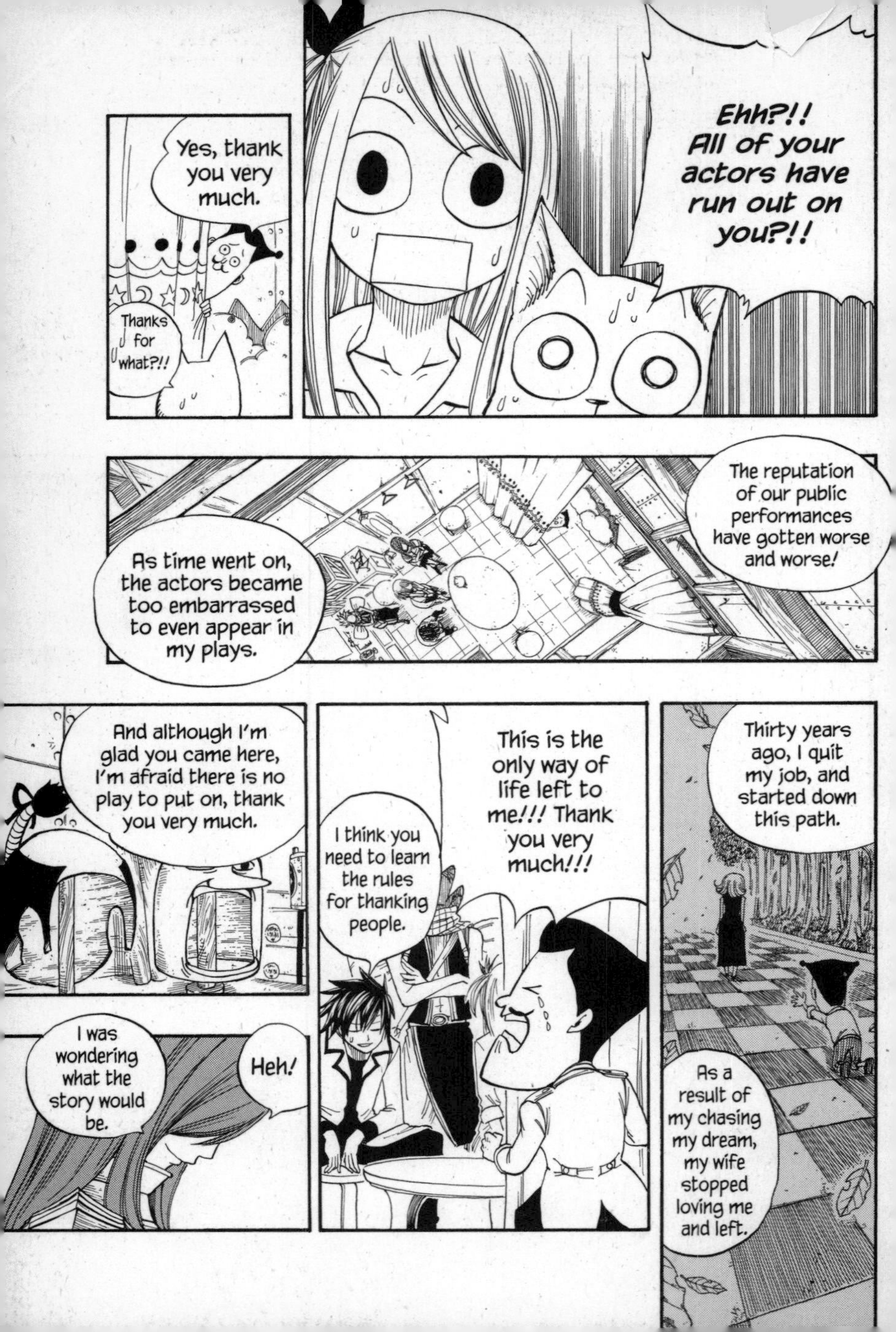
Ehh?!! All of your actors have run out on you?!!
Yes, thank you very much.
Thanks for what?!!
The reputation of our public performances have gotten worse and worse!
As time went on, the actors became too embarrassed to even appear in my plays.
Thirty years ago, I quit my job, and started down this path.
As a result of my chasing my dream, my wife stopped loving me and left.
This is the only way of life left to me!!! Thank you very much!!!
I think you need to learn the rules for thanking people.
And although I'm glad you came here, I'm afraid there is no play to put on, thank you very much.
Heh!
I was wondering what the story would be.

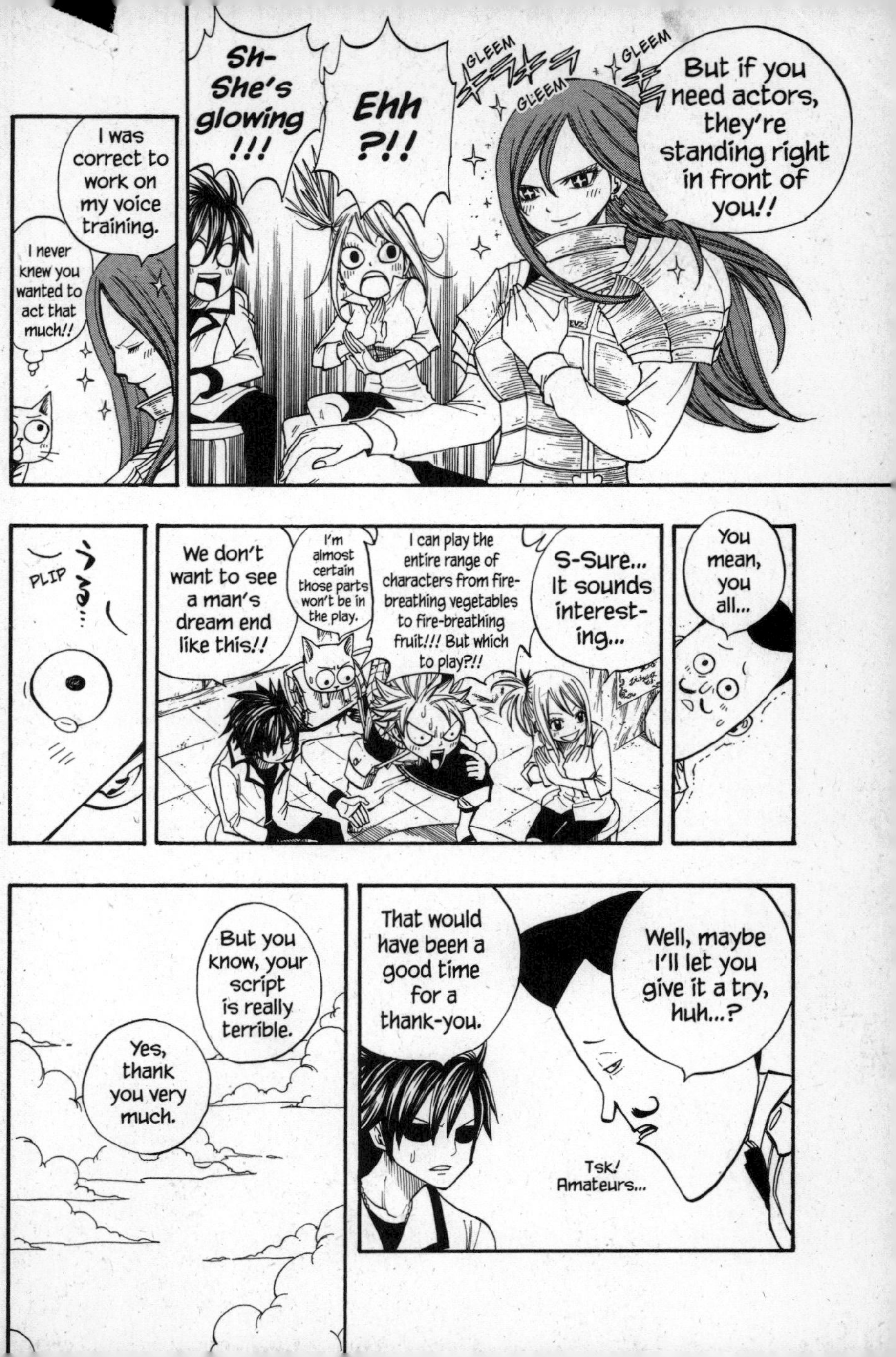
GLEEM
GLEEM
GLEEM
But if you need actors, they're standing right in front of you!!
Ehh?!!
Sh- She's glowing!!!
I was correct to work on my voice training.
I never knew you wanted to act that much!!
You mean, you all...
S-Sure... It sounds interest-ing...
I can play the entire range of characters from fire-breathing vegetables to fire-breathing fruit!!! But which to play?!!
I'm almost certain those parts won't be in the play.
We don't want to see a man's dream end like this!!
PLIP
Well, maybe I'll let you give it a try, huh...?
That would have been a good time for a thank-you.
Tsk! Amateurs...
But you know, your script is really terrible.
Yes, thank you very much.

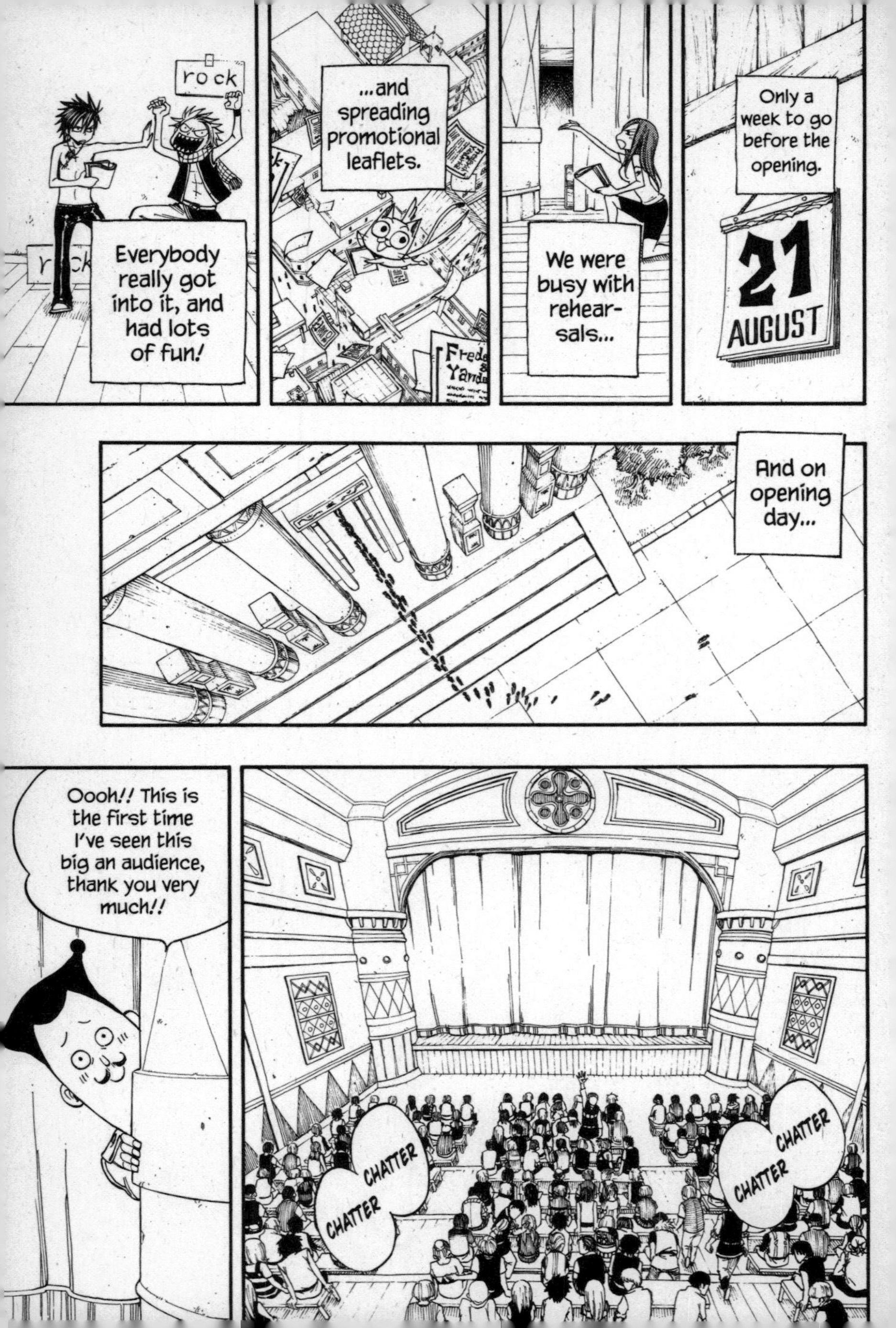
Only a week to go before the opening.
21
AUGUST
We were busy with rehearsals...
...and spreading promotional leaflets.
rock
Everybody really got into it, and had lots of fun!
And on opening day...
CHATTER CHATTER
CHATTER CHATTER
Oooh!! This is the first time I've seen this big an audience, thank you very much!!

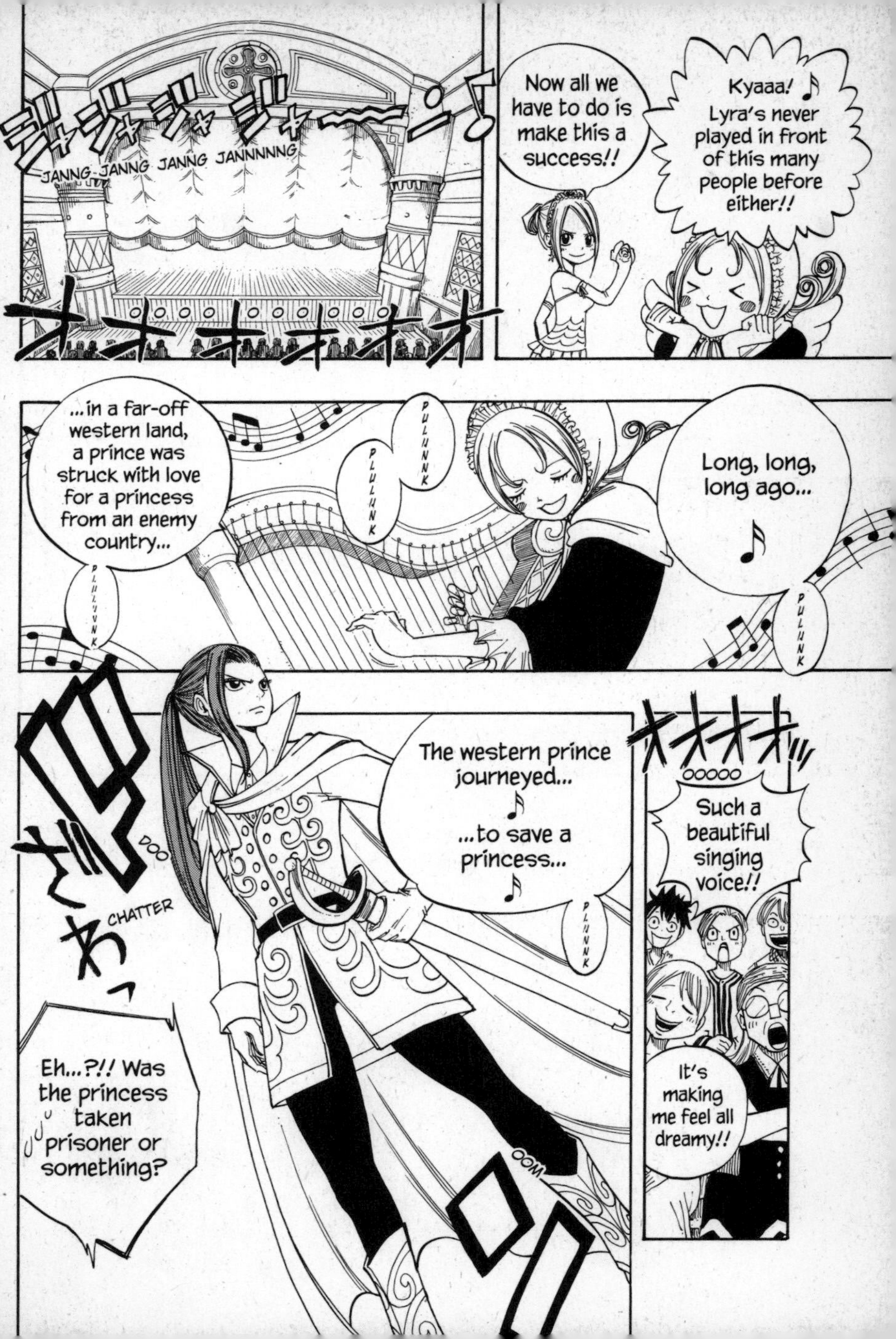
Kyaaa! ♪ Lyra's never played in front of this many people before either!!
Now all we have to do is make this a success!!
JANNG-JANNG JANNG JANNNNNG
Long, long, long ago... ♪
PLULUNK
PLULUNK
...in a far-off western land, a prince was struck with love for a princess from an enemy country...
PLULUNK
PLULUNK
OOOOO
Such a beautiful singing voice!!
It's making me feel all dreamy!!
The western prince journeyed... ♪ ...to save a princess... ♪
PLUNNK
DOO
CHATTER
OOM
Eh...?!! Was the princess taken prisoner or something?

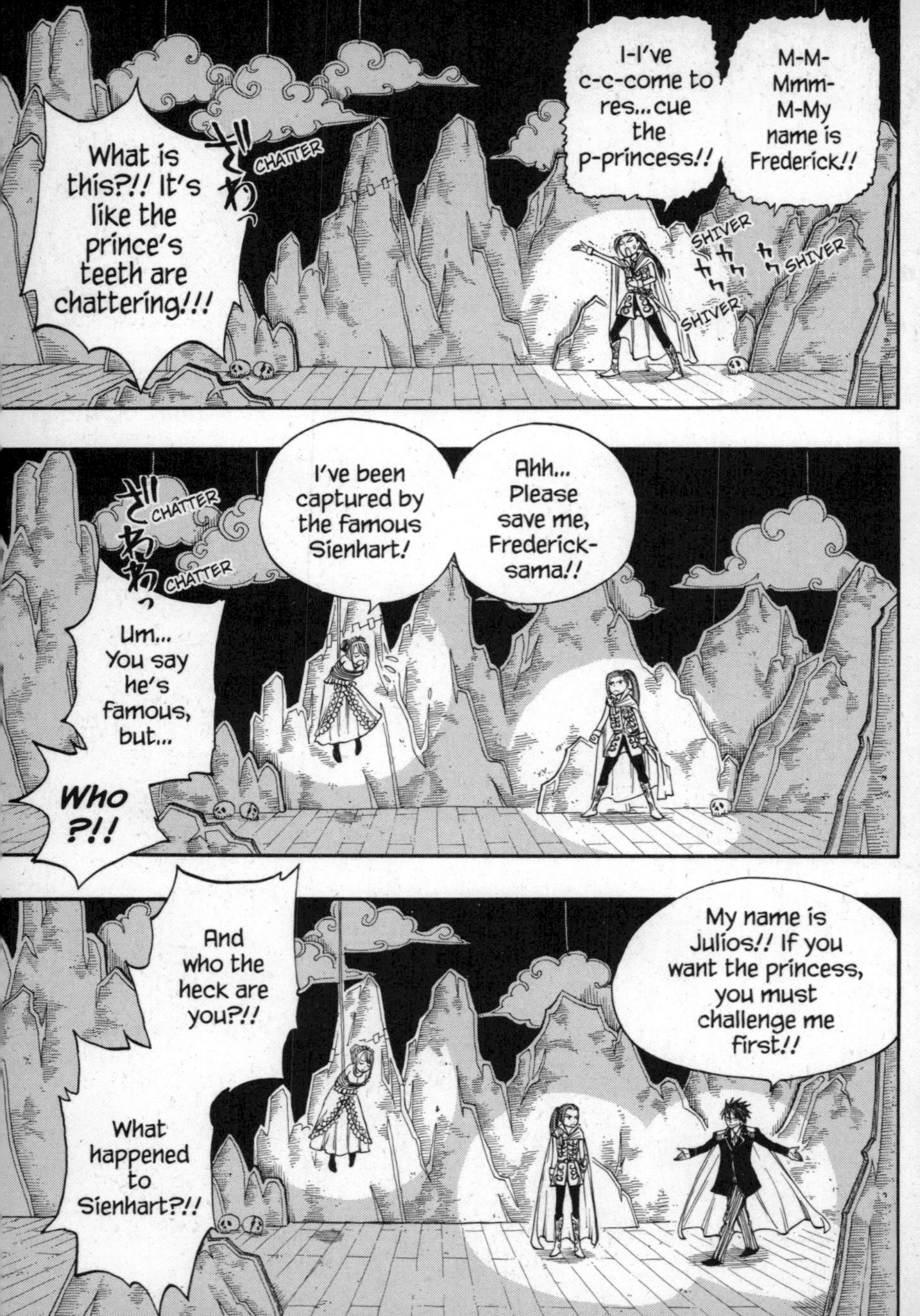
M-M-Mmm-M-My name is Frederick!!
I-I've c-c-come to res...cue the p-princess!!
SHIVER
SHIVER
SHIVER
CHATTER
What is this?!! It's like the prince's teeth are chattering!!!
Ahh... Please save me, Frederick-sama!!
I've been captured by the famous Sienhart!
CHATTER
CHATTER
Um... You say he's famous, but...
Who?!!
My name is Julios!! If you want the princess, you must challenge me first!!
And who the heck are you?!!
What happened to Sienhart?!!

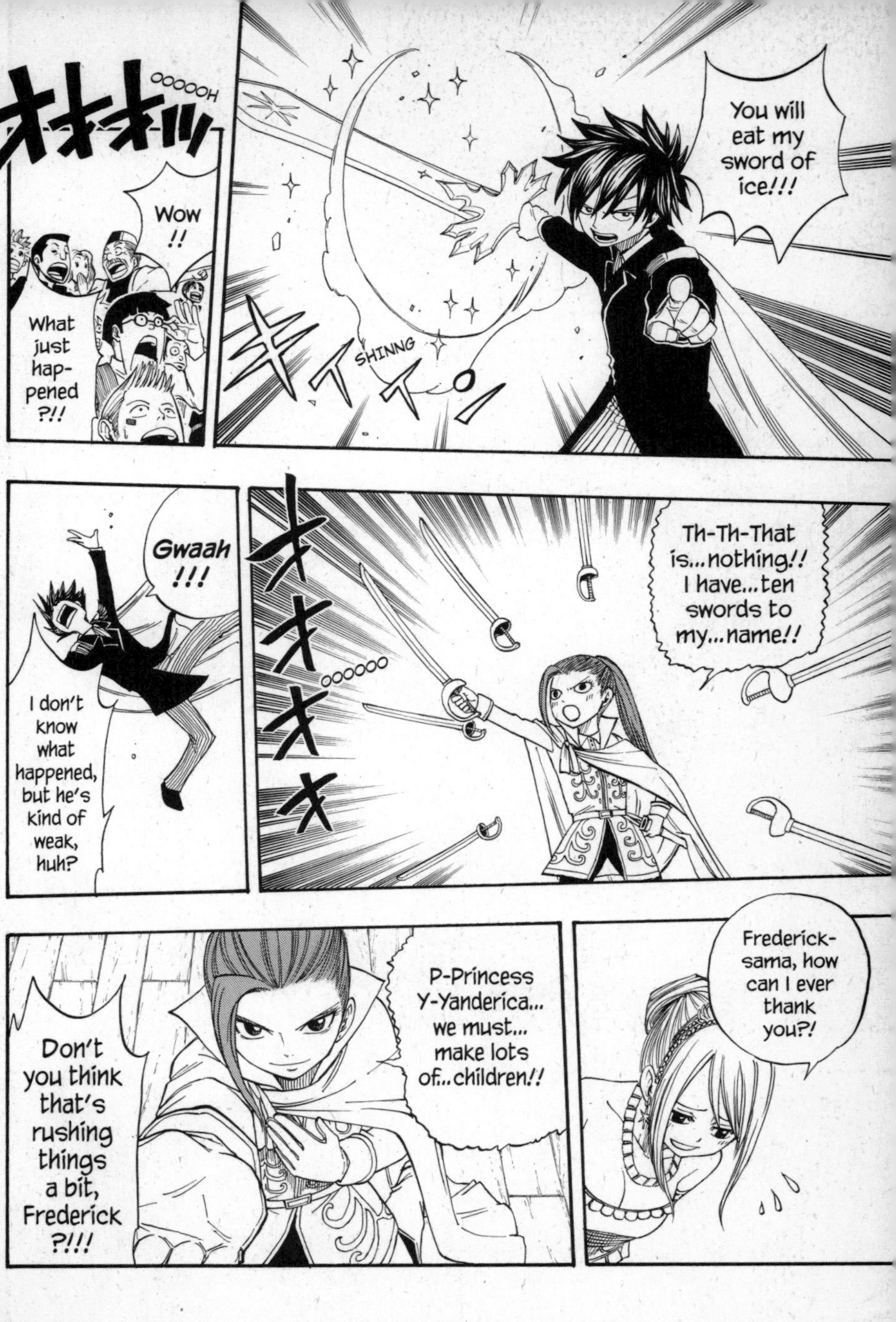
You will eat my sword of ice!!!
SHINNG
OOOOOH
Wow!!
What just hap-pened?!!
Th-Th-That is...nothing!! I have...ten swords to my...name!!
OOOOOO
Gwaah!!!
I don't know what happened, but he's kind of weak, huh?
Frederick-sama, how can I ever thank you?!
P-Princess Y-Yanderica... we must... make lots of...children!!
Don't you think that's rushing things a bit, Frederick?!!!

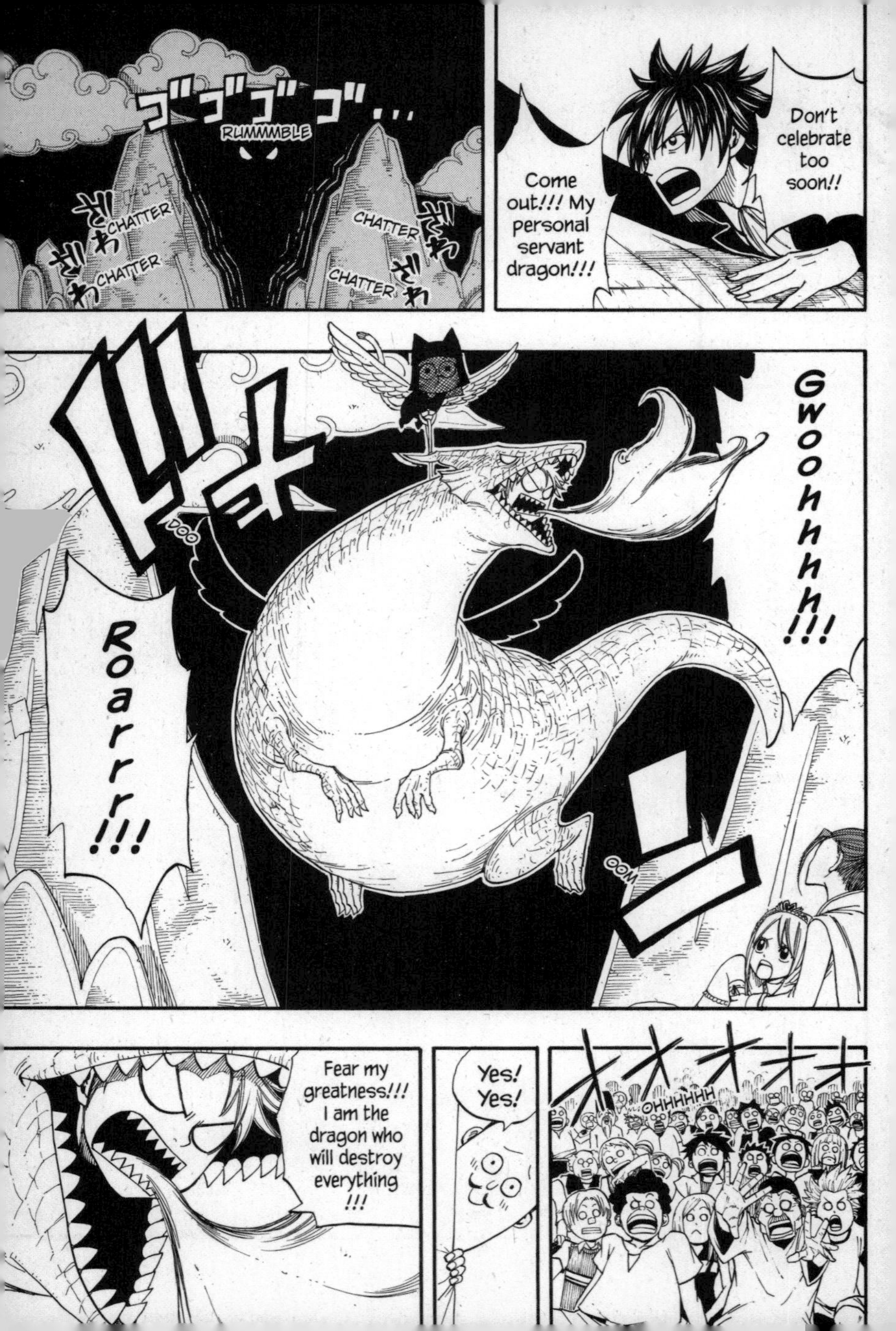

Don't celebrate too soon!!
Come out!!! My personal servant dragon!!!
ゴゴゴゴ…
RUMMMBLE
CHATTER
CHATTER
CHATTER
CHATTER
Gwoohhhhh!!!
DOO
OOM
Roarrr!!!
オオオオオ
OHHHHHH
Yes! Yes!
Fear my greatness!!! I am the dragon who will destroy everything!!!

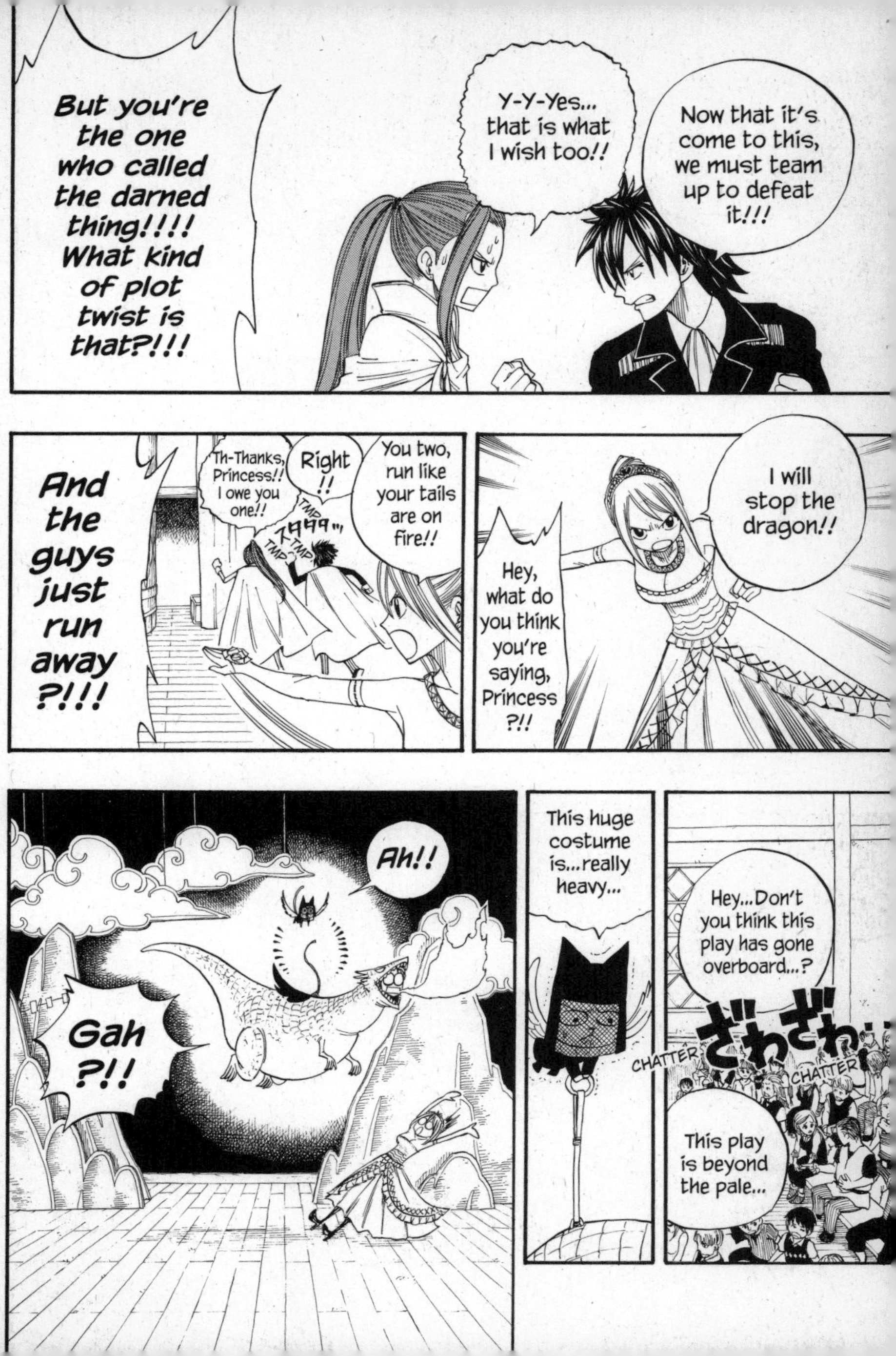
Now that it's come to this, we must team up to defeat it!!!
Y-Y-Yes... that is what I wish too!!
But you're the one who called the darned thing!!!! What kind of plot twist is that?!!!
I will stop the dragon!!
Hey, what do you think you're saying, Princess?!!
You two, run like your tails are on fire!!
Right!!
Th-Thanks, Princess!! I owe you one!!
TMP TMP TMP
And the guys just run away?!!!
Hey...Don't you think this play has gone overboard...?
ざわざわ
CHATTER CHATTER
This play is beyond the pale...
This huge costume is...really heavy...
Ah!!
Gah?!!

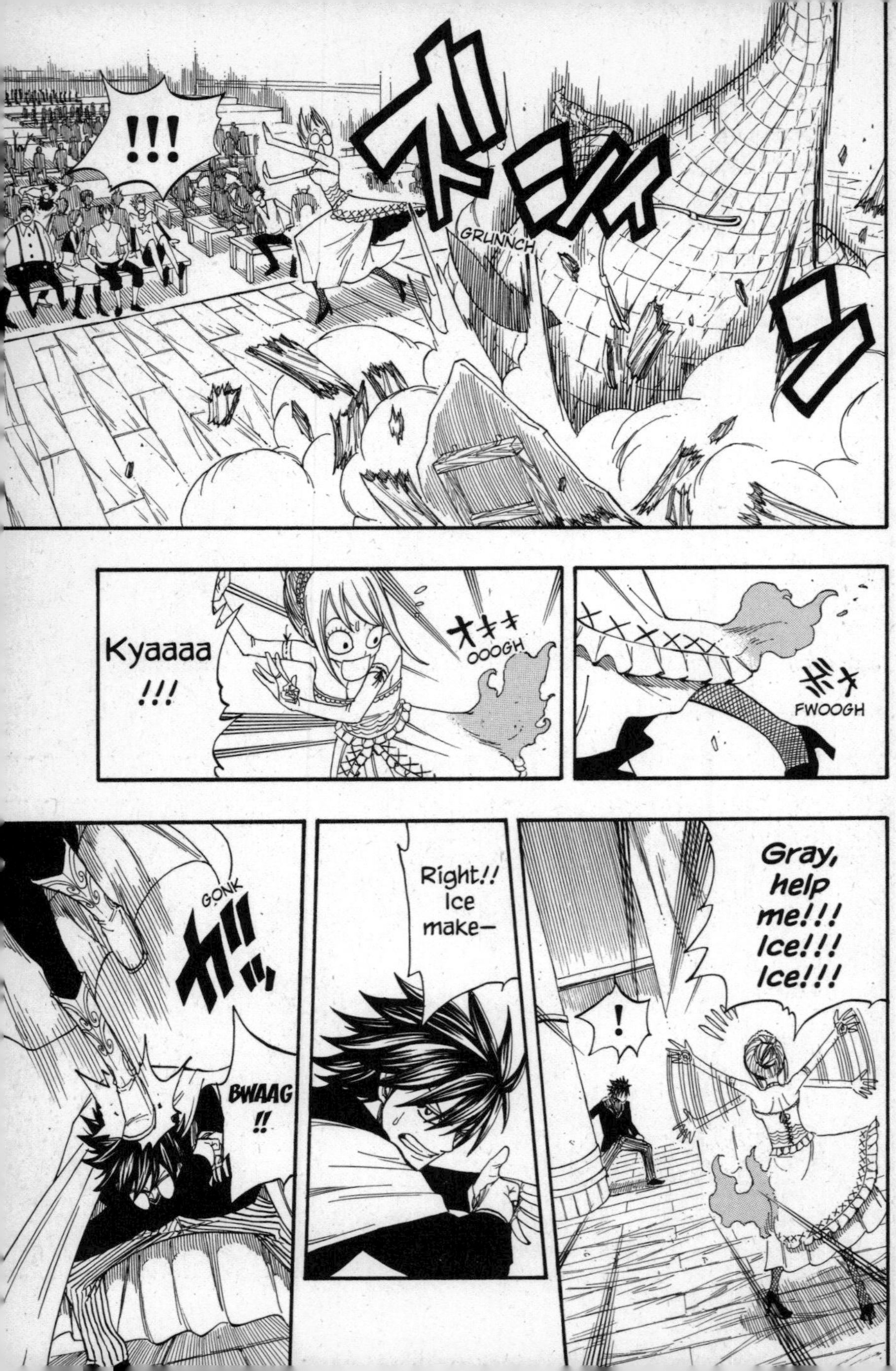
GRUNNCH
!!!
FWOOGH
OOOGH
Kyaaaa!!!
Gray, help me!!! Ice!!! Ice!!!
!
Right!! Ice make—
GONK
BWAAG!!

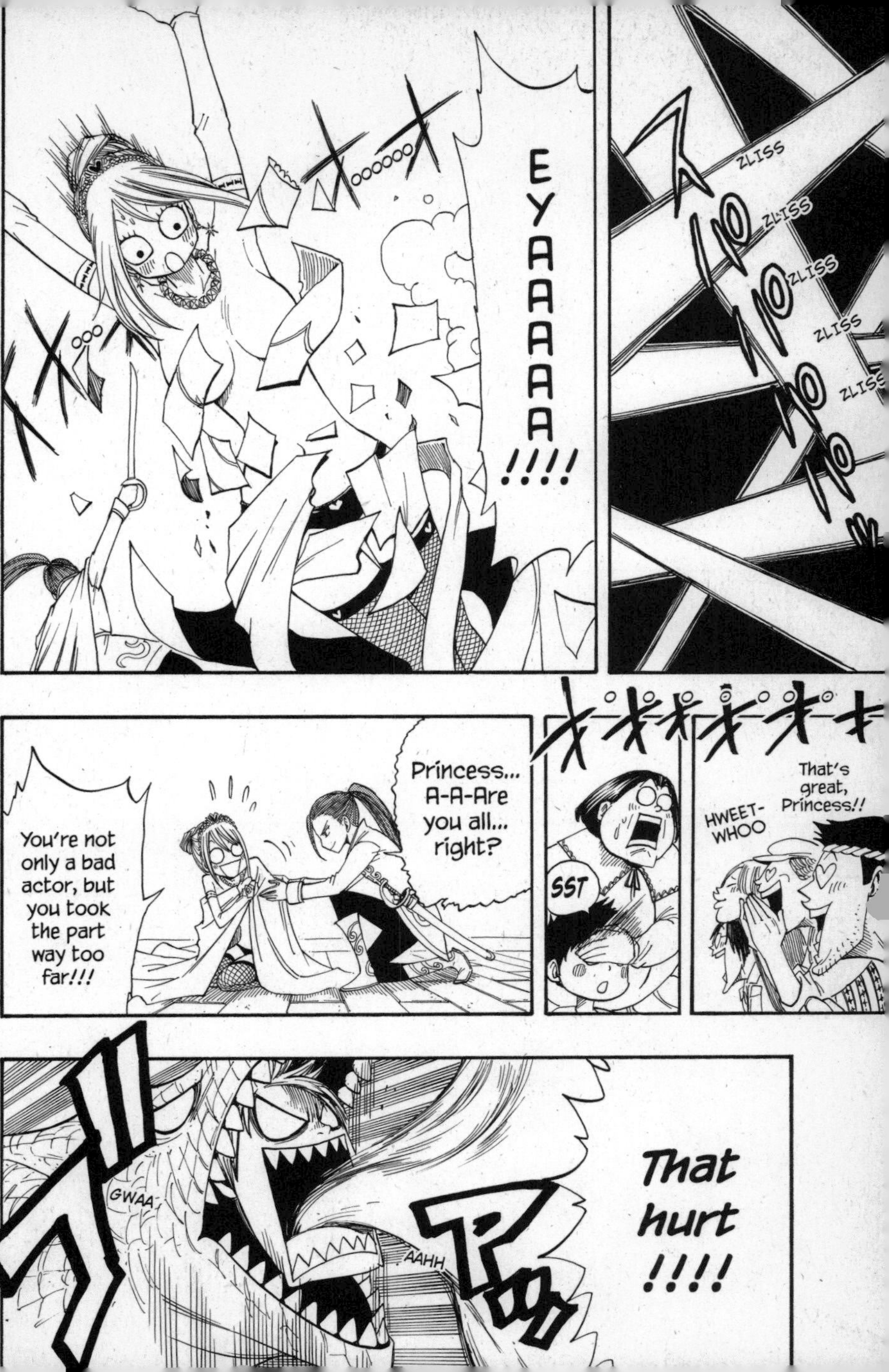
ZLISS
ZLISS
ZLISS
ZLISS
ZLISS
EYAAAAAA!!!!
That's great, Princess!!
HWEET-WHOO
SST
Princess... A-A-Are you all... right?
You're not only a bad actor, but you took the part way too far!!!
That hurt!!!!
GWAA
AAHH

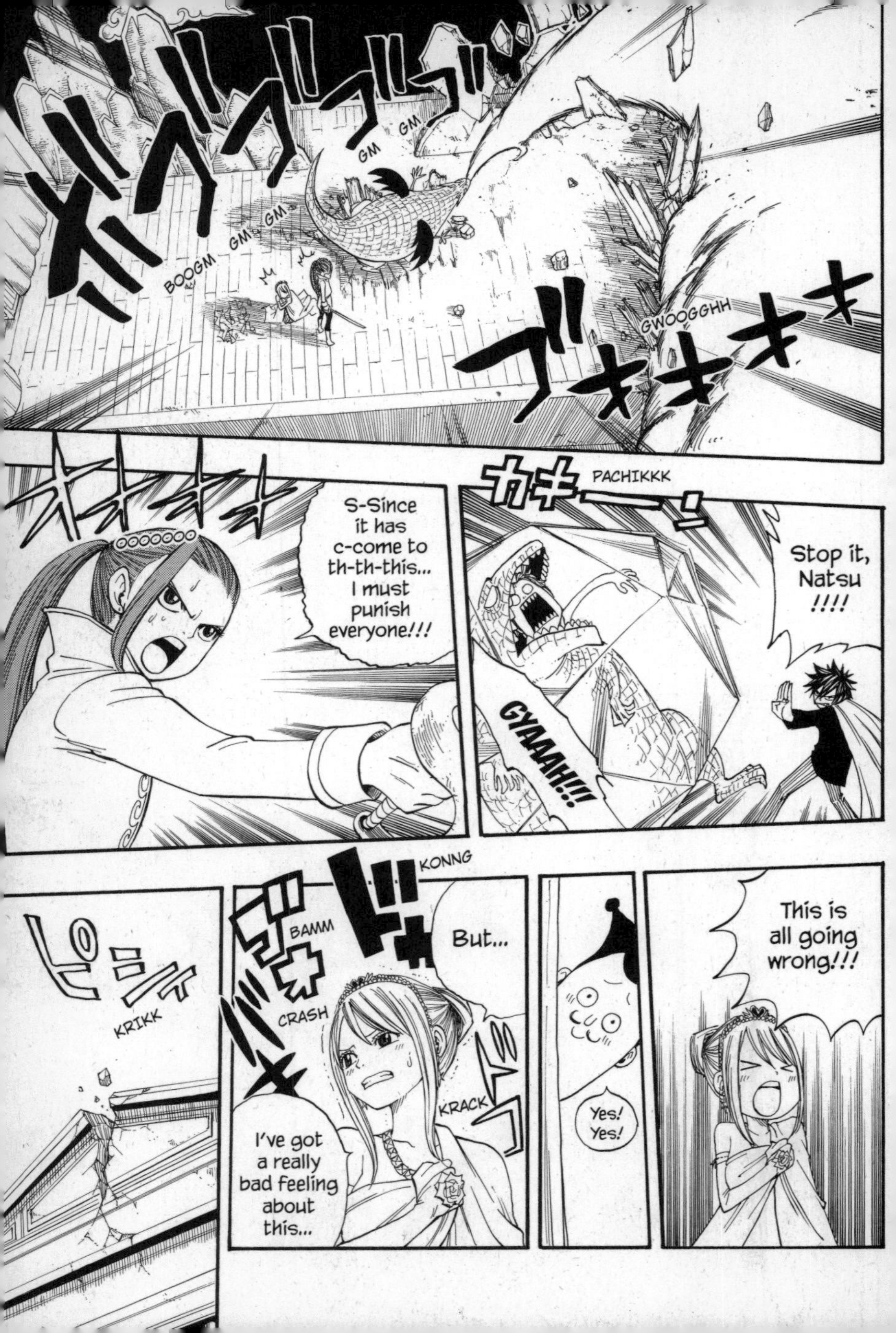
GM GM
GM GM
BOOGM
GWOOGGHH
PACHIKKK
Stop it, Natsu!!!!
GYAAAH!!!!
S-Since it has c-come to th-th-this... I must punish everyone!!!
This is all going wrong!!!
Yes! Yes!
KONNG
But...
BAMM
CRASH
KRACK
I've got a really bad feeling about this...
KRIKK

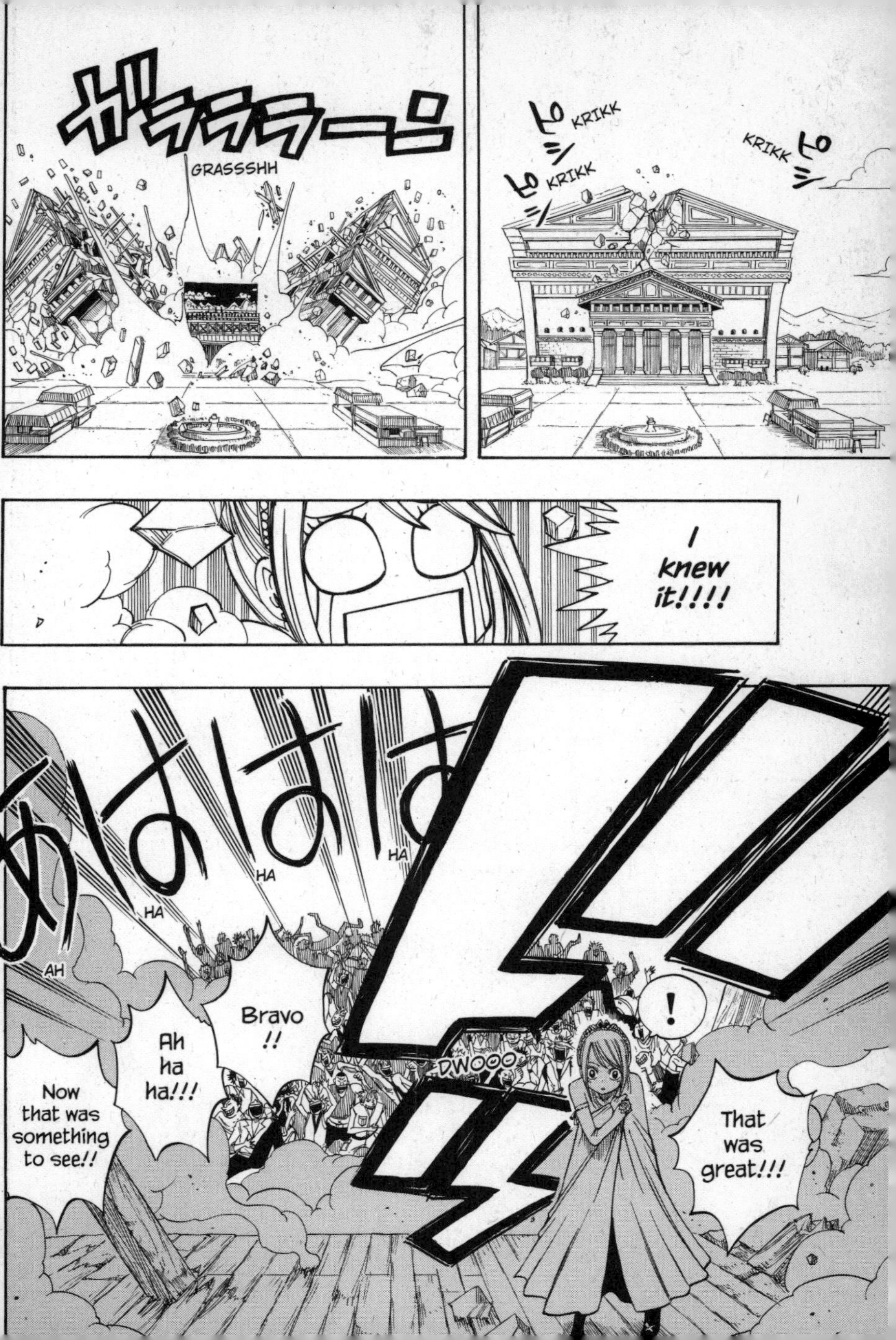

ピシ
KRIKK
ピシ
KRIKK
ピシ
KRIKK
GRASSSHH
I knew it!!!!
!
That was great!!!
DWOOO
Bravo!!
Ah ha ha!!!
Now that was something to see!!
あははは
HA
HA
HA
AH

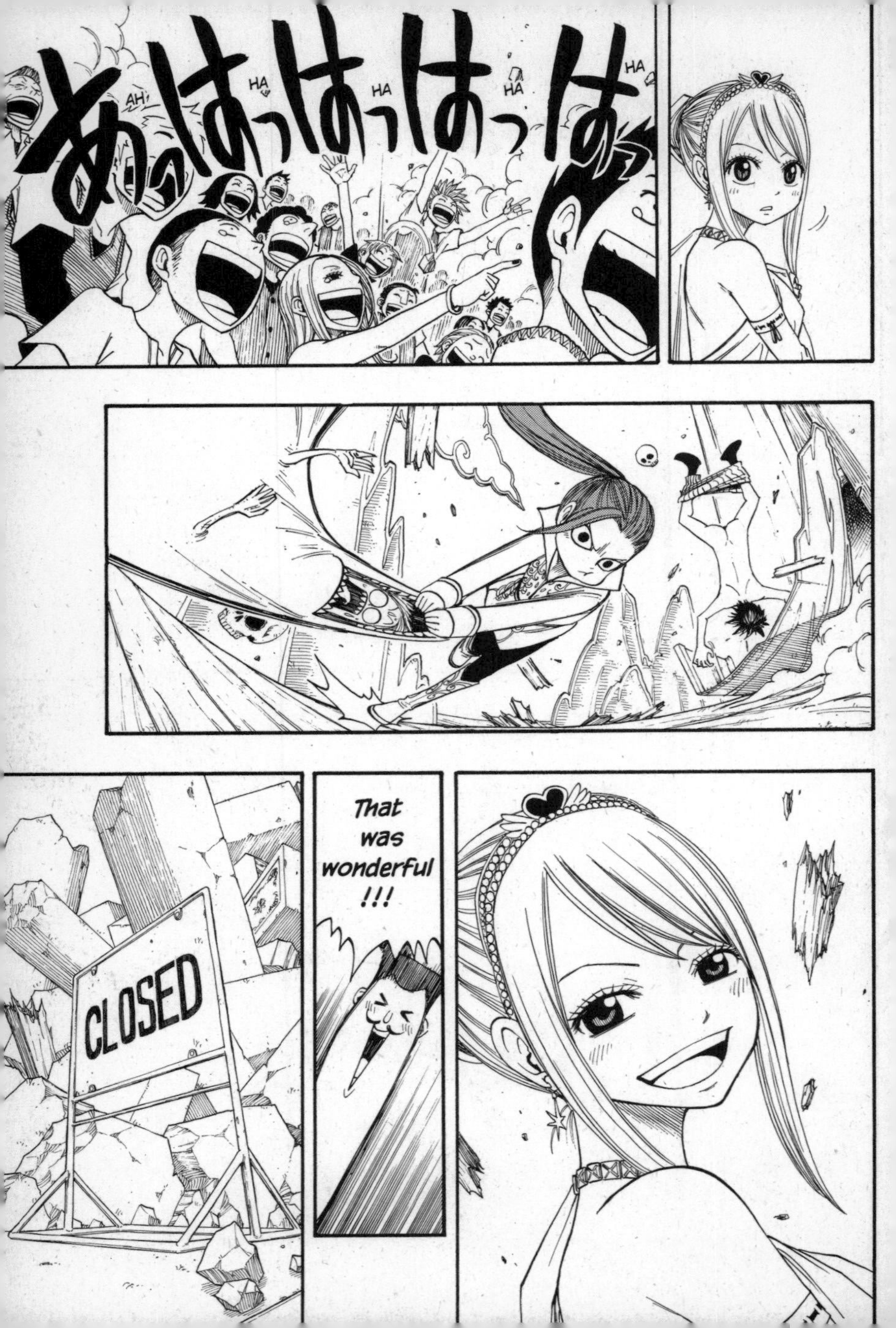
あっはっはっはっはっ
AH HA HA HA HA
That was wonderful !!!
CLOSED

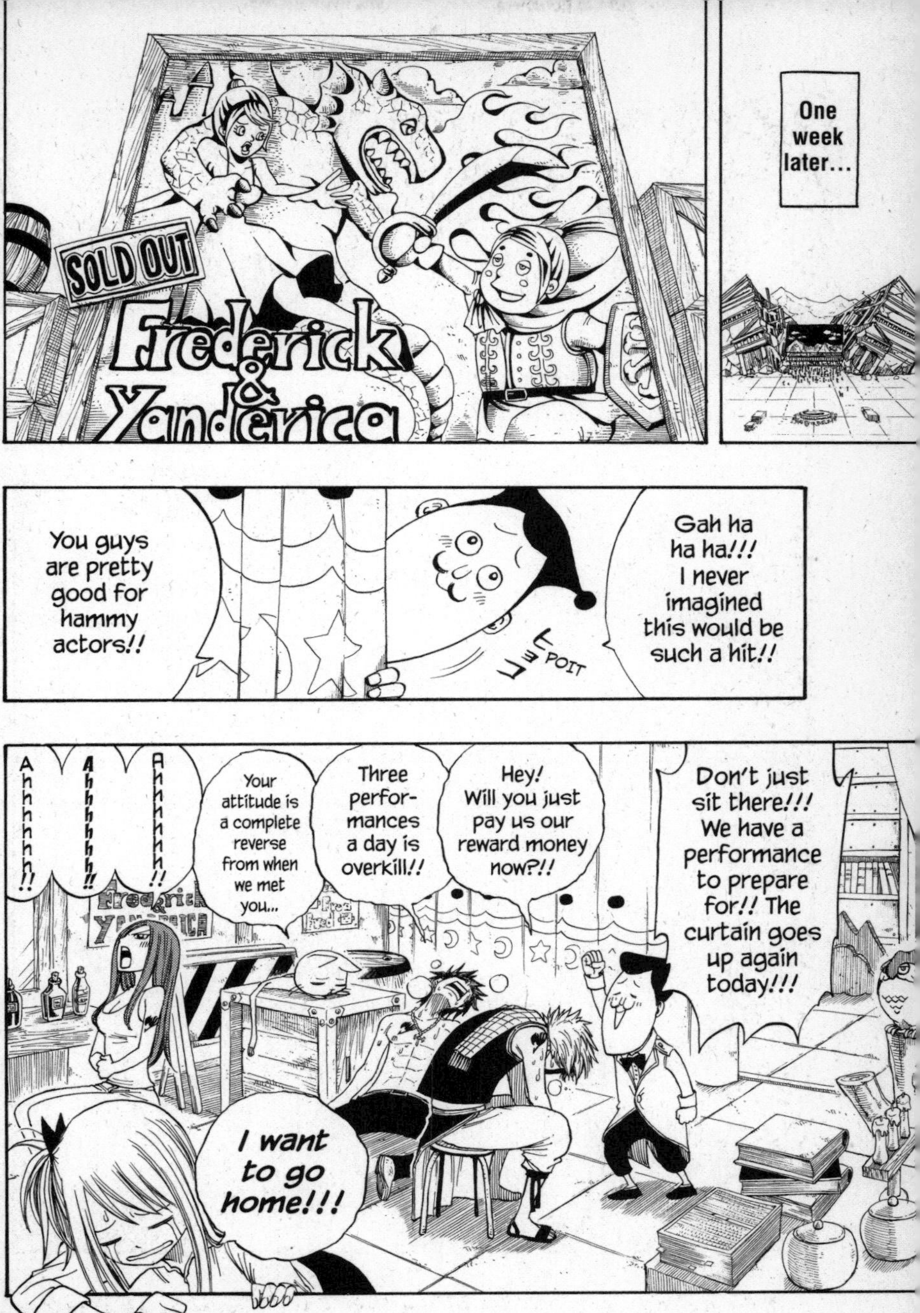
One week later...
SOLD OUT
Frederick & Yanderica
Gah ha ha ha!!! I never imagined this would be such a hit!!
POIT
You guys are pretty good for hammy actors!!
Don't just sit there!!! We have a performance to prepare for!! The curtain goes up again today!!!
Hey! Will you just pay us our reward money now?!!
Three perfor-mances a day is overkill!!
Your attitude is a complete reverse from when we met you...
Ahhhhhh!!
Ahhhhhhh!!
Ahhhhhhh!!
I want to go home!!!

FAIRY TAIL

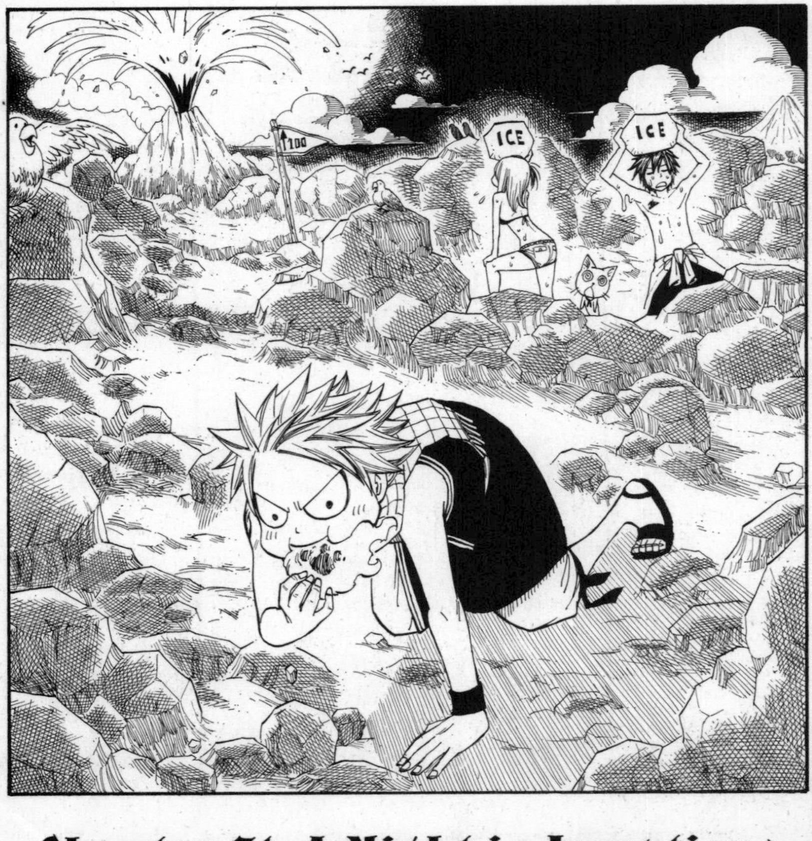
ICE
ICE
100

Chapter 71: A Night in Impatiens

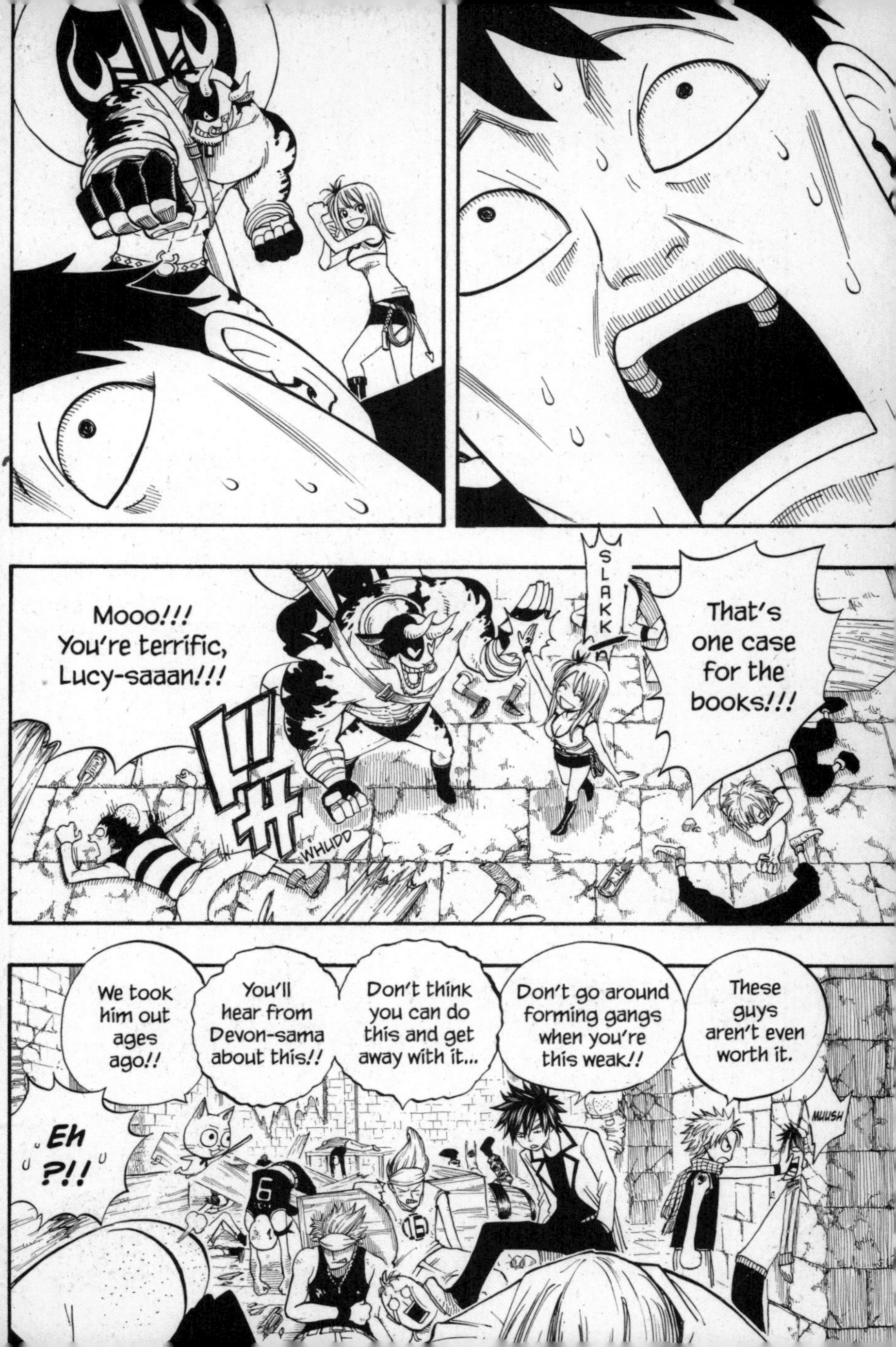
That's one case for the books!!!
SLAKK
Mooo!!! You're terrific, Lucy-saaan!!!
WHUDD
These guys aren't even worth it.
MUUSH
Don't go around forming gangs when you're this weak!!
Don't think you can do this and get away with it...
You'll hear from Devon-sama about this!!
We took him out ages ago!!
Eh ?!!

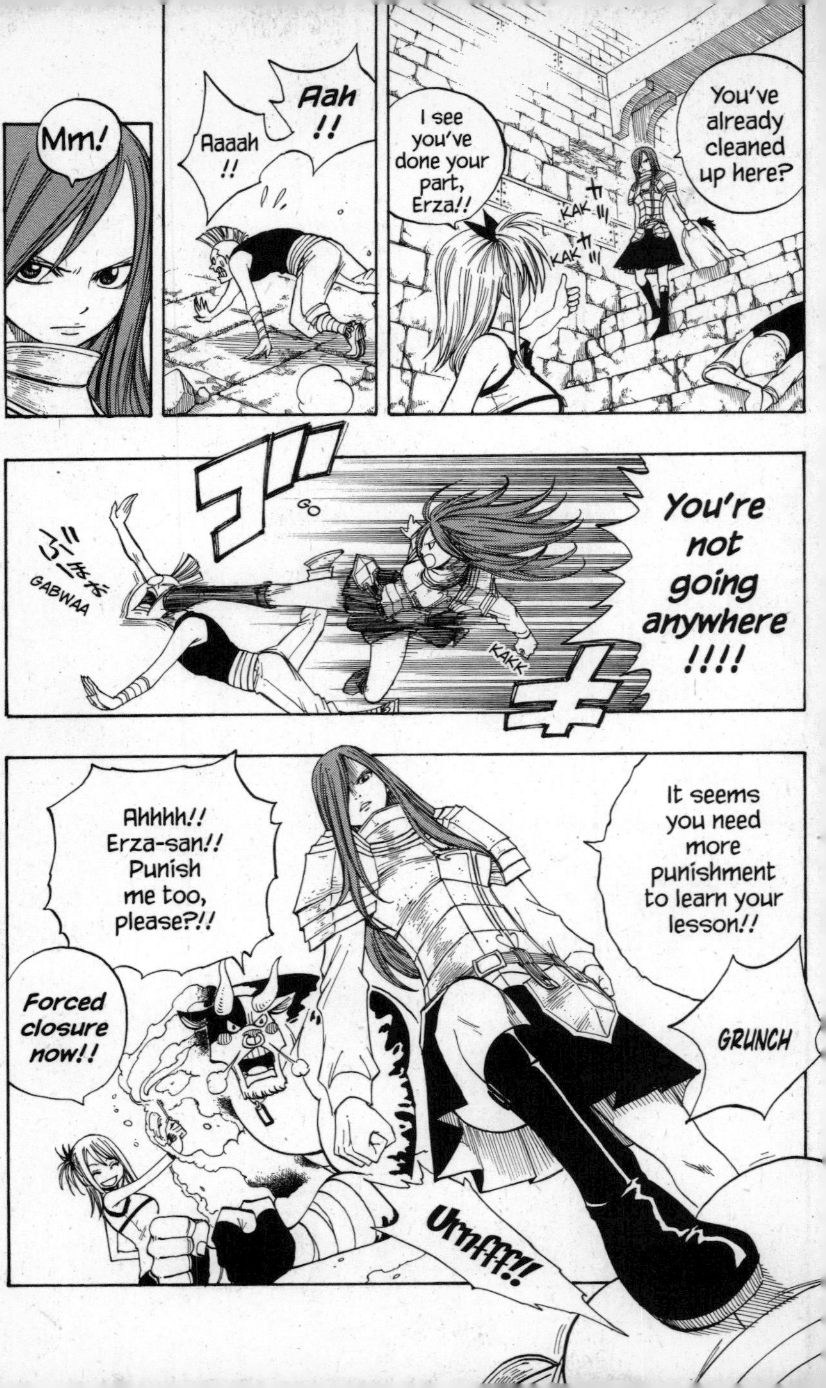
You've already cleaned up here?
I see you've done your part, Erza!!
KAK
KAK
Aah!!
Aaaah!!
Mm!
You're not going anywhere!!!!
GO
KAKK
GABWAA
It seems you need more punishment to learn your lesson!!
GRUNCH
Ahhhh!! Erza-san!! Punish me too, please?!!
Forced closure now!!
Urmfff!!

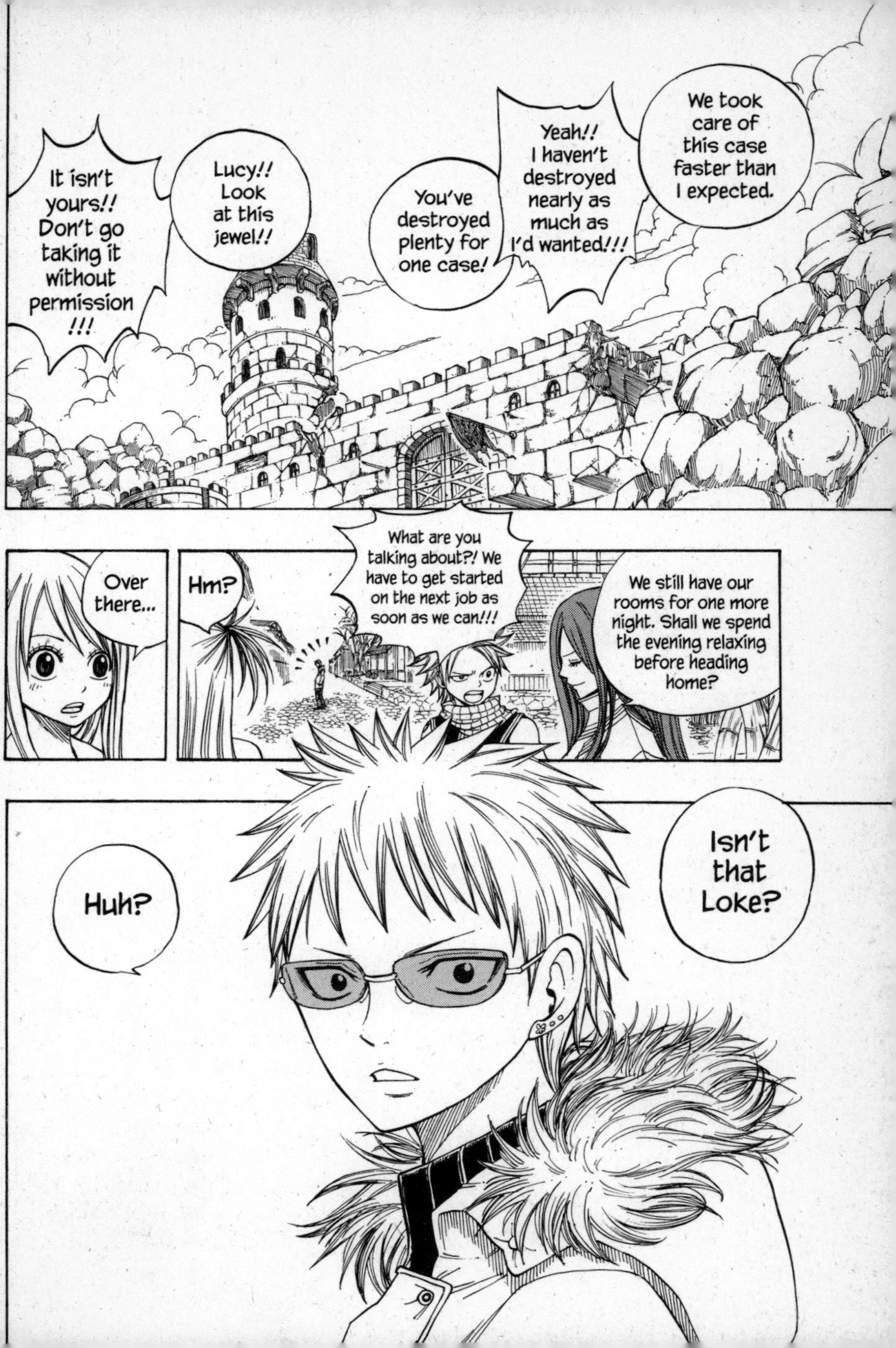
We took care of this case faster than I expected.
Yeah!! I haven't destroyed nearly as much as I'd wanted!!!
You've destroyed plenty for one case!
Lucy!! Look at this jewel!!
It isn't yours!! Don't go taking it without permission!!!
We still have our rooms for one more night. Shall we spend the evening relaxing before heading home?
What are you talking about?! We have to get started on the next job as soon as we can!!!
Hm?
Over there...
Isn't that Loke?
Huh?

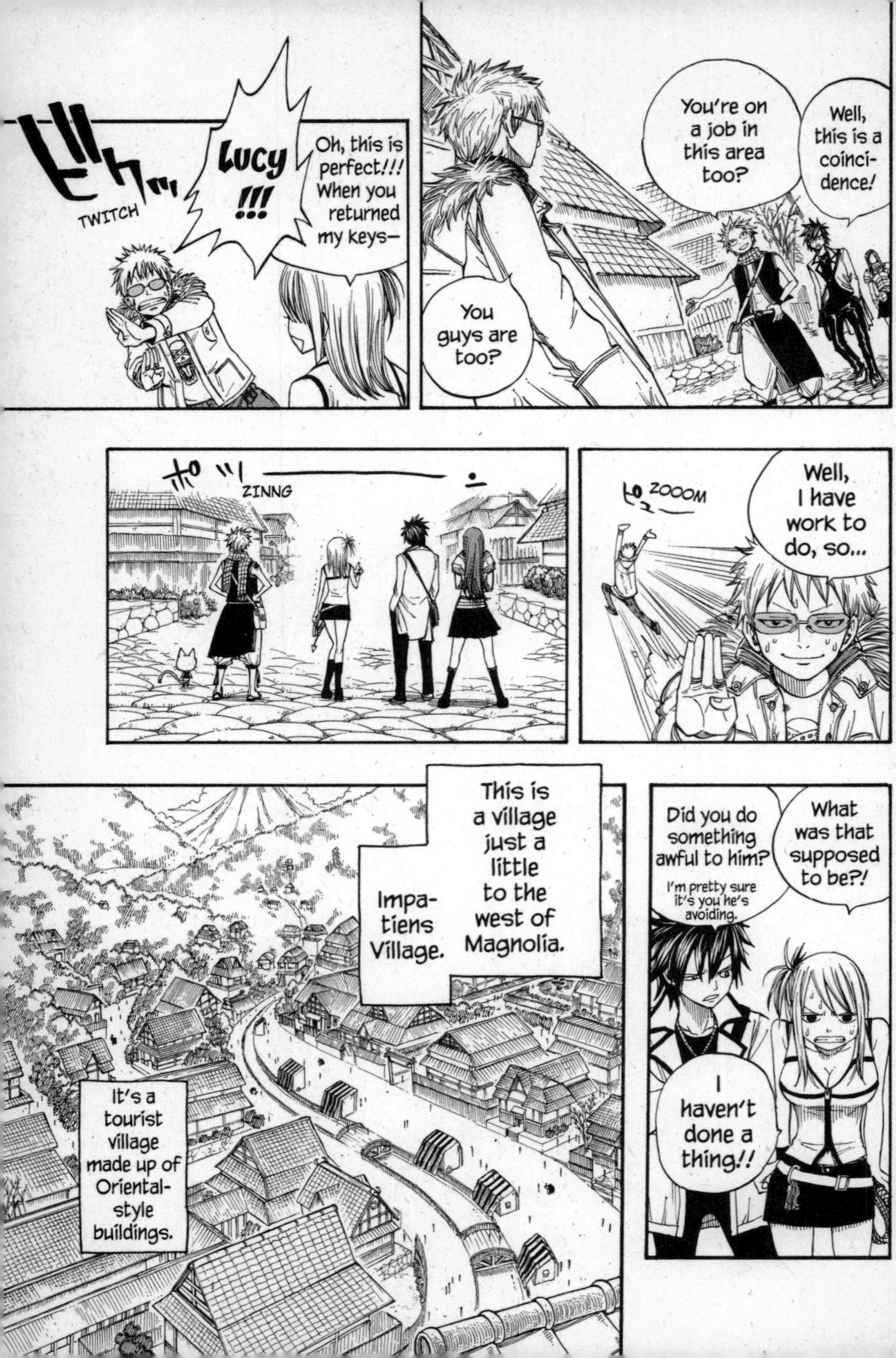
Well, this is a coincidence!
You're on a job in this area too?
You guys are too?
Oh, this is perfect!!! When you returned my keys—
Lucy!!!
TWITCH
Well, I have work to do, so...
ZOOOM
ZINNG
What was that supposed to be?!
Did you do something awful to him?
I'm pretty sure it's you he's avoiding.
I haven't done a thing!!
This is a village just a little to the west of Magnolia.
Impatiens Village.
It's a tourist village made up of Oriental-style buildings.

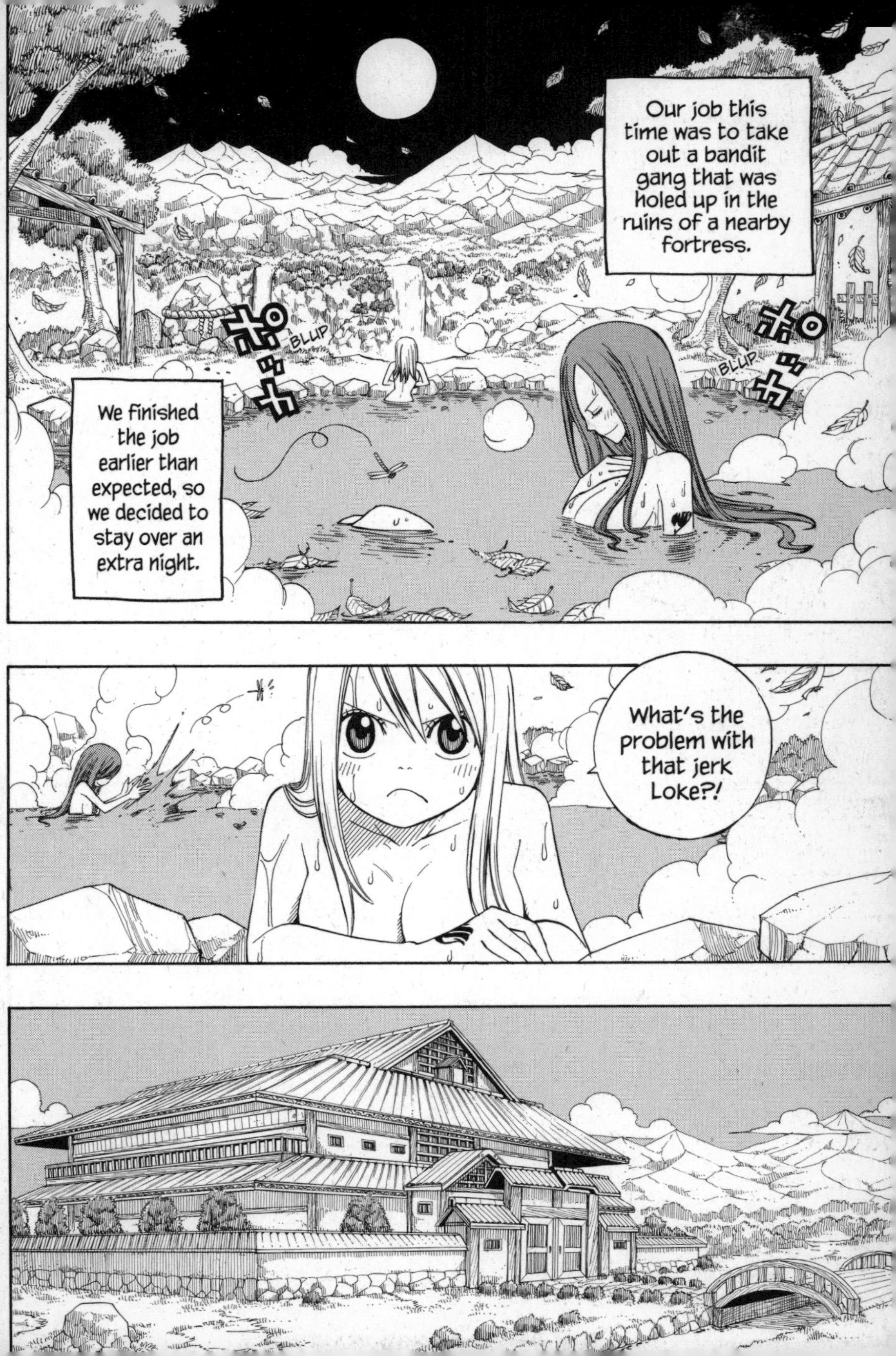
Our job this time was to take out a bandit gang that was holed up in the ruins of a nearby fortress.
BLUP
BLUP
We finished the job earlier than expected, so we decided to stay over an extra night.
What's the problem with that jerk Loke?!

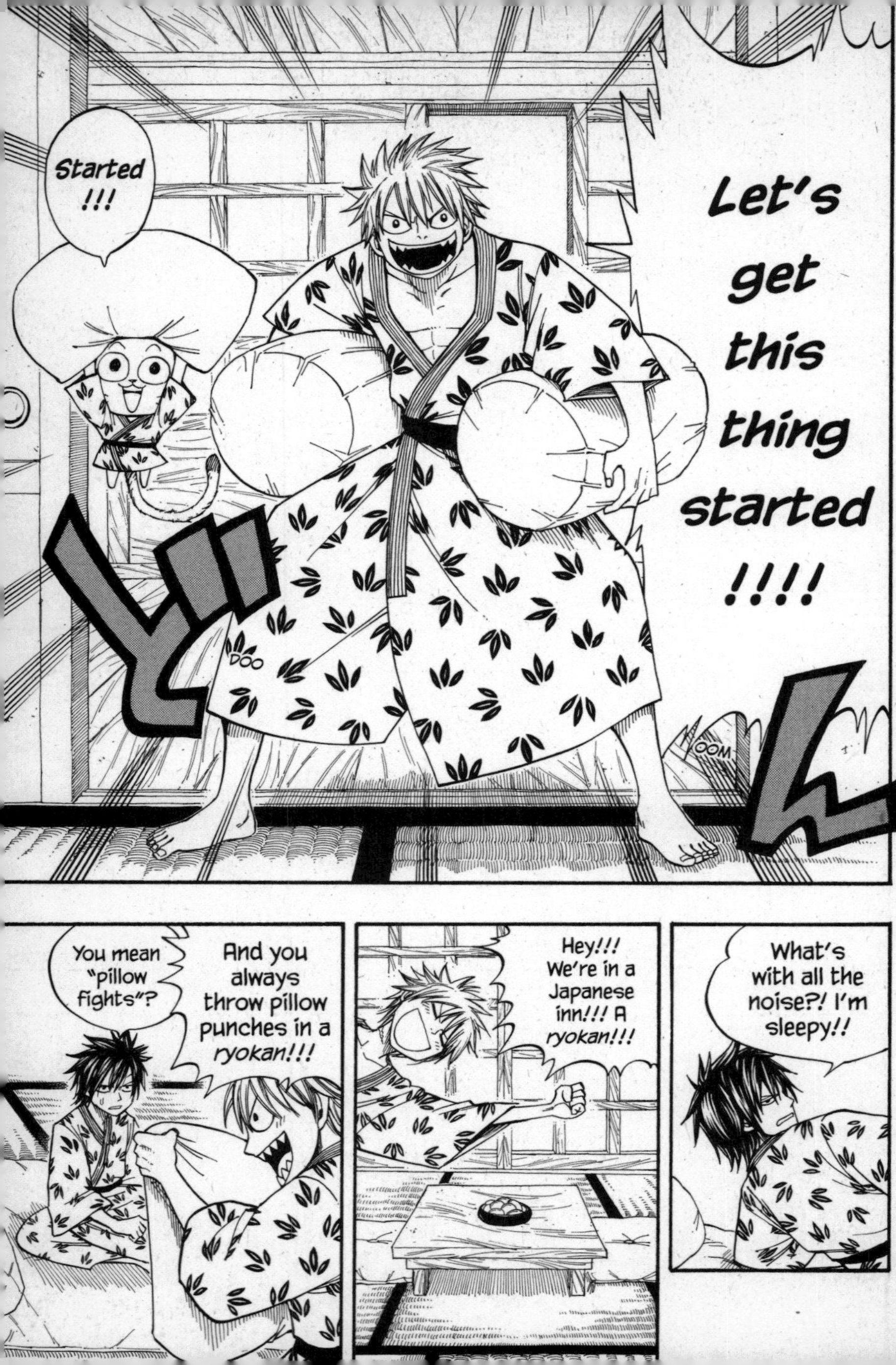
Let's get this thing started!!!!
Started!!!
OOM
DOO
What's with all the noise?! I'm sleepy!!
Hey!!! We're in a Japanese inn!!! A *ryokan*!!!
And you always throw pillow punches in a *ryokan*!!!
You mean "pillow fights"?

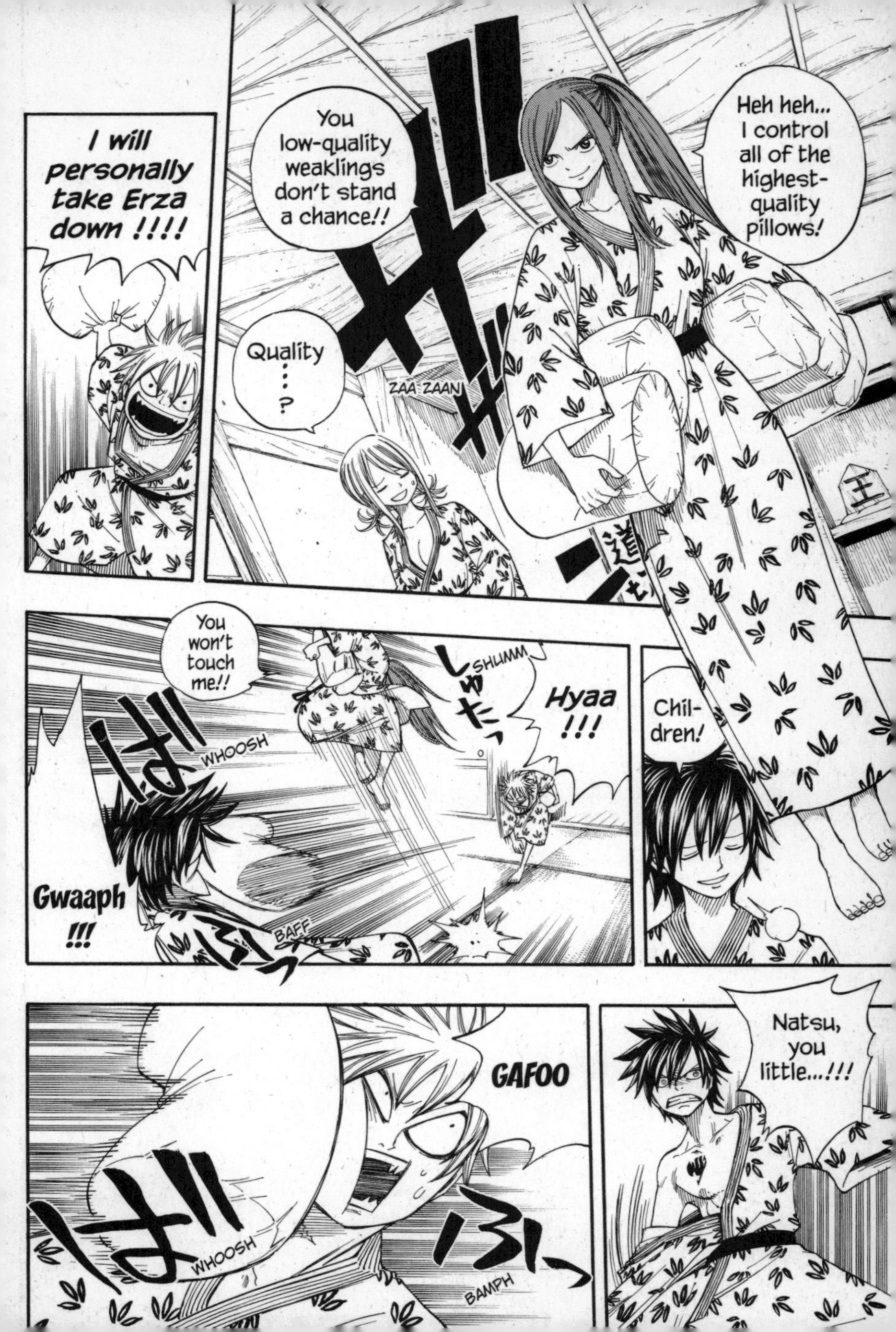

Heh heh... I control all of the highest-quality pillows!
You low-quality weaklings don't stand a chance!!
ZAA ZAAN
Quality...?
I will personally take Erza down!!!!
Children!
Hyaa!!!
SHUMM
You won't touch me!!
WHOOSH
Gwaaph!!!
BAFF
Natsu, you little...!!!
GAFOO
WHOOSH
BAMPH

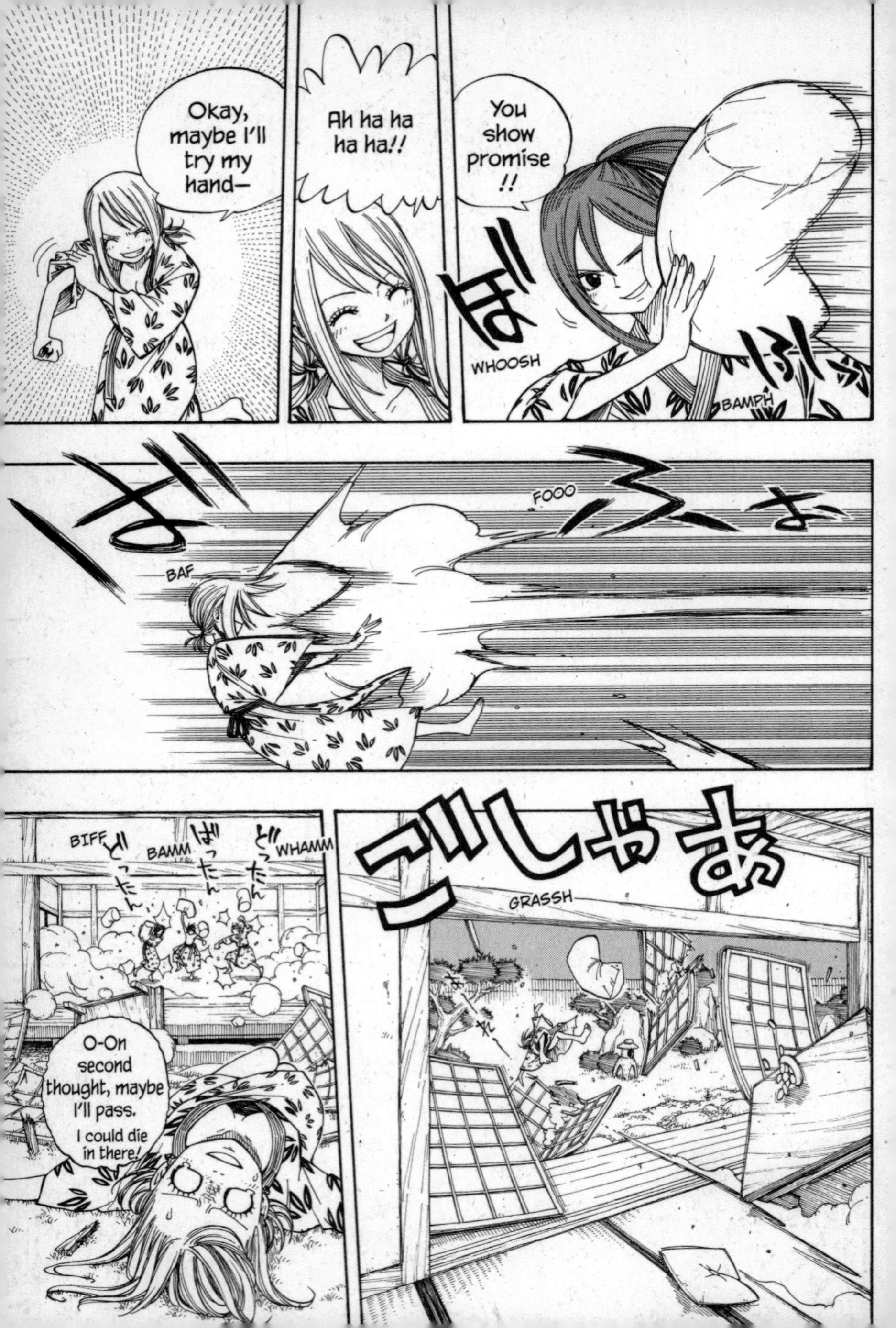
You show promise!!
WHOOSH
BAMPH
Ah ha ha ha!!
Okay, maybe I'll try my hand—
FOOO
BAF
ごしゃあ
GRASSH
WHAMM
どったん
BAMM
ばったん
BIFF
どったん
O-On second thought, maybe I'll pass.
I could die in there!

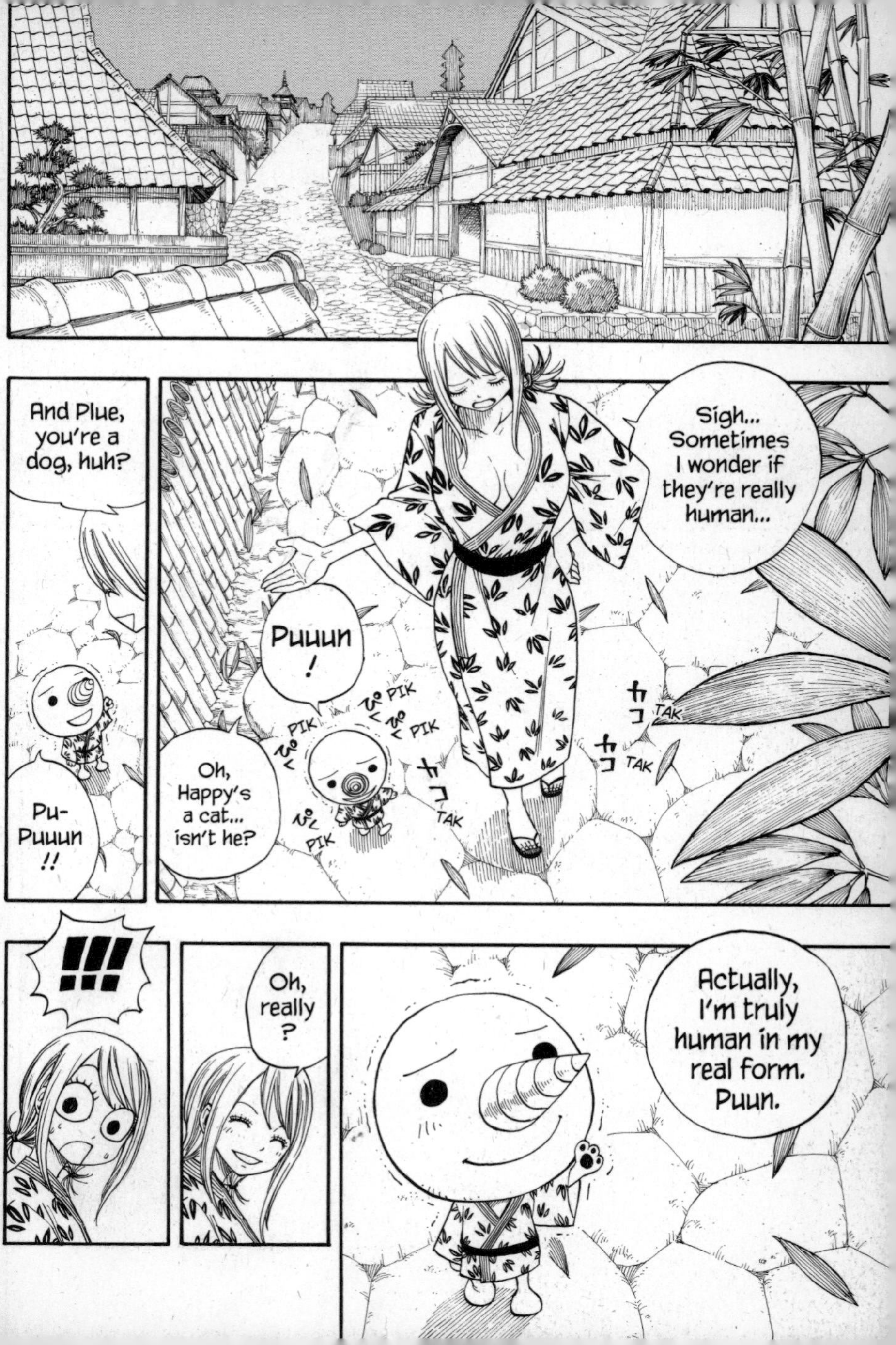
Sigh... Sometimes I wonder if they're really human...
Puuun!
PIK PIK
PIK PIK
TAK
TAK
TAK
Oh, Happy's a cat... isn't he?
And Plue, you're a dog, huh?
Pu-Puuun!!
Actually, I'm truly human in my real form. Puun.
Oh, really?
!!!

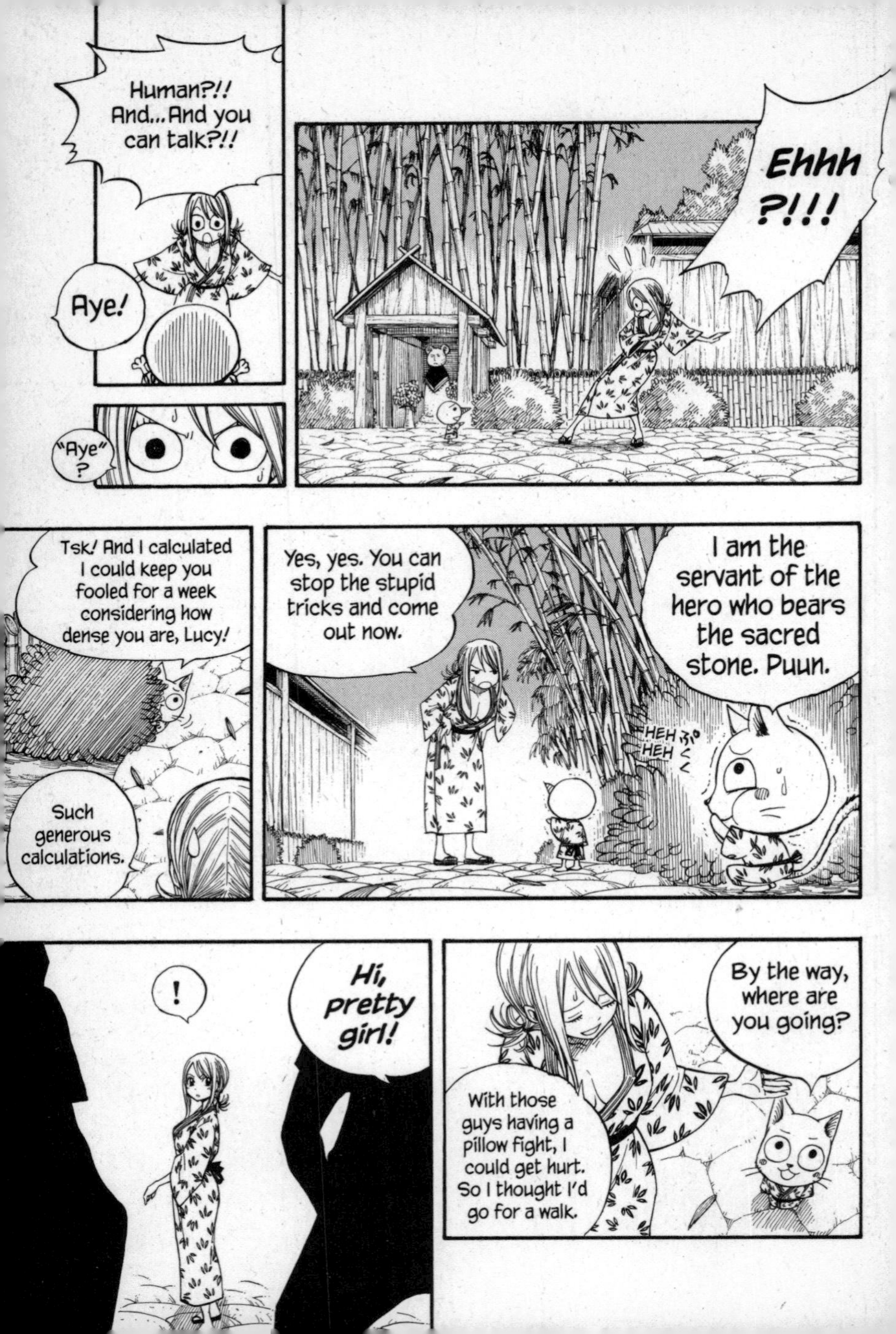
Ehhh ?!!!
Human?!! And...And you can talk?!!
Aye!
"Aye"?
I am the servant of the hero who bears the sacred stone. Puun.
HEH HEH
Yes, yes. You can stop the stupid tricks and come out now.
Tsk! And I calculated I could keep you fooled for a week considering how dense you are, Lucy!
Such generous calculations.
By the way, where are you going?
With those guys having a pillow fight, I could get hurt. So I thought I'd go for a walk.
Hi, pretty girl!
!

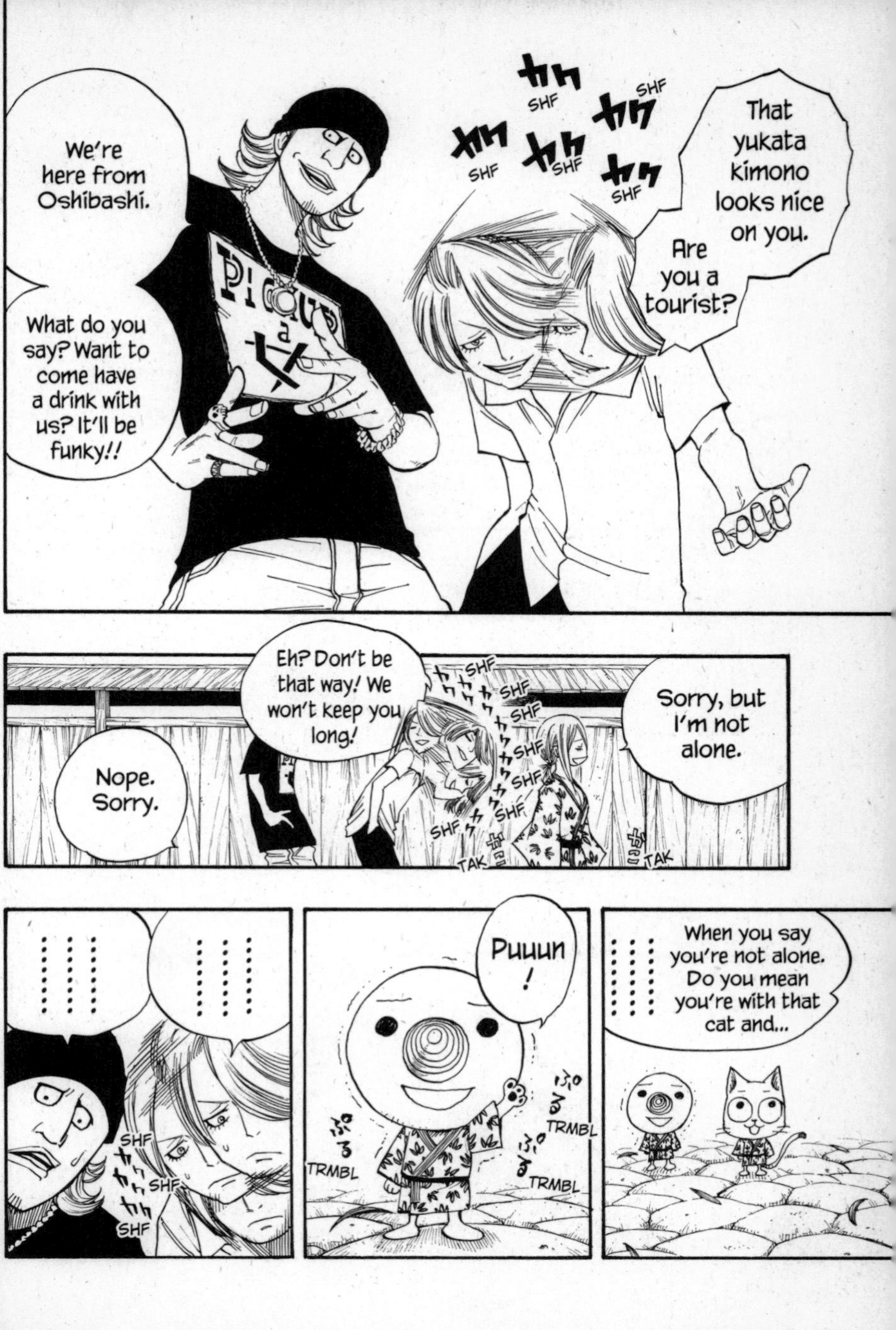

That yukata kimono looks nice on you.
Are you a tourist?
SHF
SHF
SHF
SHF
SHF
We're here from Oshibashi.
What do you say? Want to come have a drink with us? It'll be funky!!
Sorry, but I'm not alone.
TAK
Eh? Don't be that way! We won't keep you long!
SHF
SHF
SHF
SHF
SHF
SHF
SHF
TAK
Nope. Sorry.
When you say you're not alone. Do you mean you're with that cat and...
Puuun!
TRMBL
TRMBL
TRMBL
......!!!
......!!!
SHF
SHF
SHF

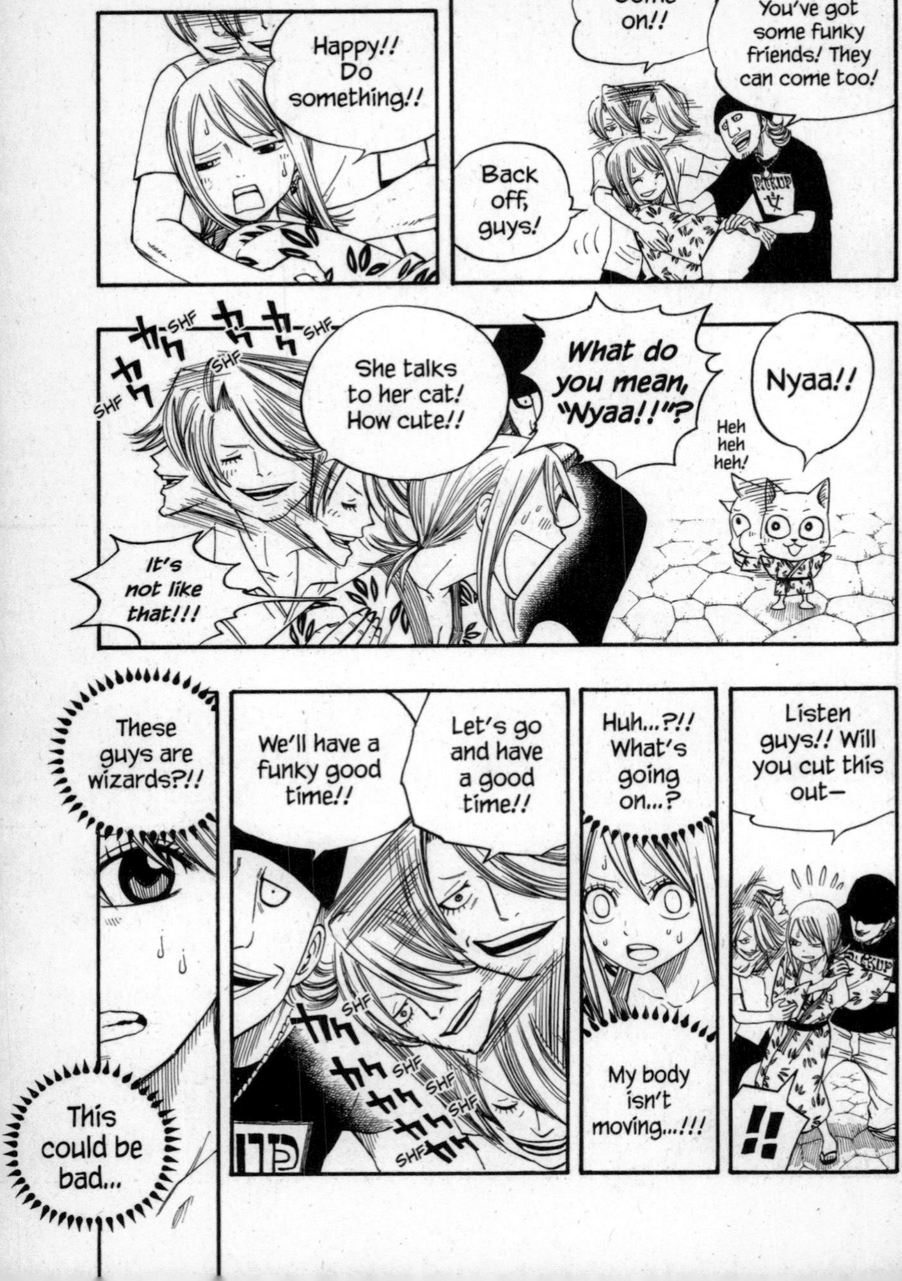
S-Sure... You've got some funky friends! They can come too!
Come on!!
Back off, guys!
Happy!! Do something!!
Nyaa!!
Heh heh heh!
What do you mean, "Nyaa!!"?
She talks to her cat! How cute!!
SHF SHF SHF SHF
It's not like that!!!
Listen guys!! Will you cut this out–
!!
Huh...?!! What's going on...?
My body isn't moving...!!!
Let's go and have a good time!!
We'll have a funky good time!!
SHF SHF SHF SHF
These guys are wizards?!!
This could be bad...

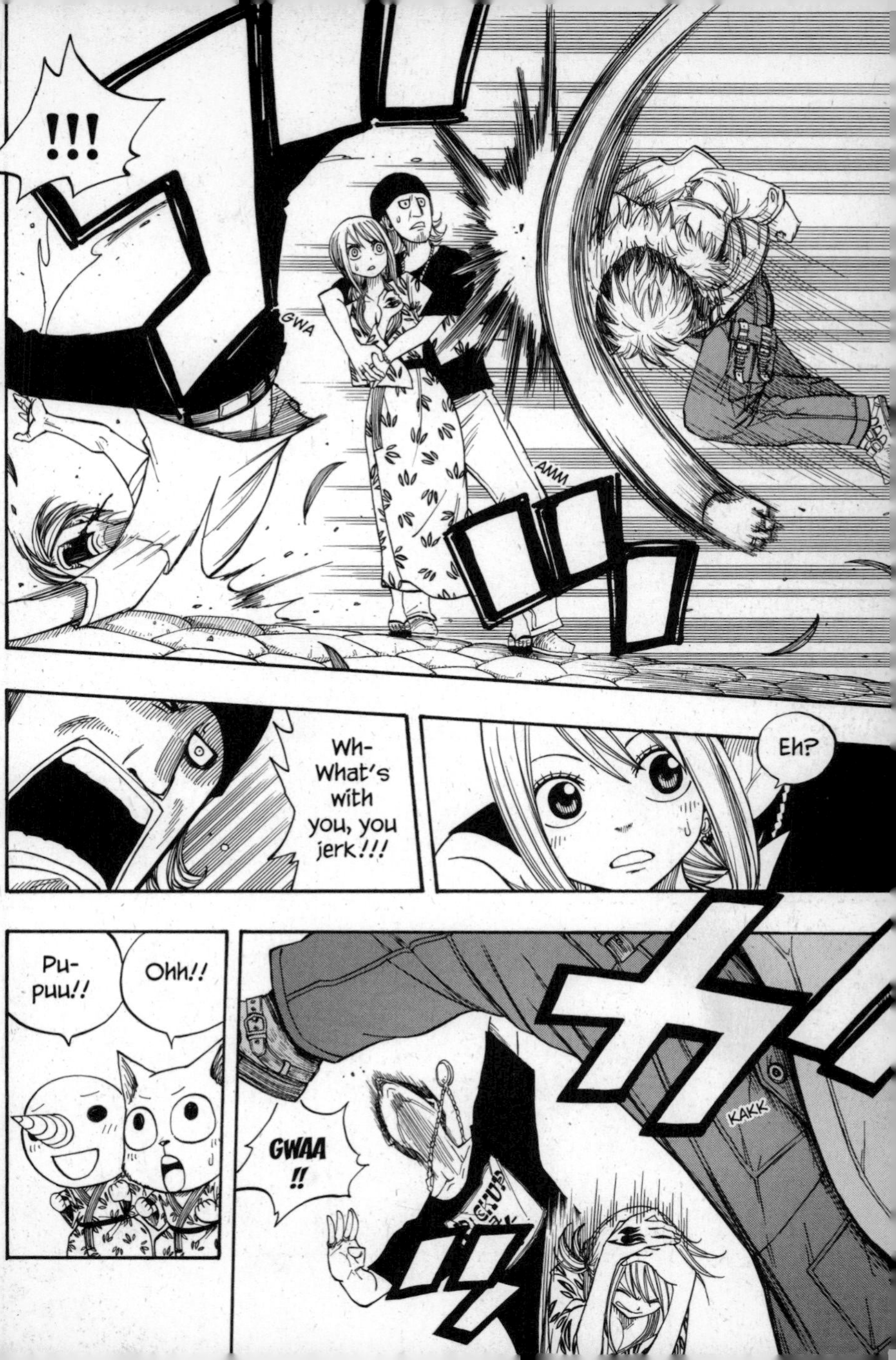
!!!
GWA
AMM
Eh?
Wh- What's with you, you jerk!!!
KAKK
GWAA !!
Ohh!!
Pu- puu!!

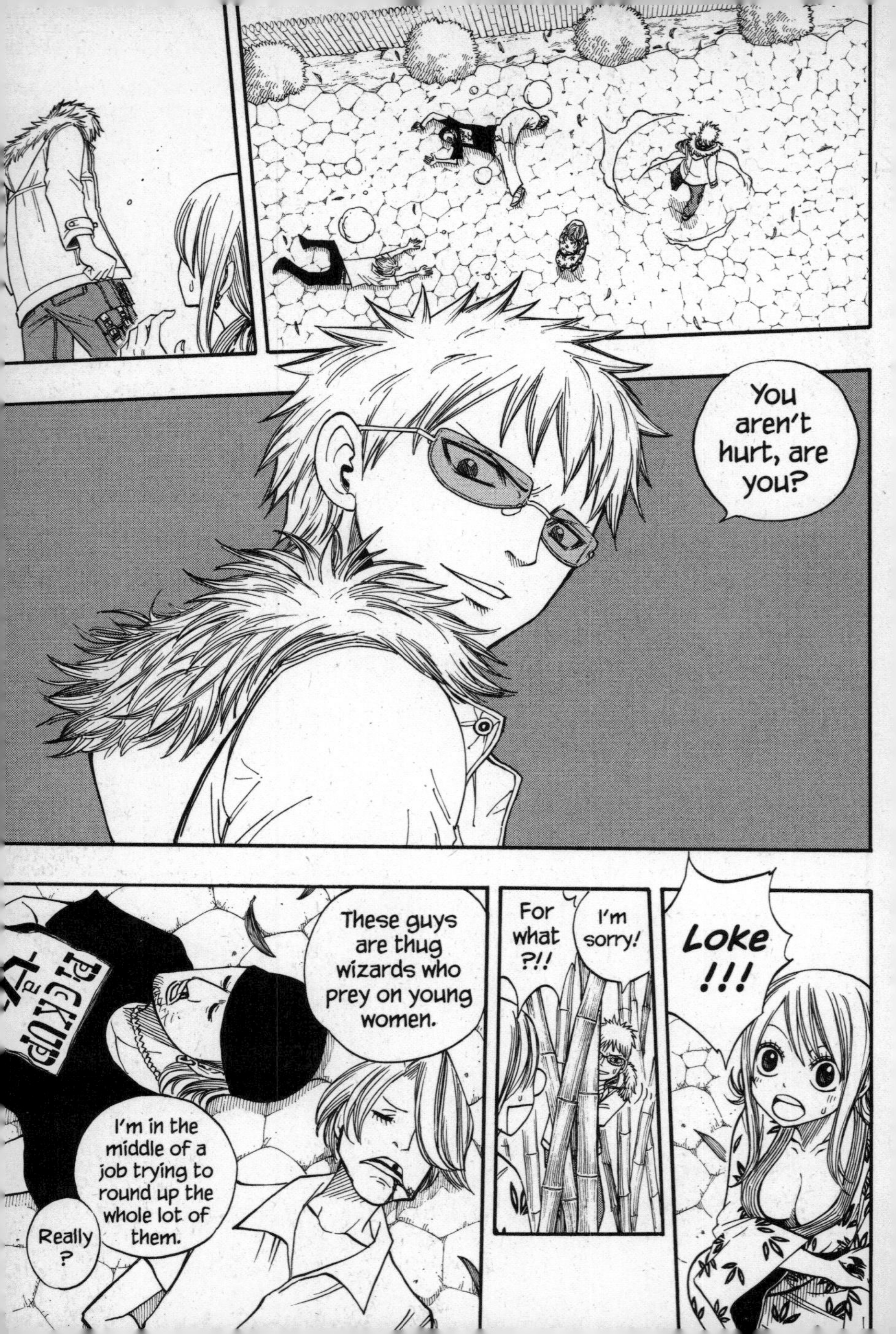
You aren't hurt, are you?
Loke!!!
I'm sorry!
For what?!!
These guys are thug wizards who prey on young women.
I'm in the middle of a job trying to round up the whole lot of them.
Really?

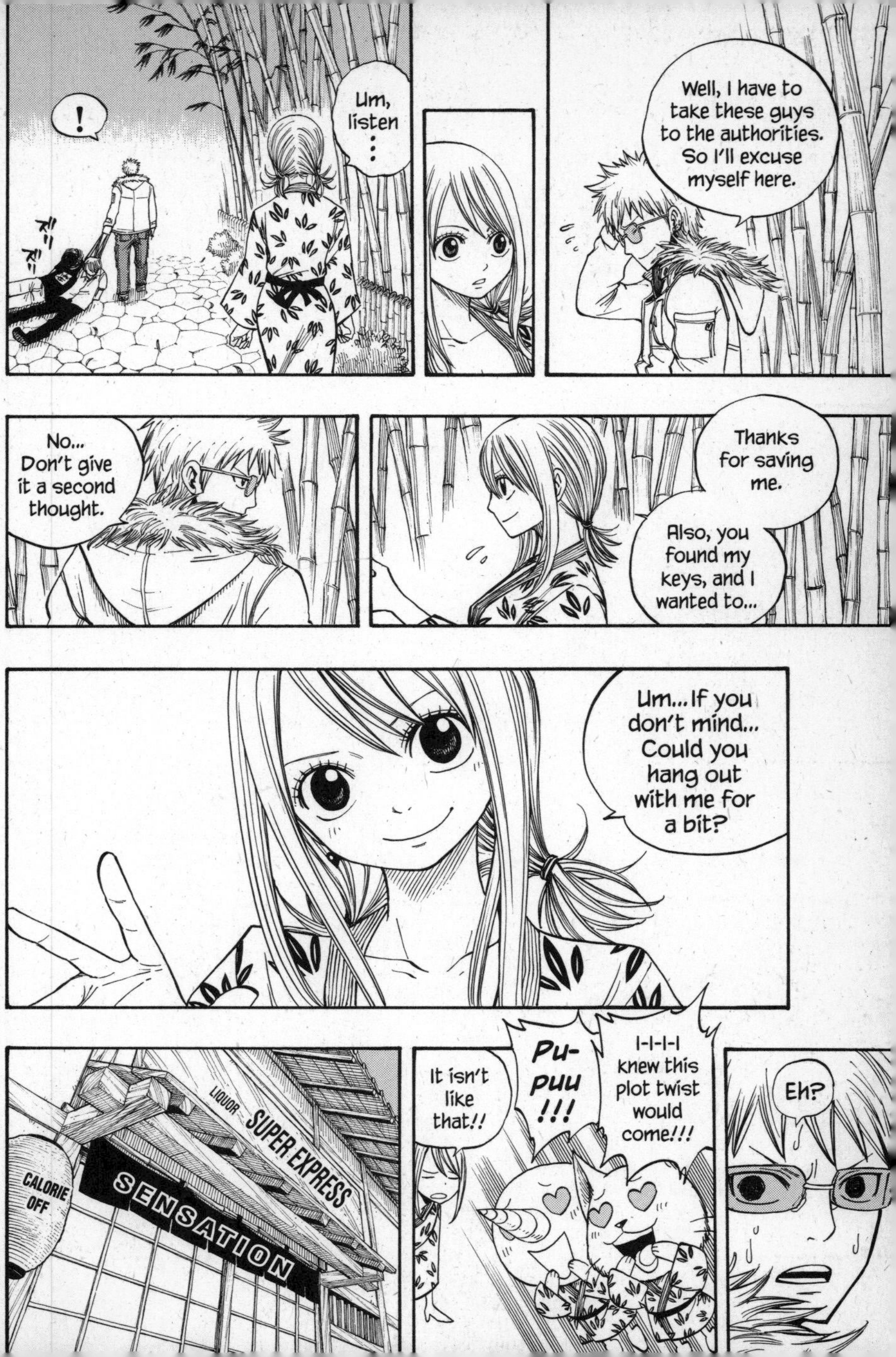
Well, I have to take these guys to the authorities. So I'll excuse myself here.
Um, listen...
!
Thanks for saving me.
Also, you found my keys, and I wanted to...
No... Don't give it a second thought.
Um...If you don't mind... Could you hang out with me for a bit?
Eh?
I-I-I-I knew this plot twist would come!!!
Pu-puu!!!
It isn't like that!!
LIQUOR
SUPER EXPRESS
SENSATION
CALORIE OFF

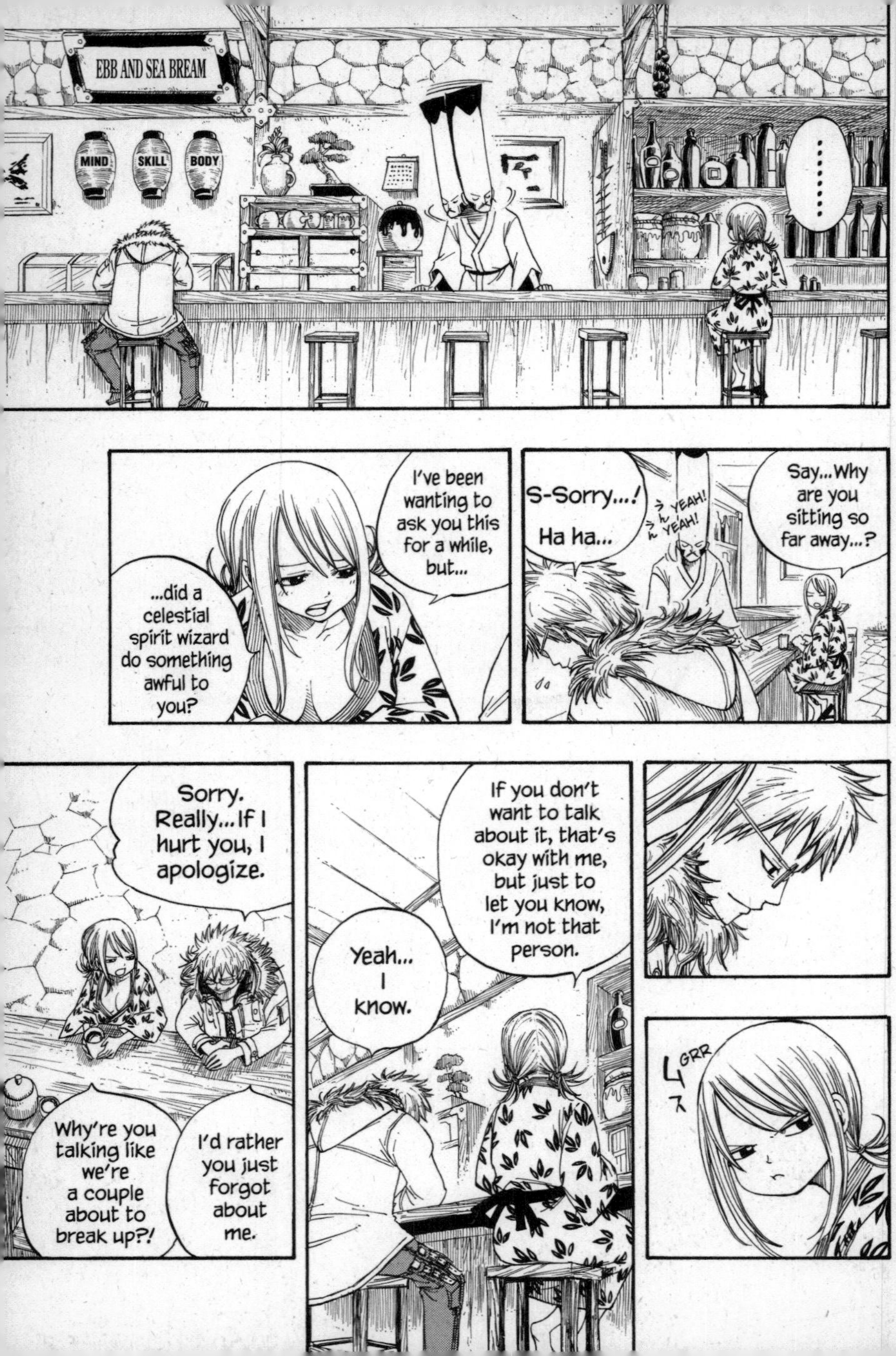
EBB AND SEA BREAM
MIND
SKILL
BODY
......
Say...Why are you sitting so far away...?
S-Sorry...!
Ha ha...
うん YEAH!
うん YEAH!
I've been wanting to ask you this for a while, but...
...did a celestial spirit wizard do something awful to you?
ム GRR
If you don't want to talk about it, that's okay with me, but just to let you know, I'm not that person.
Yeah... I know.
Sorry. Really...If I hurt you, I apologize.
I'd rather you just forgot about me.
Why're you talking like we're a couple about to break up?!

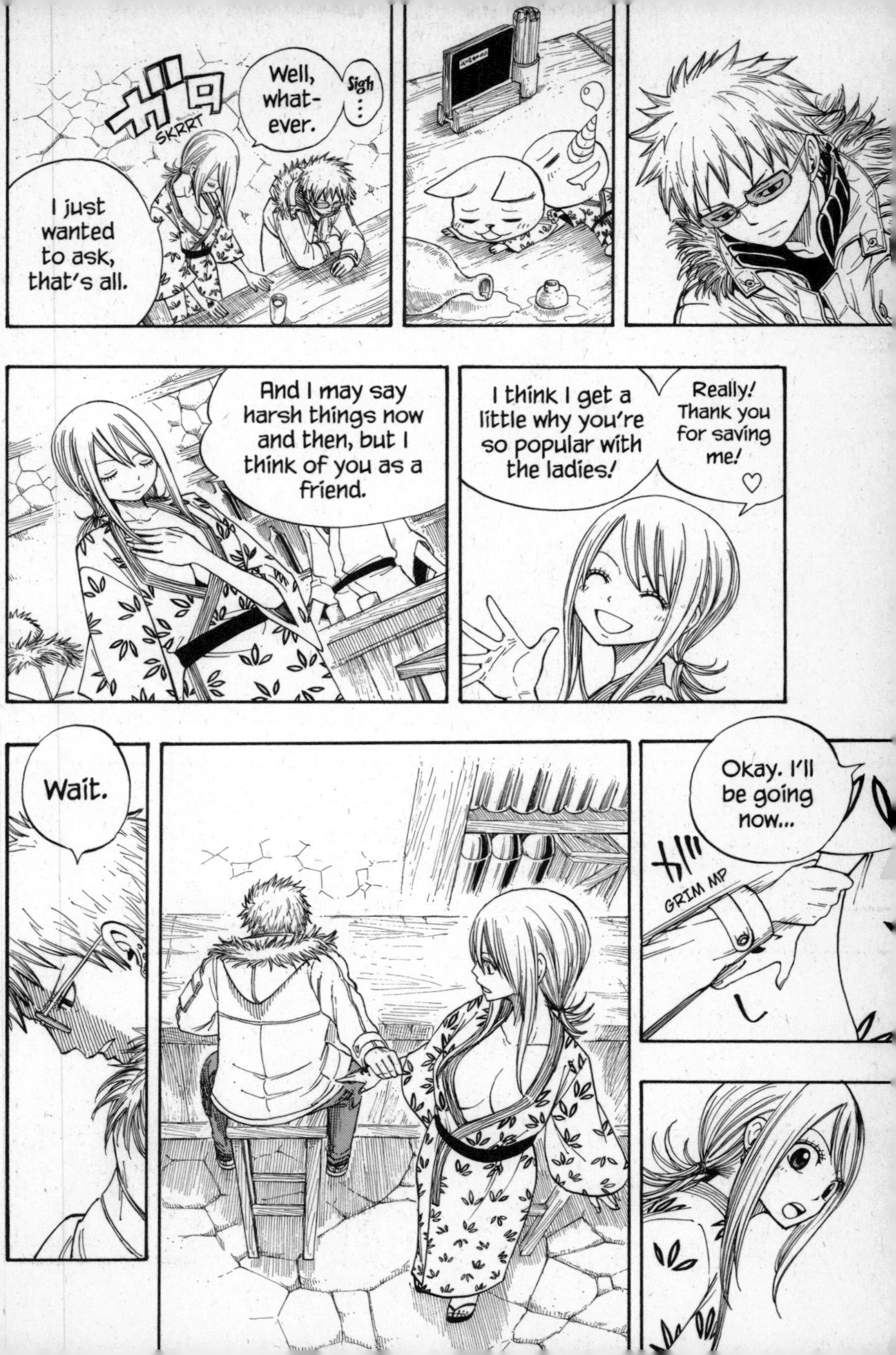
Sigh...
Well, whatever.
SKRRT
I just wanted to ask, that's all.
Really! Thank you for saving me! ♡
I think I get a little why you're so popular with the ladies!
And I may say harsh things now and then, but I think of you as a friend.
Okay. I'll be going now...
GRIM MP
Wait.

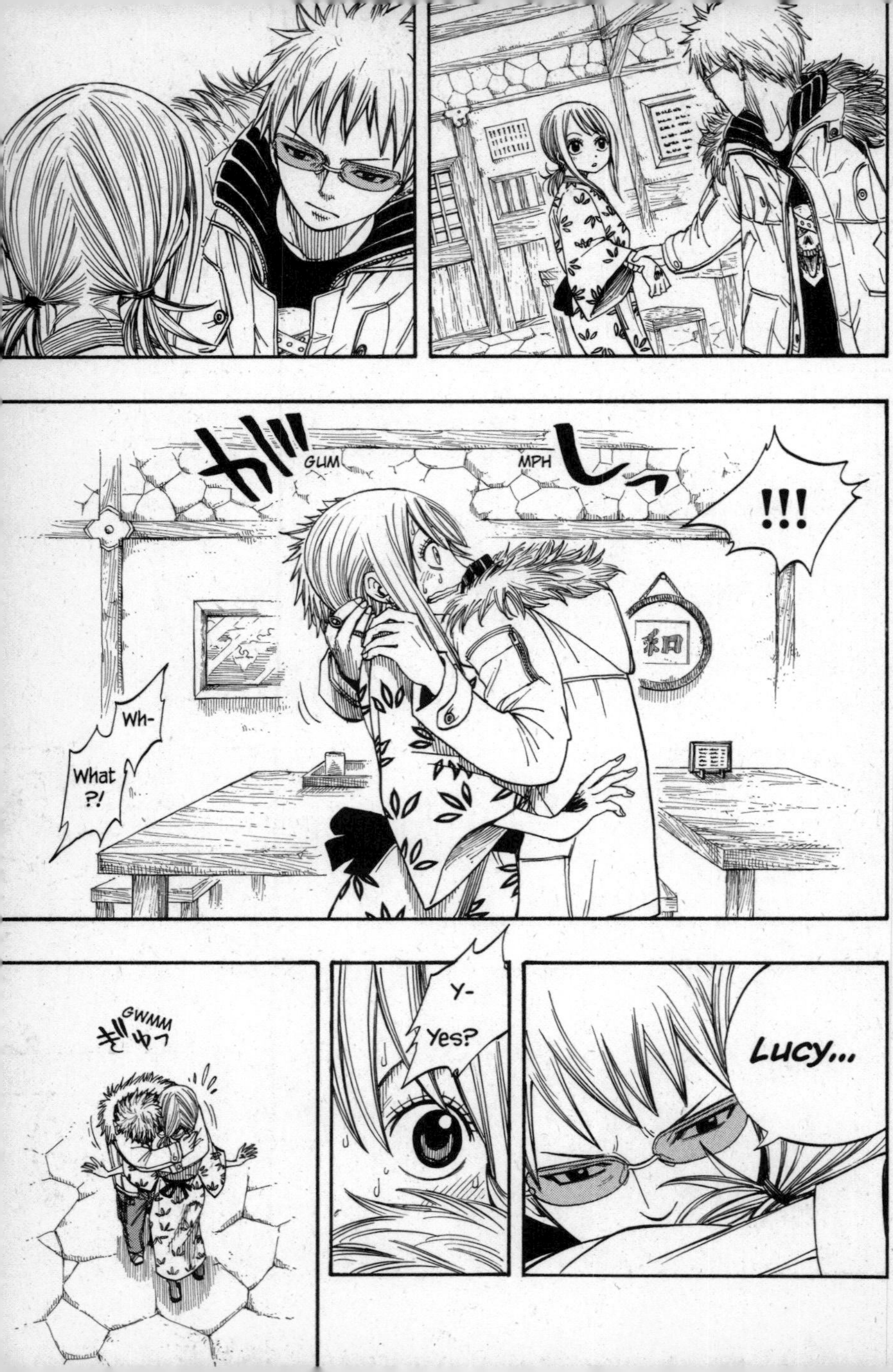

ガッ
GUM
しっ
MPH
!!!
Wh-
What ?!
Lucy...
Y-
Yes?
ぎゅっ
GWMM

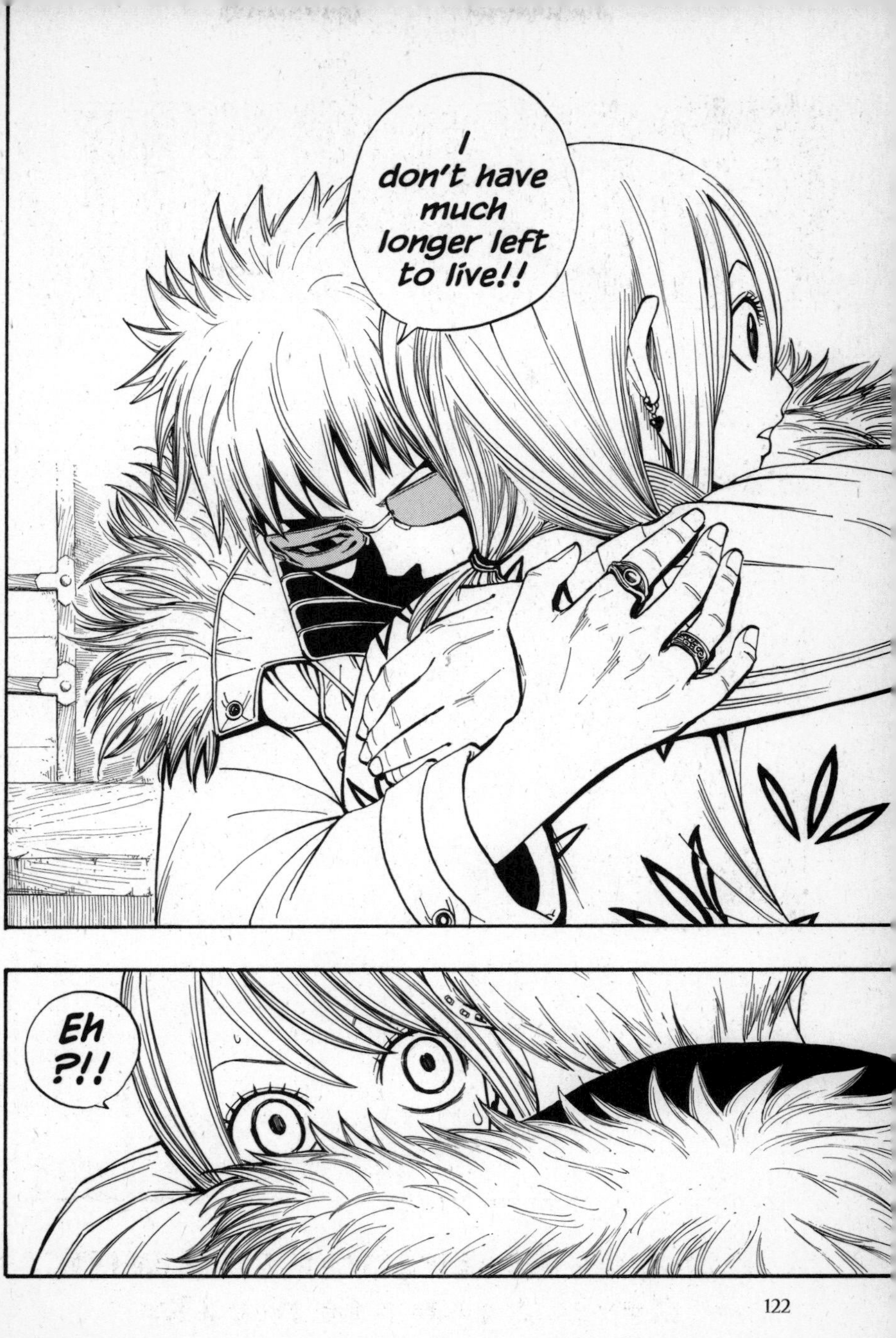
I don't have much longer left to live!!
Eh ?!!

FAIRY TAIL

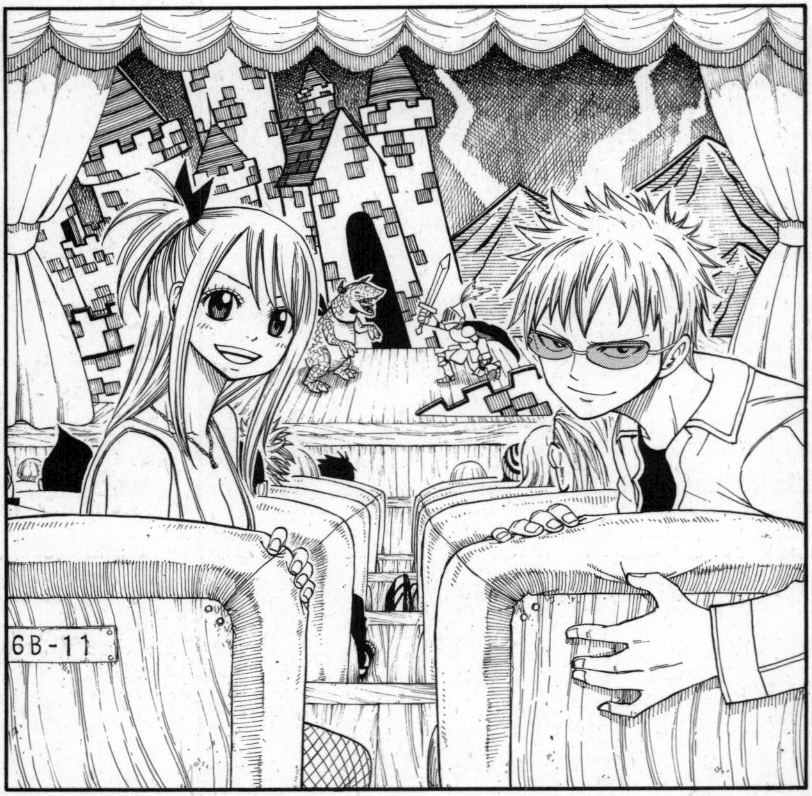
6B-11

Chapter 72: The Star That Will Never Return to the Sky

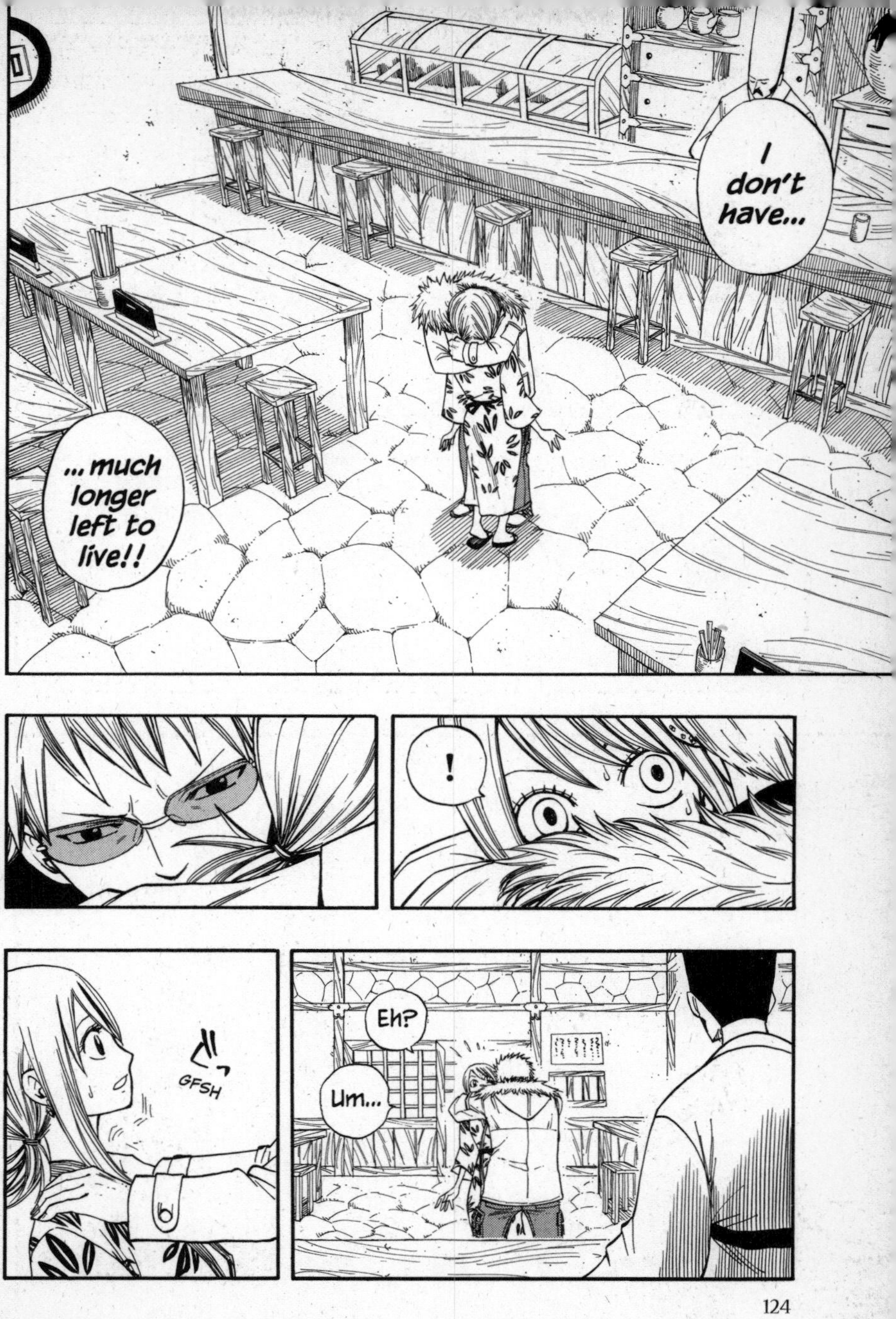
I don't have...
...much longer left to live!!
!
Eh?
Um...
GFSH

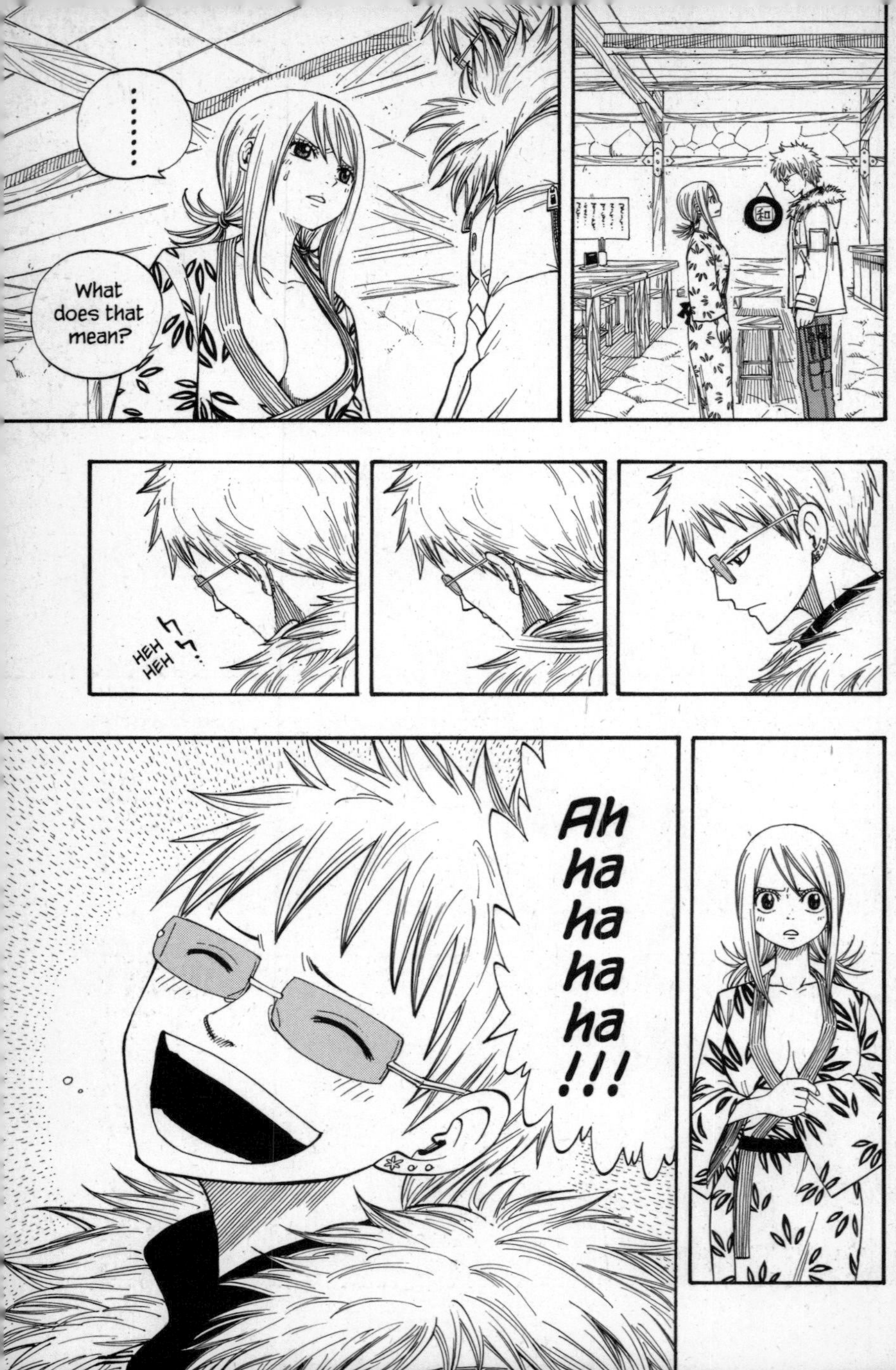
和
......
What does that mean?
HEH HEH...
Ah ha ha ha ha ha!!!

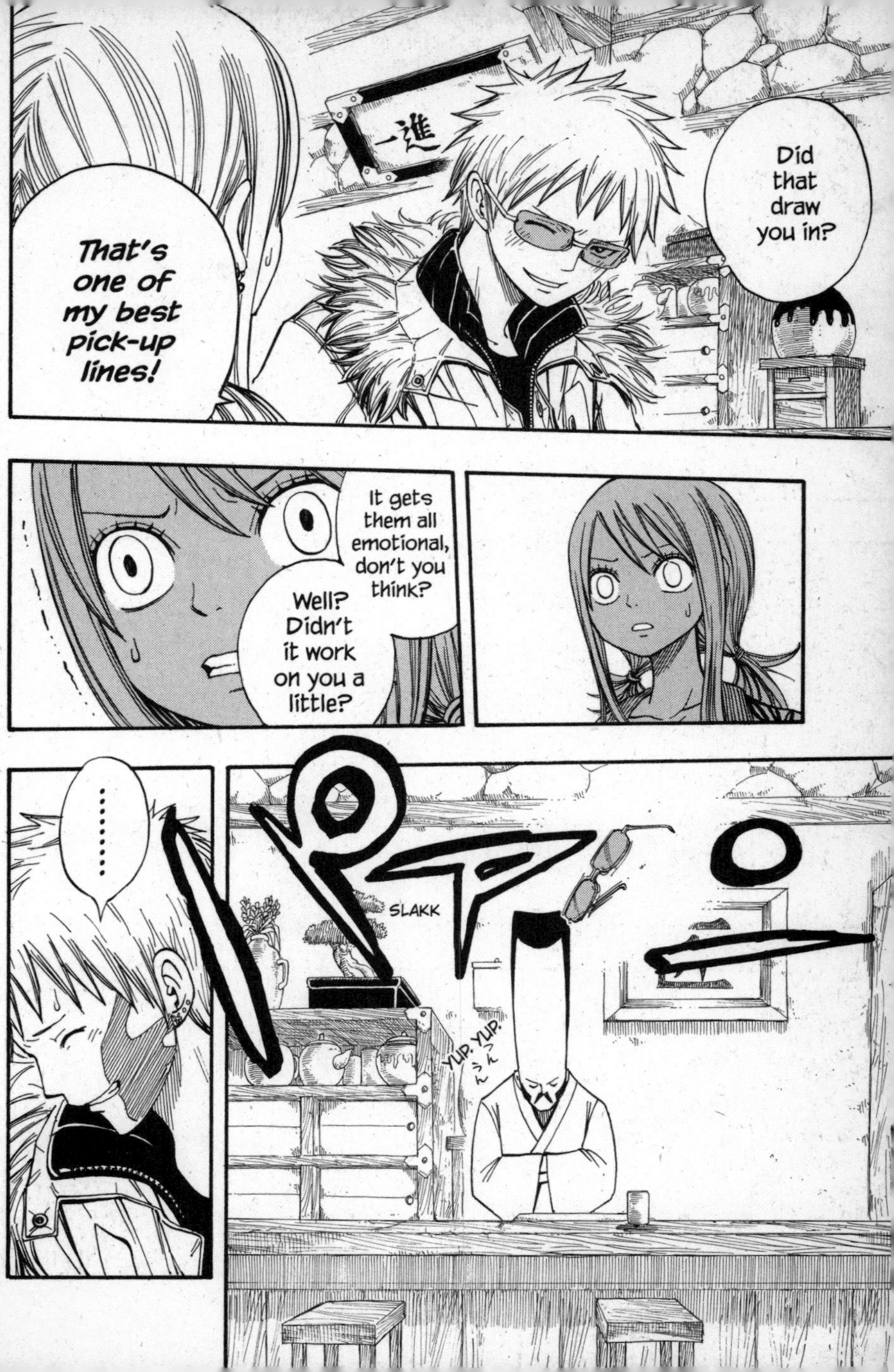
Did that draw you in?
一進
That's one of my best pick-up lines!
It gets them all emotional, don't you think?
Well? Didn't it work on you a little?
SLAKK
YUP. YUP.
うん うん
……

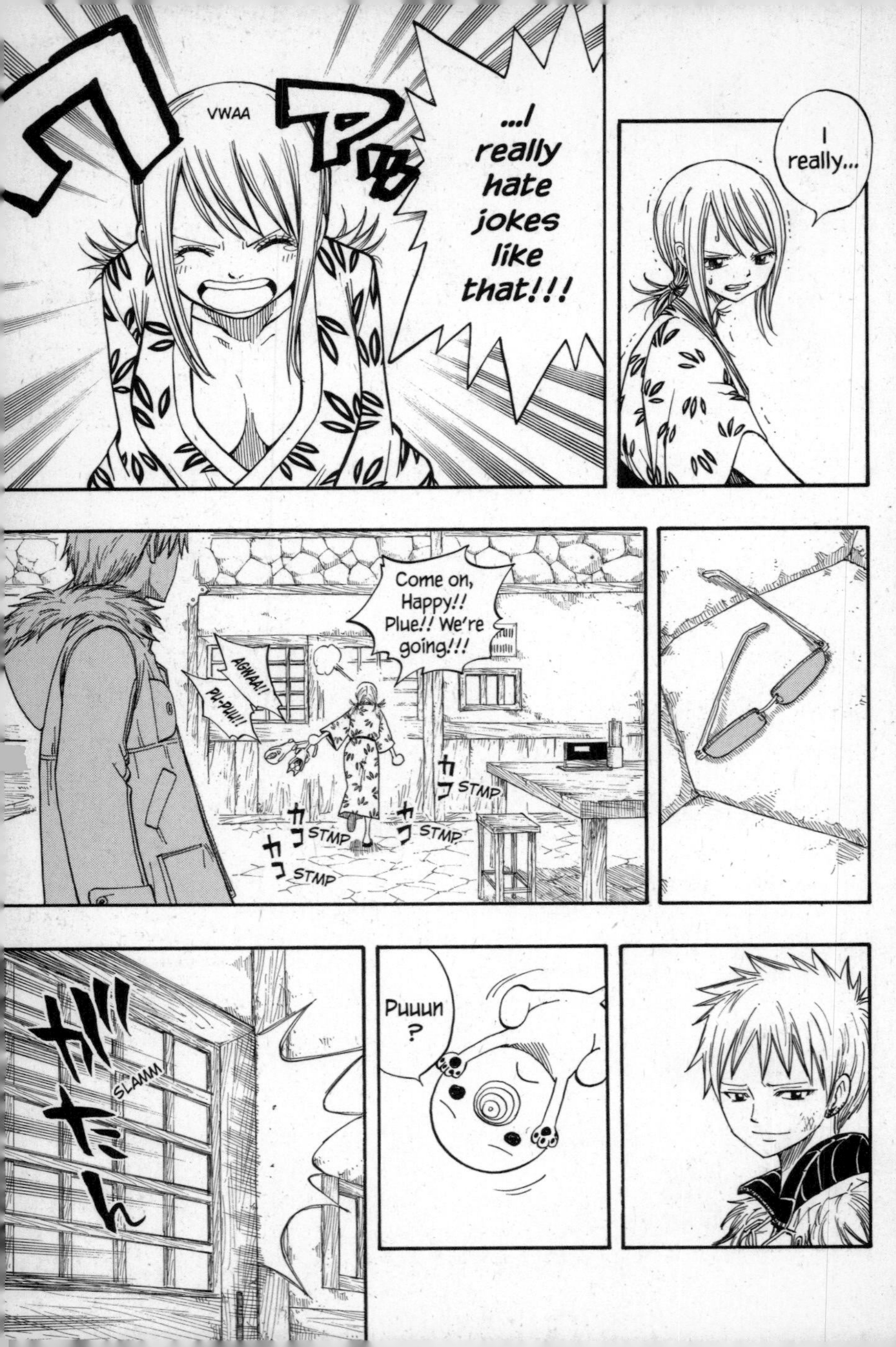
I really...
VWAA
...I really hate jokes like that!!!
Come on, Happy!! Plue!! We're going!!!
AGWAA!!
PU-PUU!!
STMP
STMP
STMP
STMP
Puuun ?
SLAMM

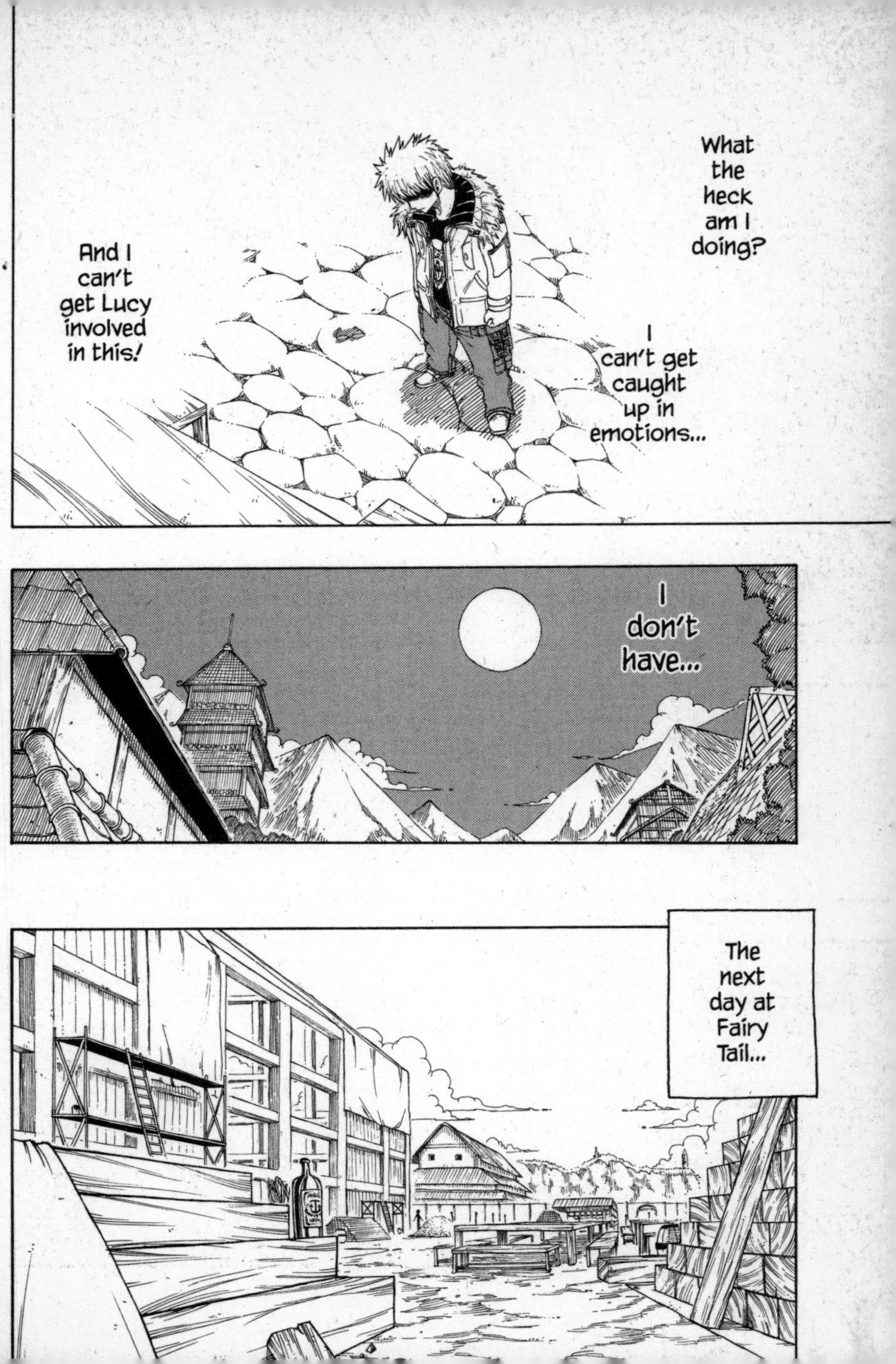
What the heck am I doing?
I can't get caught up in emotions...
And I can't get Lucy involved in this!
I don't have...
The next day at Fairy Tail...

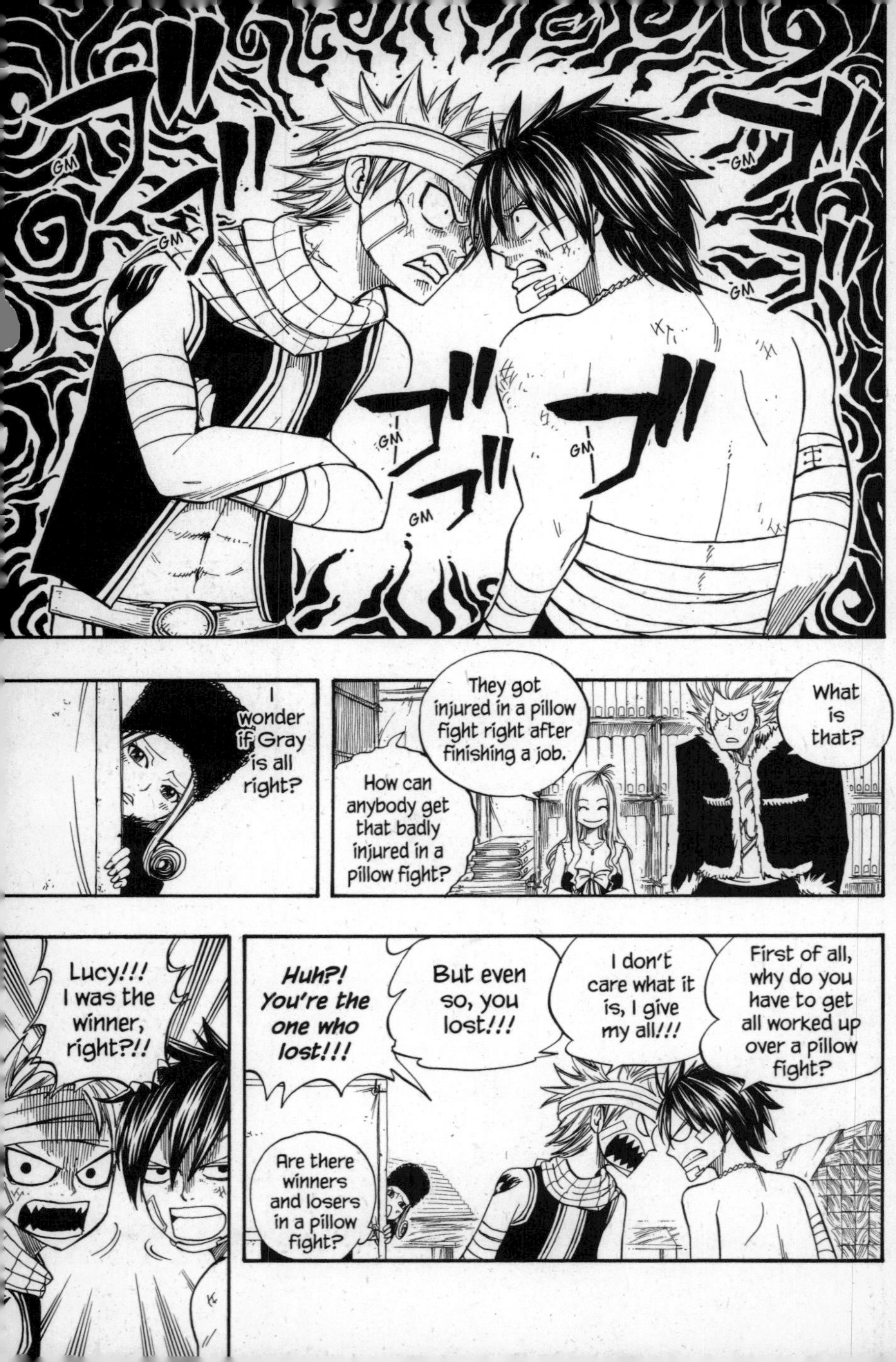
GM
GM
GM
GM
GM
GM
What is that?
They got injured in a pillow fight right after finishing a job.
How can anybody get that badly injured in a pillow fight?
I wonder if Gray is all right?
First of all, why do you have to get all worked up over a pillow fight?
I don't care what it is, I give my all!!!
But even so, you lost!!!
Huh?! You're the one who lost!!!
Are there winners and losers in a pillow fight?
Lucy!!! I was the winner, right?!!

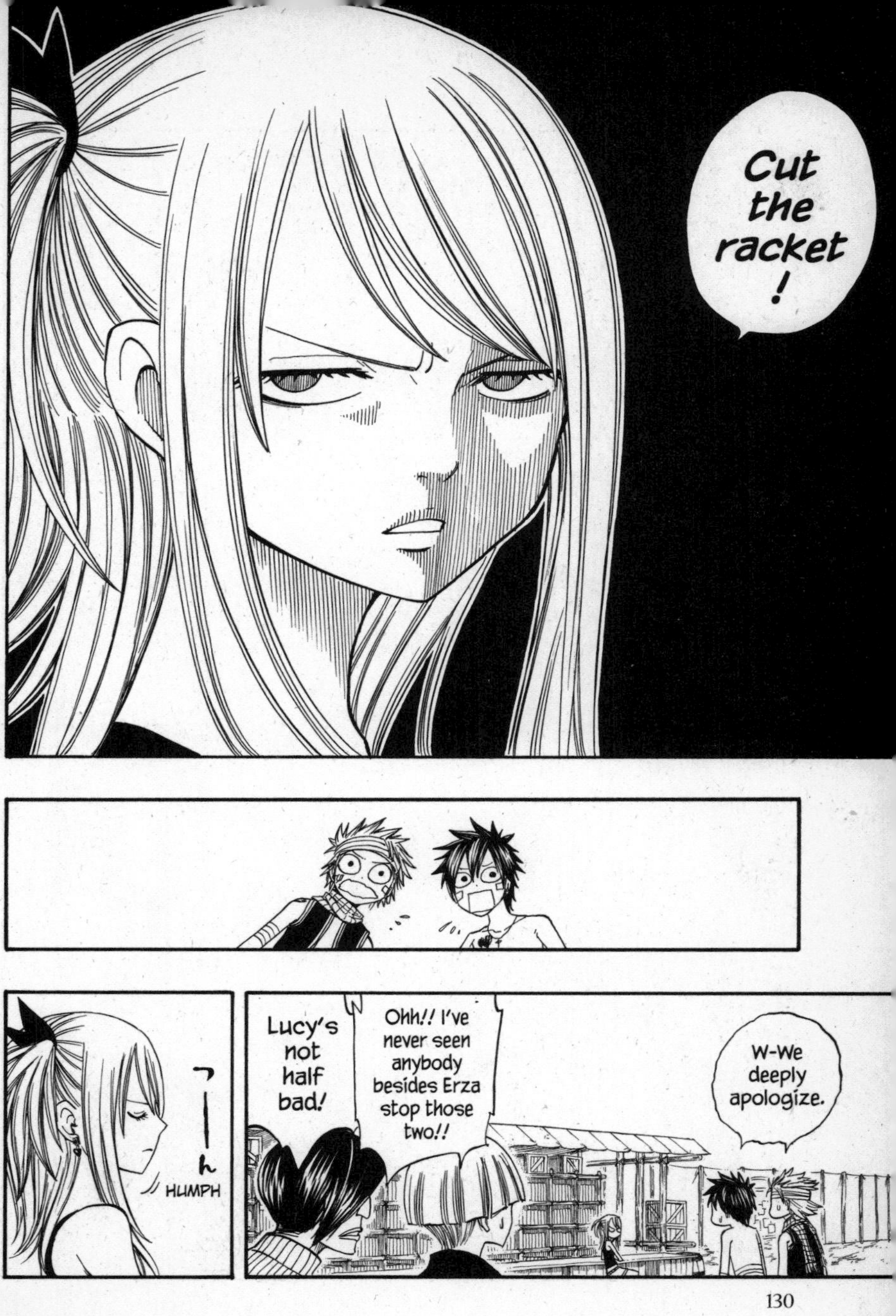
Cut the racket!
W-We deeply apologize.
Ohh!! I've never seen anybody besides Erza stop those two!!
Lucy's not half bad!
HUMPH

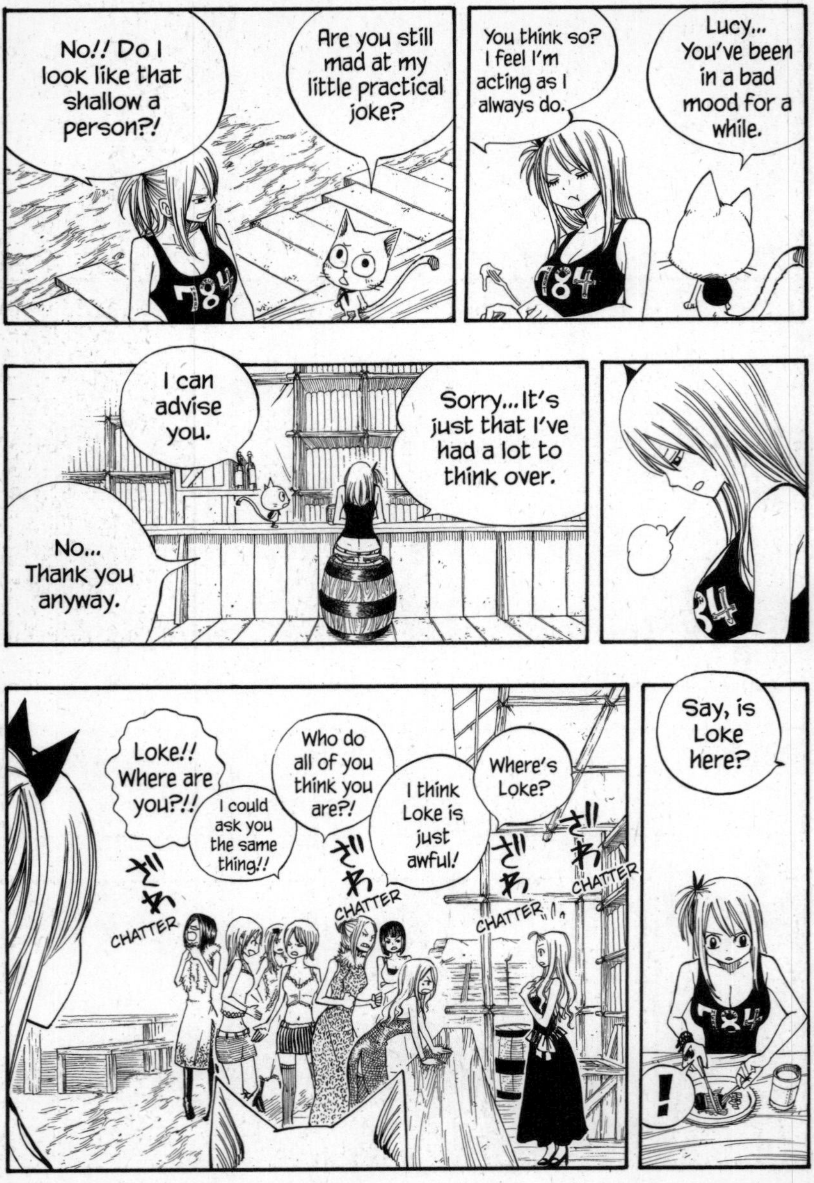
Lucy... You've been in a bad mood for a while.
You think so? I feel I'm acting as I always do.
Are you still mad at my little practical joke?
No!! Do I look like that shallow a person?!
Sorry...It's just that I've had a lot to think over.
I can advise you.
No... Thank you anyway.
Say, is Loke here?
!
ざわ
CHATTER
Where's Loke?
ざわ
CHATTER
I think Loke is just awful!
Who do all of you think you are?!
ざわ
CHATTER
I could ask you the same thing!!
Loke!! Where are you?!!
ざわ
CHATTER

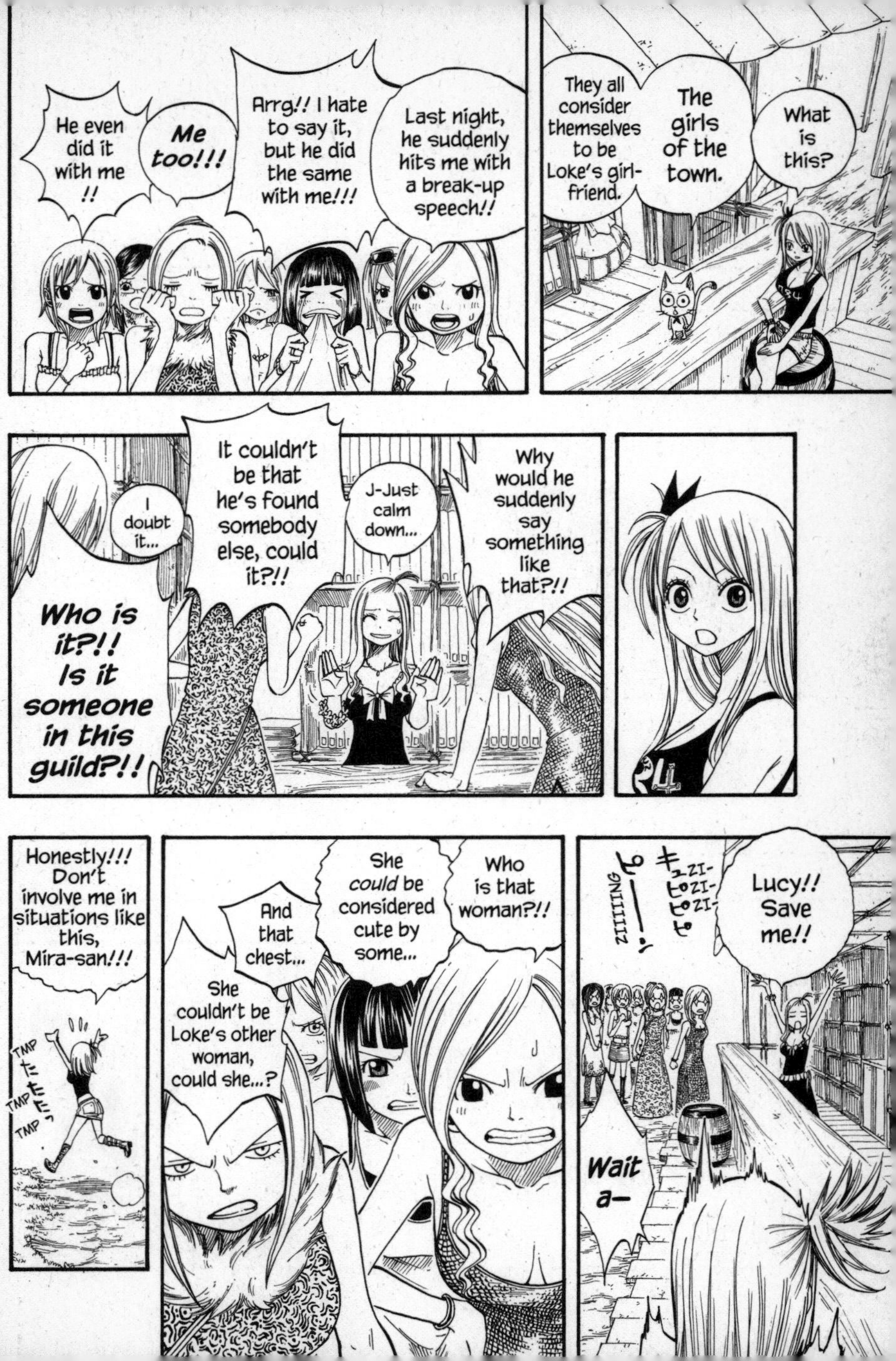
What is this?
The girls of the town.
They all consider themselves to be Loke's girl-friend.
Last night, he suddenly hits me with a break-up speech!!
Arrg!! I hate to say it, but he did the same with me!!!
Me too!!!
He even did it with me!!
Why would he suddenly say something like that?!!
J-Just calm down...
It couldn't be that he's found somebody else, could it?!!
I doubt it...
Who is it?!! Is it someone in this guild?!!
Lucy!! Save me!!
ZI-ZI-ZI-
ZIIIING
Wait a—
Who is that woman?!!
She *could* be considered cute by some...
And that chest...
She couldn't be Loke's other woman, could she...?
Honestly!!! Don't involve me in situations like this, Mira-san!!!
TMP TMP TMP

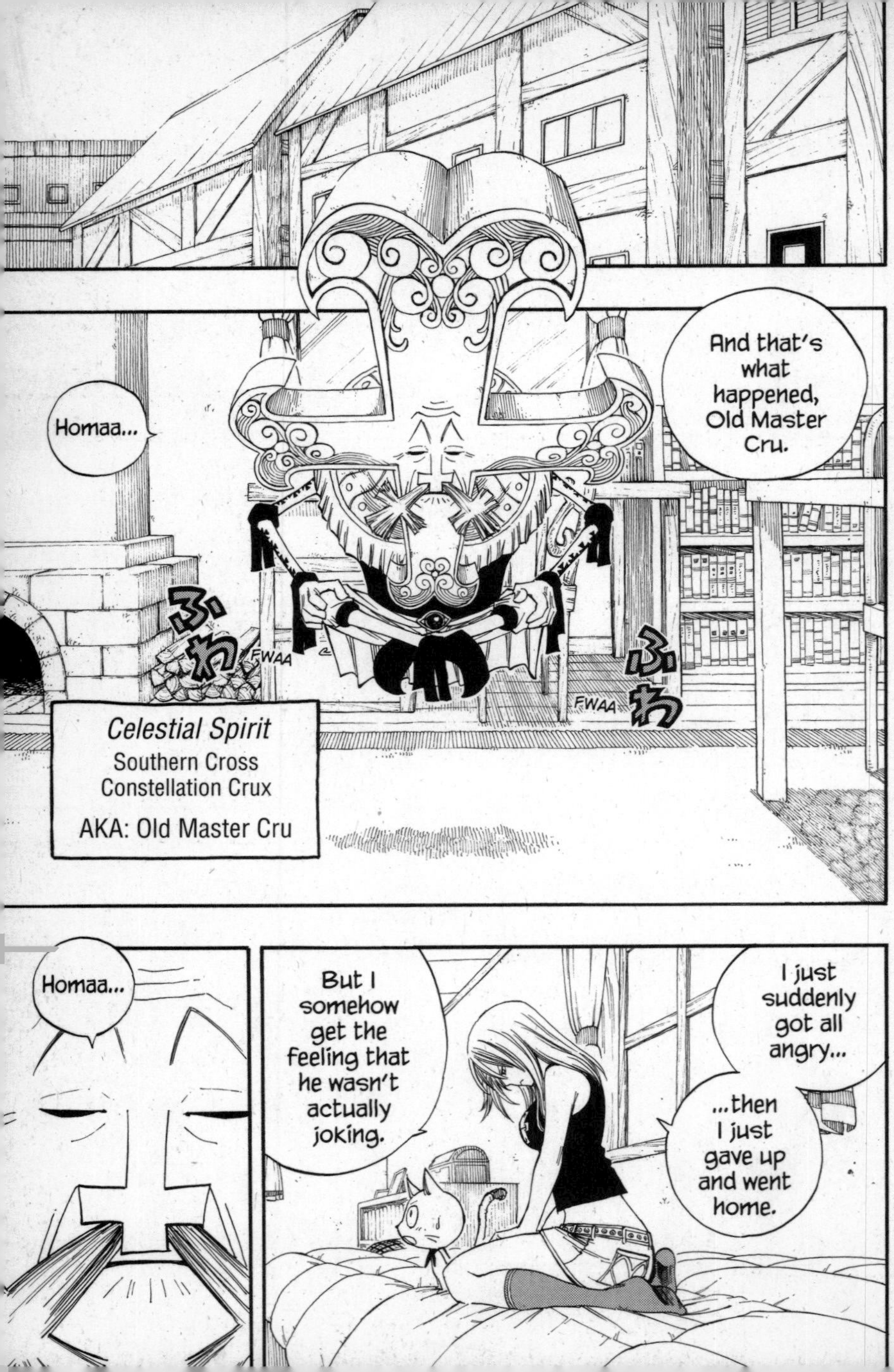
And that's what happened, Old Master Cru.
Homaa...
ふわ FWAA
ふわ FWAA
Celestial Spirit
Southern Cross Constellation Crux
AKA: Old Master Cru
I just suddenly got all angry...
...then I just gave up and went home.
But I somehow get the feeling that he wasn't actually joking.
Homaa...

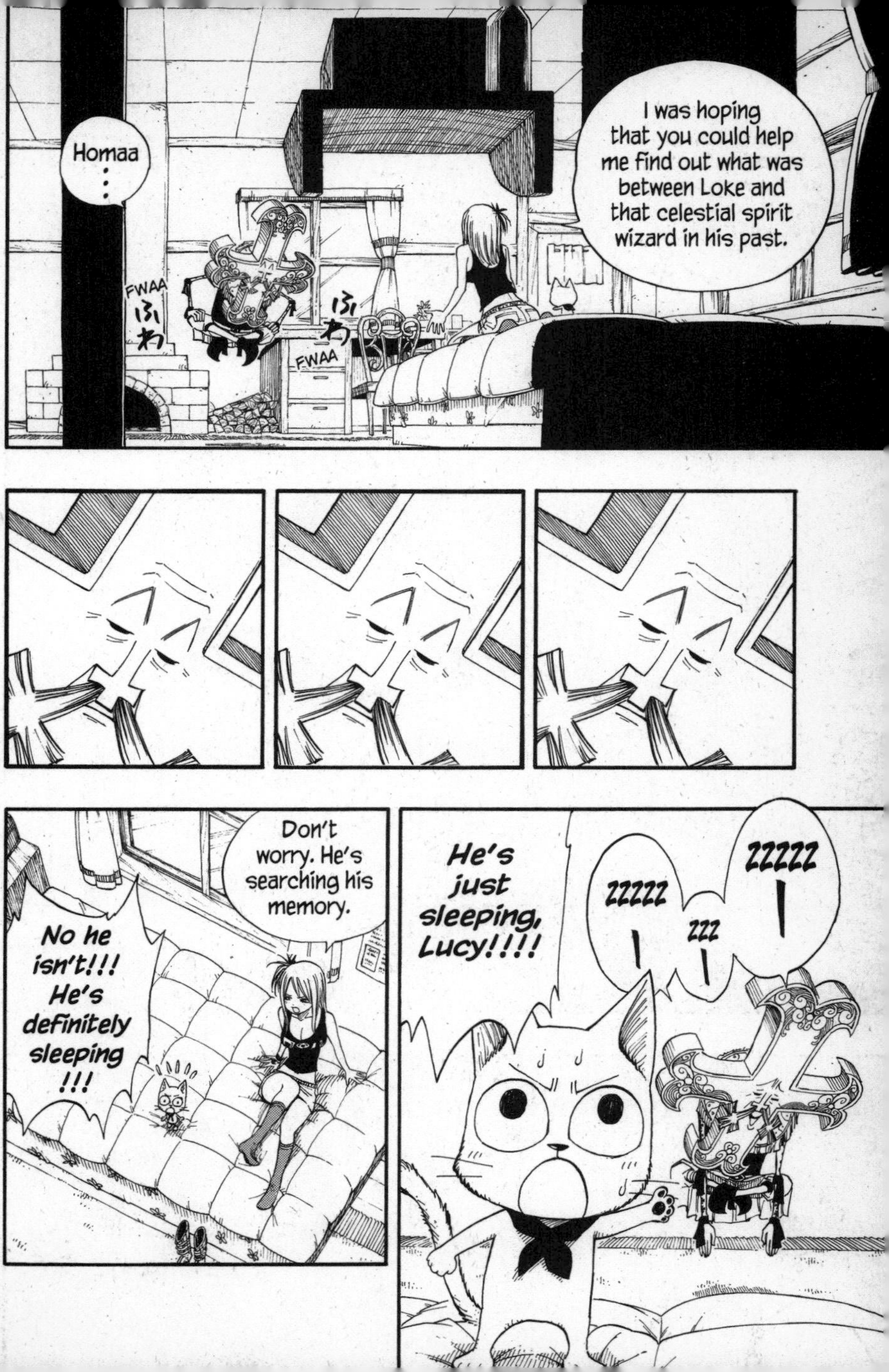
I was hoping that you could help me find out what was between Loke and that celestial spirit wizard in his past.
Homaa...
ふわ
FWAA
FWAA
ふわ
ZZZZZ
ZZZ
ZZZZZ
He's just sleeping, Lucy!!!!
Don't worry. He's searching his memory.
No he isn't!!! He's definitely sleeping !!!

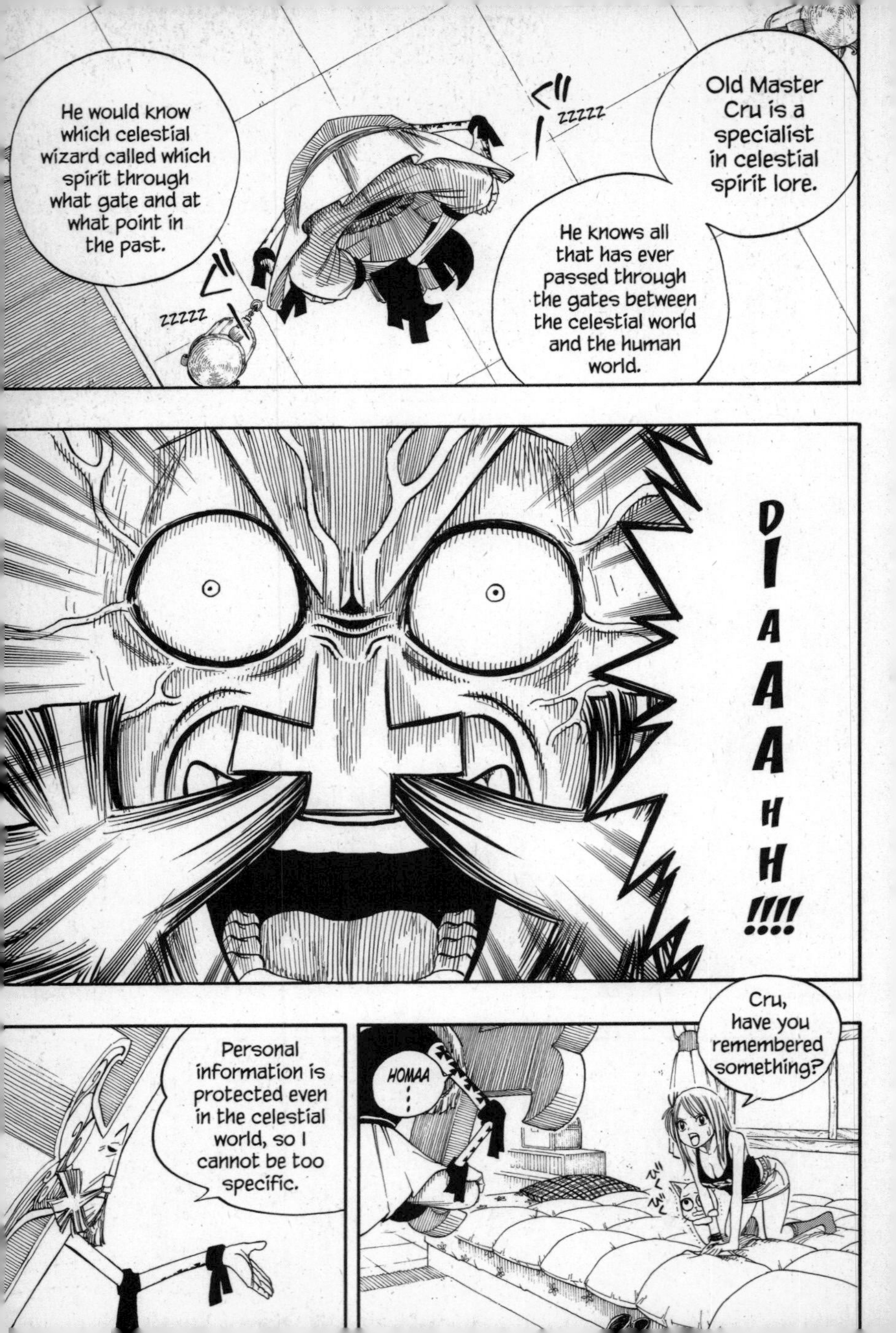
Old Master Cru is a specialist in celestial spirit lore.
He knows all that has ever passed through the gates between the celestial world and the human world.
ZZZZZ
He would know which celestial wizard called which spirit through what gate and at what point in the past.
ZZZZZ
DIAAAAHH!!!!
Cru, have you remembered something?
HOMAA ...
Personal information is protected even in the celestial world, so I cannot be too specific.

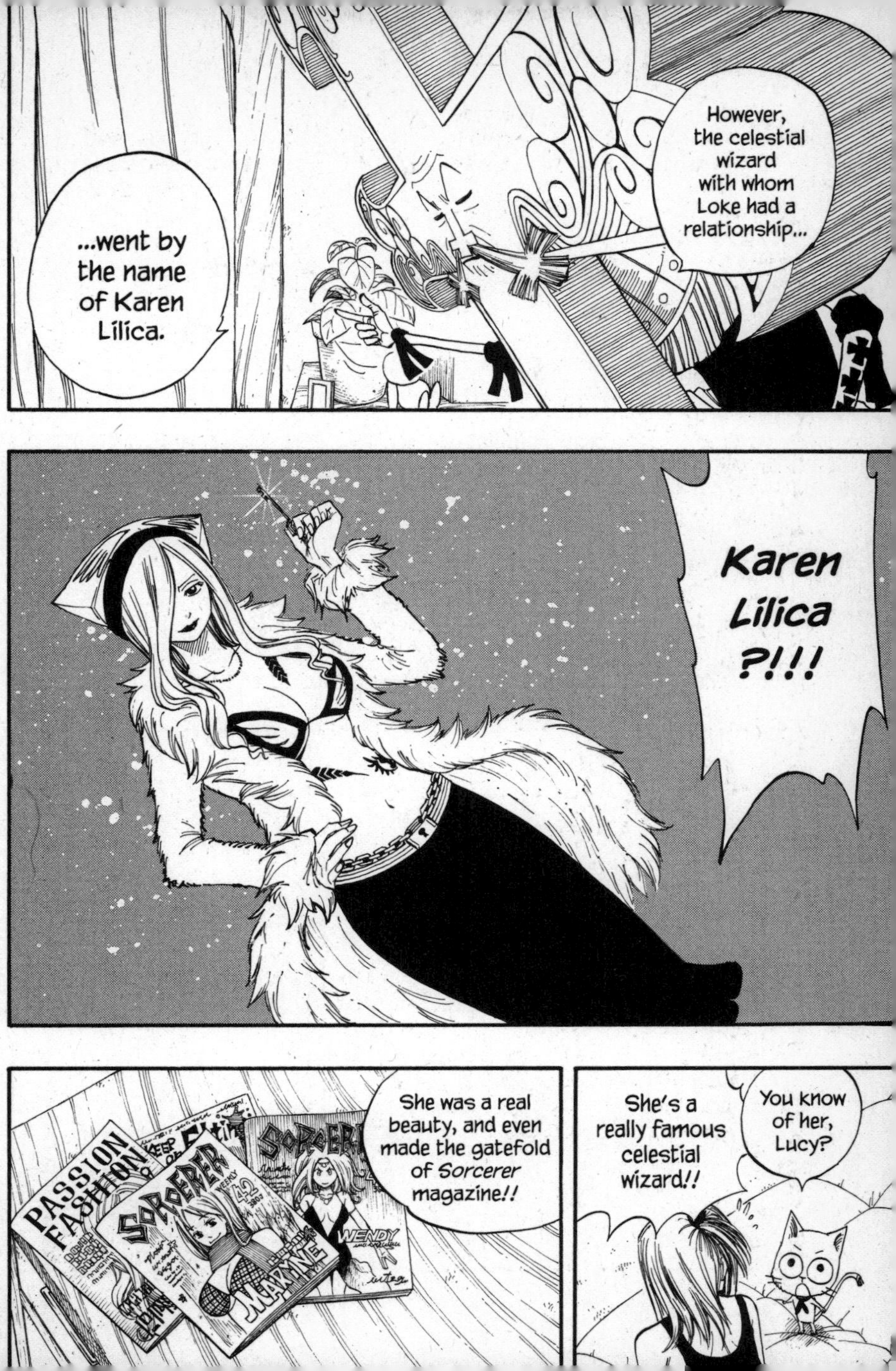
However, the celestial wizard with whom Loke had a relationship...
...went by the name of Karen Lilica.
Karen Lilica ?!!!
You know of her, Lucy?
She's a really famous celestial wizard!!
She was a real beauty, and even made the gatefold of *Sorcerer* magazine!!
PASSION FASHION
SORCERER
WEEKLY
42
MARINE
WENDY

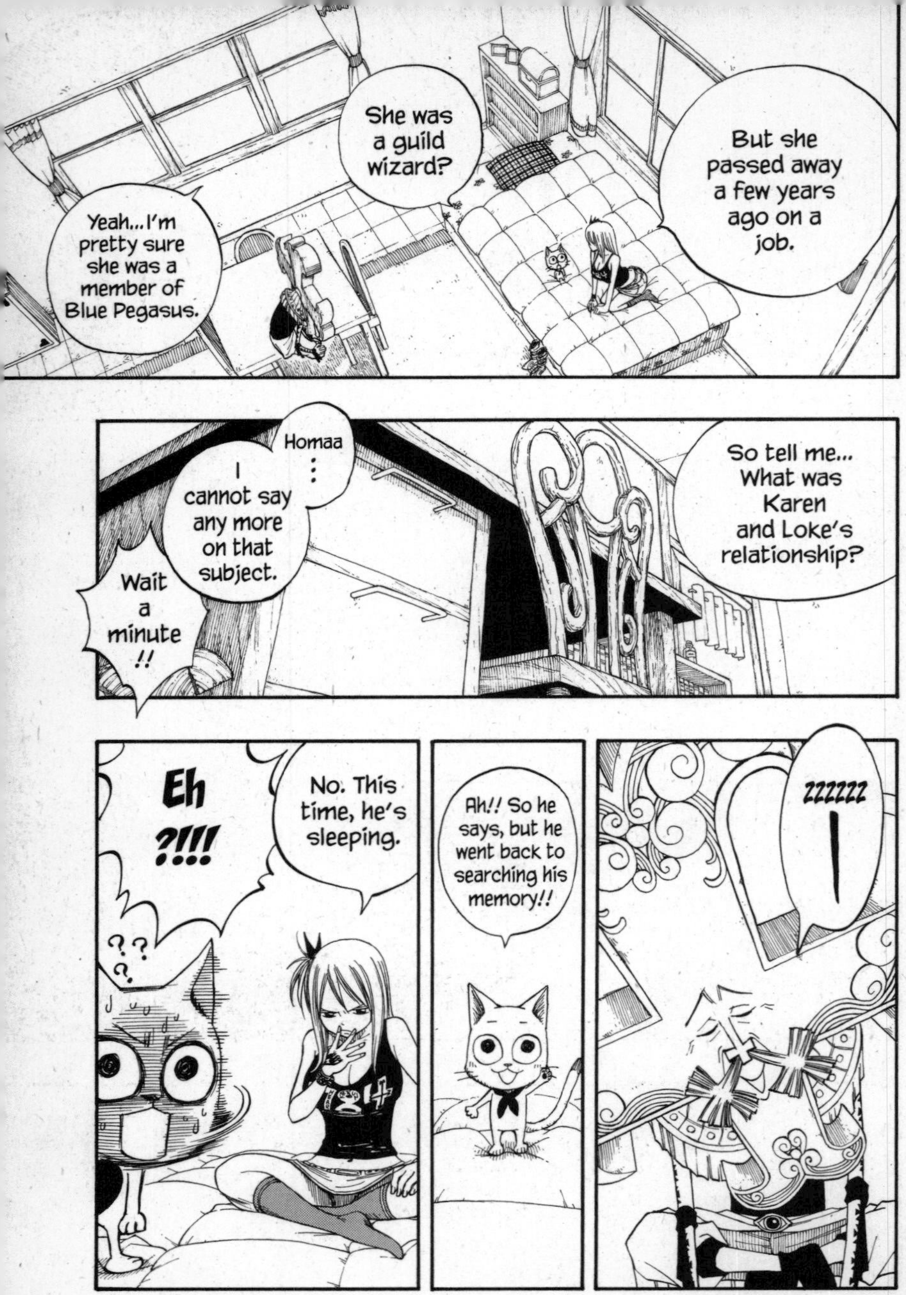
But she passed away a few years ago on a job.
She was a guild wizard?
Yeah...I'm pretty sure she was a member of Blue Pegasus.
So tell me... What was Karen and Loke's relationship?
Homaa... I cannot say any more on that subject.
Wait a minute!!
ZZZZZZ
Ah!! So he says, but he went back to searching his memory!!
No. This time, he's sleeping.
Eh ?!!!
???

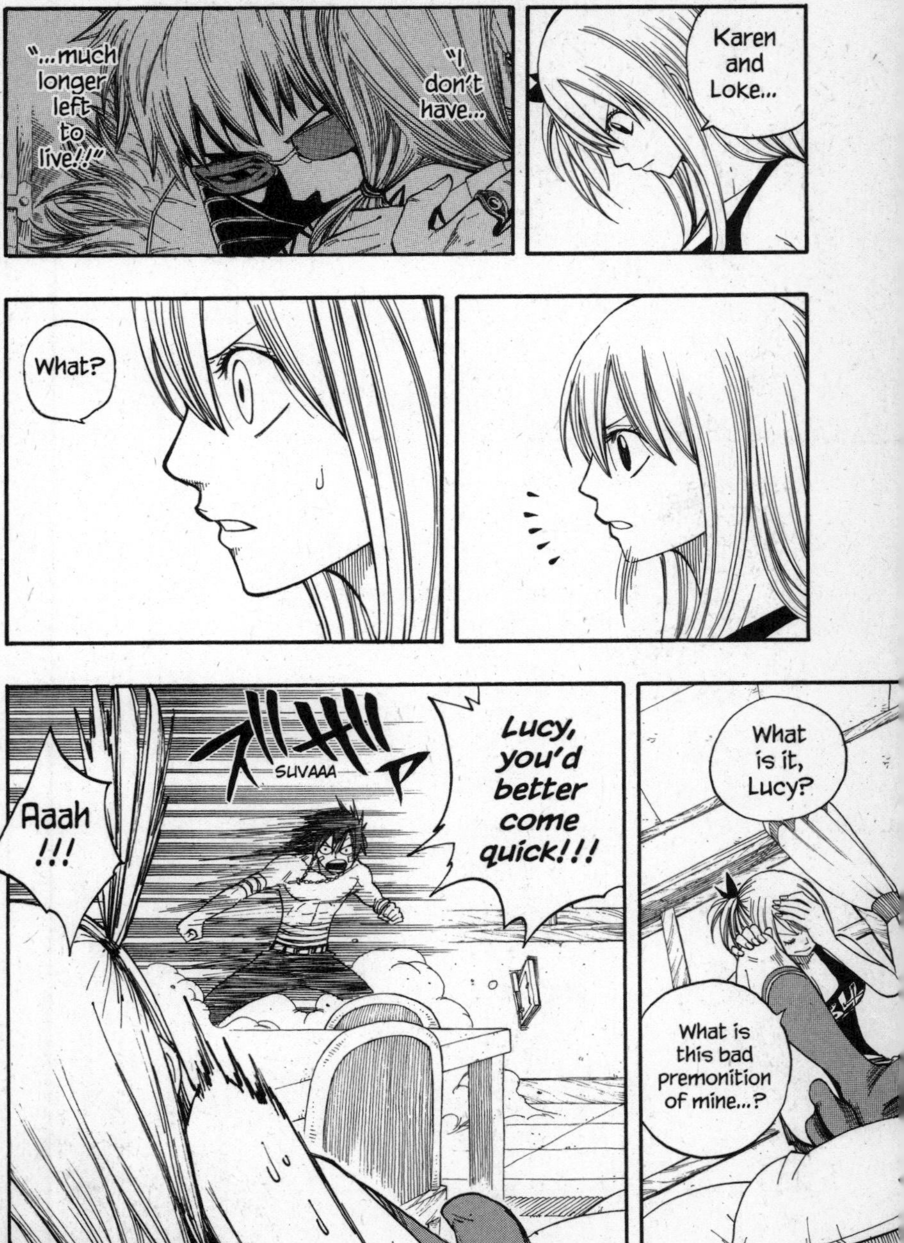
Karen and Loke...
"I don't have...
"...much longer left to live!!"
What?
What is it, Lucy?
What is this bad premonition of mine...?
Lucy, you'd better come quick!!!
SUVAAA
Aaah!!!

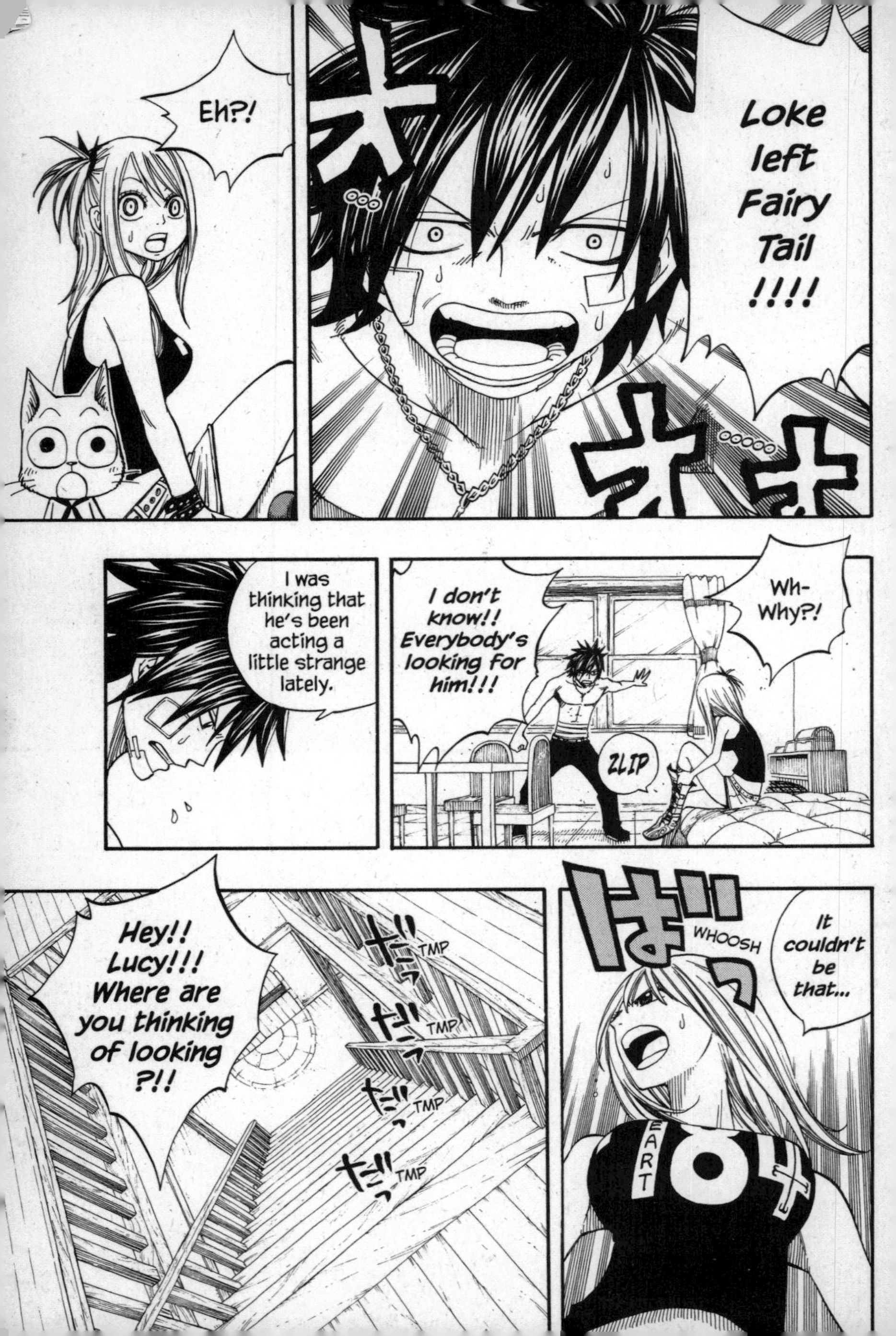
Loke left Fairy Tail !!!!
Eh?!
Wh- Why?!
I don't know!! Everybody's looking for him!!!
ZLIP
I was thinking that he's been acting a little strange lately.
はっ
WHOOSH
It couldn't be that...
Hey!! Lucy!!! Where are you thinking of looking ?!!
TMP
TMP
TMP
TMP

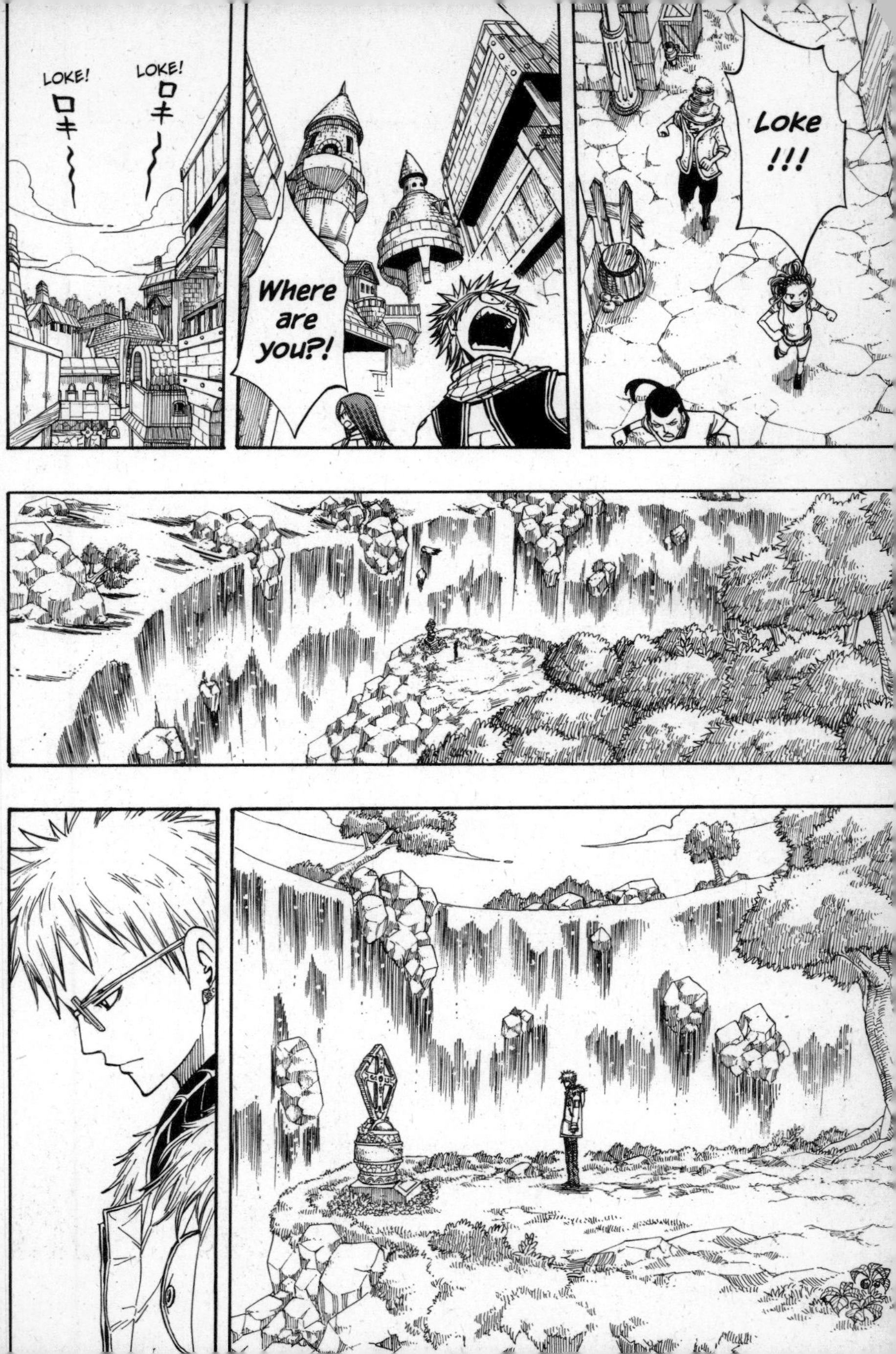
Loke !!!
Where are you?!
LOKE!
ロキ～～
LOKE!
ロキ～～

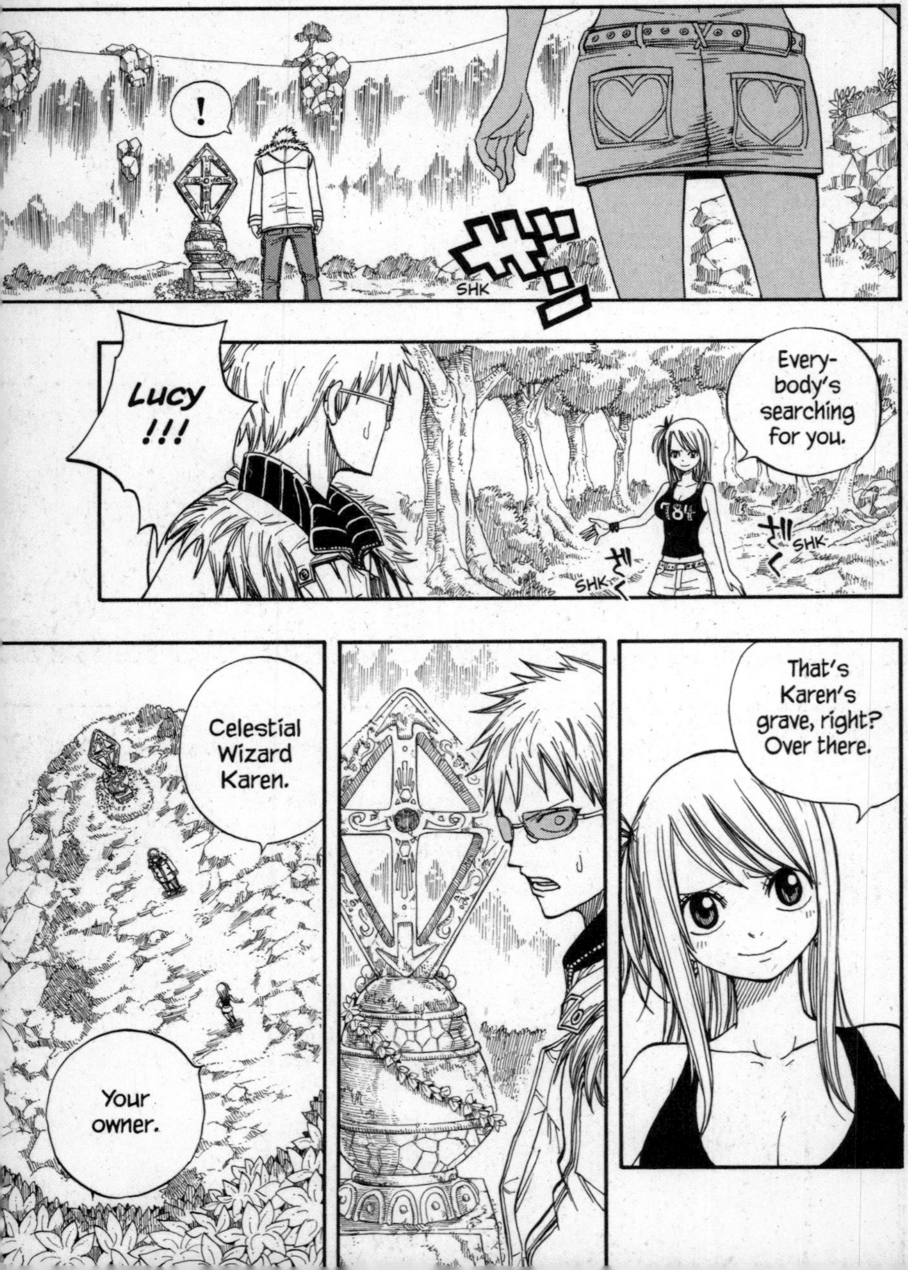
SHK
!
Every-body's searching for you.
SHK
SHK
Lucy !!!
That's Karen's grave, right? Over there.
Celestial Wizard Karen.
Your owner.

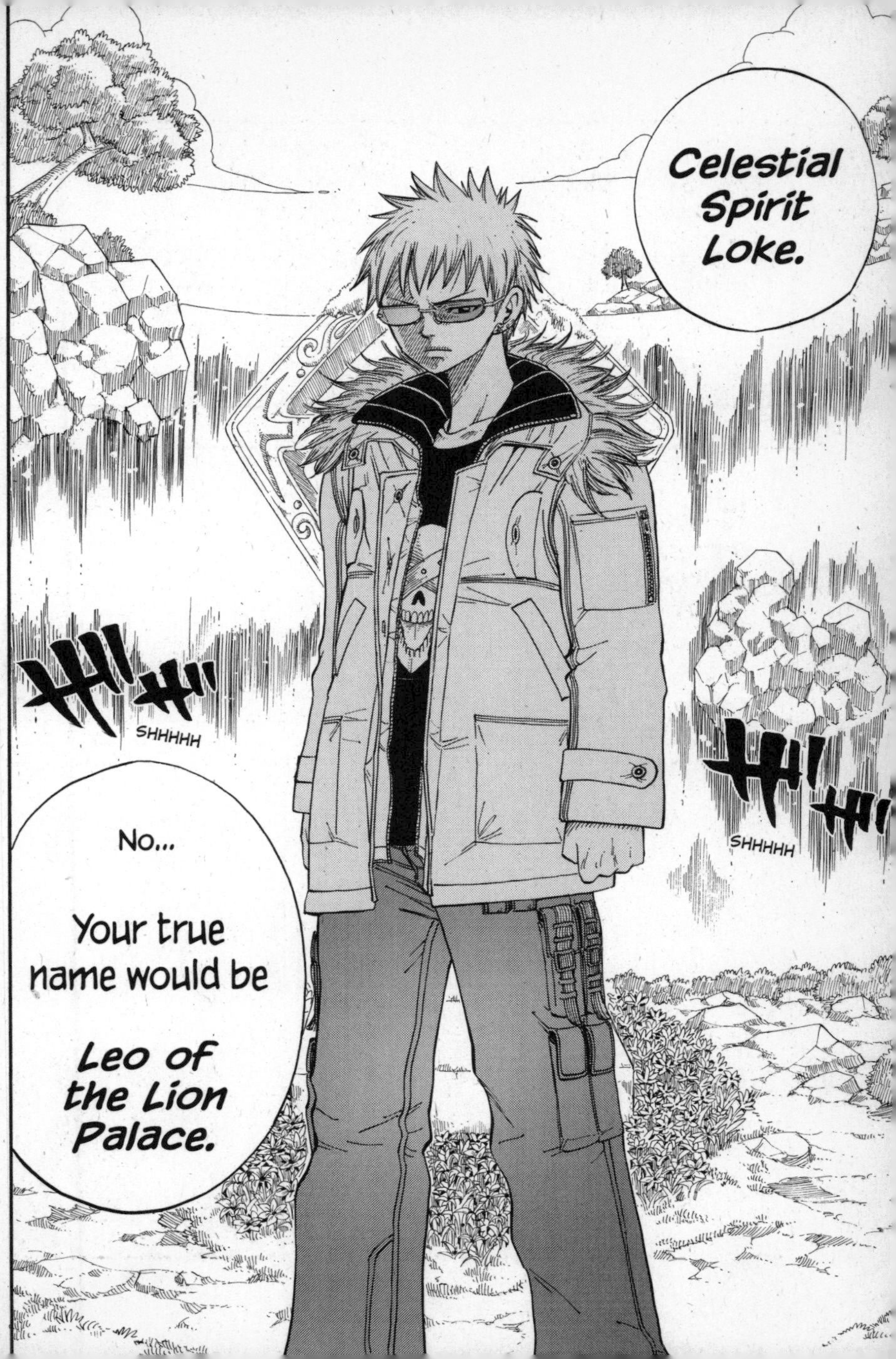
Celestial Spirit Loke.
SHHHHH
SHHHHH
No... Your true name would be Leo of the Lion Palace.

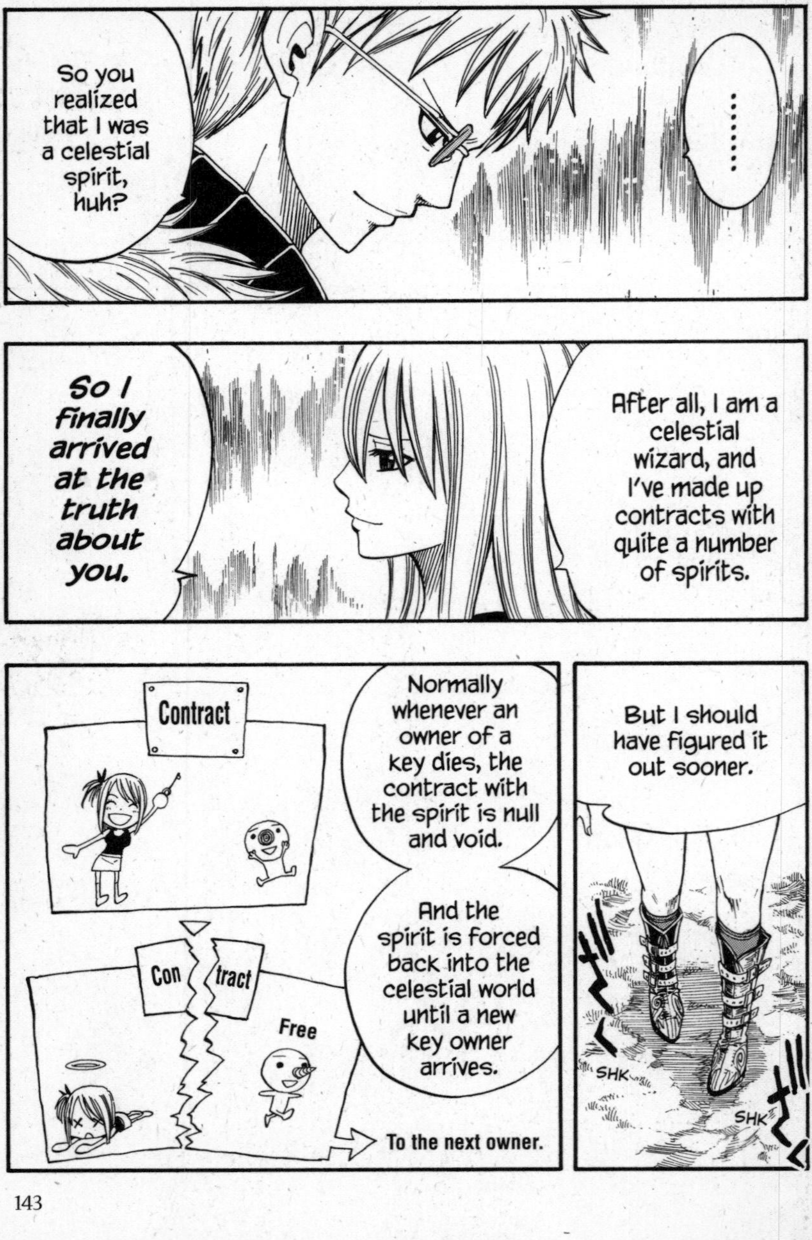
……
So you realized that I was a celestial spirit, huh?
After all, I am a celestial wizard, and I've made up contracts with quite a number of spirits.
So I finally arrived at the truth about you.
But I should have figured it out sooner.
SHK
SHK
Normally whenever an owner of a key dies, the contract with the spirit is null and void.
And the spirit is forced back into the celestial world until a new key owner arrives.
Contract
Con tract
Free
To the next owner.

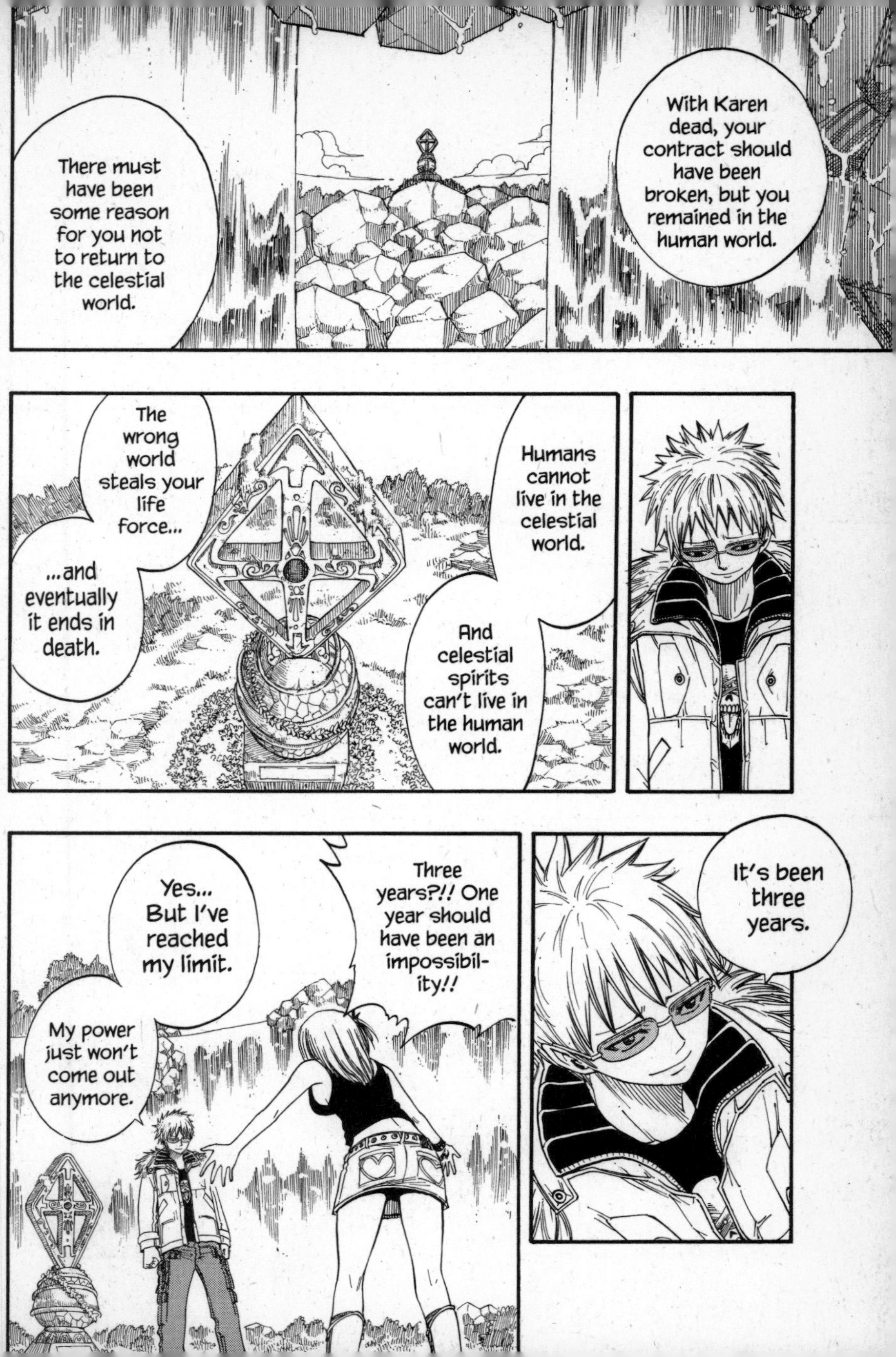
With Karen dead, your contract should have been broken, but you remained in the human world.
There must have been some reason for you not to return to the celestial world.
Humans cannot live in the celestial world.
And celestial spirits can't live in the human world.
The wrong world steals your life force...
...and eventually it ends in death.
It's been three years.
Three years?!! One year should have been an impossibil-ity!!
Yes... But I've reached my limit.
My power just won't come out anymore.

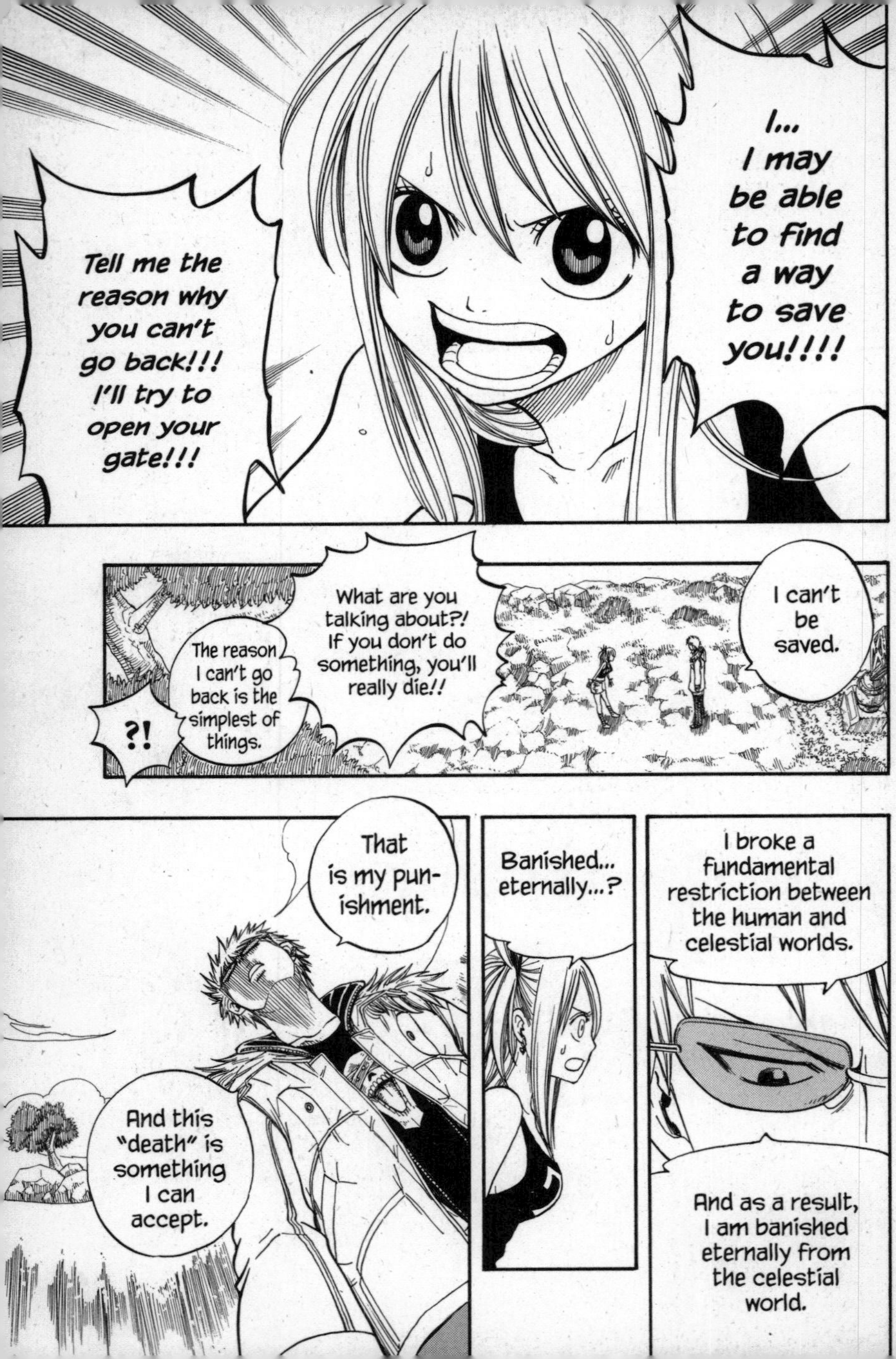
I... I may be able to find a way to save you!!!!
Tell me the reason why you can't go back!!! I'll try to open your gate!!!
I can't be saved.
What are you talking about?! If you don't do something, you'll really die!!
The reason I can't go back is the simplest of things.
?!
I broke a fundamental restriction between the human and celestial worlds.
And as a result, I am banished eternally from the celestial world.
Banished... eternally...?
That is my pun-ishment.
And this "death" is something I can accept.

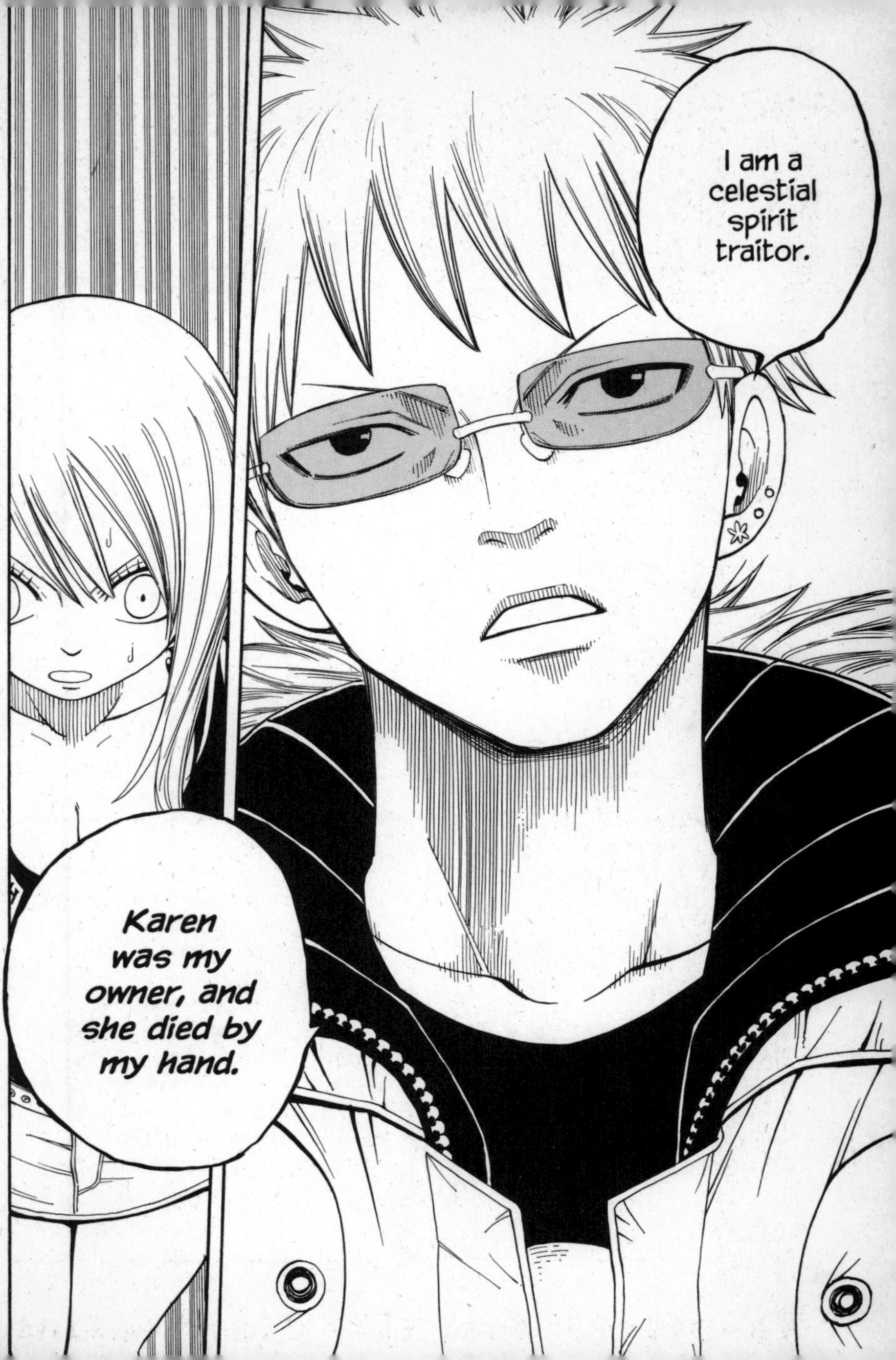
I am a celestial spirit traitor.
Karen was my owner, and she died by my hand.

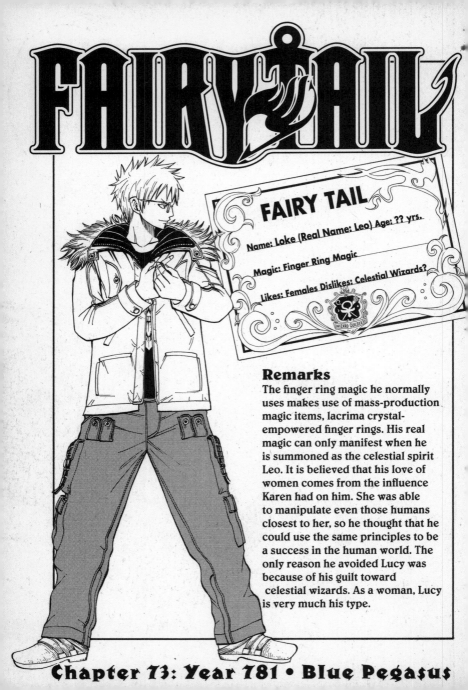

FAIRY TAIL

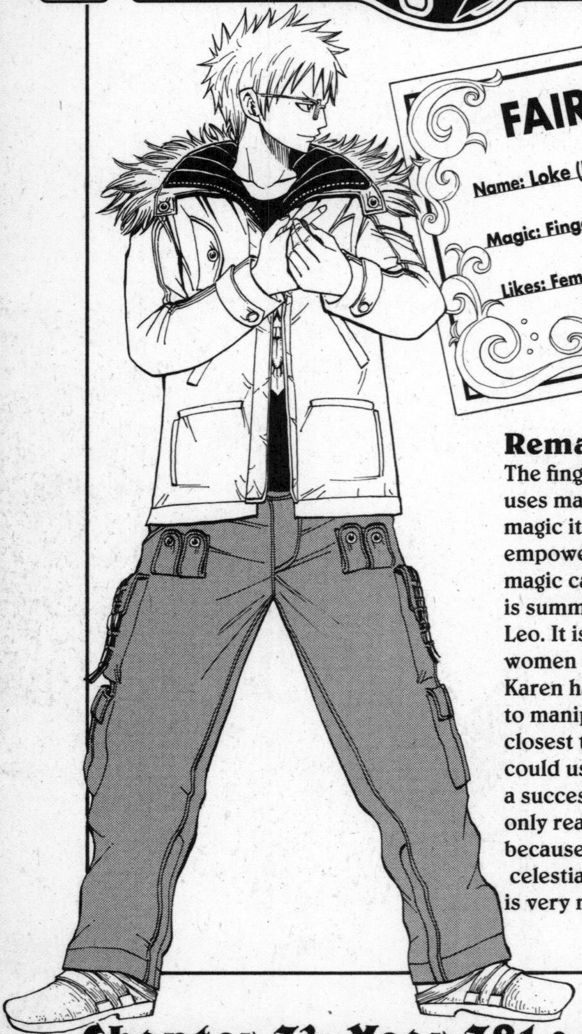

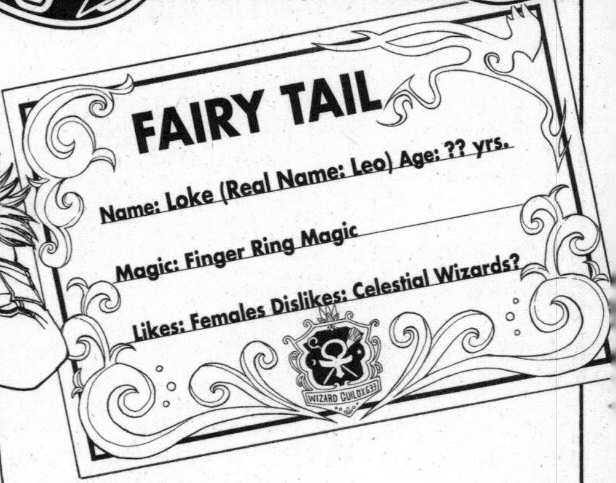
FAIRY TAIL
Name: Loke (Real Name: Leo) Age: ?? yrs.
Magic: Finger Ring Magic
Likes: Females Dislikes: Celestial Wizards?
WIZARD GUILDX633

Remarks

The finger ring magic he normally uses makes use of mass-production magic items, lacrima crystal-empowered finger rings. His real magic can only manifest when he is summoned as the celestial spirit Leo. It is believed that his love of women comes from the influence Karen had on him. She was able to manipulate even those humans closest to her, so he thought that he could use the same principles to be a success in the human world. The only reason he avoided Lucy was because of his guilt toward celestial wizards. As a woman, Lucy is very much his type.

Chapter 73: Year 781 • Blue Pegasus

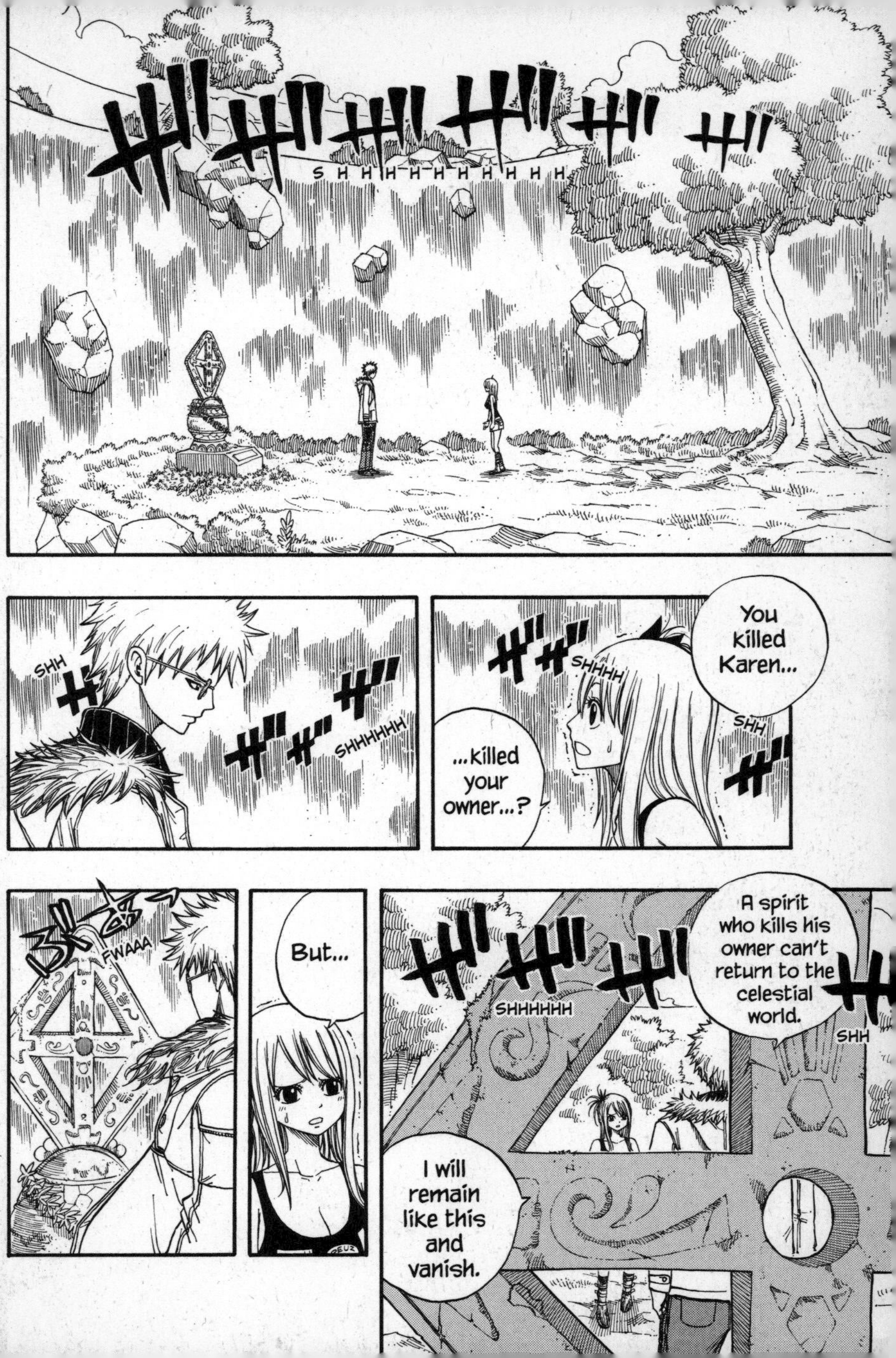
S H H H H H H H H H H H
SHHHH
You killed Karen...
...killed your owner...?
SHH
SHH
SHHHHHH
SHH
A spirit who kills his owner can't return to the celestial world.
SHHHHHH
I will remain like this and vanish.
But...
FWAAA

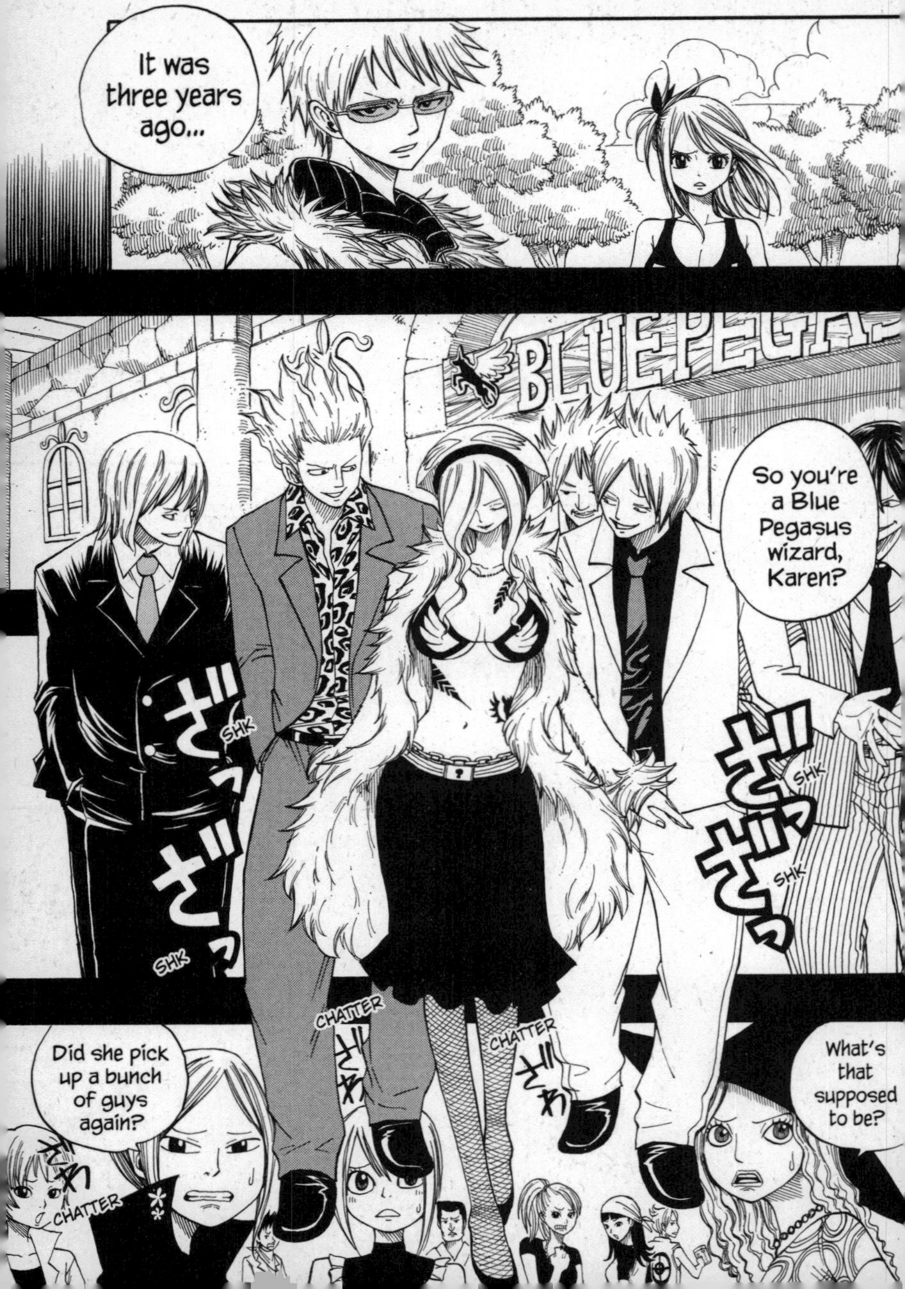
It was three years ago...
BLUE PEGA
So you're a Blue Pegasus wizard, Karen?
SHK
SHK
SHK
SHK
CHATTER
CHATTER
CHATTER
What's that supposed to be?
Did she pick up a bunch of guys again?

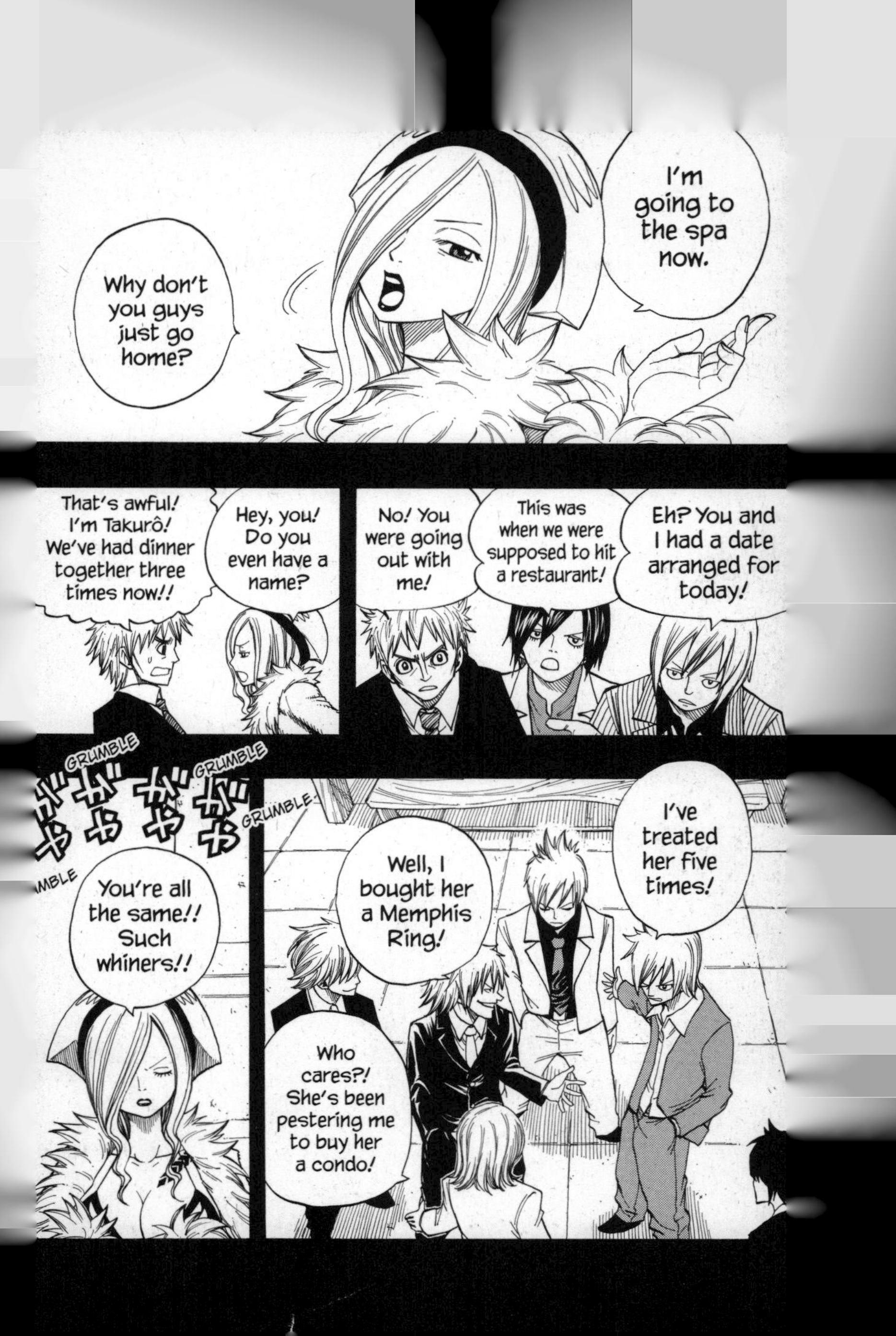
I'm going to the spa now.
Why don't you guys just go home?
Eh? You and I had a date arranged for today!
This was when we were supposed to hit a restaurant!
No! You were going out with me!
Hey, you! Do you even have a name?
That's awful! I'm Takurô! We've had dinner together three times now!!
I've treated her five times!
Well, I bought her a Memphis Ring!
Who cares?! She's been pestering me to buy her a condo!
GRUMBLE
GRUMBLE
GRUMBLE
You're all the same!! Such whiners!!

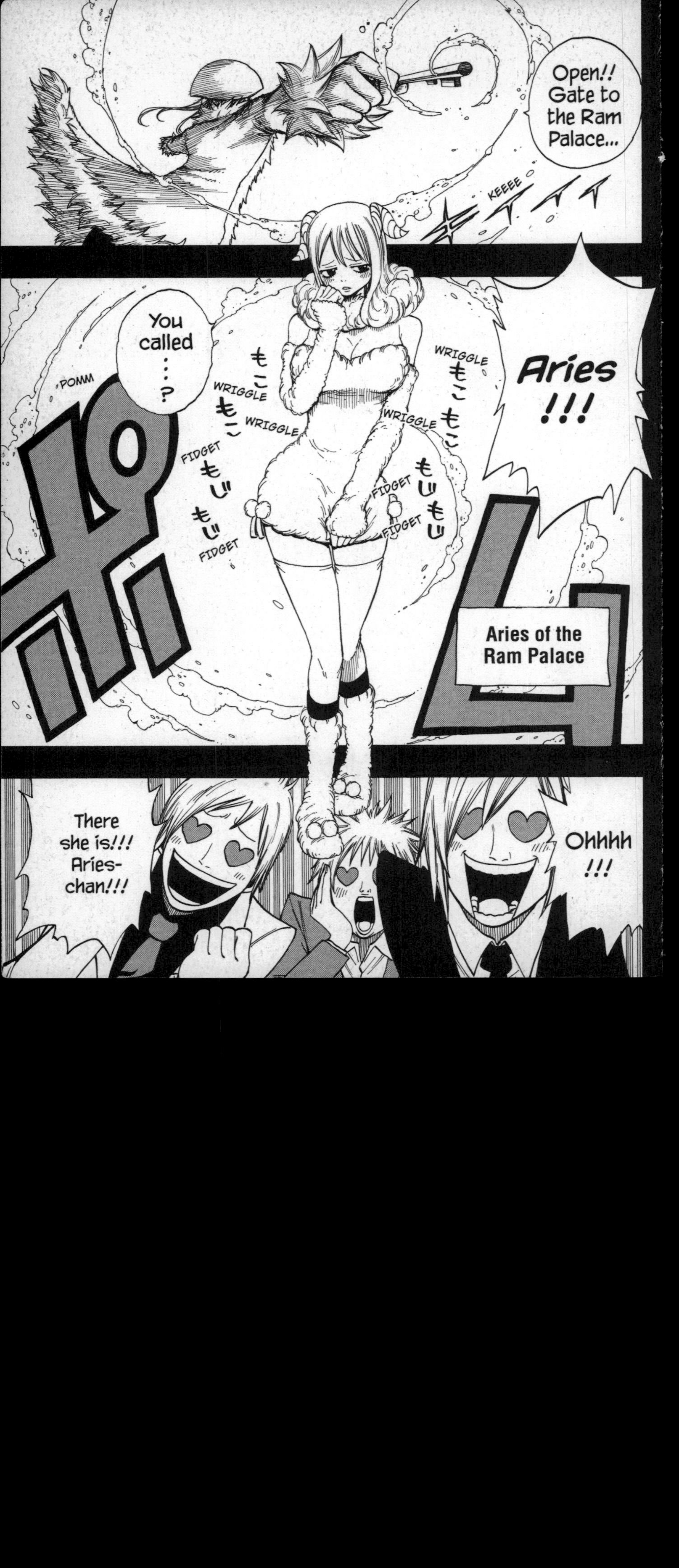
Open!! Gate to the Ram Palace...
KEEEE
Aries!!!
You called...?
POMM
WRIGGLE
WRIGGLE
WRIGGLE
WRIGGLE
FIDGET
FIDGET
FIDGET
FIDGET
Aries of the Ram Palace
Ohhhh!!!
There she is!!! Aries-chan!!!

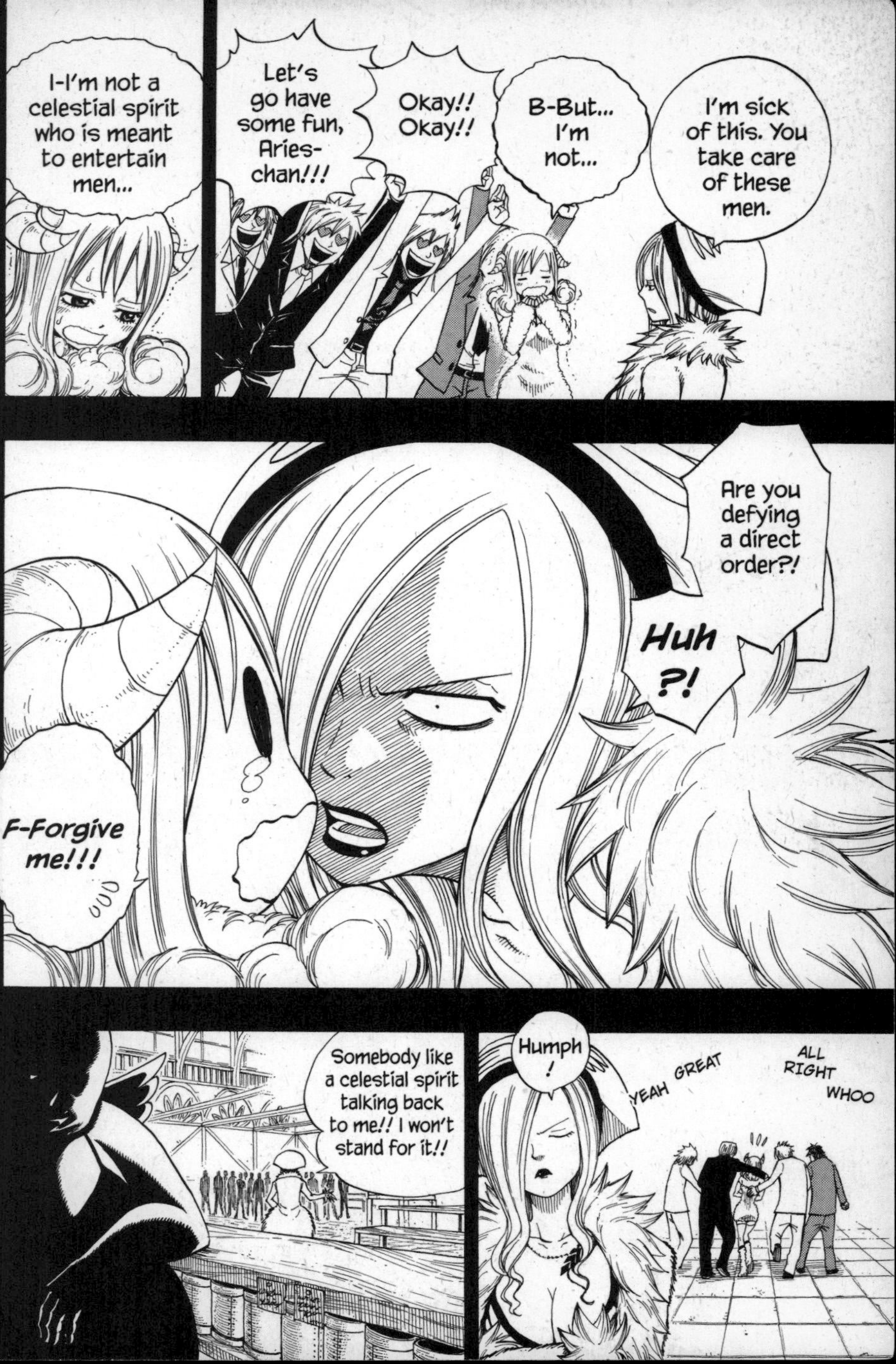
I'm sick of this. You take care of these men.
B-But... I'm not...
Okay!! Okay!!
Let's go have some fun, Aries-chan!!!
I-I'm not a celestial spirit who is meant to entertain men...
Are you defying a direct order?!
Huh ?!
F-Forgive me!!!
Humph!
ALL RIGHT
WHOO
GREAT
YEAH
Somebody like a celestial spirit talking back to me!! I won't stand for it!!

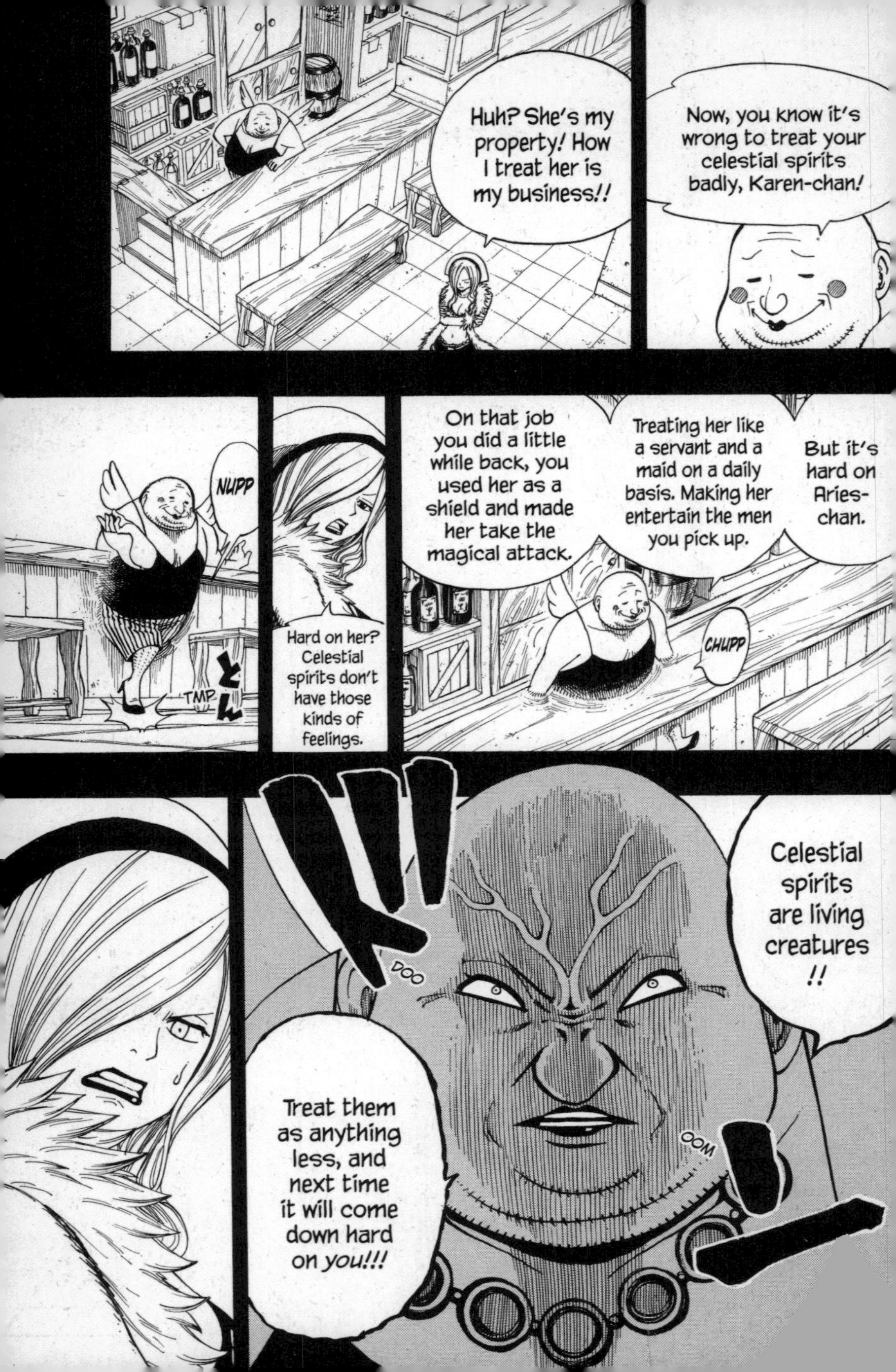
Now, you know it's wrong to treat your celestial spirits badly, Karen-chan!
Huh? She's my property! How I treat her is my business!!
But it's hard on Aries-chan.
Treating her like a servant and a maid on a daily basis. Making her entertain the men you pick up.
On that job you did a little while back, you used her as a shield and made her take the magical attack.
CHUPP
Hard on her? Celestial spirits don't have those kinds of feelings.
NUPP
TMP
とん
Celestial spirits are living creatures!!
DOO
OOM
Treat them as anything less, and next time it will come down hard on *you*!!!

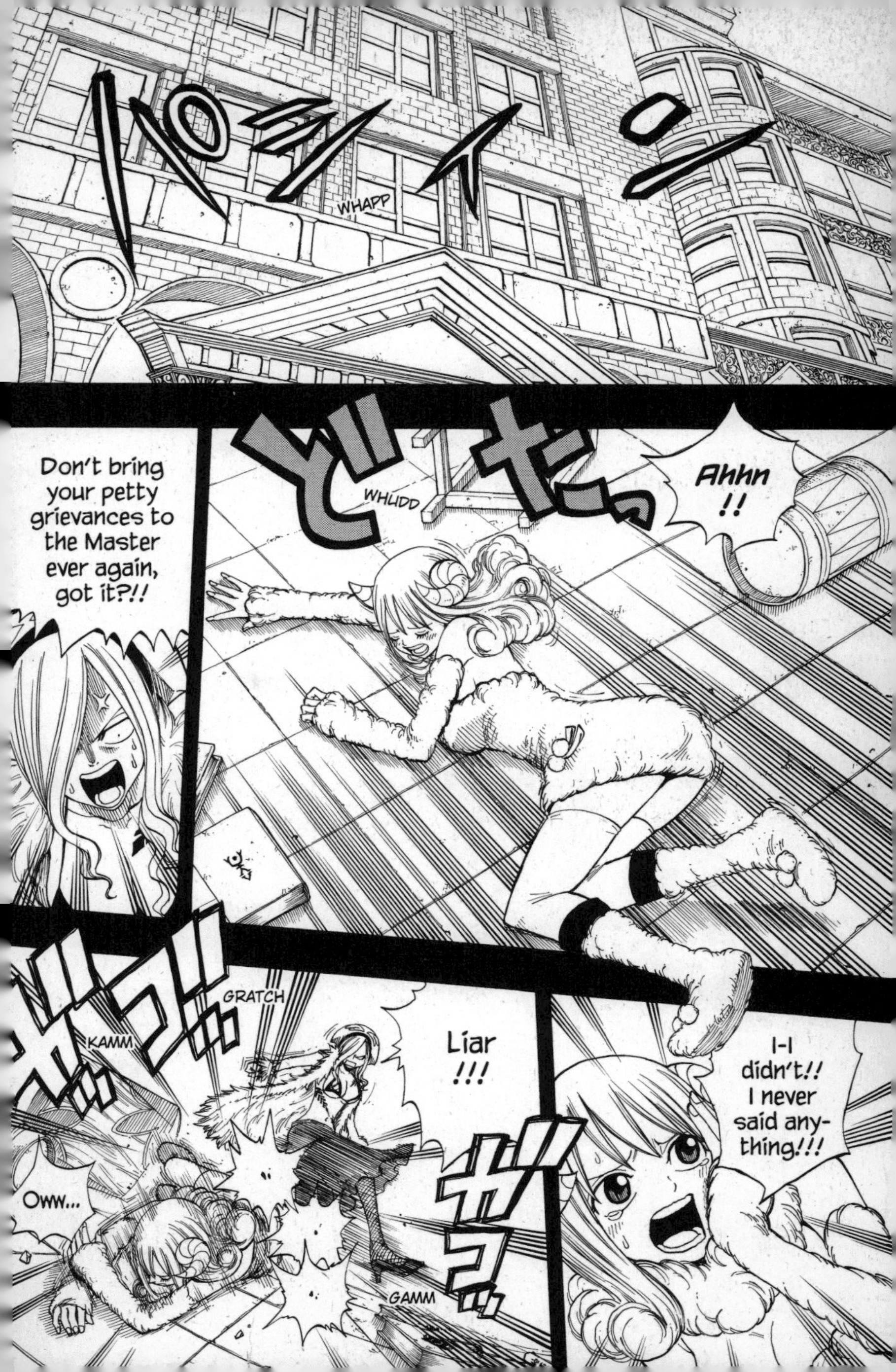
WHAPP
Ahhn!!
WHUDD
Don't bring your petty grievances to the Master ever again, got it?!!
I-I didn't!! I never said any-thing!!!
Liar!!!
GRATCH
KAMM
GAMM
Oww...

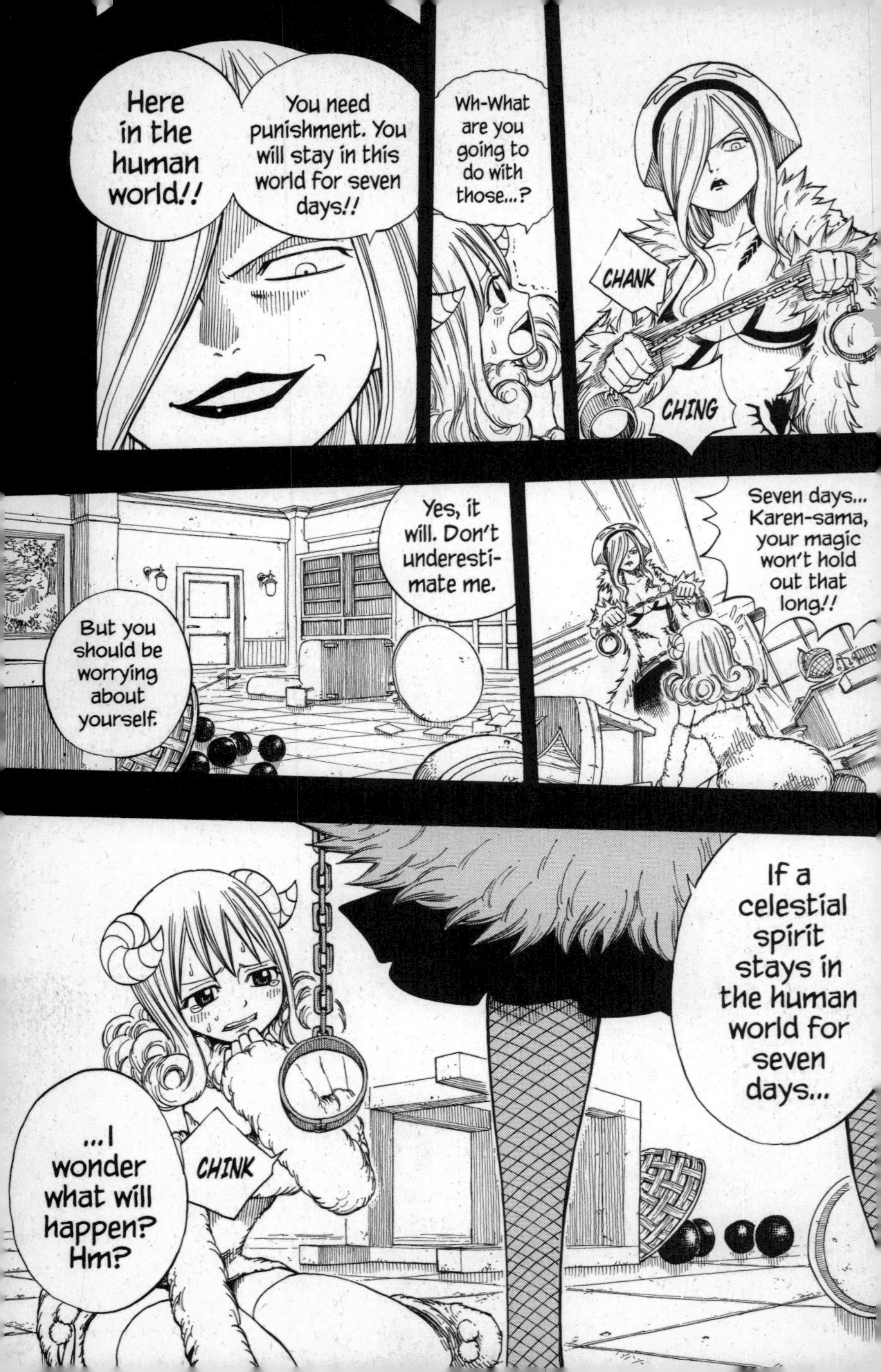
CHANK
CHING
Wh-What are you going to do with those...?
You need punishment. You will stay in this world for seven days!!
Here in the human world!!
Seven days... Karen-sama, your magic won't hold out that long!!
Yes, it will. Don't underestimate me.
But you should be worrying about yourself.
If a celestial spirit stays in the human world for seven days...
CHINK
...I wonder what will happen? Hm?

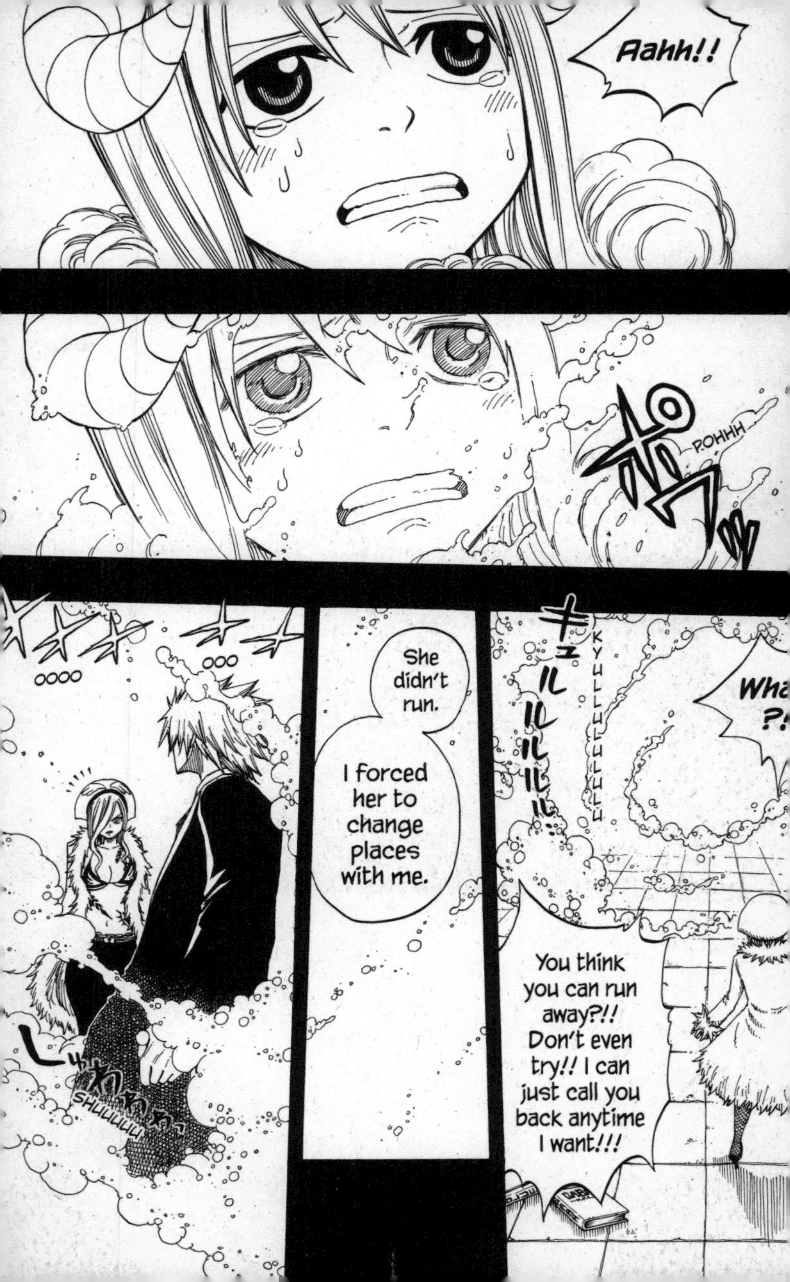
Aahh!!
POHHH
Wha ?!
KYULLULULULU
You think you can run away?!! Don't even try!! I can just call you back anytime I want!!!
She didn't run.
I forced her to change places with me.
OOO
OOOO
SHUUUUU

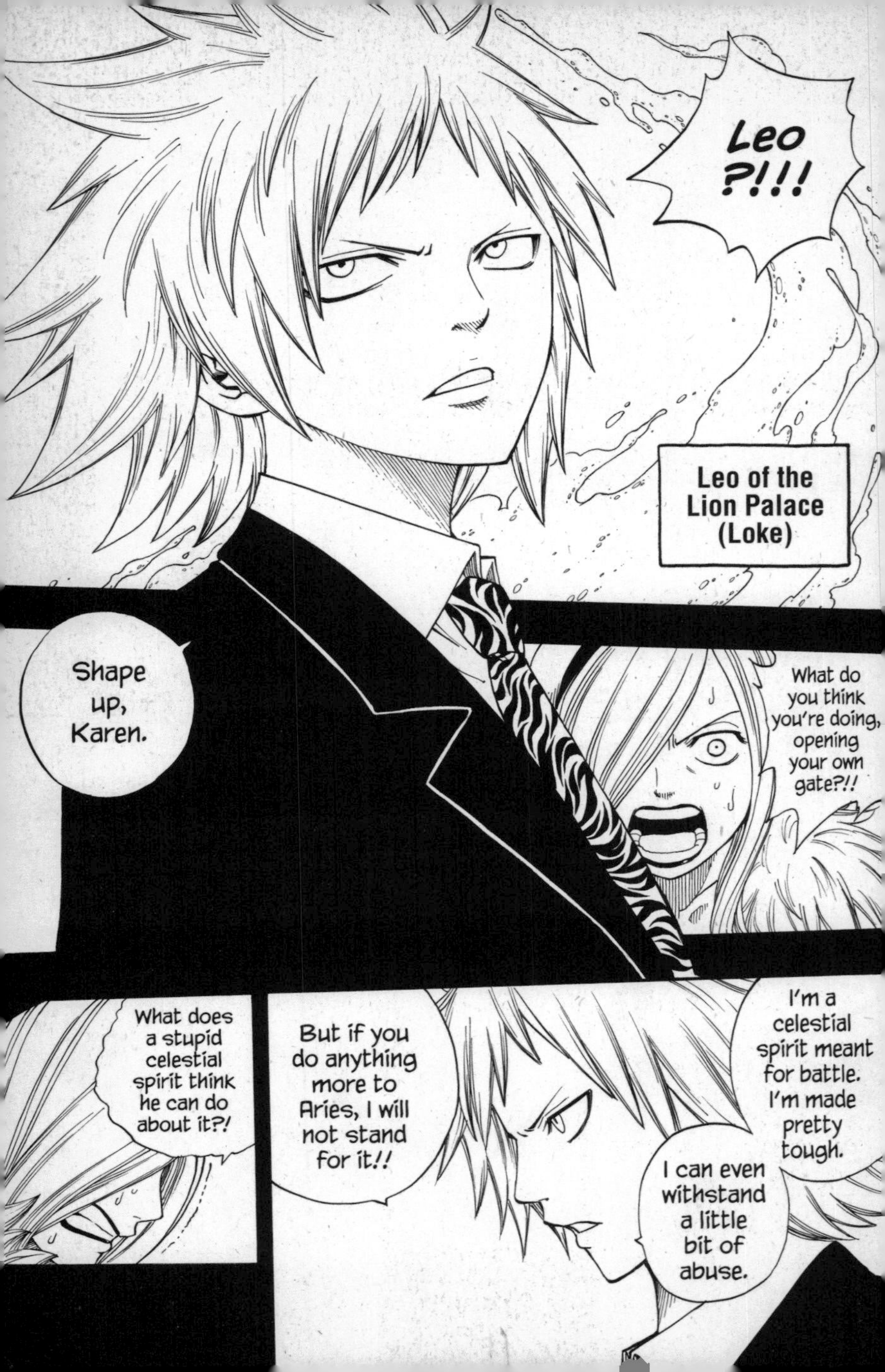
Leo ?!!!
Leo of the Lion Palace (Loke)
What do you think you're doing, opening your own gate?!!
Shape up, Karen.
I'm a celestial spirit meant for battle. I'm made pretty tough.
I can even withstand a little bit of abuse.
But if you do anything more to Aries, I will not stand for it!!
What does a stupid celestial spirit think he can do about it?!

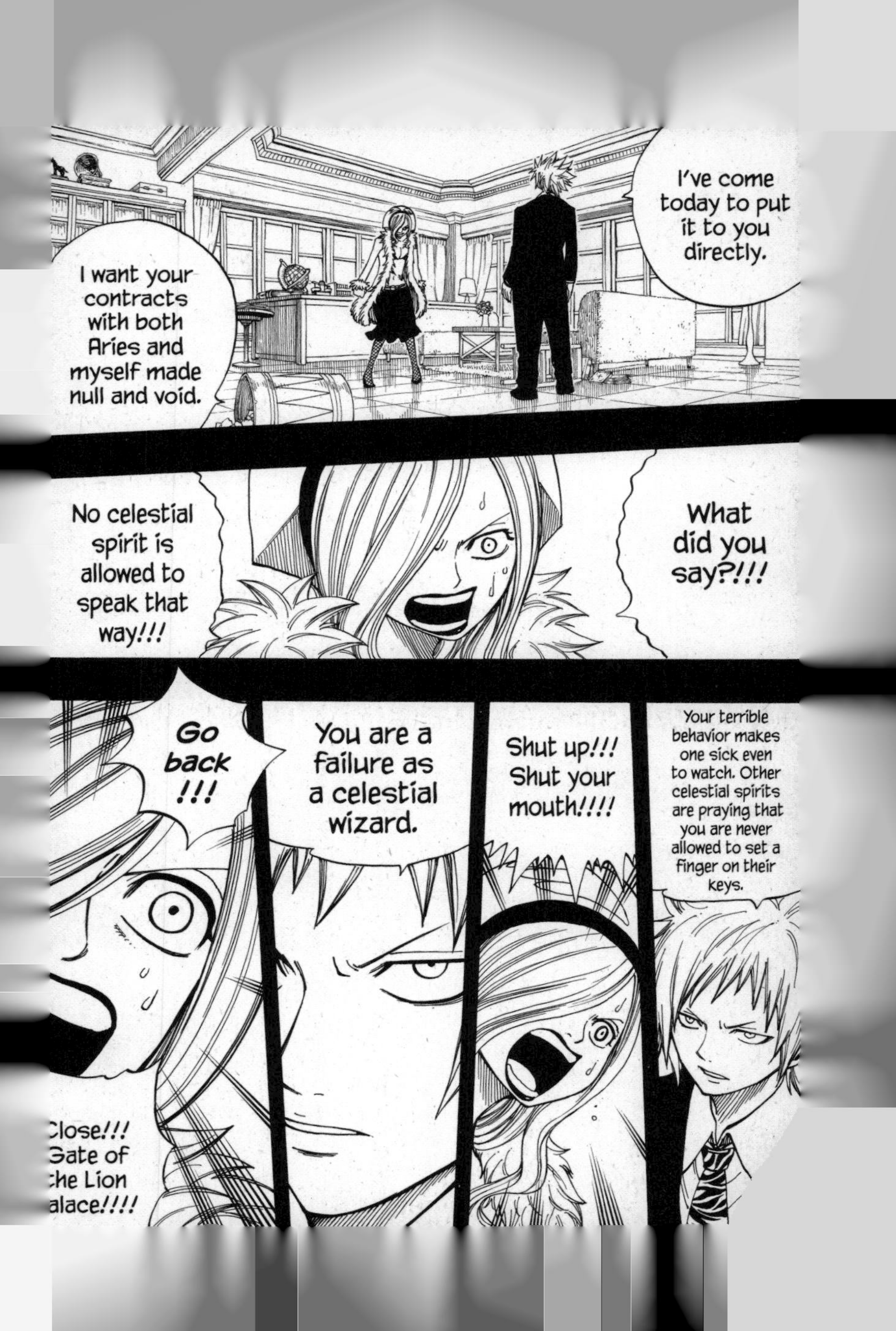
I've come today to put it to you directly.
I want your contracts with both Aries and myself made null and void.
What did you say?!!!
No celestial spirit is allowed to speak that way!!!
Your terrible behavior makes one sick even to watch. Other celestial spirits are praying that you are never allowed to set a finger on their keys.
Shut up!!! Shut your mouth!!!!
You are a failure as a celestial wizard.
Go back!!!
Close!!! Gate of he Lion alace!!!!

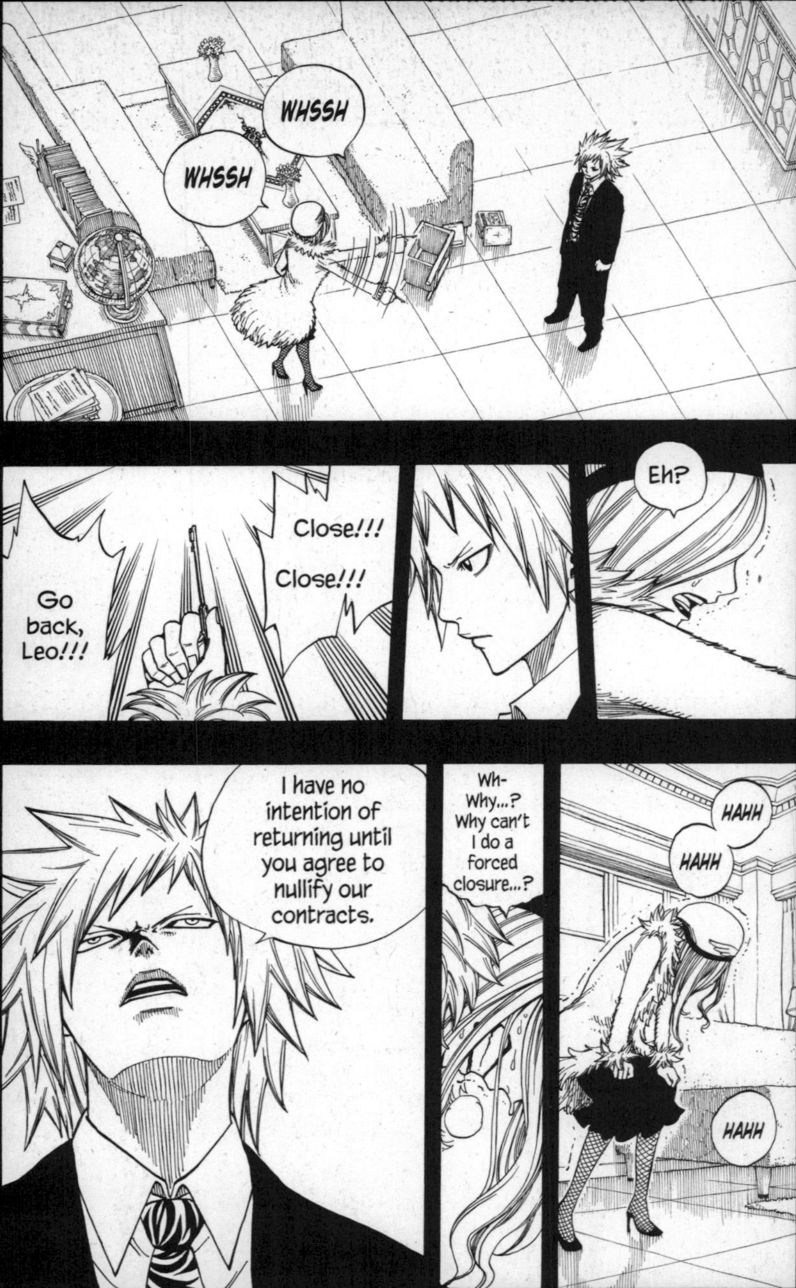
WHSSH
WHSSH
Eh?
Close!!!
Close!!!
Go back, Leo!!!
HAHH
HAHH
HAHH
Wh- Why...? Why can't I do a forced closure...?
I have no intention of returning until you agree to nullify our contracts.

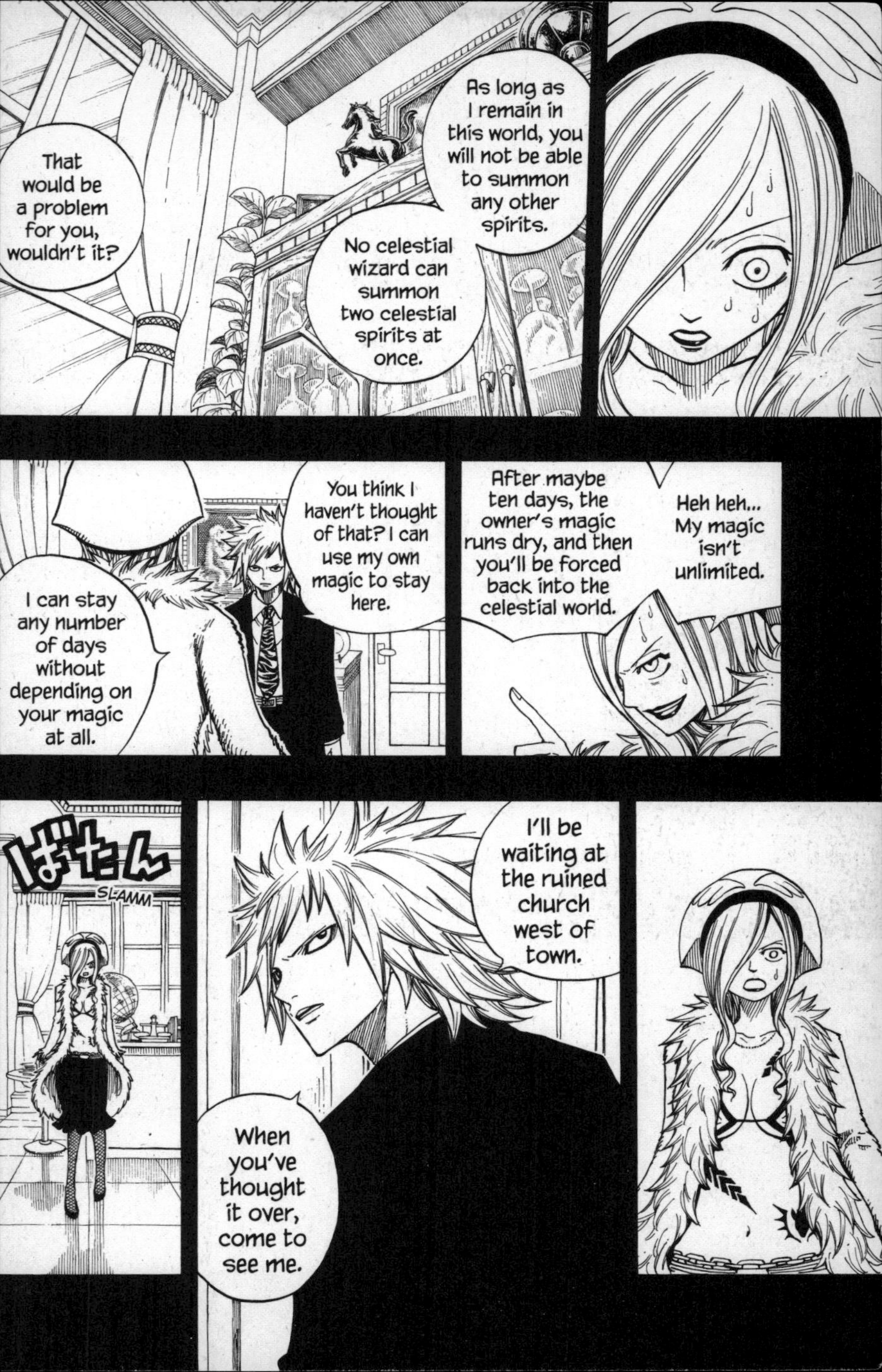
As long as I remain in this world, you will not be able to summon any other spirits.
No celestial wizard can summon two celestial spirits at once.
That would be a problem for you, wouldn't it?
Heh heh... My magic isn't unlimited.
After maybe ten days, the owner's magic runs dry, and then you'll be forced back into the celestial world.
You think I haven't thought of that? I can use my own magic to stay here.
I can stay any number of days without depending on your magic at all.
I'll be waiting at the ruined church west of town.
When you've thought it over, come to see me.
ばたん
SLAMM

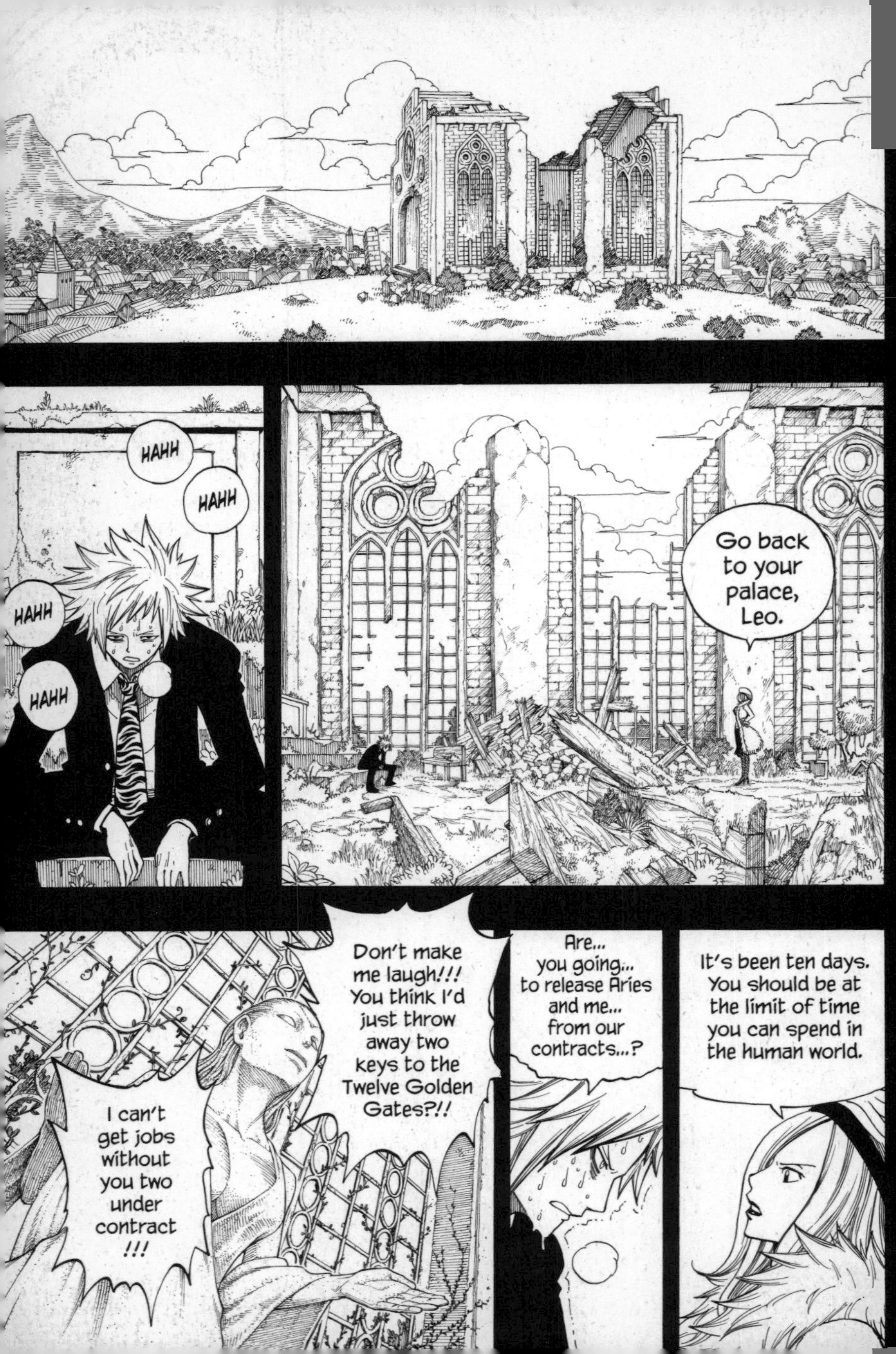
Go back to your palace, Leo.
HAHH
HAHH
HAHH
HAHH
It's been ten days. You should be at the limit of time you can spend in the human world.
Are... you going... to release Aries and me... from our contracts...?
Don't make me laugh!!! You think I'd just throw away two keys to the Twelve Golden Gates?!!
I can't get jobs without you two under contract!!!

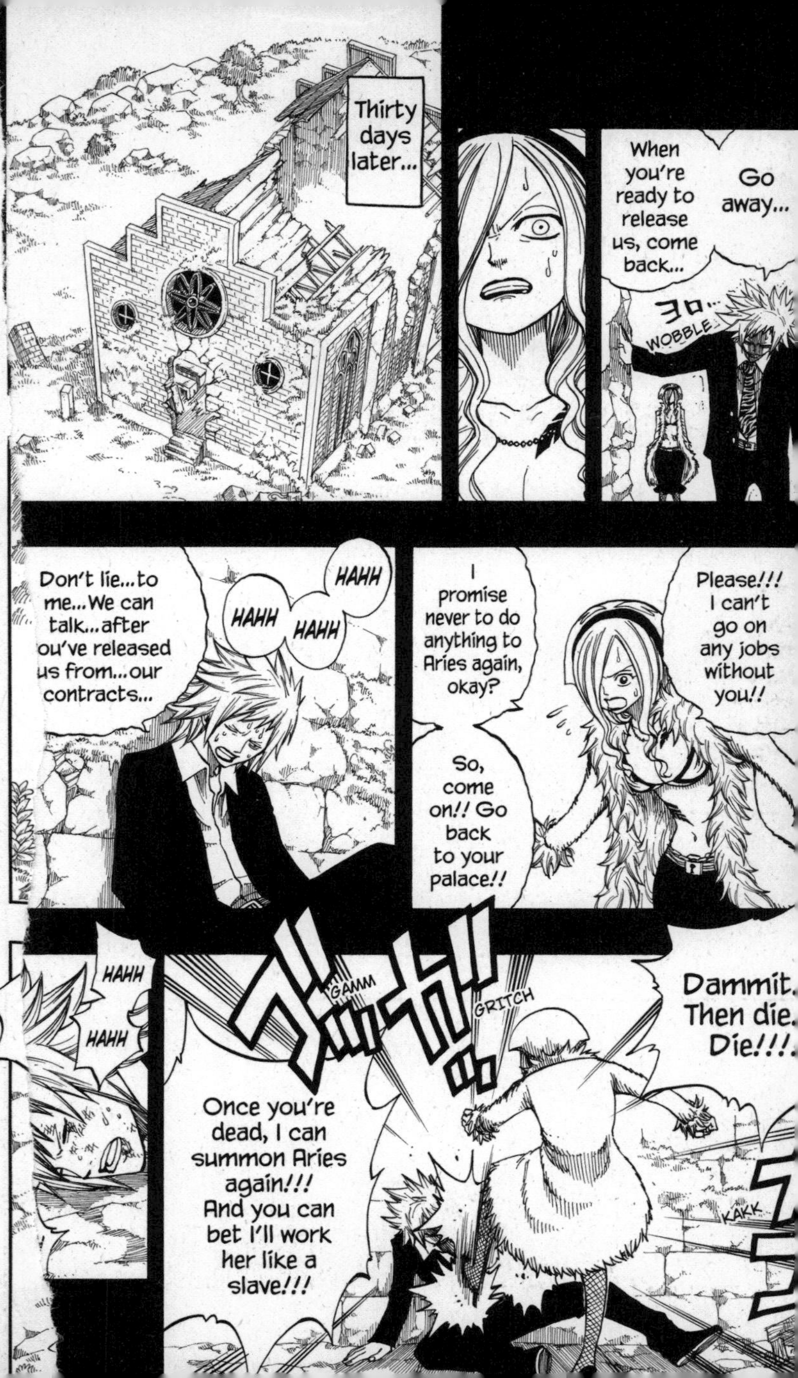
Go away...
When you're ready to release us, come back...
ヨロ… WOBBLE
Thirty days later...
Please!!! I can't go on any jobs without you!!
I promise never to do anything to Aries again, okay?
So, come on!! Go back to your palace!!
HAHH
HAHH
HAHH
Don't lie...to me...We can talk...after ou've released us from...our contracts...
Dammit. Then die. Die!!!
KAKK
GRITCH
GAMM
Once you're dead, I can summon Aries again!!! And you can bet I'll work her like a slave!!!
HAHH
HAHH

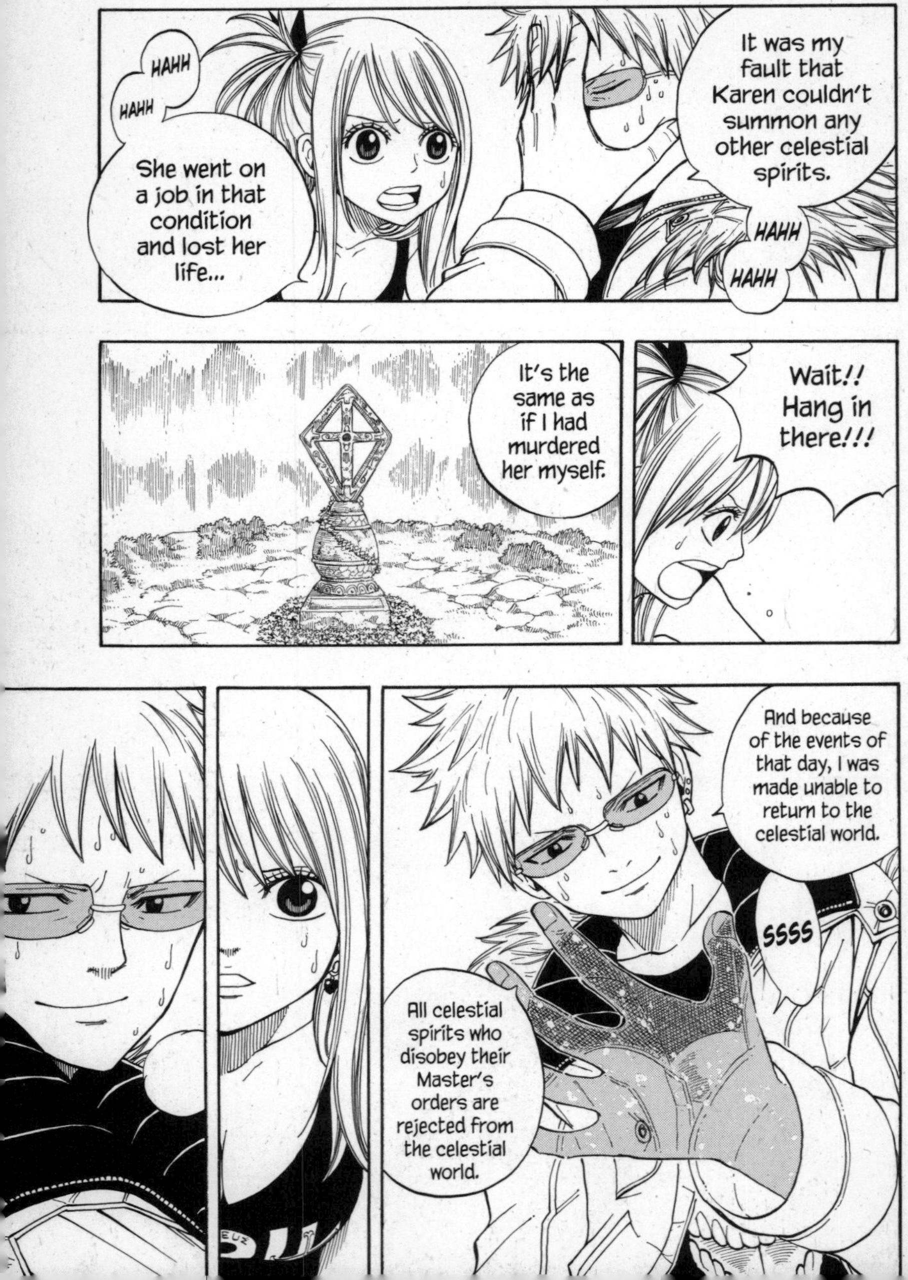

It was my fault that Karen couldn't summon any other celestial spirits.
HAHH
HAHH
HAHH
HAHH
She went on a job in that condition and lost her life...
Wait!! Hang in there!!!
It's the same as if I had murdered her myself.
And because of the events of that day, I was made unable to return to the celestial world.
SSSS
All celestial spirits who disobey their Master's orders are rejected from the celestial world.

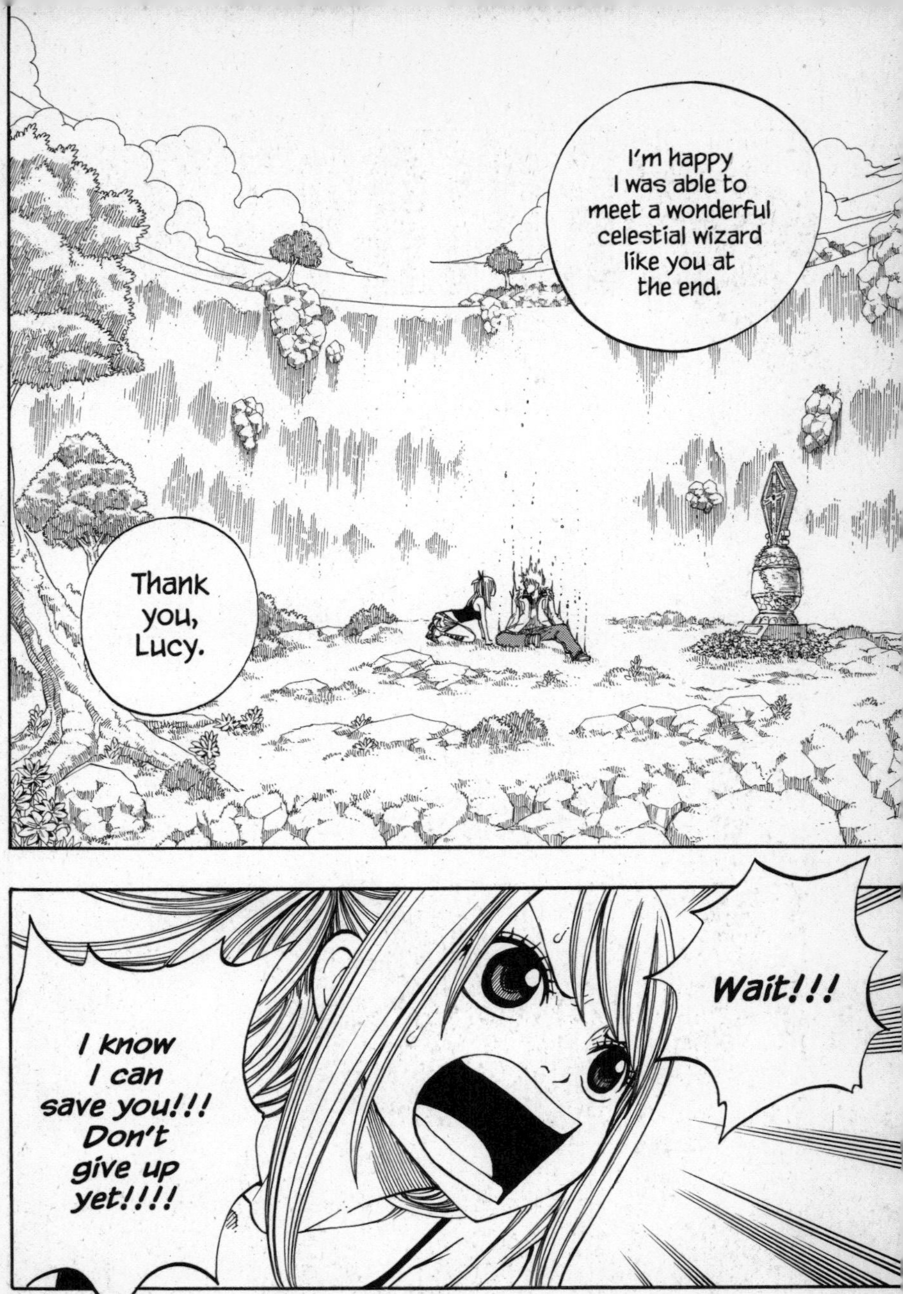
I'm happy I was able to meet a wonderful celestial wizard like you at the end.
Thank you, Lucy.
Wait!!!
I know I can save you!!! Don't give up yet!!!!

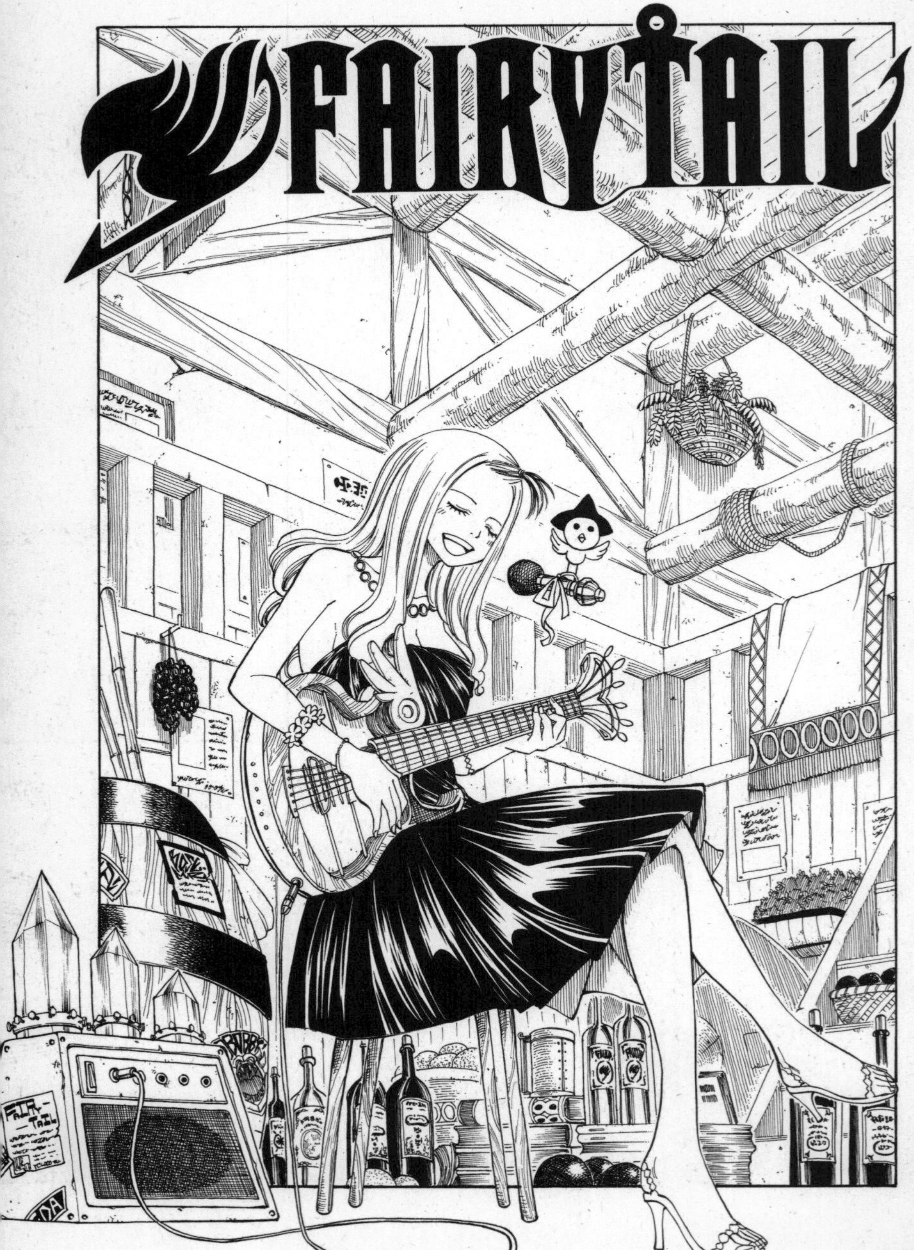
FAIRY TAIL

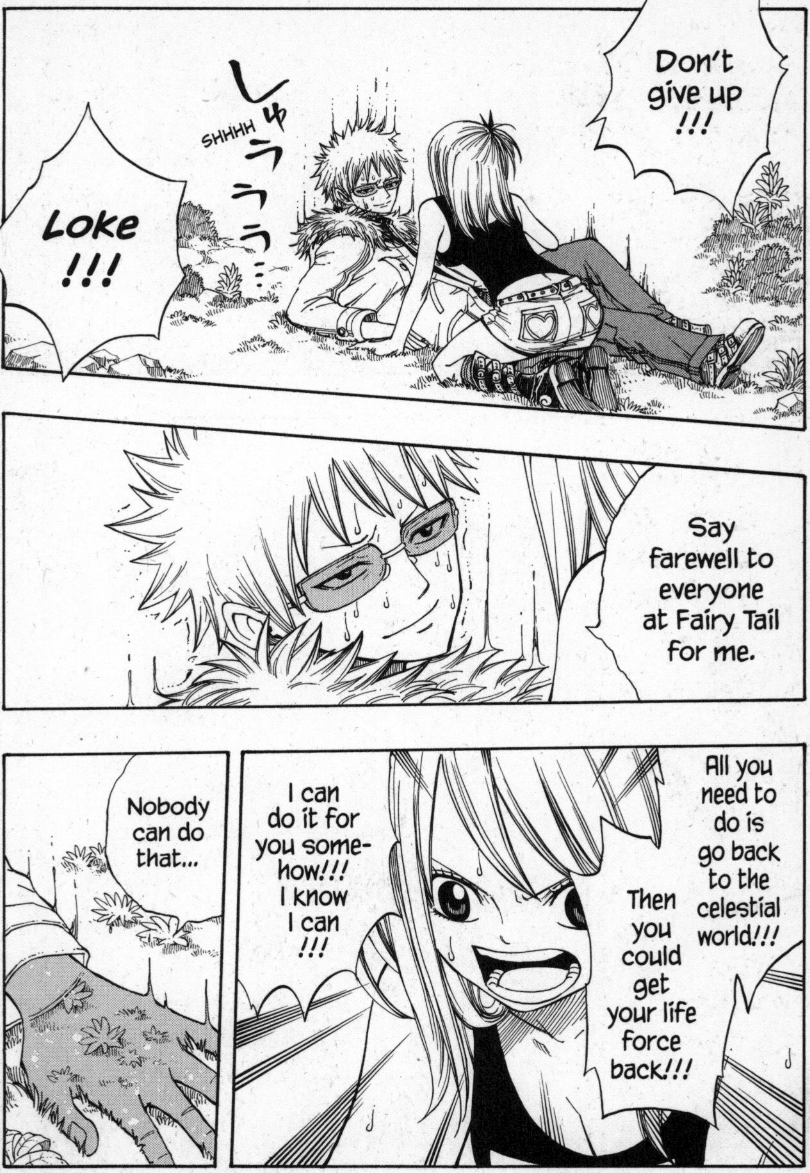
Don't give up !!!
しゅラララ…
SHHHH
Loke !!!
Say farewell to everyone at Fairy Tail for me.
All you need to do is go back to the celestial world!!!
Then you could get your life force back!!!
I can do it for you some-how!!! I know I can !!!
Nobody can do that...

Chapter 74: Celestial Spirit King

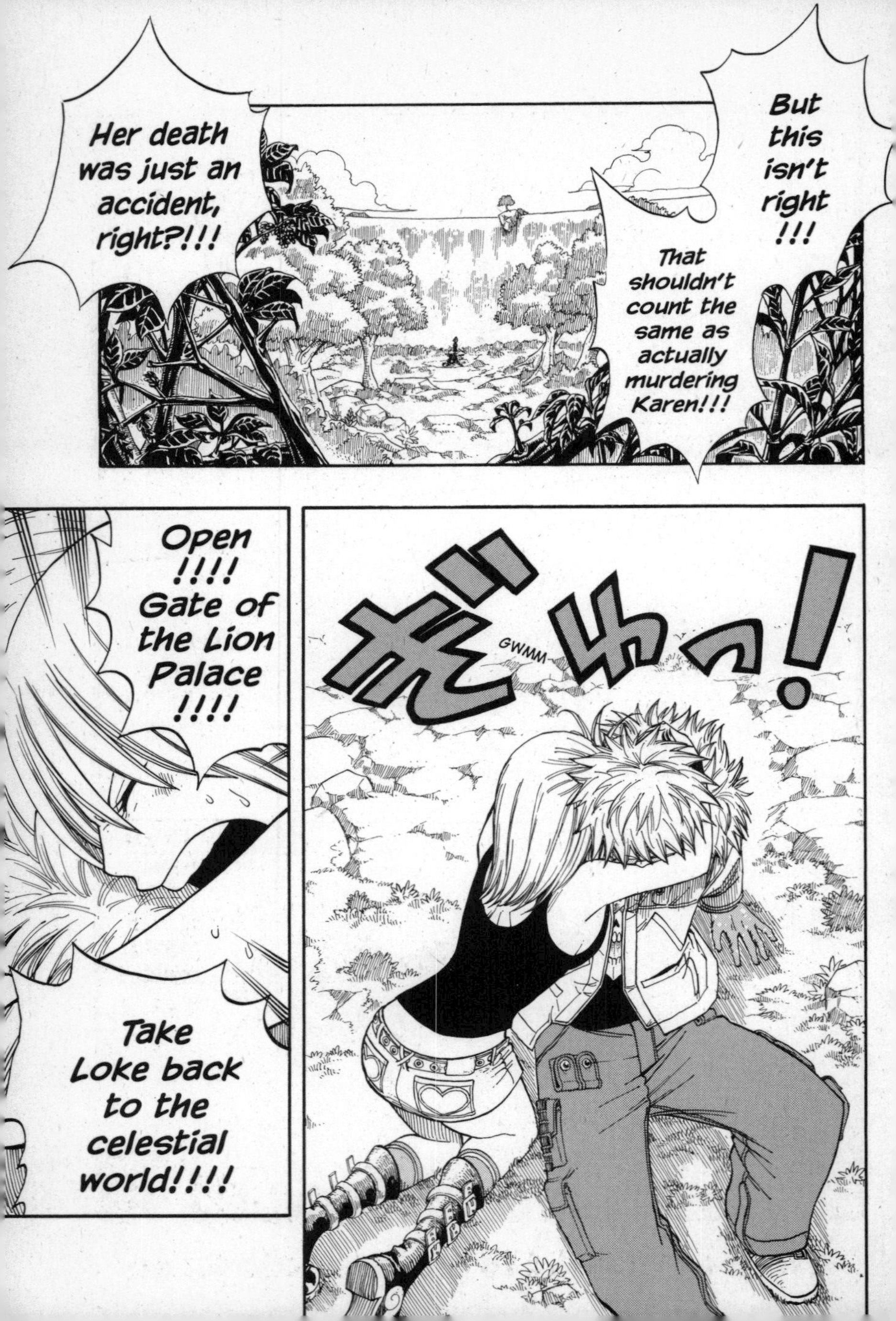
But this isn't right!!!
That shouldn't count the same as actually murdering Karen!!!
Her death was just an accident, right?!!!
GWMM
Open!!!! Gate of the Lion Palace!!!!
Take Loke back to the celestial world!!!!

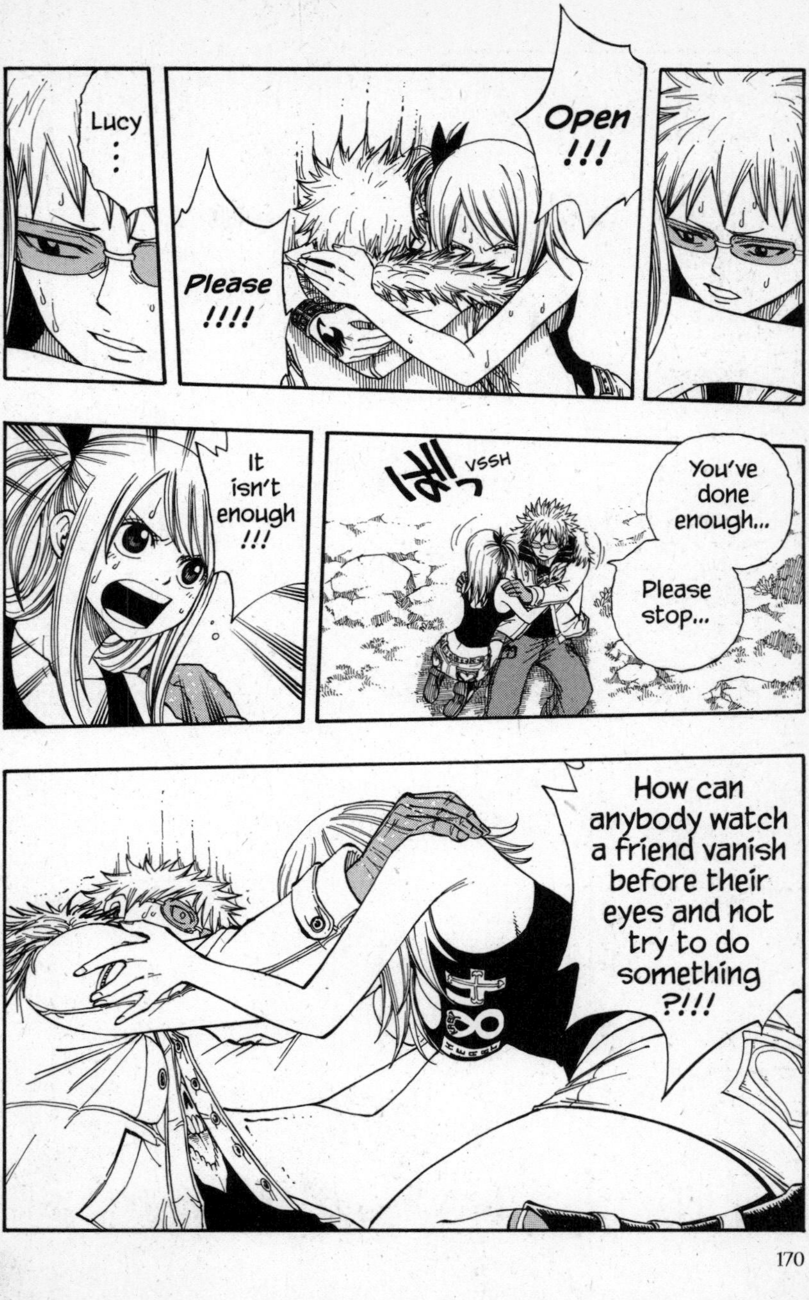
Open !!!
Please !!!!
Lucy ...
VSSH
You've done enough...
Please stop...
It isn't enough !!!
How can anybody watch a friend vanish before their eyes and not try to do something ?!!!

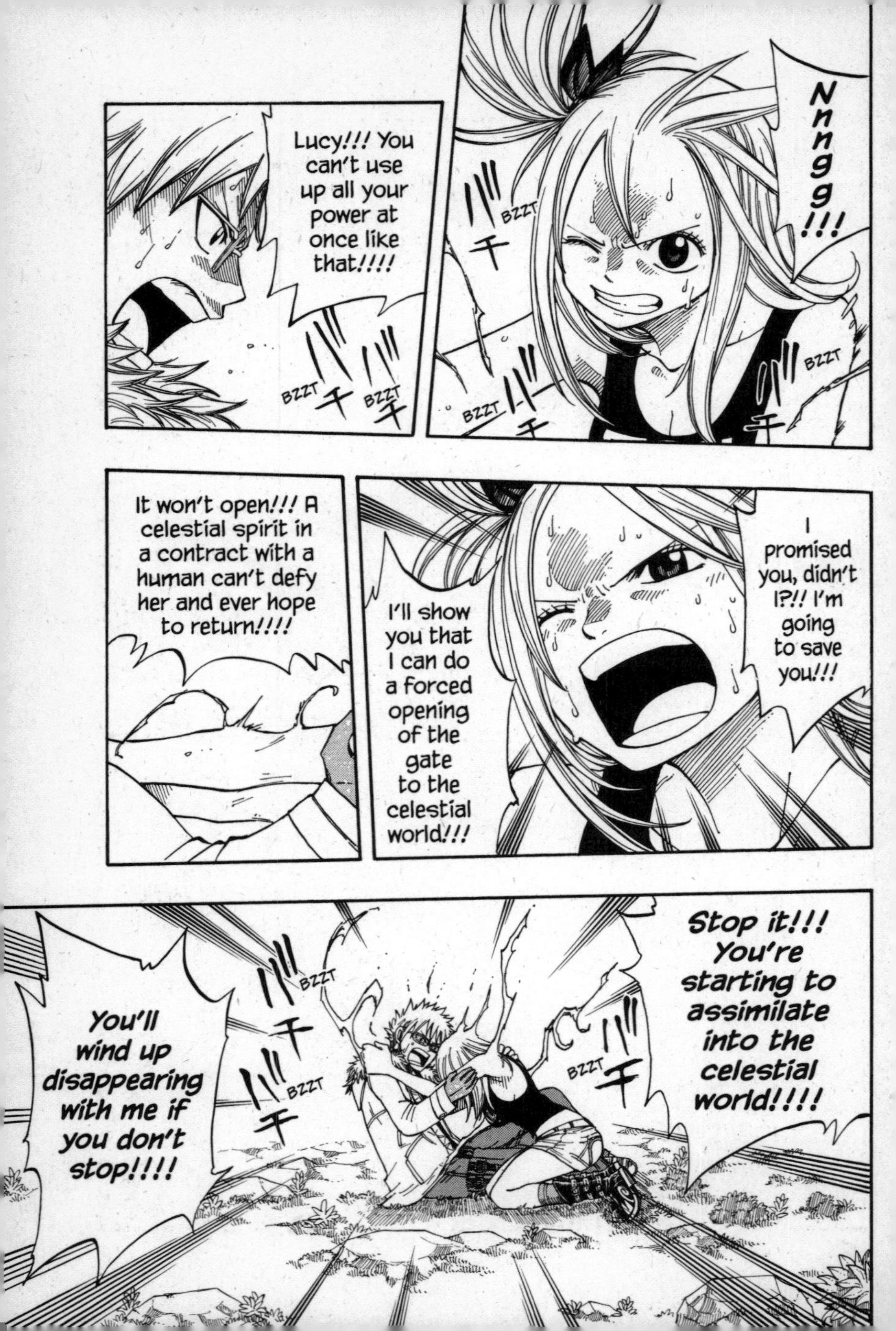
Nnngg!!!
BZZT
BZZT
BZZT
Lucy!!! You can't use up all your power at once like that!!!!
BZZT
BZZT
I promised you, didn't I?!! I'm going to save you!!!
I'll show you that I can do a forced opening of the gate to the celestial world!!!
It won't open!!! A celestial spirit in a contract with a human can't defy her and ever hope to return!!!!
Stop it!!! You're starting to assimilate into the celestial world!!!!
BZZT
BZZT
BZZT
You'll wind up disappearing with me if you don't stop!!!!

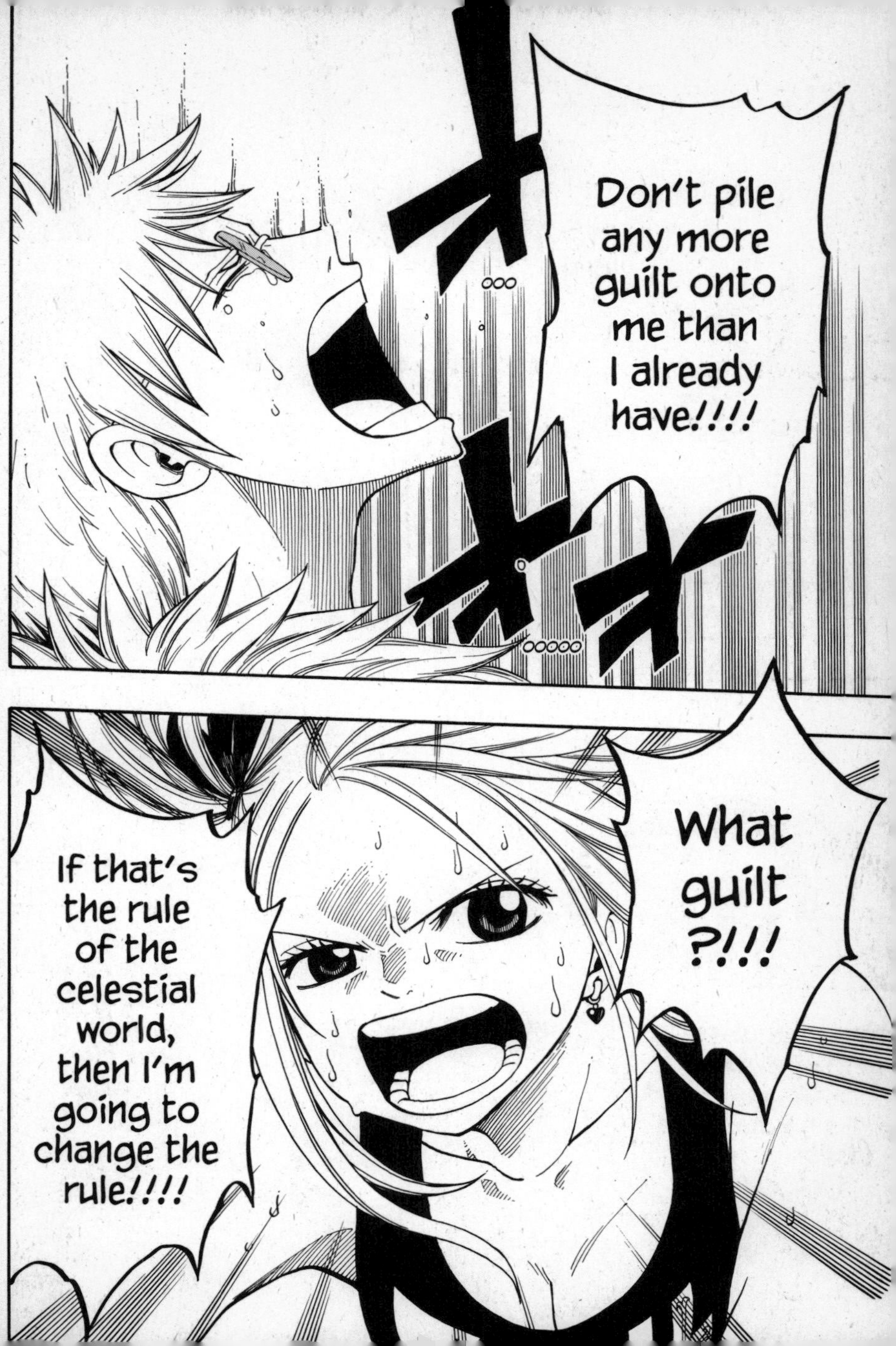
Don't pile any more guilt onto me than I already have!!!!
What guilt ?!!!
If that's the rule of the celestial world, then I'm going to change the rule!!!!

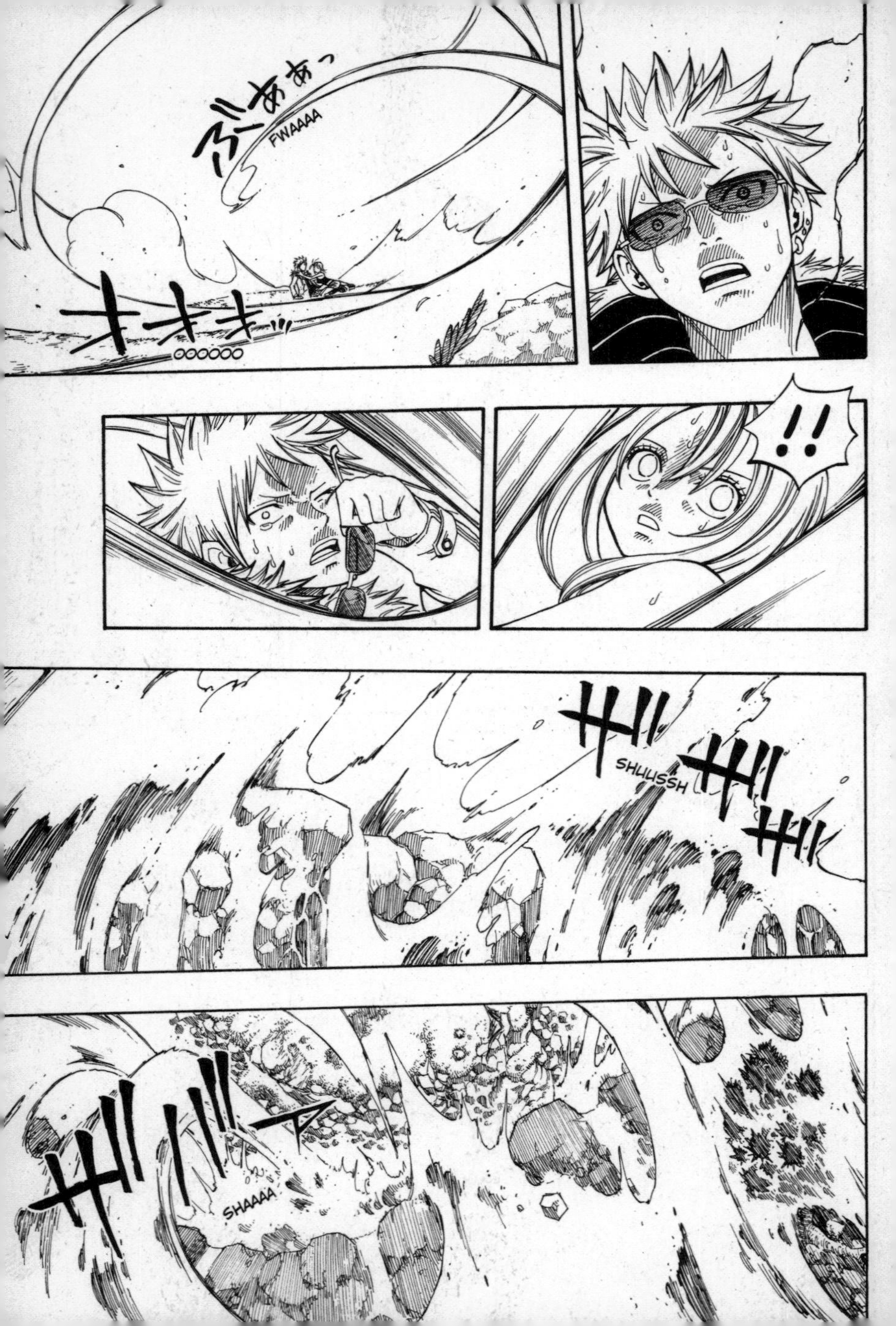
ふぁあっ
FWAAAA
OOOOOO
!!
SHUUSSH
SHAAAA

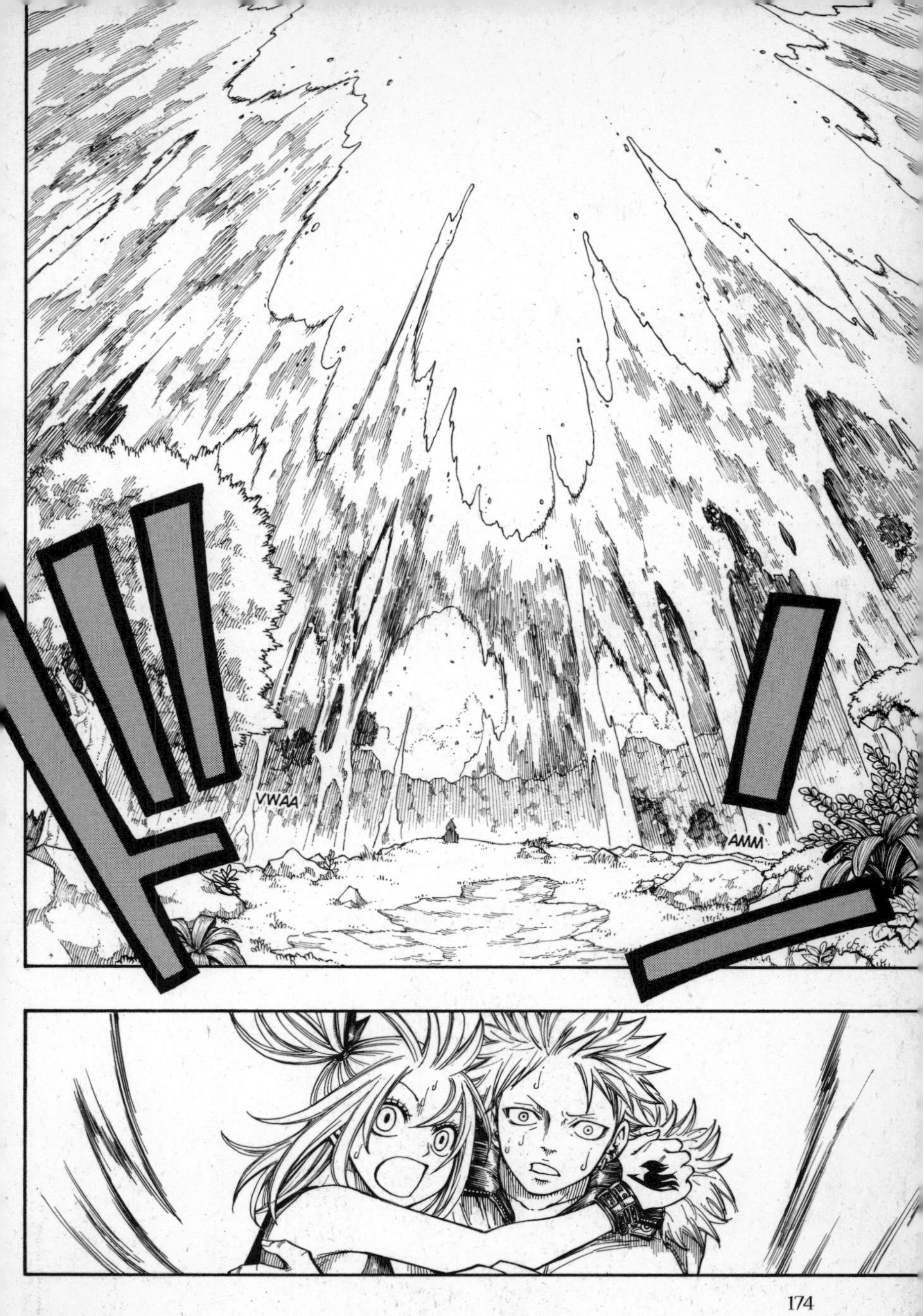
VWAA
AMM

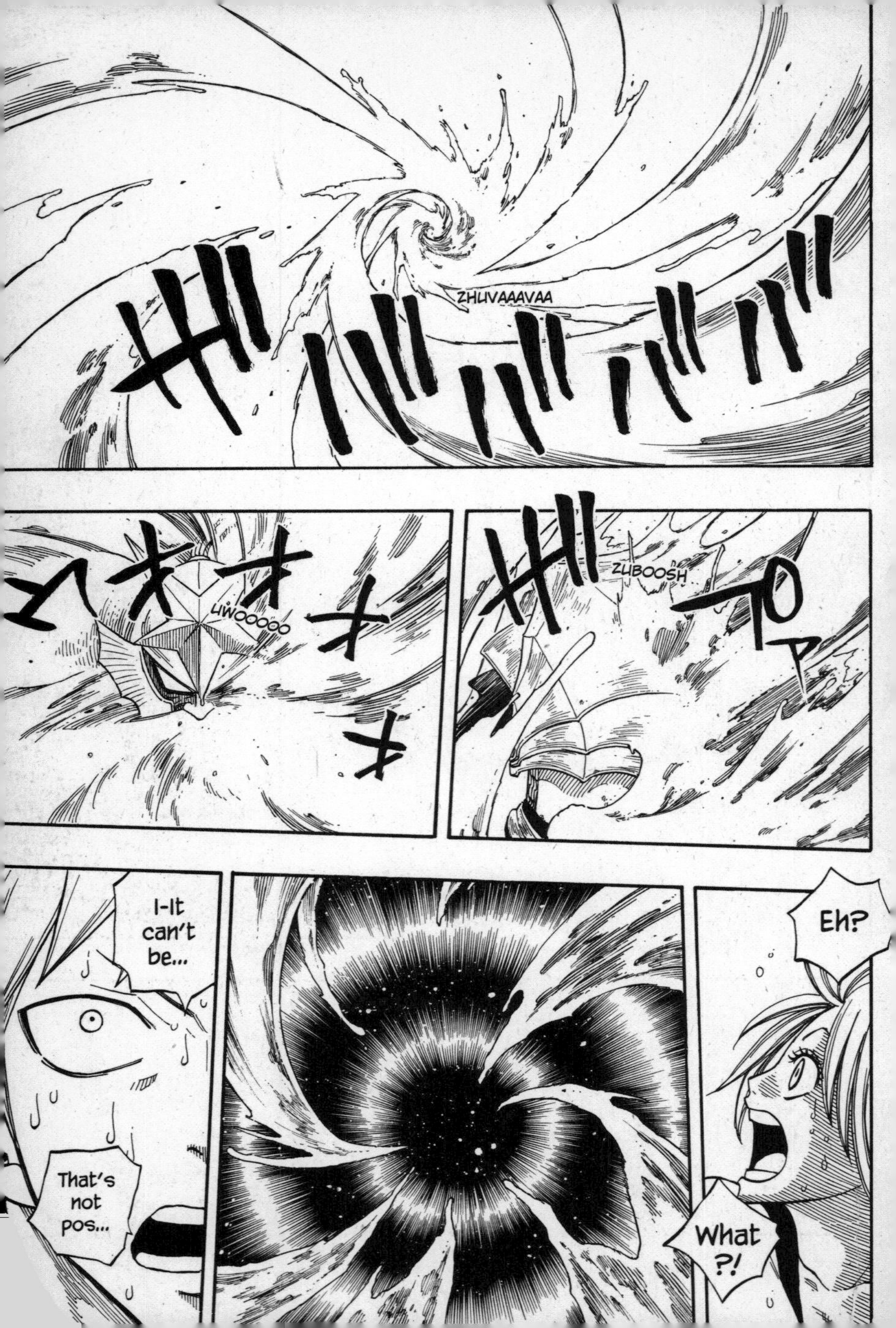
ZHUVAAAVAA
ZUBOOSH
UWOOOOO
Eh?
What?!
I-It can't be...
That's not pos...

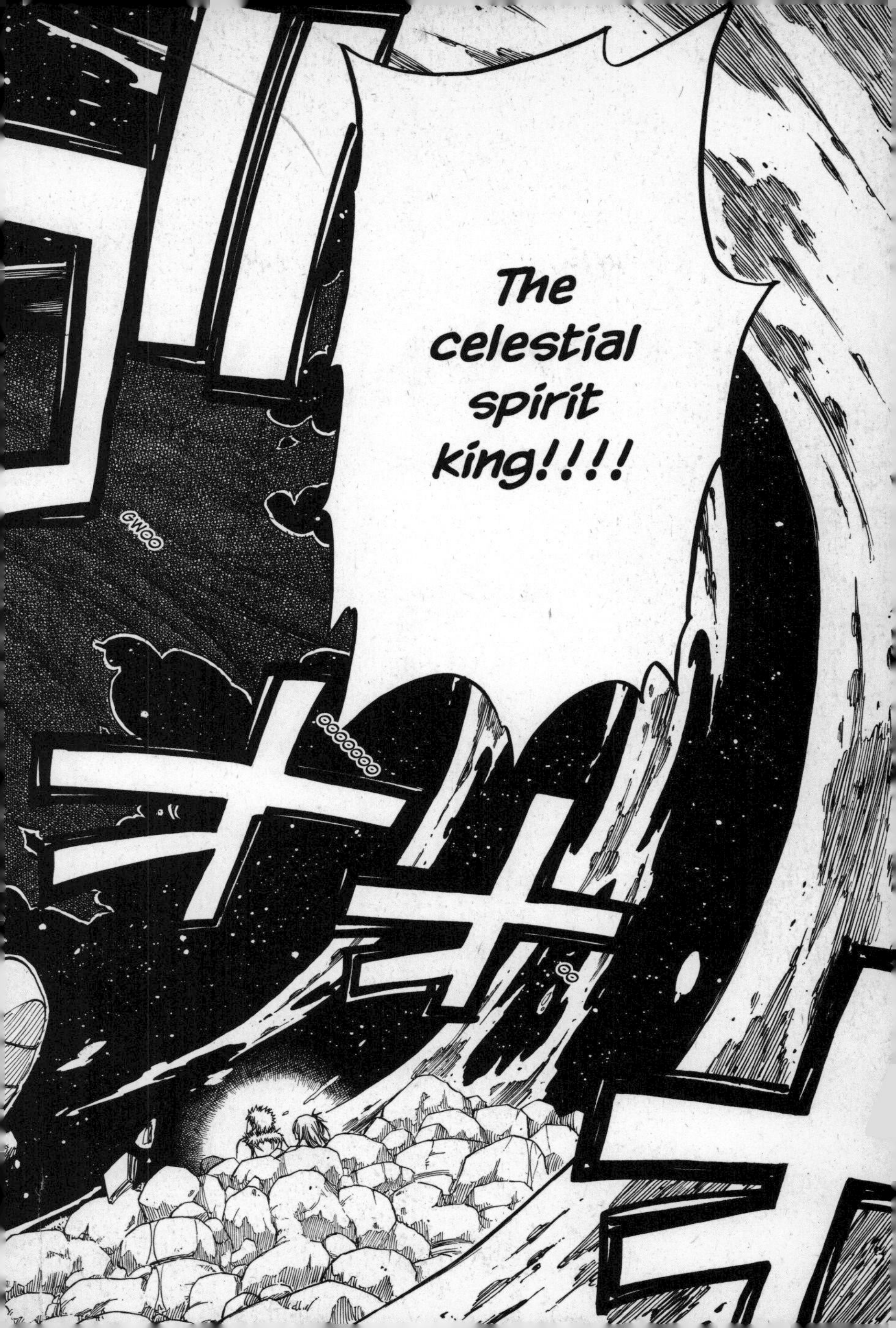
The celestial spirit king!!!!
GWOO
OOOOOOO
OO

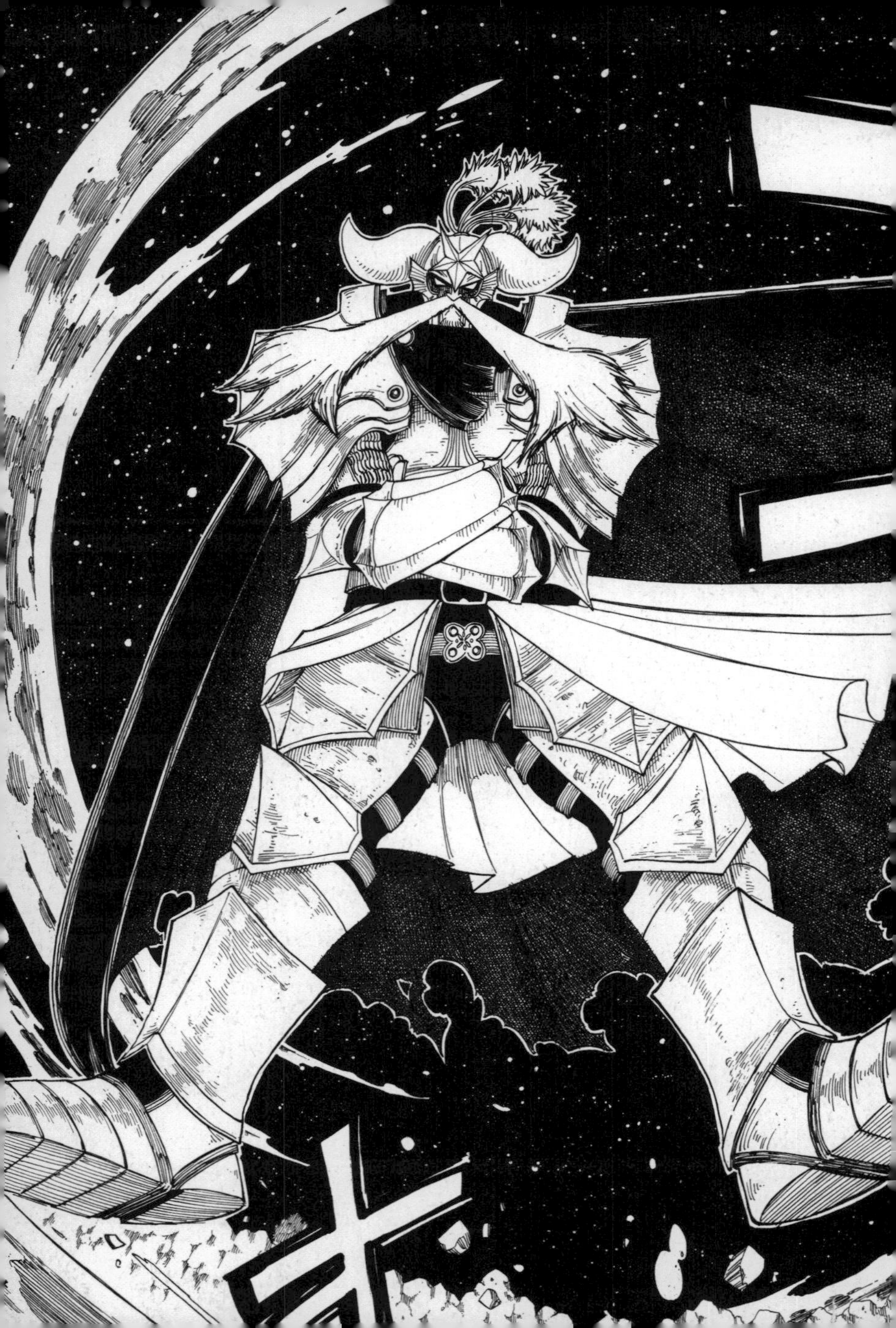

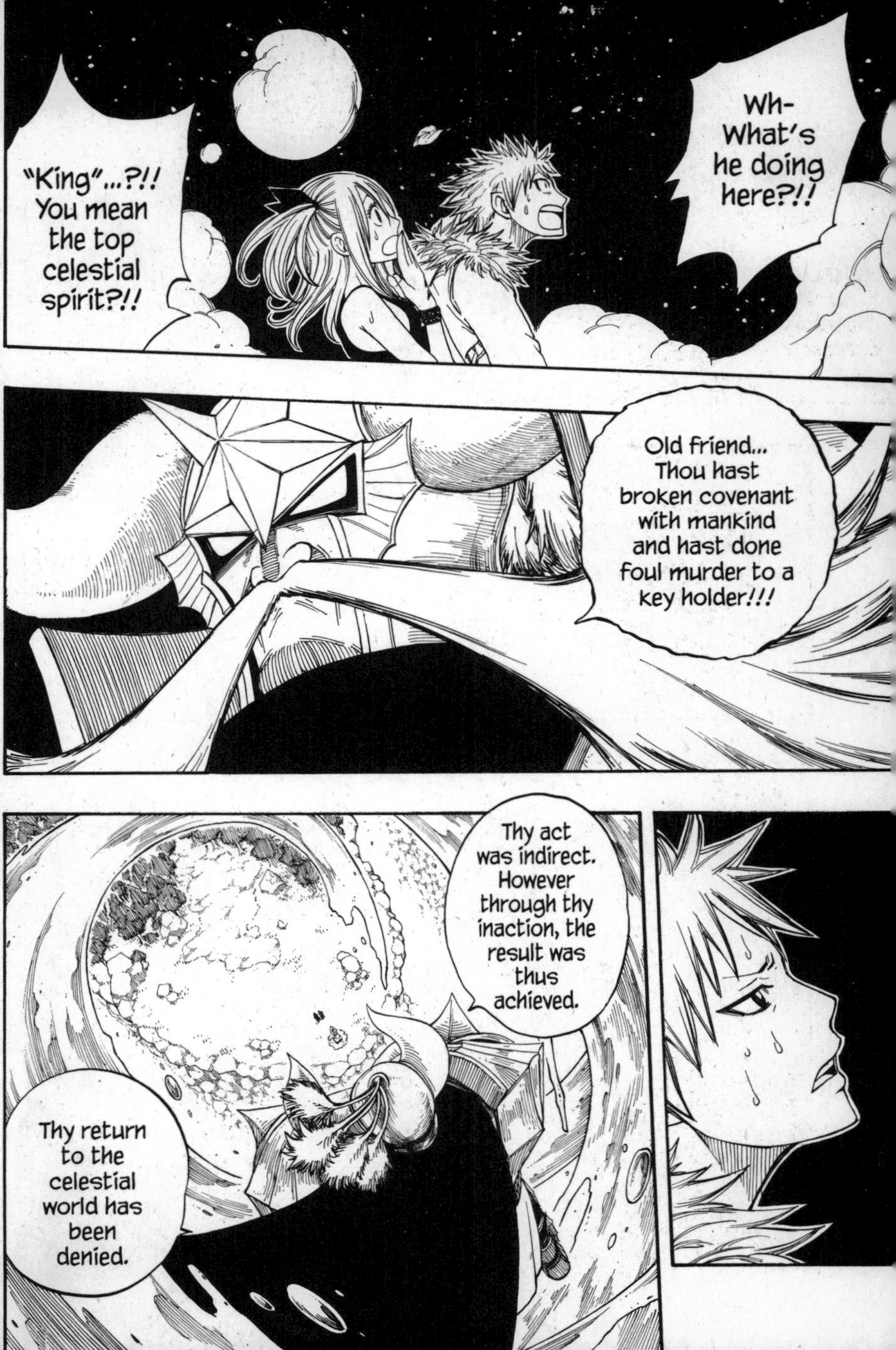
Wh- What's he doing here?!!
"King"...?!! You mean the top celestial spirit?!!
Old friend... Thou hast broken covenant with mankind and hast done foul murder to a key holder!!!
Thy act was indirect. However through thy inaction, the result was thus achieved.
Thy return to the celestial world has been denied.

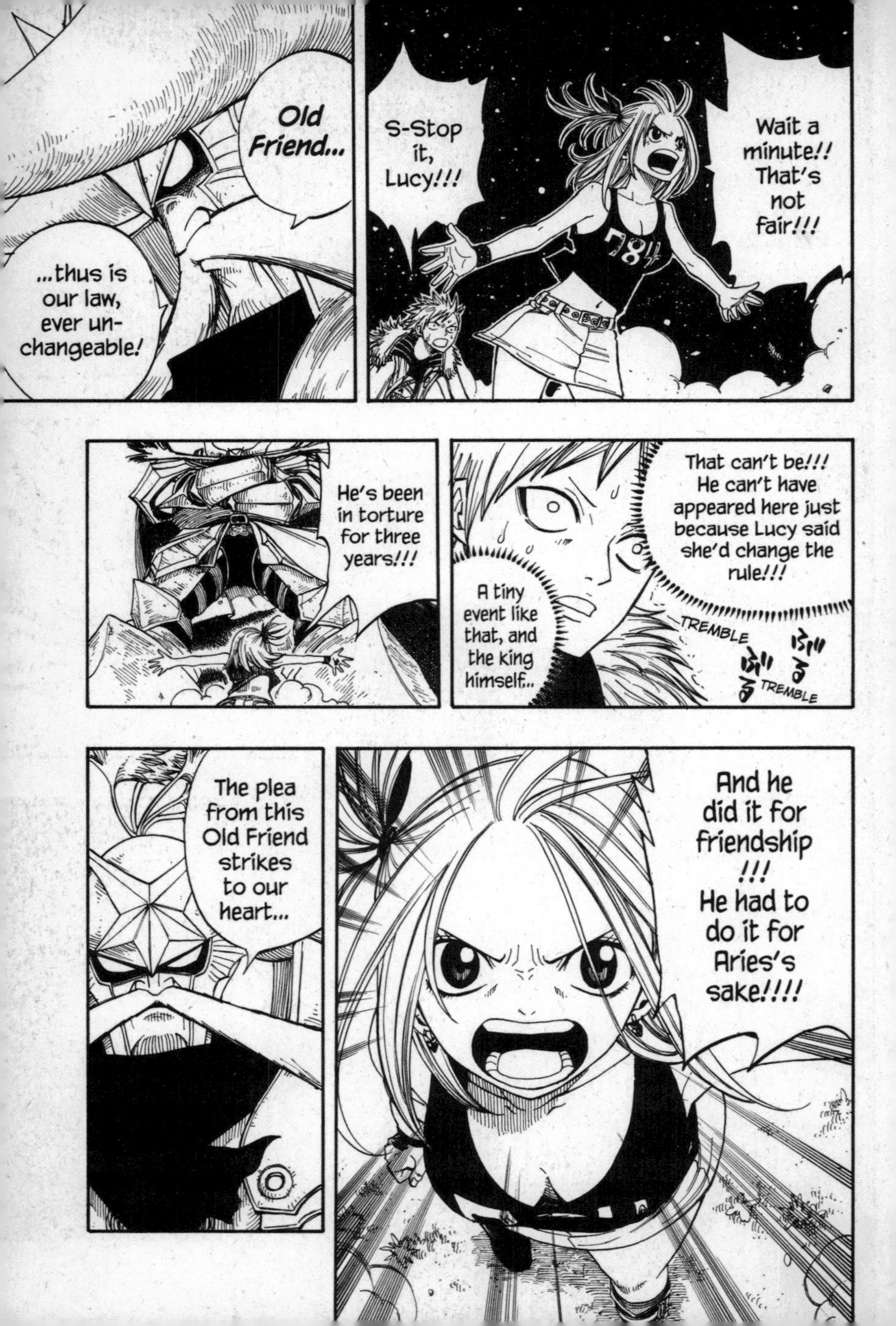
Wait a minute!! That's not fair!!!
S-Stop it, Lucy!!!
Old Friend...
...thus is our law, ever un-changeable!
That can't be!!! He can't have appeared here just because Lucy said she'd change the rule!!!
A tiny event like that, and the king himself...
TREMBLE
ぶる
ぶる
TREMBLE
He's been in torture for three years!!!
And he did it for friendship!!! He had to do it for Aries's sake!!!!
The plea from this Old Friend strikes to our heart...

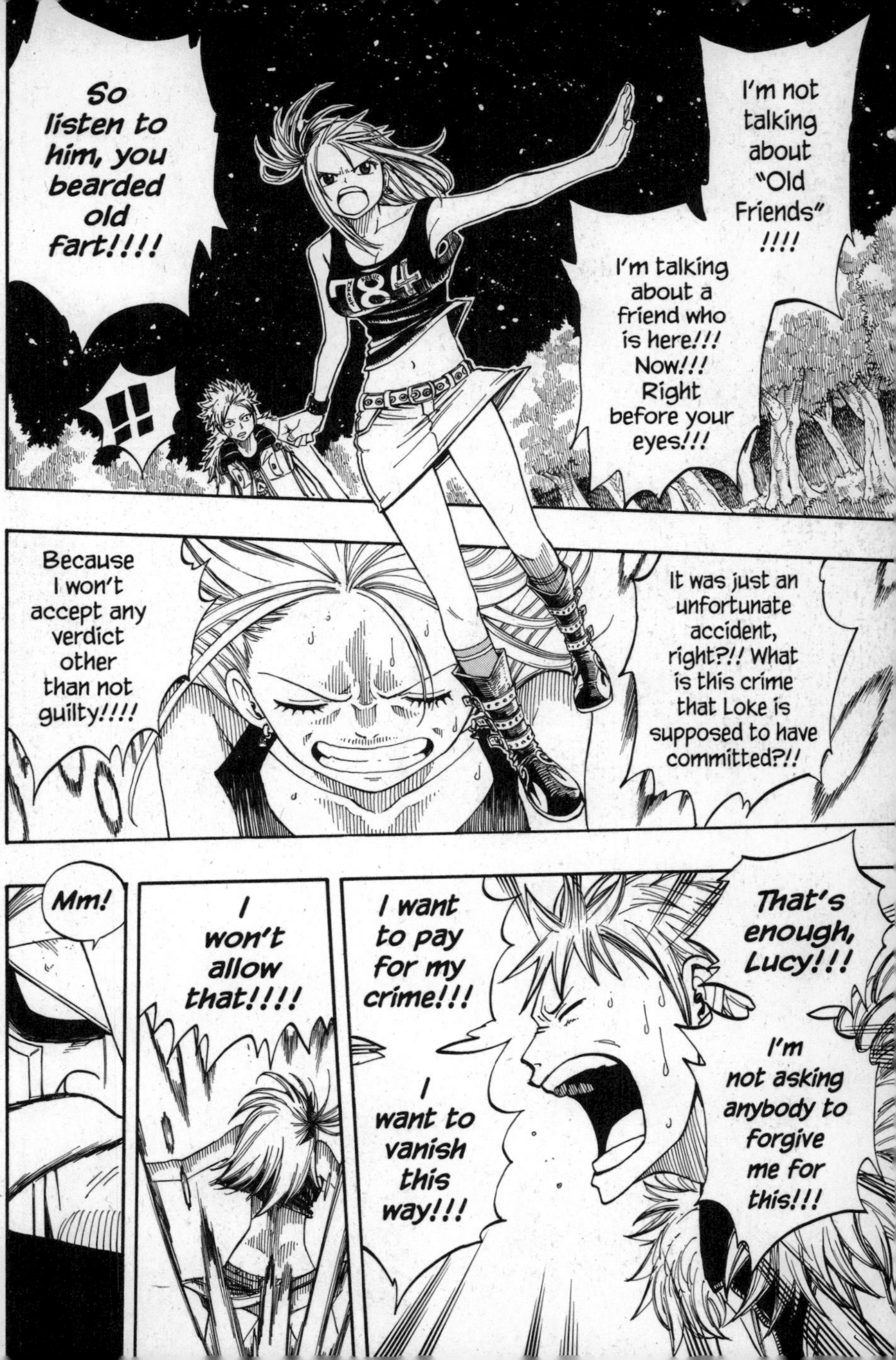
I'm not talking about "Old Friends"!!!!
I'm talking about a friend who is here!!! Now!!! Right before your eyes!!!
So listen to him, you bearded old fart!!!!
!!
It was just an unfortunate accident, right?!! What is this crime that Loke is supposed to have committed?!!
Because I won't accept any verdict other than not guilty!!!!
That's enough, Lucy!!!
I'm not asking anybody to forgive me for this!!!
I want to pay for my crime!!!
I want to vanish this way!!!
I won't allow that!!!!
Mm!

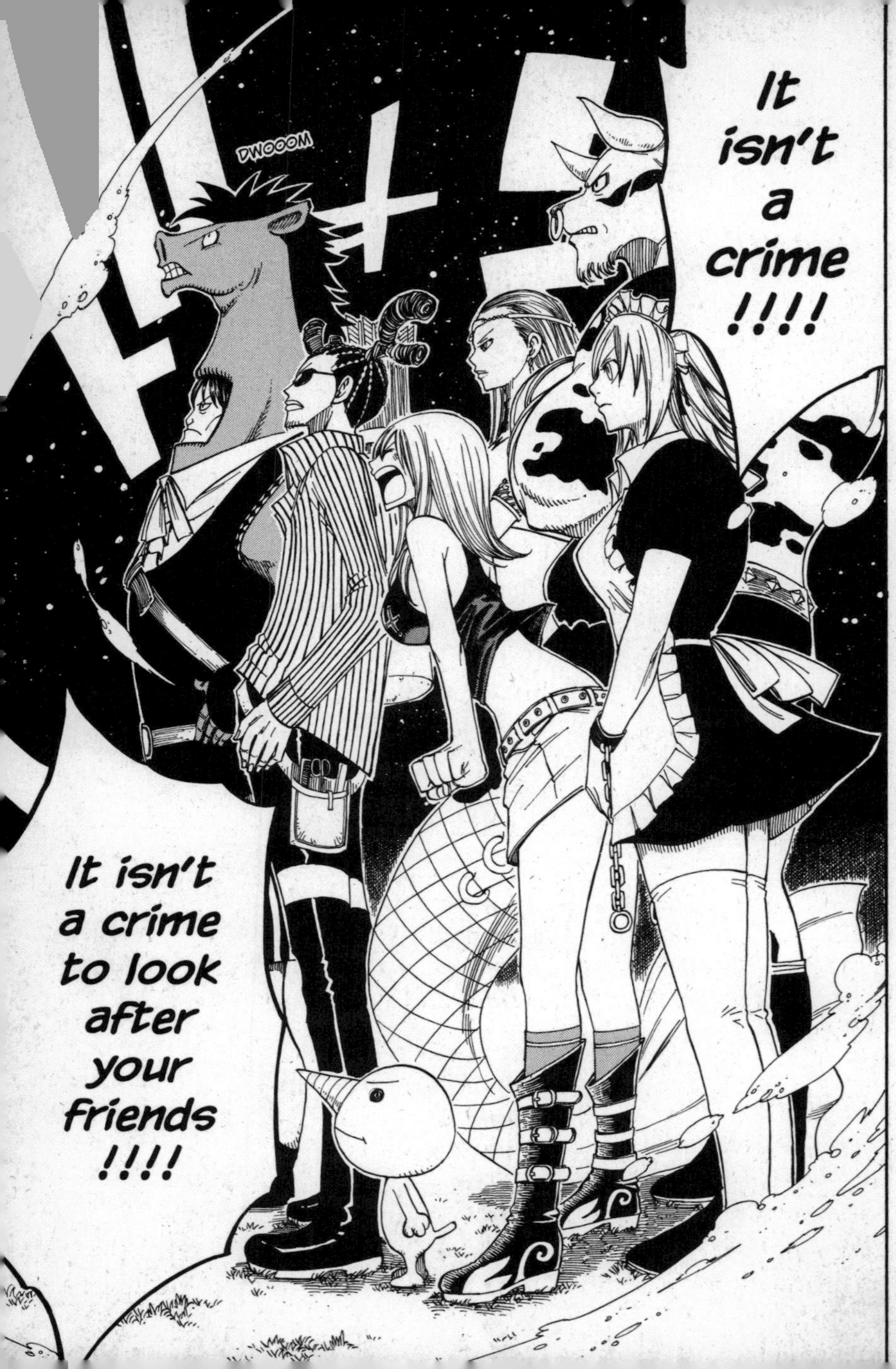
It isn't a crime !!!!
DWOOOM
It isn't a crime to look after your friends !!!!

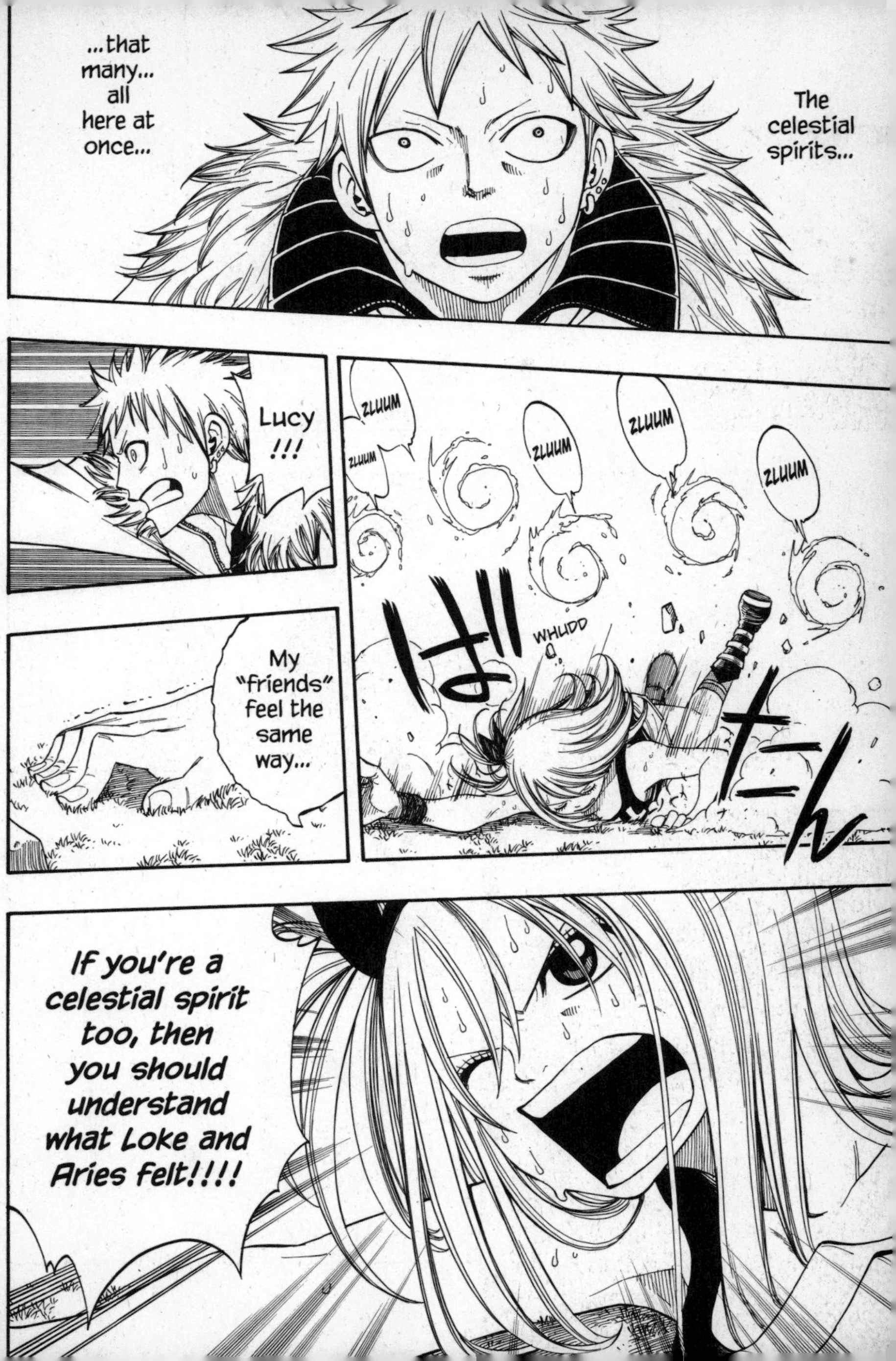
The celestial spirits...
...that many... all here at once...
ZLUUM
ZLUUM
ZLUUM
ZLUUM
ZLUUM
WHUDD
ばたん
Lucy !!!
My "friends" feel the same way...
If you're a celestial spirit too, then you should understand what Loke and Aries felt!!!!

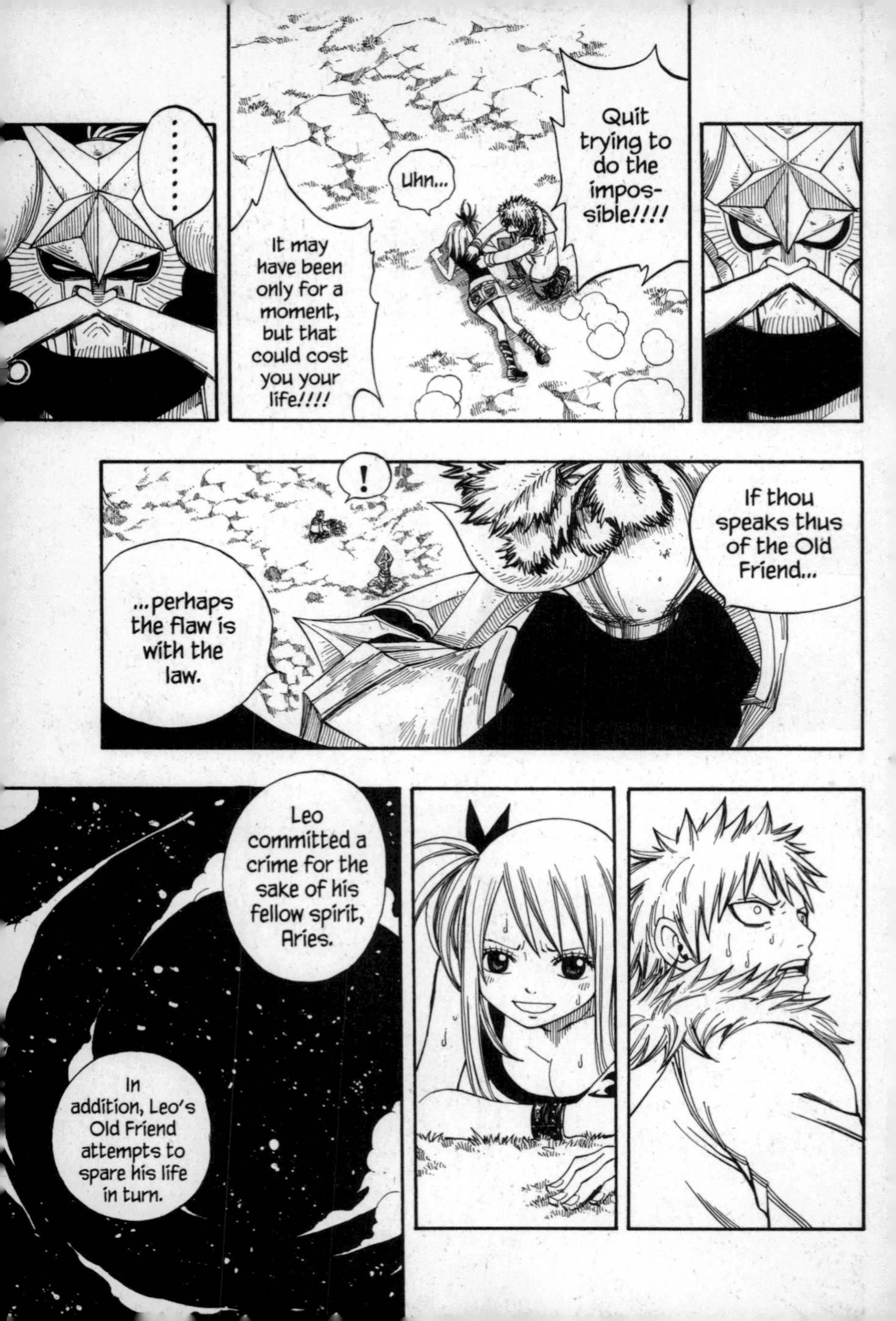
Quit trying to do the impos-sible!!!!
Uhn...
It may have been only for a moment, but that could cost you your life!!!!
......
If thou speaks thus of the Old Friend...
!
...perhaps the flaw is with the law.
Leo committed a crime for the sake of his fellow spirit, Aries.
In addition, Leo's Old Friend attempts to spare his life in turn.

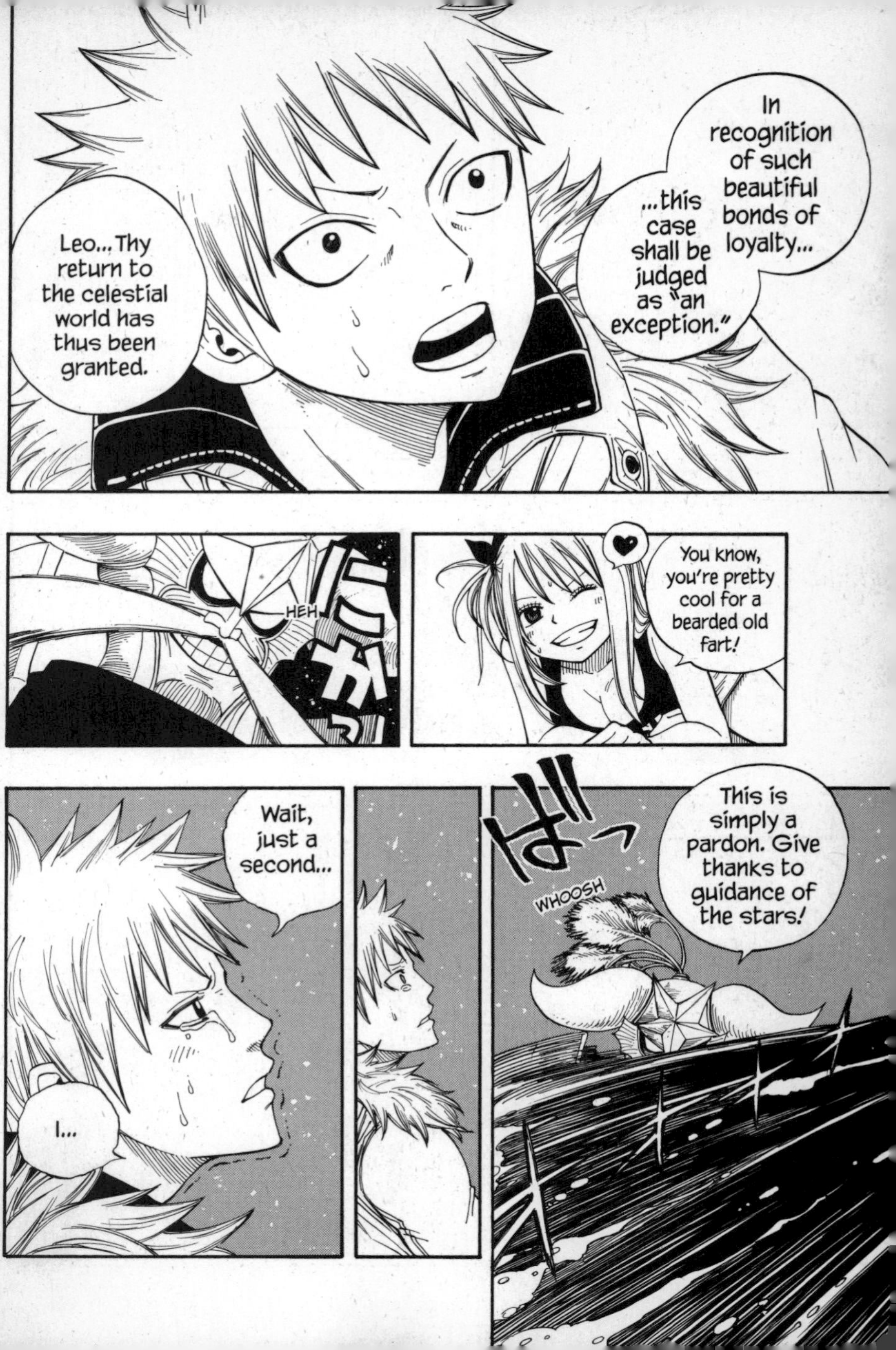
In recognition of such beautiful bonds of loyalty...
...this case shall be judged as "an exception."
Leo... Thy return to the celestial world has thus been granted.
You know, you're pretty cool for a bearded old fart!
HEH
This is simply a pardon. Give thanks to guidance of the stars!
WHOOSH
Wait, just a second...
I...

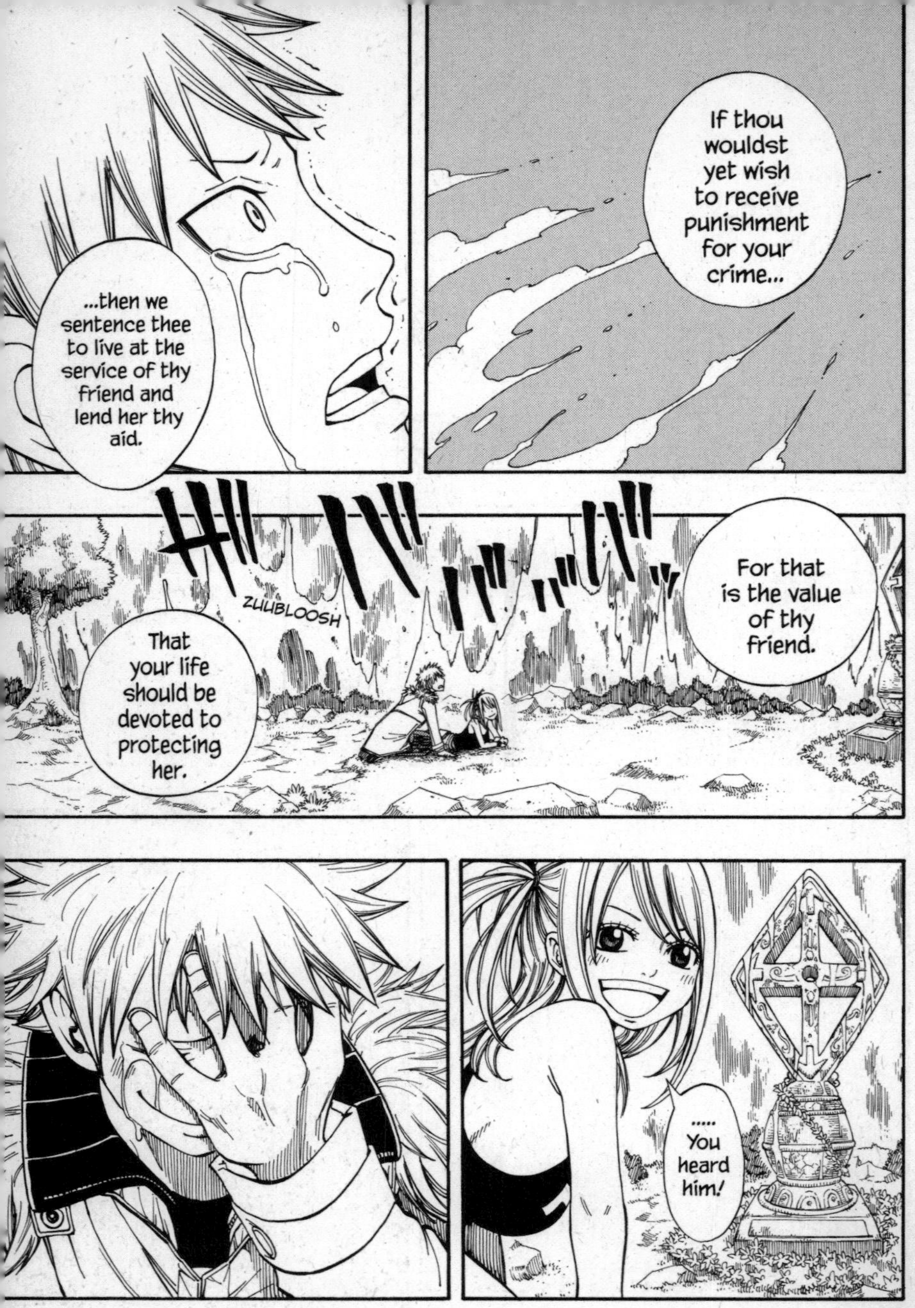
If thou wouldst yet wish to receive punishment for your crime...
...then we sentence thee to live at the service of thy friend and lend her thy aid.
For that is the value of thy friend.
ZUUBLOOSH
That your life should be devoted to protecting her.
..... You heard him!

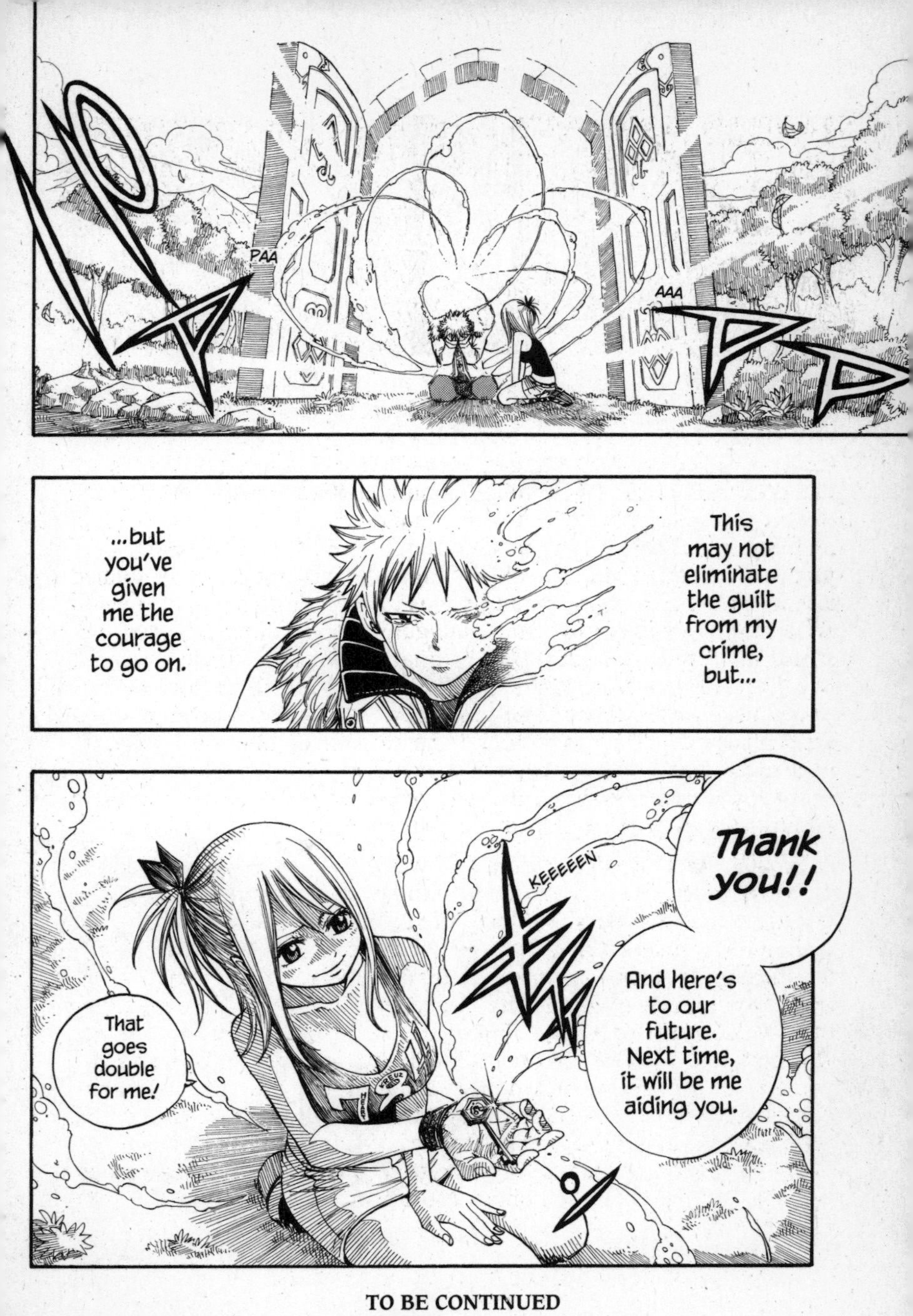
PAA
AAA
This may not eliminate the guilt from my crime, but...
...but you've given me the courage to go on.
Thank you!!
KEEEEEN
And here's to our future. Next time, it will be me aiding you.
That goes double for me!

TO BE CONTINUED

AFTERWORD

Man, am I busy!! Yeah, for a manga-ka that's a great thing to be able to say, but I'm way too busy!! If you want to know why, it's because I have another manga series—this time a monthly series. I've done this in the past, doing a monthly and a weekly series at the same time, but this time there are so many more pages required than last time! So the pace is so much different than before. By the way, when I was only doing a weekly manga, the amount of work equaled twenty pages of manga, twenty pages of *name* (the Japanese term for a rough-sketched story and dialogue), plus a couple of color pieces and small, odd jobs. But the quantity of work I had last week was forty-three manga pages, sixty-nine pages of *name,* four color pages, and tons of those small, odd jobs. What the heck was that week all about?!! The only thing I can do is laugh about it!! Yeah, it was an unusually heavy week that included a short story, so the page numbers were artificially high, but even so, my regular work week is about twice as busy as before. Man! It's unbelievable!!

Recently I met another creator, and was asked what my motivation is for doing all of that work. I don't know how to answer that question. I never even considered the concept of motivation. Of course, I love manga, and that's why I draw it. But that's the basic assumption for any manga-ka. In my case, maybe it includes journeyman-style training. That probably sums it up. I've been doing this work for over ten years, but I can't seem to get good at drawing. (Ha ha!) Is it true that if I draw a lot, I'll become better? Normally, you'd think so...Anyway, I'm busy! Really busy! And that's what comes out of my mouth when I'm talking to the people around me, but inside I'm having so much fun, I can hardly contain it! I can draw a whole lot of manga! My manga will be read by a whole lot of people! That's probably my motivation, huh?

: By the way, I entered six years ago bringing Elfman and Lisanna with me.

Erza: Natsu entered seven years ago, and Gray had entered even before I did.

Lucy: Huh? You guys have been in the guild a long time! It hasn't even been a year for me!

Erza: The story of my life before Fairy Tail is touched on in Volume 10.

Mira: I'm interested in learning about that!

 : What was that? You just casually throw a preview of the next volume into the conversation?

Mira: Okay, the final question.

Who is the heroine of Fairy Tail? Lucy or Erza?

 : **!!!**

Mira: Nobody cares who the "heroine" is, right?

Lucy: What do you mean "nobody"?! I mean, people would automatically assume it's me, right?

 : Well...I feel a little embarrassed by being addressed as the heroine, but...Am I truly being looked upon in that fashion?

Lucy: Wait a minute!! What are you blushing for?!!

Mira: Certainly at first glance, one would think it's Lucy, but I hear that Erza has more fans.

 : *You're kidding!!!*

Erza: Is that so?

Lucy: Wait!! Just look at the cover for Volume 9! It's me!! All me!! I carry the entire cover all by myself!!

Mira: If you look closely, you see an awful lot of celestial spirits there too.

Erza: Lucy, did you know? They included a poster of me in *Weekly Magazine*.

Lucy: Waaaaaah!!

Erza: And that was only me. Heh heh...

Lucy: Waaaaaaaaaahh!

Mira: Well, none of this bickering will settle the matter. So why don't we ask the author directly?

------- *And so...* -------

Mashima: You're asking who the heroine is?

Lucy: It's me, right?! You love drawing pictures of me, don't you?!!

Erza: Do not forget that you drew a poster that was me and me alone.

Mashima: I give up. I think it's okay for the readers to decide who they think the heroine is for themselves.

Mira: Exactly! Nobody cares who it is! ♥

Mashima: Frankly, I think it's okay for the heroine to be Tomeko from Tokekko Restaurant.

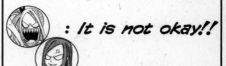 : *It is not okay!!*

Special Request
Explain the Mysteries...
... of Fairy Tail

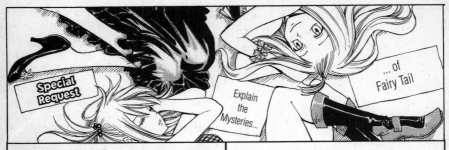

From the Counter at Fairy Tail...

: All you readers out there, hello! ♥

: Hello! You're in a good mood today, Lucy!

Lucy: Sure! It's the ninth volume, and the stories were all about me!! It's like Volume 9 was drawn especially for me! ♥

Mira: That's what it means to be a heroine, I guess, huh? Well, while you're in such a good mood, let's get started on the questions.

How many sets of armor total can Erza requip into?

Lucy: That question is pretty painful...er...I mean a sharp question!

Mira: The two of us can't answer it, so let's call in the woman herself. Introducing our special guest, Erza!

: Mm.

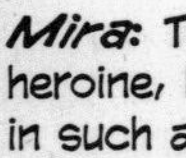

Lucy: Don't just say, "Mm"! If you don't come up with some greeting, you'll lose popularity points!

Erza: No...Well...I suppose I am not used to this...Uh...Hello.

Mira: So about the question we just heard. Erza, how many suits of armor do you have?

Erza: Many.

: Wait a second! None of the readers will really count that as an answer! You're going to have to do better than that to increase your point score!

Mira: What are popularity points exactly?

Erza: I have more than a hundred different types. I haven't counted them all myself, but I also count within their ranks dresses and kimono.

Lucy: Requipping is such a great concept! Dressing must be a breeze!

Mira: On to the next question.

I am Erza. Nice to meet you.

How long has Erza been in the Fairy Tail guild?

: Eight years. That brings back memories.

Continued on the

The Fairy Tail Guild d'Art is an explosion of fan art! Please send in your black-and-white art on large postcard stock!! Those chosen to be published will get a signed mini poster! ♪ Make sure you write your real name and address on the back of your postcard!

D'ART

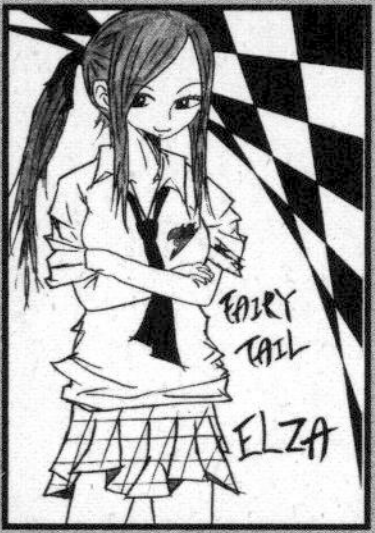
FAIRY TAIL
ELZA

▼ An Erza in a school uniform, huh? Just a little while ago I drew a side story like that.

Gunma Prefecture, Kayo

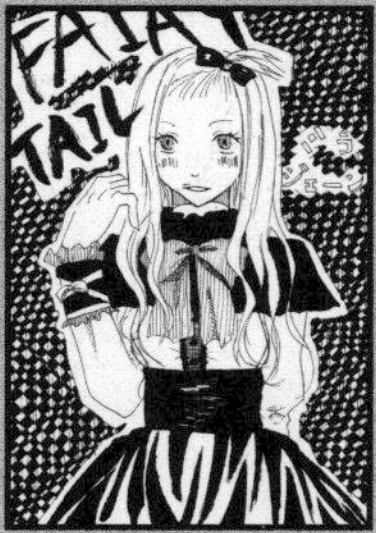
TAIL

▼ This one's very cute!! And well done!

Iwate Prefecture, Kô Minamikaze

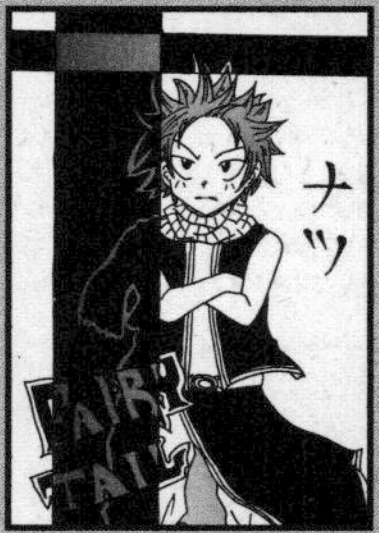
ナツ
FAIRY TAIL

▼ Whoa! This one has some great artistic sense!

Iwate Prefecture, Sena Minazuki

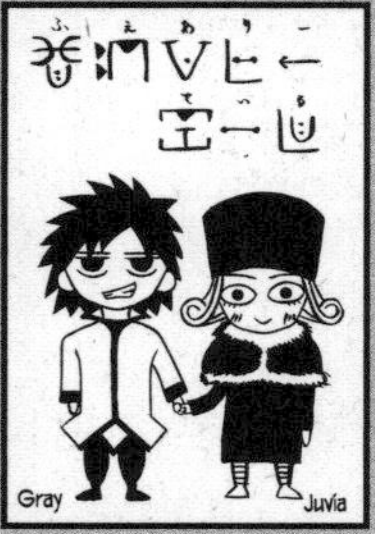
Gray
Juvia

▼ It seems that the battle between these two has gotten itself a good reputation.

Hyôgo Prefecture, Kôsuke Shimoda

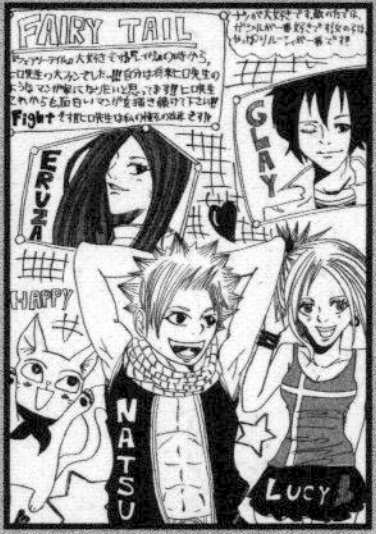
FAIRY TAIL
GLAY
HAPPY
NATSU
LUCY

▼ A fan from my previous work. I'm so happy I could cry!

Hokkaido, Seiryu Tanaka

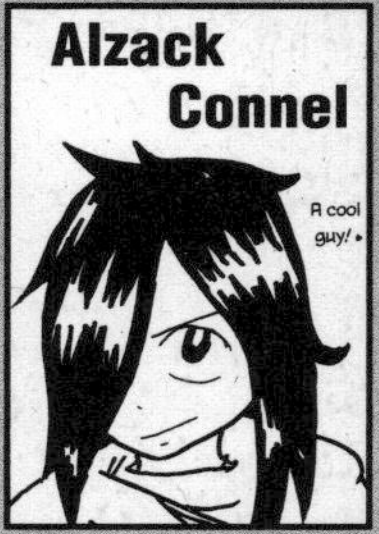
Alzack Connel
A cool guy!

▼ Are you a part of the Gloomy Character Fan Club? Maybe not, huh?

Aichi Prefecture, Chiibô

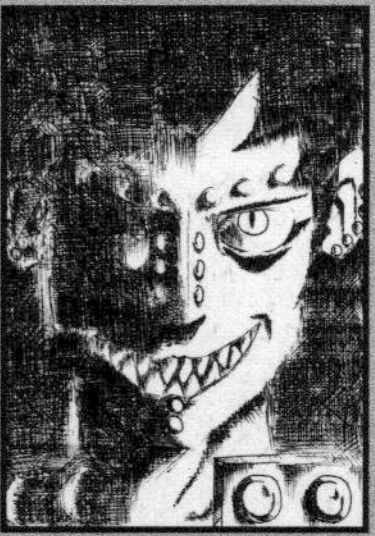

▼ Whoa! Gajeel's scary! This is one page that's got him pinned!

Niigata Prefecture, Tomohiko Enamoto

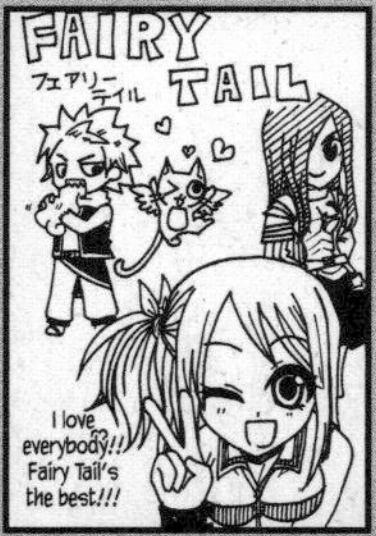
FAIRY TAIL
フェアリーテイル
I love everybody!!! Fairy Tail's the best!!!

▼ Thank you!! Keep on rooting for me, please!

Chiba Prefecture, Koharu

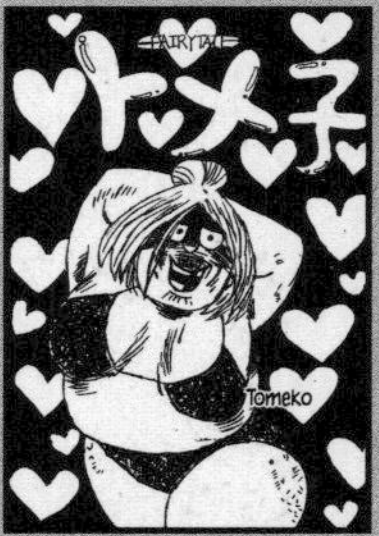
FAIRY TAIL
トメ子
Tomeko

▼ And there's Tomeko!!! One came!!! Yeah, but actually there are about twenty other pictures of her! (Ha ha!)

Ishikawa Prefecture, Natsu vs. Haru

Send to Hiro Mashima c/o DEL REY MANGA, 1745 Broadway, New York, NY 10019, delreymanga@randomhouse.com*

*Del Rey Manga will make its best efforts to get your letter to the author but cannot guarantee a response. Original artwork cannot be returned.

GUILD

Any letters and postcards you send with your personal information, such as your name, address, postal code, and other information, will be handed over, as is, to the author. When you send mail, please keep that in mind.

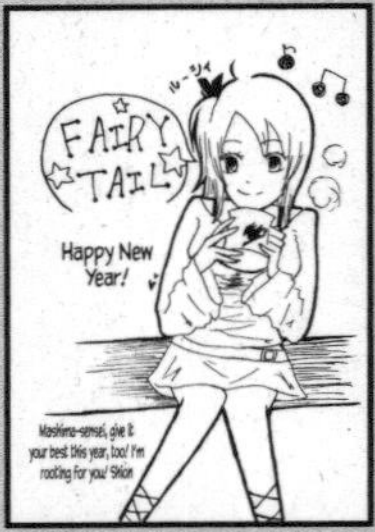
FAIRY TAIL
Happy New Year!
Mashima-sensei, give it your best this year, too! I'm rooting for you! Shion
Miyagi Prefecture, Shion

▲ Happy New Year's to you! And thanks for all of the New Year's cards!

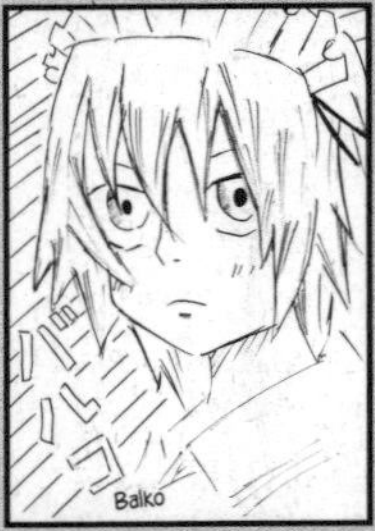
Balko
Shizuoka Prefecture, Junichi Iwahori

▲ Ehh? By the way, it's Balgo. Although Balko makes a nice girl's name.

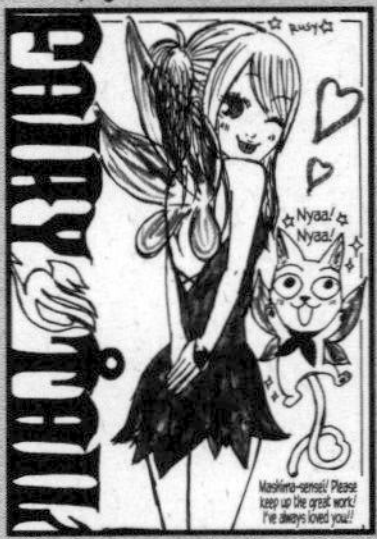
Nyaa! Nyaa!
Mashima-sensei! Please keep up the great work! I've always loved you!!
Shizuoka Prefecture, Kahori Matsushima

▲ Wow, that's cute! Is she doing cosplay as a fairy?

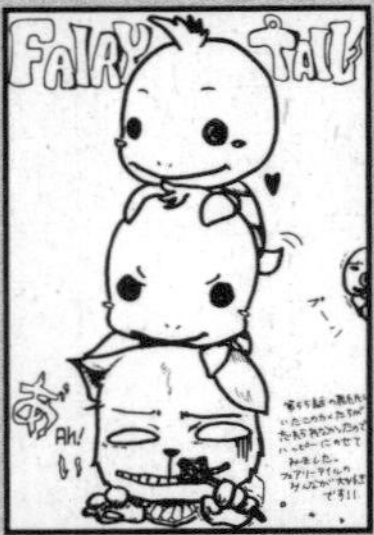
FAIRY TAIL
Ah!
Miyazaki Prefecture, Sayuri

▲ A-Another rare character...We only saw it on a splash page once...

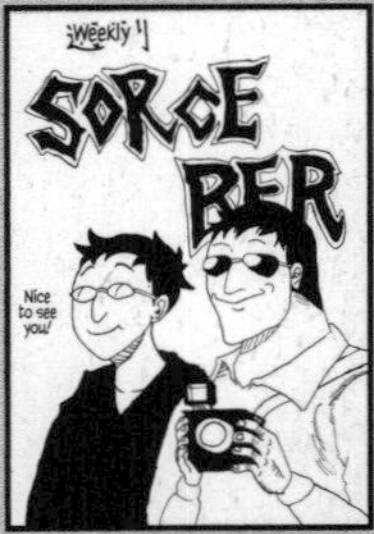
Weekly
SORCERER
Nice to see you!
Hyôgo Prefecture, Puririn

▲ These appeared in a limited edition publication. Actually they're based on editors of mine.

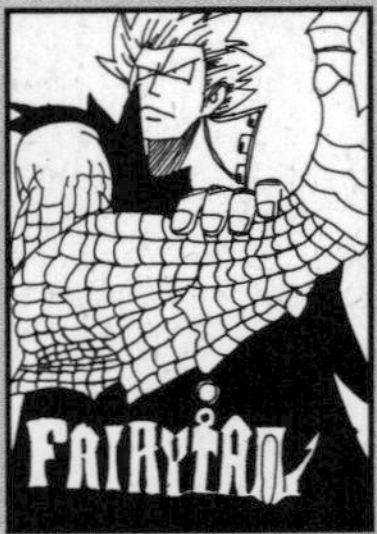
FAIRYTAIL
Ibaragi Prefecture, Masahiro Ishizaki

▲ I wonder when his next active appearance will be...?

Rejection Corner

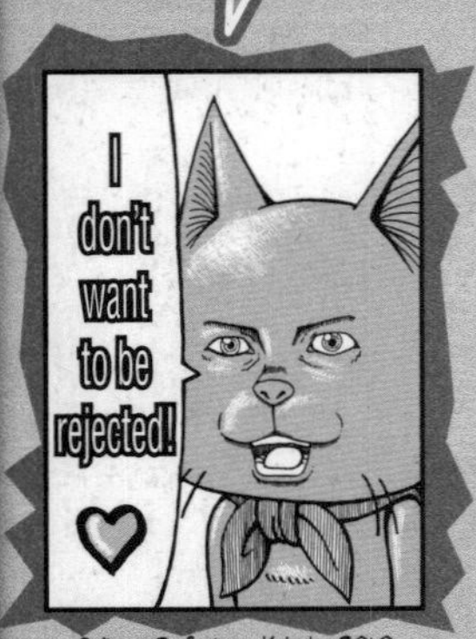
I don't want to be rejected!
Saitama Prefecture, Keisuke Gôtô

▲ You can't get everything you want!

About the Creator

HIRO MASHIMA was born May 3, 1977, in the Nagano prefecture. His series *Rave Master* has made him one of the most popular manga artists in America. *Fairy Tail*, currently being serialized in *Weekly Shōnen Magazine*, is his latest creation.

Translation Notes

Japanese is a tricky language for most Westerners, and translation is often more art than science. For your edification and reading pleasure, here are notes on some of the places where we could have gone in a different direction in our translation of the work, or where a Japanese cultural reference is used.

General Notes:
Wizard

In the original Japanese version of *Fairy Tail*, you'll find panels in which the English word "wizard" is part of the original illustration. So this translation has taken that as its inspiration and translated the word *madôshi* as "wizard." But *madôshi*'s meaning is similar to certain Japanese words that have been borrowed by the English language, such as judo (the soft way) and kendo (the way of the sword). *Madô* is the way of magic, and *madôshi* are those who follow the way of magic. So although the word "wizard" is used in the original dialogue, a Japanese reader would be likely to think not of traditional Western wizards such as Merlin or Gandalf, but of martial artists.

Names

Hiro Mashima has graciously agreed to provide official English spellings for just about all of the characters in *Fairy Tail*. Because this version of *Fairy Tail* is the first publication of most of these spellings, there will inevitably be differences between these spellings and some of the fan interpretations that may have spread throughout the Web or in other fan circles. Rest assured that the spellings contained in this book are the spellings that Mashima-sensei wanted for *Fairy Tail*.

Bento, page 34

The traditional boxed lunch of Japan usually features a main course on a bed of rice and includes pickled veggies, salad, cooked egg, and other foods along with sweet beans for dessert. Women are known for waking up early and fixing elaborate bento boxes. Single girls prepare them for themselves or their boyfriends, while mothers fix bento boxes for their children's school lunches.

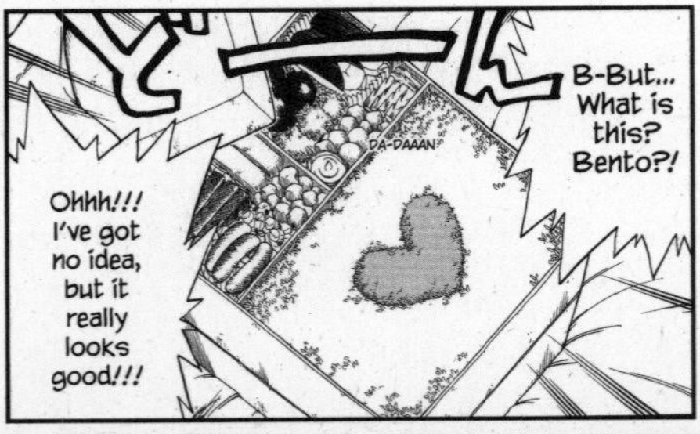
B-But... What is this? Bento?!
DA-DAAAN
Ohhh!!! I've got no idea, but it really looks good!!!

Feminist, page 36

In America, the word "feminist" has taken on nuances of a radical activist for women's rights. In Japan, the connotations are much broader, spanning the range from activist to someone who simply likes women.

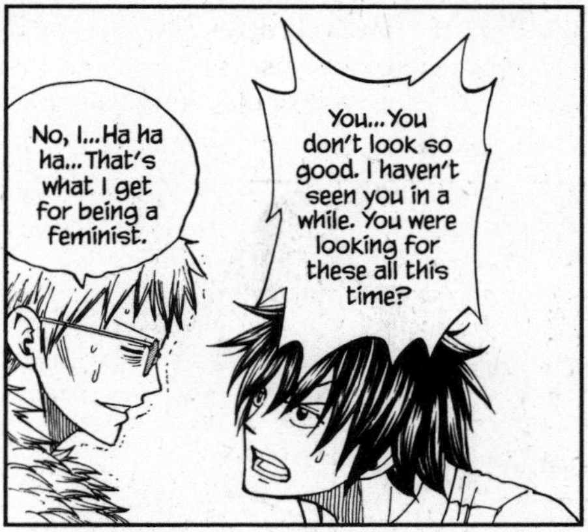
You...You don't look so good. I haven't seen you in a while. You were looking for these all this time?
No, I...Ha ha ha...That's what I get for being a feminist.

Passionate Fish, page 45

The title of the top book the librarian is holding was written in Japanese, *Jônetsu-gyo*, which means "Passionate Fish" or "Passion Fish." One might assume that, as translator, I would use the name of the movie, *Passion Fish*, for the translation, but it did not seem appropriate in this instance. When the movie came out, the Japanese title was not in Japanese, but instead used the English words in Japanese *katakana* characters, *Passhon Fisshu*. Since Mashima-sensei didn't use the proper name for the movie title, it seemed wrong for the translation to use the proper title of the movie either.

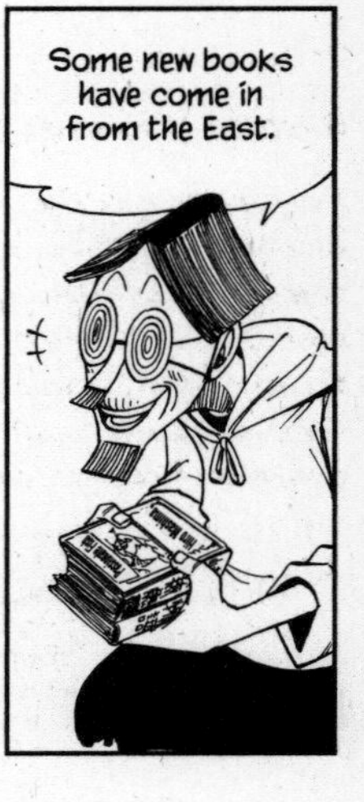
Some new books have come in from the East.

Mabô and Yanbô, page 66

There are many types of nicknames in Japanese, and this is one example. One takes the first syllable of the name and adds *bô* to the end (or *nbô* depending on phonics and the whim of the one assigning the nickname). This is generally a nickname used by men for male friends, and although it is still heard now and again, the popularity of that nickname declined decades ago. The use of the nicknames indicate that Master Makarov and Yajima are either old, very close friends, or former classmates.

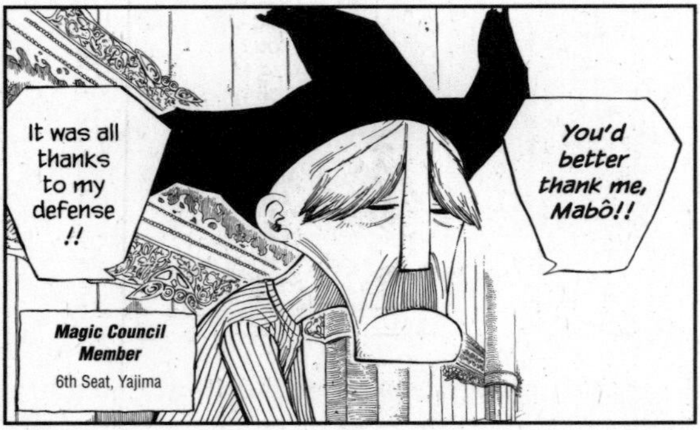
You'd better thank me, Mabô!!
It was all thanks to my defense !!
Magic Council Member
6th Seat, Yajima

Ramen, *chashu* pork, page 66

The Chinese barbecue pork, *char siu*, is pronounced *chashu* in Japan, and the most common dish associated with *chashu* is ramen. One can order *chashu* Ramen as a menu item in most ramen restaurants/Chinese restaurants in Japan, or one can order extra *chashu* to be added to other ramen dishes such as Miso Ramen. *Chashu* consists of thin slices of pork (usually pork shoulder), and one usually only receives two or three slices per ramen dish.

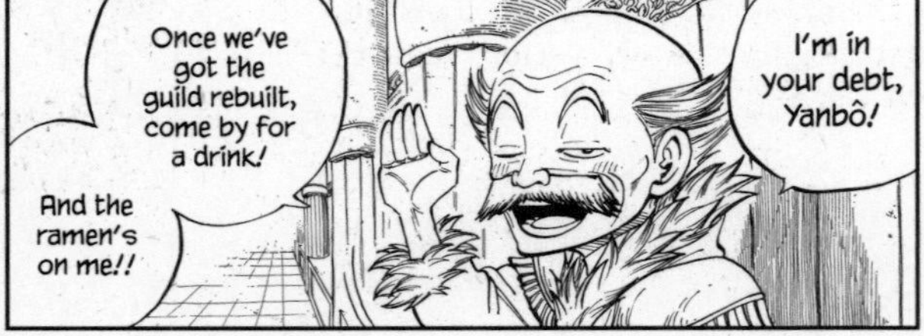
I'm in your debt, Yanbô!
Once we've got the guild rebuilt, come by for a drink!
And the ramen's on me!!

Ebb and Sea Bream, page 119

There is a phrase in Japanese, *isshin-ittai*, which means "ebb and flow." Of course it refers to the tides, but it also indicates the ups and downs of one's life. But in Japanese pun-loving fashion, here the normal *kanji* for *tai* has been replaced with a different *kanji*, also pronounced *tai*, but meaning "sea bream." Not the easiest pun to try to translate, but since English has few uses for the word "ebb" in any other context than "ebb and flow," juxtaposing "ebb and" with "sea bream" gives one the idea that someone is trying to make a joke—no matter how less-than-hilarious the pun was in this English translation.

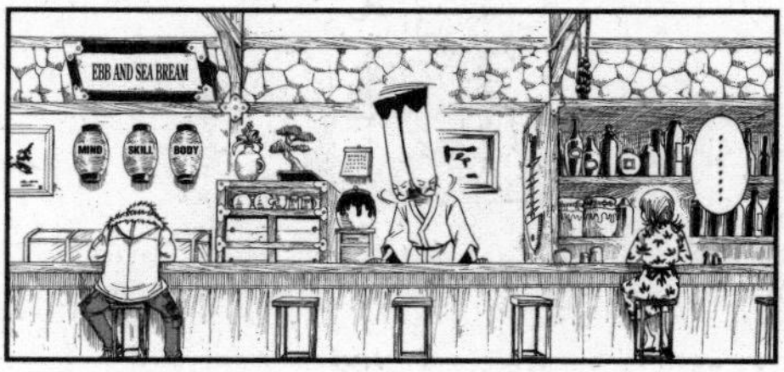
EBB AND SEA BREAM
MIND
SKILL
BODY

Homaa, page 133

This is simply one of those mumbling vocalizations that old men make in between sentences and phrases. I left the sound the same as in the Japanese.

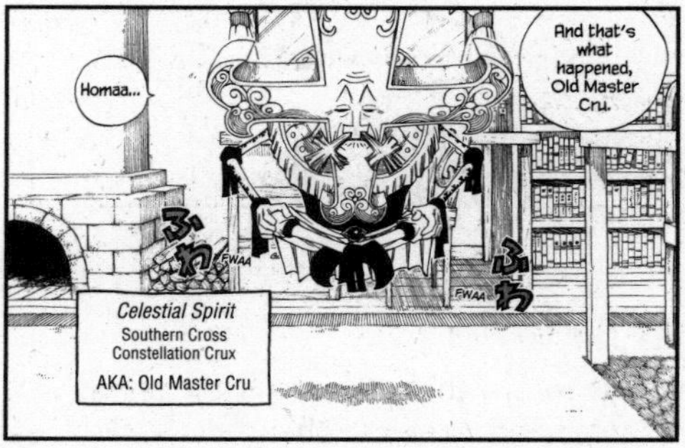
And that's what happened, Old Master Cru.
Homaa...
FWAA
FWAA
Celestial Spirit
Southern Cross Constellation Crux
AKA: Old Master Cru

Memphis Ring, page 150

The Memphis Ring is a magic item that can be found in the Japanese massively multi-player role-playing game (MMRPG), Strugarden Neo. The item is a finger ring with enough power to defeat a boss in the game.

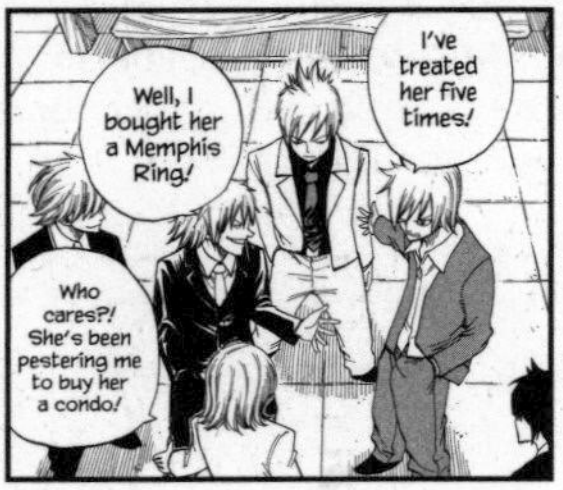
I've treated her five times!
Well, I bought her a Memphis Ring!
Who cares?! She's been pestering me to buy her a condo!

Old Friend, page 178

In Japanese, the celestial spirit king used the term *furuki tomo*, which is a rather archaic way of saying "old friend." I was unable to find any other instances where this phrase was used in Japanese history or literature, so I can't claim to be an expert in the nuances of this phrase. Only that he used it as a way of saying "you" in the Japanese—even to Lucy who he had just met. The rest of his speech was rather archaic as well, and so the translation used "thees," "thous," and similar language to convey that concept.

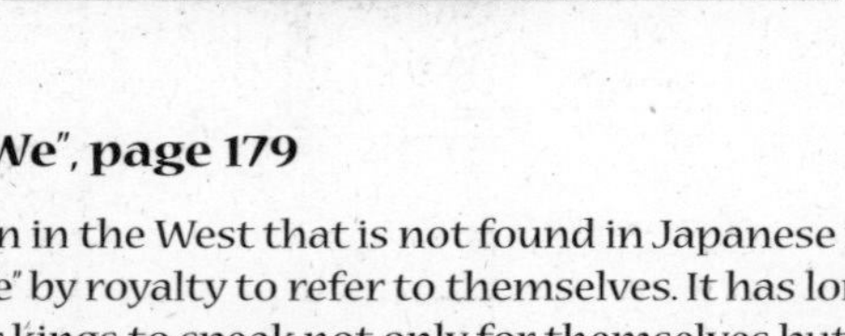
Old Friend... Thou hast broken covenant with mankind, and have done foul murder to a key holder!!!

The Royal "We", page 179

One convention in the West that is not found in Japanese is the use of the word "we" by royalty to refer to themselves. It has long been the custom for kings to speak not only for themselves but, since they are (supposedly) a living embodiment of their country and people, they speak for everyone. Therefore, kings have been known to use the pronoun "we" when referring to themselves.

Preview of Volume 10

We're pleased to present you with a preview from volume 10. Please check our website (www.delreymanga.com) to see when this volume will be available in English. For now you'll have to make do with Japanese!

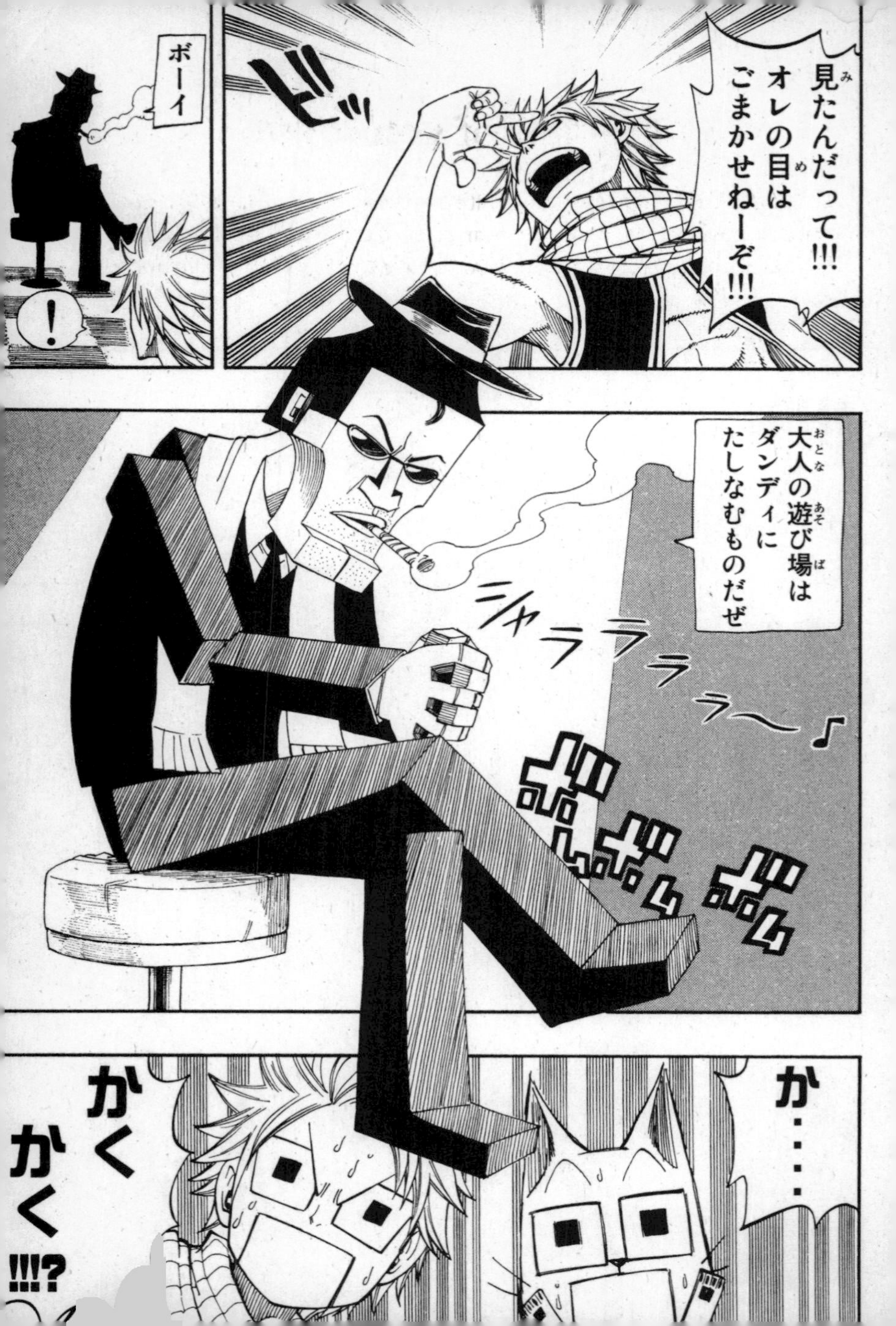
見たんだって!!! オレの目はごまかせねーぞ!!!
ビッ
ボーイ
!
大人の遊び場はダンディにたしなむものだぜ
シャラララララ～♪
ボム
ボム
ボム
か・・・・
かくかく!!!?

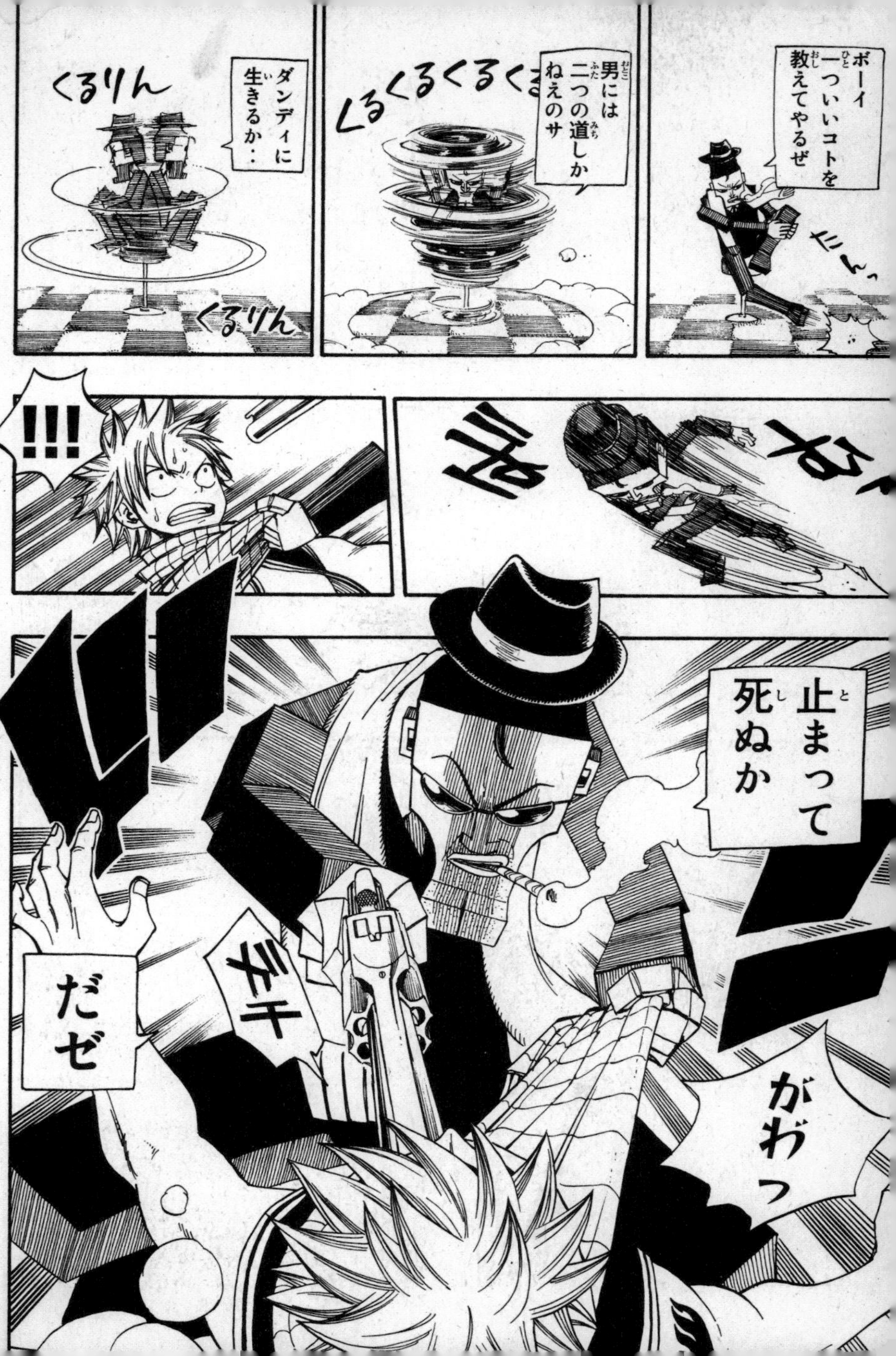
ボーイ
一つ いいコトを
教えてやるぜ
たんっ
くるくるくるくる
男には
二つの道しか
ねえのサ
くるりん
ダンディに
生きるか・・
くるりん
!!!
止まって
死ぬか
だぜ
がわっ

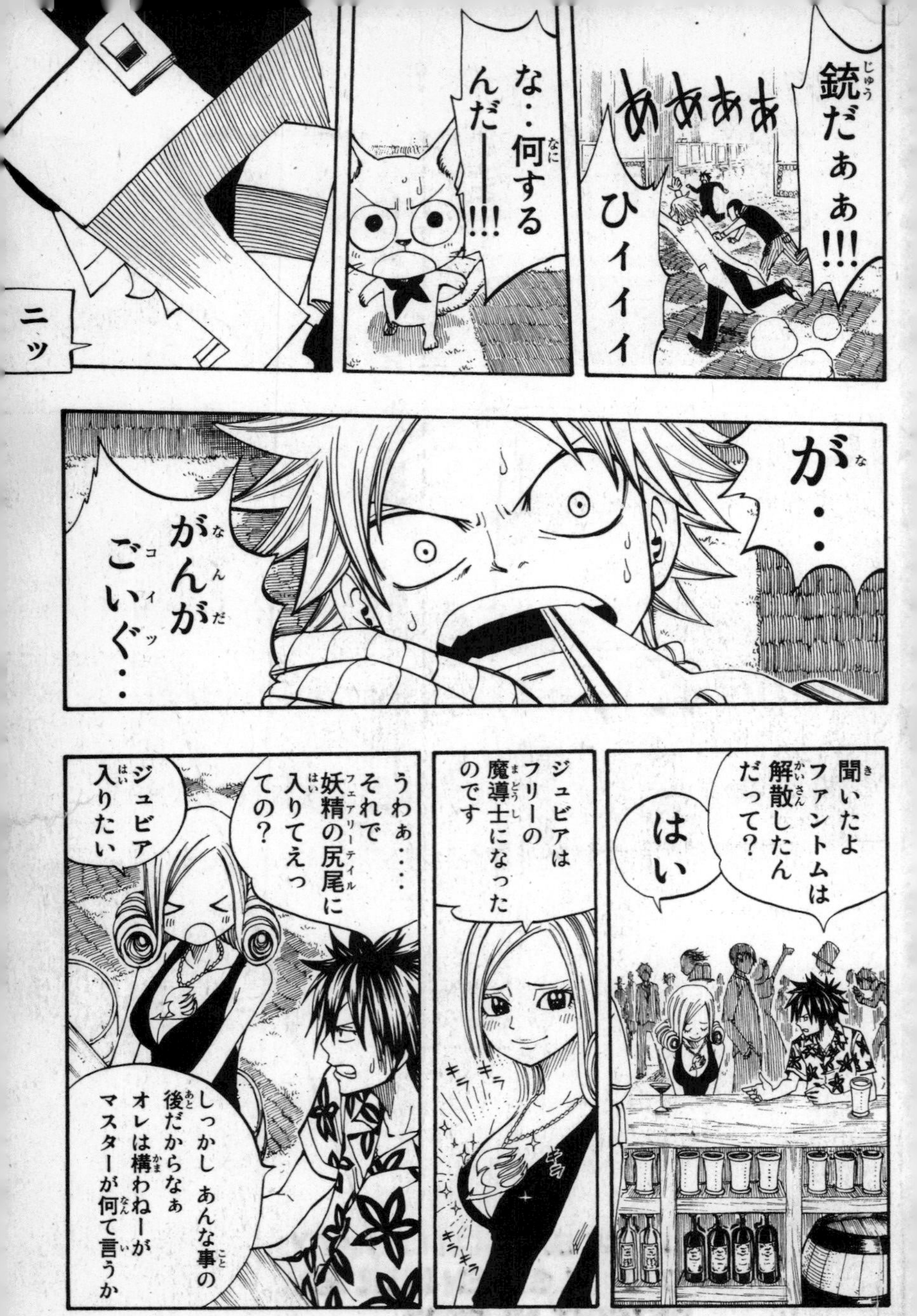
銃だぁぁ!!!
ああああ
ひイイイ
な・・何するんだ――!!!
ニッ
が・・
がんがごいぐ・・
聞いたよ ファントムは解散したんだって?
はい
ジュビアはフリーの魔導士になったのです
キラ キラ
キラ キラ
うわぁ・・・・それで妖精の尻尾に入りてえっての?
ジュビア入りたい
しっかし あんな事の後だからなぁ オレは構わねーが マスターが何て言うか

TOMARE!

止まれ

[STOP!]

You're going the wrong way!

Manga is a completely different type of reading experience.

To start at the *beginning*, go to the *end*!

That's right! Authentic manga is read the traditional Japanese way—from right to left, exactly the opposite of how American books are read. It's easy to follow: Just go to the other end of the book and read each page—and each panel—from right side to left side, starting at the top right. Now you're experiencing manga as it was meant to be!